Neuropsychoanalysis of the Inner Mind

This comprehensive and well-curated collection explores how neuroscience can be integrated into psychoanalytic thinking and practice, reexamining the biological science within psychological (sexuality, pleasure, and dreams), social (pornography), and psychopathological (learning and attention disorders, anhedonia) phenomena relevant to therapists and analysts.

Neuropsychoanalysis of the Inner Mind stands out for its focus on the emotional-motivational aspects of the mind, which are considered through the lenses of affective neuroscience, psychoanalytic theory and neuropsychoanalysis, and is important reading for scholars and psychologists interested in the topics originally addressed by Freud in his 1895 publication Project for a Scientific Psychology.

Teodosio Giacolini, Psychologist, Clinical Supervisor and Docent in psychodynamic psychotherapy in Postgraduate School in Child and Adolescent Neuropsychiatry, Department of Neuroscience and Mental Health, Policlinico Umberto I-Sapienza University Hospital of Rome. Full member of Italian Psychoanalytical Society (SPI) and International Psychoanalytical Association (IPA). Member and Coordinator (together C.P.) of the regional group of The International Neuropsychoanalysis Association (NPSA). Author of books and papers in national and international journals.

Cristiana Pirrongelli, MD, Psychiatrist specialized in both basic and clinical research, author of national and international publications. She is a full member of Italian Psychoanalytic Association (SPI) and International Psychoanalytic Association (IPA). Since 2014, she has been teaching Ethics in Psychoanalysis and is part of the Deontological Board of SPI. Member and Coordinator (with T.G.) of the regional group of The International Neuropsychoanalysis Association (NPSA). Editor of SPIWEB (National Website of the Italian Psychoanalytic Association), Research and Neuroscience section.

Neuropsychoanalysis of the Inner Mind

A Biological Understanding of Human Mental Function

Edited by
Teodosio Giacolini and
Cristiana Pirrongelli

Routledge
Taylor & Francis Group

LONDON AND NEW YORK

First published 2022
by Routledge
2 Park Square, Milton Park, Abingdon, Oxon OX14 4RN

and by Routledge
605 Third Avenue, New York, NY 10158

Routledge is an imprint of the Taylor & Francis Group, an informa business

British Library Cataloguing-in-Publication Data
A catalogue record for this book is available from the British Library

Library of Congress Cataloging-in-Publication Data
Names: Giacolini, Teodosio, editor. | Pirrongelli, Cristiana, editor.
Title: Neuropsychoanalysis of the inner mind : a biological understanding of human mental function / edited by Teodosio Giacolini and Cristiana Pirrongelli.
Description: Abingdon, Oxon ; New York, NY : Routledge, 2022. | Includes bibliographical references and index. | Summary: "This comprehensive and well curated collection explores how neuroscience can be integrated into psychoanalytic thinking and practice, reexamining the biological science within psychological (sexuality, pleasure, dreams), social (pornography), and psychopathological (learning and attention disorders, anhedonia) phenomena relevant to therapists and analysts. Neuropsychoanalysis of the Inner Mind stands out for its focus on the emotional-motivational aspects of the mind, which are considered through the lenses of affective neuroscience, psychoanalytic theory and neuropsychoanalysis, and is important reading for scholars and psychologists interested in the topics originally addressed by Freud in his 1895 publication Project for a Scientific Psychology"— Provided by publisher.
Identifiers: LCCN 2021027255 (print) | LCCN 2021027256 (ebook) | ISBN 9781032056920 (hardback) | ISBN 9781032056937 (paperback) | ISBN 9781003198741 (ebook)
Subjects: LCSH: Psychoanalysis—Methodology. | Neuropsychiatry. | Neuropsychology.
Classification: LCC RC506 .N487 2022 (print) | LCC RC506 (ebook) | DDC 616.89/17—dc23
LC record available at https://lccn.loc.gov/2021027255
LC ebook record available at https://lccn.loc.gov/2021027256

ISBN: 978-1-032-05692-0 (hbk)
ISBN: 978-1-032-05693-7 (pbk)
ISBN: 978-1-003-19874-1 (ebk)

DOI: 10.4324/9781003198741

Typeset in Times New Roman
by codeMantra

**In memory of Professor Jaak Panksepp,
pioneer of Affective Neuroscience**

Contents

PART TWO
Clinical aspects   123

Contents

PART TWO
Clinical aspects 123

Foreword

Mark Solms

The late Jaak Panksepp (1943–2017) and I co-chaired the International Neuropsychoanalysis Society since its inception in 2000 at its first annual Congress held in London, the topic of which was "Emotion". We decided to start our scientific and mutually educational journey with this topic, the very foundation of our two sister disciplines, Affective Neuroscience and Psychoanalysis.

I welcome the efforts of the colleagues that co-authored this book, who recognize the necessity, power and utility of a phenomenal level of analysis of the mental apparatus. We trust that the neuropsychoanalytic study of psychological states can profoundly enrich a fully integrated cross-species affective neuroscience, thereby illuminating many mental and neurobiological processes in humans.

The foundation of psychoanalysis by Freud was preceded by his deep interest in the neurobiological functioning of the mind, of which *The Project for a Scientific Psychology* (1895) represented his most complex effort. Freud soon gave up on the ideal of studying mental functions on a physiological basis, given the limited development of neuroscience at the time. Consequently, he proceeded to study the mental organ through functional instruments and categories, which he named Metapsychology. In my recent work, I wrote: *"Freud's 'Project for a Scientific Psychology' is the Rosetta Stone of neuropsychoanalysis.* It was the foundational text for the whole of what became known as metapsychology....(it) *was the first attempt – Freud's own attempt – to achieve what the whole interdisciplinary endeavour called neuropsychoanalysis is trying to achieve today."* (Solms 2020, p. 1). Freud gave particular importance to an element derived from the biological sciences and from the study of Darwin's work, making it the fulcrum of his theoretical-clinical construction: the function called drive. Therefore, in 1933, he wrote in *New Introductory Lectures On Psychoanalysis*: *"The theory of the drives is so to say our mythology. Drives are mythical entities, magnificent in their indefiniteness"* (Freud 1933, p. 95). A few years earlier he had written: *"No knowledge would have been more valuable as a foundation for true psychological science than an approximate grasp of the common characteristics and possible distinctive features of the drives. But in no region of psychology were we groping more in the dark.*" (Freud 1920, p. 61). However, drives are for researchers – like the co-authors of this book – no longer *indefinite and dark entities*, because especially Affective Neuroscience —a term coined by J. Panksepp in 1992 – has made it possible to identify and learn more about the different instinctual emotional networks.

Freud had thus taken in the lesson learned from the father of biologists, Charles Darwin, who had identified instincts and comparative psychology as two privileged perspectives upon the study of the human mind. The development of psychoanalytical thought has gradually moved away from the 'Darwinist' Freud and from the dialogue with biological sciences in general.

The current developments in the Neurosciences, and in particular the Affective Neurosciences, enable us to resume the interrupted dialogue between psychoanalysis and neurobiology. Its most significant expression is Neuropsychoanalysis, a research paradigm that unites psychoanalysts and scholars who want to reconnect both with the Freud of the *Project for a Scientific Psychology* (1895) and with Freud as a 'comparative biologist'. It is precisely comparative biology, the pivotal aspect of Affective Neurosciences, that led to the discovery of the phylogenetic roots of the basic neural networks of emotional functions, analogous in all mammals, which drive mental functioning. "*The human infant is not a blank slate; like all other species, we are born with innate needs. These needs ('demands upon the mind to perform work', as Freud called them, his 'id') are felt and expressed as emotions. The basic emotions trigger instinctual behaviours, which are innate action plans that we perform in order to meet our needs (e.g. cry, search, freeze, flee, attack)*" (Solms 2018, p. 5). These basic emotions are the expression of the basic neural network that resides in the subcortical regions of the brain and is characterized by specific neuronal circuits and by a specific neurochemistry. Of particular relevance was the finding that various primary emotional systems and the affective states related to them (so-called reward and punishment) are the source of intentional actions, hence of mental development and of the way in which personality is structured. As I recently wrote in the Introduction to my book *The Hidden Spring*: "*Since the cerebral cortex is the seat of intelligence, almost everybody thinks that it is also the seat of consciousness. I disagree. Consciousness is far more primitive than that. It arises from a part of the brain that humans share with fishes. This is the 'hidden spring'…*" (Solms 2021). In other words, Affective Neuroscience regards emotional and affective states as the foundations of the mind. Consequently, the normal or pathological functioning of the personality should be sought in the BrainMind dynamics of these primary emotional systems. Neuropsychoanalysis was born as a response to the need to consider the mind from both a psychoanalytic and a neuroscientific perspective, laying the grounds for a deeper knowledge of the basic emotional underpinnings of psychiatric disorders. This makes it possible to develop new neuropsychologically and neurochemically based therapies, thanks to a better knowledge of their homologous emotional operations.

If primary emotions originate in the functioning of the subcortical areas of the brain, what is the role of the neocortex in the organization of mental functioning? The neocortex is the seat of the higher cognitive functions that facilitated the development, in the human species, of reflexive self-reports of its own emotional states, a mental phenomenon that Panksepp defined as 'tertiary process'. Regarding these reflexive processes of the human brain, according to Affective Neuroscience, the primary emotional experiences arising in the brainstem are processed through a secondary level – expressed mainly in the basal ganglia – that enables, through learning and memory, the extension of the primary systems into space and time, establishing the prerequisites for the operation of cortical functions and hence of higher cognitive functions.

"The fundamental contribution of the cortex to consciousness in this respect is stabilization (and refinement) of the objects of perception and generating thinking and ideas. This contribution derives from the unrivalled capacity of the cortex for representational forms of memory (in all of its varieties, both short- and long-term). To put it metaphorically, the cortex transforms the fleeting, fugitive, wave-like states of consciousness into mental solids. It generates objects. (Freud called them 'object presentations')." (Solms and Panksepp 2012, p. 165).

In conclusion, Neuropsychoanalysis attempts to understand the human mind from a neuro-evolutionary perspective and, making a fresh start from the point where Freud interrupted his Project for a Scientific Psychology, it tries to shed light on his intuitions regarding the affective roots of the human nature: "Affect was the *raison d'être* of consciousness" (Solms and Panksepp 2012, p. 152).

References

Freud, S. (1920). *Beyond the pleasure principle*. In J. Strachey (Ed. and Trans.), The Standard Edition of the Complete Psychological Works of Sigmund Freud, Volume XVIII (1920–1922) (pp. 1–64). London: The Hogarth Press and the Institute of Psycho-analysis. 1953.

Freud, S. (1933). *New Introductory Lectures on Psycho-Analysis*. The Standard Edition of the Complete Psychological Works of Sigmund Freud, Volume XXII (1932–1936): New Introductory Lectures on Psycho-Analysis and Other Works, 1–182.

Solms, M. (2021). *The Hidden Spring*: A Journey to the Source of Consciousness. Profile Books, 2021.SBN 1782835717, 9781782835714.

Solms, M. (2020). New project for a scientific psychology: General scheme. Neuropsychoanalysis. doi: 10.1080/15294145.2020.1833361.

Solms, M. (2018). The scientific standing of psychoanalysis. *BJPsych Int.* 2018 Feb; 15(1): 5–8. doi: 10.1192/bji.2017.4.

Solms, M. and Panksepp, J. (2012). The ID knows more the Ego Admits: Neuropsychoanalytic and Primal Consciousness Perspectives on the Interface Between Affective and Cognitive Neuroscience *Brain Sci.* 2012, *2*, 147–175.

Contributors

Alcaro Antonio
Psychologist and Psychotherapist, PhD and a researcher in neuroscience at the University of Rome "La Sapienza" (Psychology Department). After 10 years of collaboration with Jaak Panksepp in the field of Affective Neuroscience, he works on the emotional foundations of individual personality.

Francesco Castellet Y Ballarà
M.D. specialist both in Neurology and Psychiatry. Full Member of SPI (Società Psicoanalitica Italiana)/IPA (International Psychoanalytic Association) and Psychiatric and Psychoanalytic Consultant for ESA (European Space Agency) and EUMETSAT.

Clarici Andrea
MD, psychiatrist, psychoanalytic psychotherapist, working clinically in private psychoanalytic practice. He is also Professor in the course "Advanced Dynamic Psychology" at the Faculty of Psychology and the course of "Child Neuropsychiatry" at the Faculty of Medicine, both at the University of Triest (UNITS, Italy).

Colace Claudio
Psychologist and Psychotherapist at the Operational Unit of Psychology of the ASL of Viterbo (National Health Service Office), Italy, where he works at the Outpatient Psychology Department and at the Center for Drug Addictions of Civita Castellana. He obtained PhD in Psychology at the Department of Psychology of the University of Bologna.

Di Maggio Chiara
MD, PHD, Child and Adolescent Neuropsychiatrist.

Falci Amedeo
M.D, neuropsychiatry of child and adolescents; Full Member and Training Analyst SPI (Società Psicoanalitica Italiana)/IPA (International Psychoanalytic Association).

Fioriello Francesca
MD, Child and Adolescent Neuropsychiatrist.

Giacolini Teodosio
Psychologist, Clinical Supervisor and Docent in psychodynamic psychotherapy in Postgraduate School in Child and Adolescent Neuropsychiatry, Department of Neuroscience and Mental Health, Policlinico Umberto I-Sapienza University Hospital of Rome. Full member of Italian Psychoanalytical Society (SPI) and International Psychoanalytical Association (IPA). Member and Coordinator (together C.P.) of the regional group of The International Neuropsychoanalysis Association (NPSA). Author of books and papers in national and international journals.

Janiri Luigi
MD., neurologist and psychiatrist; Full Professor of Psychiatry at the Catholic University of Rome, Head of the Unit of Liaison Psychiatry of the Fondazione Policlinico Universitario Agostino Gemelli IRCCS hospital of Rome. Member of Italian Psychoanalytical Society (SPI)/International Psychoanalytical Association (IPA).

Mazza Marianna
MD, PhD., Psychiatrist, Member of Italian Psychoanalytical Society (SPI)/International Psychoanalytical Association (IPA). Her clinical and scientific practice is at the Department of Psychiatry of the Fondazione Policlinico Universitario Agostino Gemelli IRCCS, Catholic University in Rome, Italy.

Moccia Lorenzo
MD., PhD, Psychiatrist. His clinical and scientific practice is at the Department of Psychiatry of the Fondazione Policlinico Universitario Agostino Gemelli IRCCS, Catholic University of Rome, Italy.

Pirrongelli Cristiana
MD, Psychiatrist specialized in both basic and clinical research, author of national and international publications. She is full member of Italian Psychoanalytic Association (SPI) and International Psychoanalytic Association (IPA). Since 2014, she has been teaching Ethics in Psychoanalysis and is part of the Deontological Board of SPI. Member and Coordinator (with T.G.) of the regional group of The International Neuropsychoanalysis Association (NPSA). Editor of SPIWEB (National Website of the Italian Psychoanalytic Association), Research and Neuroscience section.

Riezzo Sara
MD, Child and Adolescent Neuropsychiatrist.

Salone Anatolia
MD., PhD in Neuroscience, Psychiatrist, member of the Italian Psychoanalytic Society (SPI)/International Psychoanalytical Association (IPA).

Spadazzi Claudia
MD., Gynaecologist, Clinical Psychologist, Sexual Therapist. Full Member Italian Psychoanalytic Society (SPI)/International Psychoanalytical Association (IPA). Co-founder of Italian Psychoanalytic Dialogues.

Zanettovich Andrea
MD, psychoanalytically oriented psychotherapist; lecturer in Dynamic Psychology at the University of Trieste; Director of Training and Research Center in Psychoanalytic psychotherapy of Trieste and Responsible for the Trieste branch of the Postgraduate School of Psychoanalytic Psychotherapy of Ravenna.

Part One
General aspects

1 Motivational/emotional systems

Synoptic tables

*Cristiana Pirrongelli, Chiara di Maggio,
Francesca Fioriello, Sara Riezzo, and
Teodosio Giacolini*

Introduction

This chapter aims to propose a quick and concise, albeit not exhaustive, view of what motivational/emotional systems are, according to Affective Neuroscience. As research shows, these systems are homologous among mammal species and are mainly wired in subcortical areas. We refer to the dimension of mental functioning that Freud described as Es. Certain areas of brain/mind functioning that were still unknown until a few years ago are now better known in their behavioral neurophysiology. Affective Neurosciences highlighted connections between emotional systems and cortical areas; these systems influence mental functioning much more through bottom-up mechanisms than through top-down connections from cortical to subcortical areas. Furthermore, these tables are also an attempt to translate psychopharmacological knowledge from the field of their use based on classical nosography to that of psychiatry, based on behavioral neurophysiological knowledge of motivational/emotional systems, in an endophenotypic analysis of the problem.

Seeking system		
	Anatomical localization	*Evolutionary function*
The SEEKING system supports the activation of every act that we perform and that requires energy. Therefore, the "seeking system" is constantly involved with the world and its processes. In animals, the SEEKING system operates with no premeditation and strategic planning. In fact, this system requires more connections with the frontal neocortex, which is	Medial bundle of the forebrain (nucleus accumbens, ventral tegmental area, mesolimbic and mesocortical areas, lateral hypothalamus, periaqueductal gray matter of the midbrain). From the ventral tegmental area (VTA) the seeing system ascends, through mesolimbic and mesocortical	The SEEKING emotional system is, according to Panksepp, the main and oldest motivational one. It generates drive impulses for exploring the world, becoming involved, interested in reality. Its activation results in intense processes of learning, producing

(Continued)

DOI: 10.4324/9781003198741-2

Seeking system

	Anatomical localization	Evolutionary function
more developed in humans. It provides a kind of "excited and euphoric anticipation".	dopaminergic pathways, to three destinations:	adaptive behaviors (basal ganglia) and knowledge (neocortex). The neuronal SEEKING system includes a reward center related to enthusiasm and euphoria of involvement but not hedonistic satisfaction. It supports the expectation that, by activating itself, we can find something "good" for our well-being and provide the energy necessary to achieve it. It participates in appetitive phases (to search, find and acquire the necessary resources, not only those aimed at consumption) present in all systems. If the system is damaged, the animal can no longer take care of itself, it goes into depression and dies.

The emotional system that Panksepp presents as seeking is involved in procurement research, exploration, investigation, curiosity, interest and expectation (the system is called in English: foraging/exploration/ investigation/curiosity/interest/ expectancy/SEEKING system). The system, says Panksepp, responds unconditionally to homeostatic imbalances (states of body necessities) and environmental incentives. It represents the reward system (together with the RAGE and FEAR systems to achieve the set goals) and it mediates the primary processes known as appetitive solicitations which lead to research by environmental exploration. Even though the exhibited behavior is comparable to the one shown during the desire phase antecedent to the act of fulfillment, the positive emotion that comes from the activation of the seeking system (Wanting) is different from the sensation of pleasure that causes the realization of the goal (Liking), representing an "anticipatory euphoria" (appetitive/ incentive behavior).

Both pleasure and reinforcement secondary to satisfaction (consummatory behavior/sensory pleasure reward) are associated with a reduction in the activity of this system. In this phase, the system deactivation allows the activation of both reinforcement processes and secondary learning, which act through motivation, thus intended as positive reinforcement. In this way, an initial neutral stimulus, thanks to the interaction with other systems, such as reinforcement, can be then classified as either irrelevant or relevant and stored in memory. At a third level, it generates

1   medial fasciculus of the forebrain and lateral hypothalamus (MFB-LH).
2   Nucleus accumbens.
3   Medial prefrontal cortex. The dopaminergic neurons of the VTA (common to the CARE system: activation of research impulses to procure food, prepare the nest, recover the puppies) receive input from other regions of the brain and send output to upper brain areas, especially towards the nucleus accumbens (involved in the development of addictions; the medial frontal neocortical regions are focused on primary emotional needs. It explains how we seek pleasant experiences and escape the pitfalls) that interacts with the medial frontal cortex and promotes simple appetitive learning. Other regions involved in the functioning of the system:

1   Noradrenergic and serotonergic system (control arousal).
2   GABAergic, glutamatergic and aceticolin systems (for more specific attention functions). Specific types of interoceptors or "need detectors" located in different medial regions of the brain and in other body organs perceive homeostatic imbalances that indicate simple bodily needs (thirst, hunger, drowsiness, body temperature) and convey these specific homeostatic messages to the seeking

specific expectations and desires, secondary to awareness. This system then mediates an intentionality that is intrinsically present within the action. The joy of the SEEKING system, identifiable with the so-called "enthusiasm", has an energizing effect and can counteract several negative emotions. It is involved in creative activities. The energy boost towards both the exploration of the environment and the research of useful resources for survival is not much connected to the satisfaction for achieving a goal, but to the rewards expectation. In fact, it does not mediate the pleasure, but the desire for it. The anticipatory urgency of different activities shares a positive sense of wanting to do and being able to do, for example, the pleasant anticipation of finding the food and the positive feeling linked to find it, provide a sense of confident expectation that compensates the negative feelings related to hunger. In humans, unlike animals, it operates with strategic planning and premeditation, since there are connections with the frontal neocortex that allow a strategic thought to elicit the system, thus generating complex learned behaviors, both instinctive and counter-instinctive (the firefighter can neutralize the fear of fire and do his/her job by adopting learned strategies). The SEEKING system promotes, in addition to strategic practical thinking, purely intellectual neocortical capacities, energizing the entire human creativity. It is activated not only in response to simple homeostatic imbalances (thirst, hunger, sleep, temperature), but also when facing more complex social needs (mediated by different interoceptors), including the need to play the company. It is in a state of almost continuous operation that keeps both men and animals in a general state of involvement with the world.

system. In addition, some sensors report changes in sex hormones and are connected to the LUST system, promoting sexual desire.

Neuromediators and endogenous activating substances	Neuromediators and endogenous inhibitory substances	Related emotions	Psychopathology	Drugs
Dopamine: It can be released in two different ways, through a "tonic" and "phasic" release. A recent research has highlighted the role of phasic dopamine release in reward processes. The tonic release refers to a slow diffusion of small concentrations of dopamine in the extracellular space, beyond the intersynaptic space, and is linked to the normal activation of dopaminergic neurons and to the release of independent-impulse dopamine in the terminal areas. In contrast, the phasic release follows a burst of activity of dopaminergic VTA neurons, following which elevated dopamine levels are released into the synaptic space to a millimolar concentration and then rapidly removed through the reuptake system. If the phasic release of dopamine can generate a transient seeking signal, the tonic release seems more related to the sustained activation of the emotional state of seeking. It could be hypothesized that	Dynorphin: Powerful and pervasive brain opioid that inactivates the system, causing a depressive state. It mediates a very distinct form of negative affect that is recruited by social loss, and demonstrably reduces the responsivity of the brain's reward-SEEKING system. Corticotropin (CRF): Elevated levels of CRF promote stress and are responsible for psychological pain and a sense of loneliness, inactivating the production of endogenous opioids. GABAergics: They inhibit the impulse to SEEKING and GABA neurons are in turn inhibited by low doses of endogenous opioids.	Interest, craving, anticipatory craving and a heightened sense of self when man feels effective in making things happen in the world, frustration when he is not satisfied.	Depression When the system is chronically hypo-activated, at behavioral, neurobiological and psychological levels, a form of hopeless depression is experienced, characterized by lethargy, anhedonia and lack of dynamism. Depression can be considered as a state of reduced involvement in aspects of the world, due to an endogenous hypofunction of the reward network or/and due to an inhibition of its secondary activity to other brain circuits, such as those involved in the processing of negative emotions (GRIEF/Separation disorder, FEAR or RAGE). Depression may also reflect an emotional despair phase following protracted PANIC arousal. Narcissistic Personality disorder, Obsessive compulsive disorder: When the dopaminergic pathways of the SEEKING system are stimulated for too long, they cause stereotyped behavior in the animal, even trivial repetitive activities in humans.	Anti-depressants -------------- Buprenorphine: mixed mu-opioid receptor agonist/ antagonist used at low doses in depressed clients who have had no relief from many accepted anti-depressants Opioids at low doses: opioid drugs can yield dopamine-independent pleasures and promote dopamine-SEEKING urges, especially at low doses. DBS /Deep Brain Stimulation treatment of the medial forebrain bundle (MFB): it might be a robust anti-depressant in treatment-resistant patients; DBS-induced affective shifts might restore "enthusiasm" in depressed patients, and help them to again engage positively with the world, alleviating amotivational dysphoria.

DA tonic levels usually strengthen the signal-to-noise ratio in neural networks, increasing the effectiveness of DA phasic release in promoting seeking signals.

If the tonic levels of DA are low, the phasic DA events are generally too weak in activating the seeking neurodynamics, and the body tends to withdraw from an active engagement in the environment. In contrast, excessive tonic levels reinforce the power of DA signals so that SEEKING expresses itself repeatedly without any connection to specific contexts or environmental events. Only a moderately high tonic level of DA is sufficient to promote the seeking patterns, guided by sensory and cognitive representations of the external environment.

Neurotensin:

It activates the neuro-modulator system, especially of dopaminergic transmission, in close association with the mesocorticolimbic dopaminergic system, whose dysfunction is hypothesized to be the basis of various psychiatric disorders such as schizophrenia.

Glutamate:

It plays a role in learning.

Endogenous Opioids:

Paranoid schizophrenia: Dopaminergic hyperactivity of the system, with increased D2 receptors, especially in the ventral layer and occasionally in the left amygdala, induces people to suspect and develop paranoid tendencies.

Antipsychotics reduce the circuits of self-stimulation of the seeking system by reducing the dopaminergic action on D2 receptors (these circuits are unstable in schizophrenic pathology).

Dependency disorders:

Substances of abuse such as dopamine and amphetamines are addictive because they directly increase the effects of dopamine, activating the impulse of seeking. Also, alcohol dependence involves capture of the ventral tegmental dopaminergic SEEKING system.

Antipsychotic drugs predominantly active on D2 receptors are indicated for paranoid schizophrenia.

Antidrepressant drugs with the possible addition of antipsychotics active on D2 receptors, are indicated for obsessive-compulsive disorder.

(*Continued*)

Neuromediators and endogenous activating substances	Neuromediators and endogenous inhibitory substances	Related emotions	Psychopathology	Drugs
They promote an affective state of well-being or positive, which leads to the search for companionship, followed by increased production of prolactin, oxytocin and IGF-1 (insulin-like grow factor-1). It is possible that low levels of endogenous opioids alone can activate the seeking system, inhibiting GABA neurons and alleviating negative emotions such as FEAR, leading to a safe haven. Acetylcholine: It creates homeostatic imbalances that activate the SEEKING system (as well as the FEAR system) Orexin: It has a probable role in supporting energy activation in animals or people, considered a modulator of positive arousal and affect.			In a neuroethological view, dependence is the result of an "emotional narrowing" due to an increasing and sometimes exclusive SEEKING research through both the memory of addictive rewards and through the desire to alleviate the dysphoric state during abstinence. Sociopathies/ withdrawal: Attachment disorders. Chronic Insomnia: Decreased modulation of seeking and selective attention systems is connected to the inability to initiate or/ and maintain sleep in patients with chronic insomnia.	

Rage system

Behaviors	Anatomical localization	Evolutionary function
Defensive-affective aggressiveness:		

Defensive-affective aggressiveness:

The activation of this system induces a behavior of aggressiveness and defense. It is provoked in animals by the frustration generated from the limitation of freedom of action and access to resources and frustration of expected rewards, when sought. It determines the activation of the fear system in the enemy that can give rise to escape, defensive-affective aggression and dorsal-vagal reactions.

It is elicited by stimulation of the area ranging from the medial hypothalamus to the PAG (periaqueductal Gray).

It is, together with the FEAR system, the other defensive system aimed at maintaining the physical integrity of the individual.
It is activated by situations of limitation or coercion of bodily movements, such as in the case of a predator's attack and frustration of the rewards expected following the activation of the SEEKING system. It is also active for territorial control. Contrary to predatory aggression, it is not necessarily directed against a specific individual. Present in men and animals.

In man, anger is an emotional state that implies both the attribution of a fault and some wrong suffered, and an impulse to correct the wrong or prevent its repetition; aggression can be an attempt to force another to undertake or to refrain from some action, against his will and not for his own good.

Appears with electrical stimulation of the dorso-lateral hypothalamus (aggression) or the antero-ventral part and PAG (counter-aggression). It ceases immediately as soon as the stimulation ends.
There is a greater presence of the testosterone receptor in the circuit that goes from the medial amygdala to the lateral hypothalamus.

It manifests itself with clear signs of anger, activation of the sympathetic autonomic nervous system and increase in muscle strength/energy.

Assertive predatory aggressiveness:
The behavior is calm, precise and guided by a strategy and does not imply activation of the autonomic nervous system. The predatory killing gives the predator a pleasant sensation (ready availability of food) while the angry aggression gives negative feelings.

It is directed towards an animal perceived as a prey; it is also called quiet-biting attack, requires planning, few signs of autonomic activation and is strictly embraced by the SEEKING system. The stimulation of its circuits in herbivores activates foraging behavior, and in humans, predatory behavior.

Intraspecies aggressiveness –for dominance:
It preferably manifests itself through the struggle between conspecifics of the herd for the supremacy of one over the others and the consequent hierarchies, above all for reproductive purposes but also for homeostatic imbalances (such as hunger) which increase the sensitivity of the choleric impulse (also for humans). It is related to behaviors of submission and of segregation within hierarchies.

(Rage: primary process, it does not need an intentional object to hate. Anger: secondary process emotion, it always has an object that is perceived as the cause of anger).

Active competition especially among males for the conquest of food and sexual resources. The signals of challenge activate in the contender similar behavior or, in case of defeat, activation of the FEAR system with escape behavior or submission.

Linked to better quality and continuity of reproduction.

Infanticide in the animal

(predator-like attitude)

Activating neuromediators	Inhibitory neuromediators	Related emotions	Psycho-pathology	Drugs
Defensive/affective aggressiveness:	Inhibitory action of opioids, serotonin and GABA.	ANGER lived unpleasantly.	Aggressiveness, easy irritability.	*SSRIs* (5-HT1B not specific), *benzodiazepines*,
P Substance also implicated in pain modulation.		SEEKING, ANGER	Paranoid personality disorder.	*Propranolol* (works by blocking
Catecholamines, excitatory amino acids, *serotonin* (via 5-HT2 receptors).	GABA and serotonin are not specific inhibitors of this system.	ANGER, SEEKING, PLAY, experienced	Obsessive-compulsive personality disorder.	beta receptors of cerebral norepinephrine), *oxytocin*,
Testosterone.	Cytokines (modulator effect through GABAa, 5-HT1a, 5-HT2, NK1 receptors).	as positive emotions. FEAR, experienced as a negative emotion.	Cluster B personality disorder.	*opioids*, *lithium* (increases the synthesis of serotonin and decreases the release of norepinephrine).
Acetylcholine, glutamate, nitric oxide synthetase, cytokines.			Psychopathy, antisocial personality disorder.	*Antiepileptics* act through action on GABA receptors:
IL-1 interleukin (family of activating cytokines both in PAG and in the medial hypothalamus through the 5-HT2 receptor).	Low levels of serotonin stimulate dysphoric anger but also pictures of the depressive mirror.		Mood-mania disorders, narcissistic personality disorder, antisocial disorder.	*Pregabalin* (GABA receptor), *Gabapentin* (GABA receptor), *Valproic acid, Topiramate, Carbamazepine, Oxcarbazepine,* etc.
IL-2 interleukin (family of activating cytokines if injected into the PAG; they act through NK1 receptors) *Vasopressin.*				Antipsychotics (rec. D2): *Clozapine, Olanzapine* (high in the serotonin and dopamine receptors).
cholecystokinin (modulator role, acts through CCKB receptors).				*Antipsychotics old and new generation e.g.:* *Quetiapine* (antagonist DA and 5-HT receptors in serotonin receptors).
Predatory/assertive aggressiveness:				*Substance P Antagonist drugs*: *Aprepitant* is a selective receptor antagonist for the substance P (NK1 receptor), (probably through GABAergic neurons).
Biogenic amines, dopamine/ catecholamines, adrenaline, linked to the activation of seeking system.				Other substances that inhibit NK1 receptors:
Intraspecies aggressiveness - for dominance:				*Hormonal therapies.*
Testosterone and vasopressin, (which bind the system to lust), dopamine, serotonin (if high promotes dominance, if low dysphoric aggression and depression), catecholamines.				*Thyroid hormones* *Cannabinoids/Cannabidiol* *Zolpidem* *Ethanol* *Cytokines* *Excitatory amino acids that act on NMDA + receptorsEnkephalines -Deep brain stimulation*

Fear system

	Anatomical localization	Evolutionary function
The system of fear specifically organizes the models of natural behavior of escape and evasion. Fear is a negative condition characterized by worry, generalized nervousness, tension that gives the individual the message that his own safety is in danger. It is always accompanied by autonomous events (autonomic nervous system activation) as well as behavioral. Produces terror when the system is activated hastily. It produces chronic anxiety when weaker and longer-lasting activation is present. Primary or innate fear: congenital sensory inputs within the fear system.

This system is strongly interconnected with other emotional systems, especially with RAGE. The fact that the two systems are so strongly linked could be explained evolutionarily. In fact, one of the functions of anger is to cause fear in our competitors, and one of the functions of fear is to reduce the impact of rabid behavior by opponents who threaten us. In this system, pain plays an important role and, in fact, it is able to activate the system of FEAR. However, | From the central and lateral amygdala to the medial hypothalamus; periaqueductal gray matter. It goes from the central areas of the amygdala to the anterior and medial hypothalamus, surrounding the third ventricle, and from there to the areas located dorsally of the PAG, inside the mesencephalon.

When the frightening stimuli are far away the medial frontal cortex and the amygdala are active, in these cases the individual could hide himself and remain motionless (Freezing).

When a frightening predator is very close to the lower regions, especially the PAG areas, they take over, forcing the individual to flee. | At low activation levels it generates bodily tension and trembling immobilization.

If the activation is intense it can cause a dynamic escape pattern to explode. Porges' Polyvagal Theory rethinks the functioning of the Autonomic Nervous System not in terms of antagonism between the sympathetic and parasympathetic system, but in terms of response hierarchies. The vagus nerve consists of a family of nerves: the dorso-vagal branch and the ventro-vagal branch, in turn, divided into two components, a viscero-motor component, which regulates the viscera above the diaphragm, and a somato-component motor.

The first circuit that appears (the most archaic logenetically) is the one called dorso-vagal, connected with the regulation of the vegetative processes and the functioning of the organs placed below the diaphragm. It is activated in extreme danger conditions, creating a state of slowing down to immobilization (the defense of reptiles), and therefore determines a state of immobility that does not arise from a condition of security, but from extreme fear. In higher mammals, this condition of immobilization with fear is linked to mental dulling and the loss of sense of control and the underlying emotions are sadness, disgust, embarrassment and of course, fear until dissociation.

A subsequent phylogenetic stage led to the development of the sympathetic system, which regulates the metabolic capacity and heart rate, that is all those reactions which, at a physiological level, are linked to the attack-escape mechanism, the elective defense reaction of the mammal in front of danger; the sympathetic system, when activated, inhibits the gastrointestinal tract. |

	Anatomical localization	*Evolutionary function*
the opposite does not happen and often, indeed, it happens that the activation of the FEAR system inhibits the perception of pain. Pain perception plays a fundamental role in learning about signal conditioning.		The activation of the sympathetic system is observable through a state of mobilization: muscle tension, oxygenation, vasoconstriction and heart rate increase; the energy flows towards the front and upwards, the jaw tightens. In this case, the underlying emotions are fear and anger.
		The subsequent logenetic stage led to the development of the ventro-vagal circuit, which is specific to higher mammals and humans; it is a circuit that has a calming and restraining effect because it stops the sympathetic activity; the heart rate decelerates, but, in this case, it is an immobilization without fear, in the absence of danger.
		When the person is in a ventro-vagal state the heart rate slows down (but it is not the bradycardia due to fear, as happens in the dorso-vagal state), the breath becomes slower and deeper, the modulation of the muscles of the middle ear occurs (which improves the ability to listen and understand) and we can observe harmonious movements of the neck and head.

Activating neuromediators	Inhibitory neuromediators	Related emotions	Psycho-pathology	Drugs
Glutamate (activates the innate fear system), neuropeptide Y (seems to calm the fear system). *CRF* corticotropin re leasing factor (CRF, anxiety promoter). *DBI* (diazepam binding inhibitor, neuropeptide that appears to promote anxiety by binding to the BDZ (benzodiazepine) link sites via the GABA sites). *CCK* cholecystokinin (can activate symptoms of both anxiety and panic/suffering). *ACTH/ adrenocorticotropic hormone)* (escape or freezing reactions in animals). *Neuropeptide alfa MSH* induces different behaviors and reactions of fear. *Substance P* *Beta-carboline* (inverse agonists that decrease the affinity of the receptor for GABA being able to induce anxiety up to epileptic seizures).	endogenous benzodiazepines and "endozepine" deoxy-corticosterone (high affinity for the GABA, a complex stimulating its affinity for GABA producing anxiolytic/sedative effects in physiological conditions such as stress and pregnancy). Tyrosine	Anxiety Worry Trauma	chronic anxiety escape patterns anticipatory anxiety (conditioned fear) phobias PTSD and its variants dependent personality disorder borderline personality disorder schizotypal personality disorder paranoid personality disorder	*benzodiazepines* Direct agonists: high affinity and intrinsic activity. *imidazopyridine:* alpidem – low intrinsic activity, mainly anxiolytic action. *Zolpidem* – high intrinsic activity, predominantly hypnotic action. *SSRI (*the elevation of serotonin reduces anxiety*).* *antiepileptics* (topiramate, lamotrigine). *Oxytocin.* *Buspirone* acts on serotonin receptors. *Beta-blockers* do not act on anxiety directly but on anxiety symptoms such as palpitations and sweating. *d-cycloserine* (anti-tuberculous antibiotic) active on the glycine site of NMDA(N-methyl-D-aspartate) receptors. *Opiates* *l-dopa + psychotherapy* in PTSD can be effective carbamazepine, topiramate and other antiepileptics. *Prazosin* (not on the market in Italy) particularly effective on nightmares related to trauma and sleep problems, acetyl cholinesterase inhibitors for memory. *Methylphenidate* (acts on the loss of attention in PTSD) *Trazodone and zolpidem* first choice for sleep in PTSD. *Rapastinel* (glyx-13, bv-102) anxiolytic antidepressant not marketed in Italy active on the glycine site of NMDA receptors. *Substance p inhibitors* through receptors NK1 GR-205171 antagonist NK1 receptors and other analogous antagonists.

(Continued)

Activating neuromediators	Inhibitory neuromediators	Related emotions	Psycho-pathology	Drugs
				Flumazenil (progenitor of the competitive antagonists of the benzodiazepine site, currently used in cases of overdose)
				barbiturates, meprobamate, alcohol
				1-tyrosine
				Oxytocin
				Phenelzine
				Antihistamine (hydroxyzine)
				Buspirone
				CRH1 Antagonist GSK561679
				Glutamate
				Endocannabinoids
				Cannabinoids
				Ion channels
				Ketamine
				MDMA –
				Psychedelic substances
				Riluzole
				Xenon
				Neurosteroid aloradine
				D-cycloserine -
				L-dopa
				Purinergic receptor antagonists
				Fytochemical/Plant-based medicines
				Deep brain stimulation.

Lust system

	Behaviors	Anatomical location	Evolutionary/adaptive function
SEXUAL DESIRE (LUST), like attachment, love and devotion, describes the core of a system that generates strong physical impulses and social emotions. The evolutionary need that is at the origin of this system seems to be the preservation of animals not as individuals but as a species. For human beings, this topic is less closely related to the chemicals activated in animals, since sexuality in humans is much more linked to the mind, emotional life and to sociocultural aspects than it happens in other animals. Nevertheless, at the primary process level, the circuits of SEXUAL DESIRE are very similar. Panksepp notes that the dopamine-driven research system is also involved in the promotion, especially in finding a sexual partner.	They are specific to the sex. In the male: courtship, territoriality and rivalry between males; in the female: sociality and female sexual responsiveness, care (together with CARE).	Cortico-medial amygdala. Medial regions of the anterior hypothalamus in mammals, preoptic area of the hypothalamus (POA) in rats and interstitial nuclei of the anterior hypothalamus (INAH) in humans (in common with the CARE and PANIC systems). Nucleus of the bed of the stria terminalis (BNST). Periaqueductal gray matter of the midbrain (PAG). Even if there are brain areas of overlap, the sexual impulse has different origins and mediators in the two sexes; the organization of sexual brain circuits begins during the fetal period during which the distinction between male and female brain circuits begins. These areas are already active at an early age, but acquire full functionality with puberty.	Survival of the species, promotion of a strong immune system and longevity (equal to physical exercise). Fisher (1998) describes in mammals three neural circuits at the base of emotional-motivational systems, necessary for mating, reproduction and parenting: sexual desire or lust, attraction and attachment. These are not only associated with different neurotransmitters and/or hormones, but also with different behavioral repertoires and have evolved into different aspects of reproduction. Sexual desire has evolved primarily to motivate individuals to seek sexual union with any member of the opposite sex of the species. The neural circuits associated with attraction have motivated individuals to choose between potential partners or suitors, with a preference for species-specific individuals, focusing attention on genetically appropriate individuals. Attachment has evolved primarily to motivate individuals to sustain bonds long enough to complete parental tasks. Sexual desire is characterized by the craving for sexual gratification and is mediated by androgens and estrogens. The attraction system is characterized by specific attention given to a partner. In man, this obsessive and passionate love is also characterized by "intrusive thoughts" on the object of love and by a desire for union with this potential partner This state is mainly associated with high levels of dopamine (DA) and norepinephrine (NE) and a reduction in central serotonin (5-HT) levels. The adult male-female attachment, according to ethologists, is characterized in birds and mammals for the mutual defense of the territory and/or nesting, for reciprocal feeding and care, for maintaining closeness, separation anxiety and shared parental tasks. In humans, it is also characterized by feelings of calm, security, social comfort and emotional union. The neural circuits involved have been associated mainly with neuropeptides, oxytocin and vasopressin.

Neuromediators and endogenous activating substances	Neuromediators and endogenous inhibitory substances	Related emotions	Psychopathology	Drugs
Dopamine: supports the appetitive and research component.	An excess of prolactin inhibits, at an increasing level, the dopaminergic pathways of desire.	Erotic feelings. Jealousy.	Aggressiveness/ dominance. Sexual identity and gender disorder (the sexual aspect of the body and cerebral sexual organization may not combine with socio-cultural identity).	L-dopa (increases desire) Impotentia coeundi: testosterone if low or Selective PDE5 inhibitors such as sidenafil, tadelafil, vardenafil, (increase nitric oxide production both in the brain and in the penis, perhaps even in the clitoris, with vasodilation and smooth muscle relaxation).
Endorphins: for the "consumption" of the relationship and to satisfaction.	Increase in Sex Hormone Binding Globulin (SHBG), during oral contraceptive therapy, oral HRT, and/or diet rich in phytoestrogens.		Conduct disorders.	L-arginine: increases nitric oxide production.
LH-RH, CCK, oxytocin (in females), vasopressin (in males), steroids (+), nitric oxide (NO). GnRH and arginine-vasopressin are produced in males in the preoptic area of the hypothalamus, oxytocin in females in the ventromedial portion of the hypothalamus. Testosterone is secreted already before and after birth. With the development of the gonads during puberty, estrogen and progestogen steroids activate oxytocin in females, while in males vasopressin is reinforced by testosterone.	Thyroid hormone, if deficient, can reduce sexual desire in both sexes. Androgen hormones: peripheral modulators. Estrogen hormones: central and peripheral modulators.		Harmful behaviors. Fetishism. Sex addiction.	Baclofen different dose-dependent effects. Niacin (VitB3). GHB: it is both a drug and an aminoacid derivative that is normally found in the central nervous system; at low doses it can cause a state of euphoria, sociability, feeling of well-being, increased sexual desire.
Hormones bind by receptors to different cerebral subcortical regions, in particular to the anterior portion of the hypothalamus. In the male, this area is richer in testosterone receptors.				Bromocriptine: increases frequency, capacity, enjoyment.
Testosterone activates nitric oxide (NO) in the brain which promotes an increase in sexual ardor and male aggression. Vasopressin and oxytocin differ from each other by two amino acids.				Cannabis: increases in a large percentage of cases desire and orgasm quality through various mechanisms, in the long term inhibits desire.

Vasopressin mediates the persistence of aspects of male sexuality, such as courtship, territoriality and rivalry between males. Oxytocin stimulates social-mobility and female sexual responsiveness.

Even if in a lower way, oxytocin also promotes the care for the offspring by the parents (mainly the mother, but also the father) and in the male it determines some behaviors of sexual activation, through an action on the hippocampus.

Androstenedione: endogenous steroid with pheromonic type activity, linked to an individualistic and dominant behavior.

DHEA hormone is converted into sex hormones in a sex-specific way: effects are still controversial.

Kisspeptin-neurokin-b-dynorphin (KNDy): it activates the production of LH and modulates the puberal period.

Progestinics (moderate central inhibitors; strong inhibitors if antiandrogenic;

facilitators if androgenic).

Oxytocin (central modulator).

Vasopressin (central modulator).

Cocaine and amphetamines: generate pseudo-appetitive behaviors.

Opiates: generate feelings of satisfaction as if there had been a "pseudo-consumer" satisfaction.

Illegal Psychedelic Substances:

Psilocin:

in a certain percentage of cases, it induces a prolonged spontaneous orgasm.

LSD: possible ecstatic sexual experience.

MDMA: amphetamine which through different mechanisms favors the desire for sexual coupling, especially in the human. In the long term it inhibits desire.

2CB, 2C-I, 2C-T-2 and 2C-T-7: reinforce sexual desire through different mechanisms.

Antipsychotics:

used for pathological jealousy, conduct disorders, etc.

Male sex hormone inhibitors for paraphilias and sexual violence: medroxprogesterone acetate, cyproterone acetate, SSRI leuprolide acetate.

Long-term drugs that inhibit desire or function: Opiates, Cocaine, Cannabinoids, Alcohol, antihistamines, lipid-lowering agents, Antihypertensives, anti-depressants, anxiolytics, antipsychotics.

Care system

	Behaviors	Key brain areas	Evolutionary meaning
The CARE system (nurturance, as the ability to provide emotional and physical care to someone) produces non-sexual social bond and it could be summarized as maternal devotion; although lot of studies prove that maternal care is not a universal evidence in animal kingdom and that fathers are able to care for offspring like mothers. Laboratory researches show that a young animal's cry activates parents' brain areas linked to separation distress (GRIEF/PANIC system) and in this way parents experience offspring's pain. This important system shows that a first, primordial level of empathy between two individuals is activated by GRIEF system, an important system for sociality. Panksepp speculated that CARE system evolved from LUST system (vasotocin and other neuromodulators could have been evolve in oxytocin, which promotes female sexual desire and maternal care).	Maternal care: physical contact and somatosensory stimulation, protection, nurturance. Bases of social interaction. In accordance with Polyvagal Theory, an absent or little environmental danger promotes a most phylogenetic recent system activation, producing comfort.	Anterior hypothalamus: paraventricular nucleus (PVN), dorsal pre-optic area (dPOA); site of oxytocin production, close to LUST system areas (ventral pre-optic area). From pre-optic nucleus through the habenula to the brain stem, and part through hypothalamus to ventral tegmental area (VTA). Anterior cingulated cortex (ACC). Bed nucleus of the stria terminalis (BNST); site of oxytocin receptors and separation distress regulation (oxytocin promotes mother's distress separation feeling due to offspring cry or loss). Ventromedial hypothalamus (VMH); site of oxytocin receptors. Ventral tegmental area (VTA); site of dopamine production. Lateral mid-brain-spinal cord; site of oxytocin receptors to promote onset of lactation. Ventral vagal system.	Preferential bond building, essential to survive before getting autonomous. Each species has different bonding windows: alatricials (that are immature at birth and usually predator) have a bonding window that remains open for a long time; while for herbivores (that are mature at birth and usually, prey) bonding window is closed within few hours after birth. Prey species need to bond rapidly because they risk getting lost soon after birth.

Activating neuromodulators	Inhibitory neuromodulators	Emotions	Psychopathology	Treatments and drugs
Estrogens: they mediate oxytocin production from anterior hypothalamus cells (PVN, POA); lesions at this level inhibit maternal behavior. *Oxytocin*: it is involved in maternal behavior in the early stage of care by promoting maternal care instinct; it can inhibit the development of tolerance to opiates and increases the sensitivity of brain to opioid system, and so the gratification related to caregiving, in this way oxytocin contributes to sustain maternal behavior over time. Oxytocin production is mediated by estrogens peak at the end of pregnancy and delivery. *Endogenous opiates:*_ low doses favor positive social interactions; high doses determine indolence state, socially apathetic (like full satisfaction feeling). *Prolactin*: it induces milk production from mother's	*Testosterone*: it reduces maternal behaviors and affective modulation. *Endogenous opiates (high doses)*: they determine indolence state, socially apathetic (like full satisfaction feeling). *"Steroidsulfateaxis"*: DHEAS and DHEA levels can influence maternal behavior and psychiatric postpartum diseases	Nurturance, love, social interest.	*Autism*: autistic behaviors have been noted in young animals with medial temporal lobe damage and in those treated with opiate: lower pain sensitivity, communication, play and curiosity deficits. These observations led to speculate that autistic children have received high exposure to endogenous opioids during early development. They may continue to experience high opioid activity in certain brain circuits. This could explain the origin of low pain sensitivity and consequent tendency to self-injurious behaviors. *Post-partum psychopathology:* Steroidsulfate (STS) axis dysfunction (deficit) may be associated with post-partum psychiatric conditions, with post-partum psychosis. This axis appears to exert disproportionately large effects in the late pregnancy/early post-partum period. STS deficiency, in women, as in men, is expected to result in lower levels of circulating estrogens	*Oxytocin:* improvement in social cognition in autism spectrum disorder (preliminary studies). Craving improvement in alcohol and drugs abuse (preclinical studies) *Opioids/opiates:* improvement in social integration in autistic children *Estrogens:* *DEHA* and *DEAHS*: STS and DHEA can directly influence the expression of a molecule that has recently received attention as a possible pathophysiological mechanism in several mood disorders: Post-partum depression, personality disorders, attachment disorders, addiction disorders.

(*Continued*)

Activating neuromodulators	Inhibitory neuromodulators	Emotions	Psychopathology	Treatments and drugs

acinar glandular tissues; it contributes to maternal feelings and maternal behaviors onset. Prolactin is also able to be produced by a "sensitization process" that can take place when a female stays closer to puppies for a long time (i.e., social experience promotes the activity of this system).

Dopamine: it mediates nest building, food seeking and recovery of lost offspring.

Norepinephrine: it is involved in olfactory memory.

Noradrenaline, acetylcholine, glutamate, γ-aminobutyric acid: they are involved in maternal behavior.

"Steroidsulfateaxis": DHEAS and DHEA levels can influence maternal behavior and psychiatric post-partum diseases.

as a consequence of reduced levels of DHEA precursor and estrogens are generally thought to be protective against psychosis.

Personality disorders:

avoidant, schizoid,

paranoid, narcissistic,

antisocial.

CARE system is involved transversely in various personality disorders; in several cases lower functioning of this system is related to disease severity (i.e., narcissistic, paranoid, schizoid, schizotypic and antisocial).

Attachment disorders and addiction disorders:

effects of opioid assumption show similarities with pleasure feelings caused by caregiver closeness. Social bonding and opiate addiction share some features:

1 gratification feeling.
2 tolerance.
3 suspension distress.

Panic/grief system

	Behaviors	Key brain areas	Evolutionary meaning
The PANIC/GRIEF system is strongly linked to CARE system and it represents the complementary aspect, that is separation. Separation causes feelings of loneliness and sadness, while reunion produces feelings of comfort and safety, thanks to substances release by CARE system. Pain related to this system is different from other physical pain and, although it produces panic feeling, it does not deal with FEAR system, because they are controlled by different neural circuits and produce different behaviors. Some studies show that too long an activation of PANIC/GRIEF system could induce chronic mood disorders and could inhibit enthusiasm generated from SEEKING system. The PANIC/GRIEF system is not attributable to FEAR system. Indeed, these systems are controlled by different cortical structures and chemicals, so they also have different reactions to drugs. Moreover these systems produce different autonomic reactions: FEAR system increases tension, heart rate, sweating and gastrointestinal disturbance; while PANIC/GRIEF system causes oppression and weakness (dorsal-vagal activation).	Crying (distress vocalization), signals of care needing. If this behavior continues for a long time, it changes and signals disappear. Gradually the system deactivates, and despair appears, that is mediated by opioids kappa receptor that inhibit SEEKING system. Immobilization, dissociation (pain insensitivity). According to Polyvagal Theory, when environment is perceived as harmful and without fly or fight ways, the dorsal-vagal system (phylogenetically more ancient) is activated.	Anterior cingulated cortex (ACC), in superior species. Bed nucleus of the stria terminalis (BNST), shared with CARE and LUST systems. Dorsal pre-optic area (dPOA), shared with CARE and LUST systems. Septal ventral area (VS). Dorsomedial thalamus (DMT). Periaqueductal Gray (PAG), shared with pain sensation pathway. Dorsal-vagal system.	Survival, maintenance of social bond that is source of feeding and protection. It represents the evolution of the most archaic (not social) fly or fight system, which is activated by pain or fear.

Activating neuromodulators	Inhibitory neuromodulators	Emotions	Psychopathology	Treatments and drugs
Corticotropin releasing factor (CRF): it is produced by paraventricular nucleus of hypothalamus in response to stress, through hypothalamic pituitary adrenal axis activation (cortisol). Cortisol allows to activate body's resources to achieve reunification. The hippocampus has many cortisol receptors, involved in episodic memory. In case of stress situations, this system would allow to develop reassuring memories, both relational and spatial ones. Prolonged activation of hypothalamic pituitary adrenal axis causes exhaustion of neuromodulators (NE, 5HT, DA) and if it continues, hippocampus damage. Glutamate: it mediates crying (NMDA and kainite receptors). Opioids, kappa receptors in κ-opioid receptors (dynorphin): they produce disorientation and dissociation feelings.	Opioids, mu receptors in μ-opioid receptors (beta-endorphin) and delta receptors: endogenous opioids release if stimulated by caregiver touch. Their function is complementary to the CARE system. Oxytocin: it is released during social relationship; it reduces tolerance to endogenous opioids; its function is complementary to the CARE system. Prolactin: it reduces separation distress behaviors; its function is complementary to the CARE system. Testosterone: it is involved in reduction of sensitivity of this system during puberty.	Separation distress, sadness, panic.	*Depression:* Animal models demonstrate that offspring show distress separation after separation from caregiver, but if isolation persists, recall signals progressively decrease and it established a condition of despair and depression. The aim of this system is to preserve energetic resources. At neurochemical level, we observe increase of CRF production and hypothalamic pituitary adrenal axis activation, and accordingly reduction of norepinephrine, serotonin and dopamine reserves (that are involved in SEEKING system). Distress separation signals have adaptive functions that are to preserve physical resources, to reduce risk of being predated, to discourage the individual to move further away from the safe place.	*Antidepressants:* SSRI. SNARI SaRI NaSSA DaRI NaRI *Amisulpiride* *Dopamine* reuptake inhibitors MAO inhibitors *Opiates,* especially *buprenorphine* *Benzodiazepines,* especially *alprazolam.* Drugs that work on GABA A and B receptors, e.g.: *Phenibut* (GABA B receptors). *Cannabis and its derivates.* *Substances that bind tropomyosin B kinase receptors.* *Antagonists of substance P NK1 receptors.* Analgesics/Anti-inflammatory: *diclofenac, acetaminophen, infliximab, Acetylsalicylic acid plus SSRI,*

Substance P: recent
studies suggest
it is involved in
depression, because
NK1 receptors are
widespread in brain
areas related to
emotions and stress
reaction (like limbic
system).

Social anxiety

Panic attacks:
sudden loss of safety
feeling (rather than
sudden fear)

Agoraphobia

*Separation anxiety
disorder*

*Personality
disorders*: borderline,
dependent.

*Omega-3 supplementation,
COX-2, TFN-alfa* antagonist
etanercept inhibitor,

*Uu8 Anti-inflammatory
cytokines,*

*Purinergic receptors (P2XT)
stimulants*

Anaesthetics:

ketamine.

Orexin/Hypocretin system.

Angiotensin-II +LY354740

*P38 Mitogen-activated protein
Kinase*

Minocycline.

IFN alfa –

Typhoid vaccination

NF-kB inhibitors

Bacterial endotoxin

Deep brain stimulation

*Anti-inflammatory cholinergic
reflex activator.*

IDO antagonists.

Chemokines receptors

antagonist

Salbutamol or salmeterol.

Play system

	Anatomical location	Evolutionary function
The game is a repeated and functionally incomplete behavior that is undertaken voluntarily during good physical condition in an environment with low levels of stress. It has a "bell" shape, increases in quantity in the first period of childhood, remains stable in youth and decreases towards puberty, probably due to neurochemical changes and to the neocortical development that inhibits the subcortical structures. The joyful social engagement of the mammal is the equivalent of men's laugh, particularly high in child physical play (e.g. tickling). The laughter circuit uses the same mesolimbic, mesocortical dopaminergic pathways as SEEKING and dreams. Game categories: explorative, relational, constructive, symbolic and of struggle. The latter is fundamental and is not related to any kind of angry aggression. In fact, the game seems to be a youthful expression of aggression for dominance, but behavioral sequences are different from competitive ones: it is a fake competition that requires reciprocity in the alternation of roles. In fact, the postures of submission in social play are never kept so long that differences in rank can be established. In adults, the game converges towards a verbal exchange, a "question and	Parafascicular complex and posterior dorsomedial thalamic nucleus that make up the non-specific reticular nuclei of the thalamus. The main sensory system that provokes and supports physical play is touch ("playing or tickling skin" in specialized skin areas). Amygdala has a secondary involvement. Neocortex has a function in the symbolic/fictional game. Bilateral lesions of the thalamus reduce the desire to play. For the game, the ways that run through the non-specific reticular nuclei are more important than the specific ways of touch: the first ones convey affective feelings activated by touch, the second, cognitive information concerning tactile stimuli. Injuries of the ventro-medial hypothalamus also inhibit play, as they generate a pathological aggressiveness that limits play activities. More playful mammals tend to have wider amygdalic dimensions, however lesions in these areas hardly generate game deficits. Studies using selective play deprivation have also provided insight into the consequences of playful experiences on basal ganglia function and the role for basal ganglia in social play suggests that corticostriatal functioning benefits from playful activities.	The social game represents the evolutionary antecedent of cooperation. It allows one to perceive the other as similar to oneself. Unlike dominance-subordination systems, which emphasize inequalities between interacting individuals (care, lust), there is also a tendency to perceive oneself and the other on the basis of a similarity in social life, in order to cooperate with each other in an equal way. This trend contributes to the creation of emotional bonds such as friendship. The evolutionary reason for the impulse to the play seems to be that of learning social skills (aggression, courtship, sexuality, competition and parenting) and non-social ones (hunting, procuring food) – this would be crucial for survival and for the construction of functions at a higher level. Even a complex feeling like social dominance may have a way of emerging and being educated

answer" session. There is a "dark side of laugh", present and used only in humans, which occurs in grotesque situations in which humor is at the service of aggressive or sexual impulses, otherwise unacceptable. It is not an intrinsic aspect of the primary system of the game, but it implies more complex mental functions. The ability to engage in social play is one of the principal indicators of healthy development, both in animals and humans.

through play. The game would also have epigenetic effects on the brain: research shows that the active play of neuronal growth factors in certain areas of the brain, such as in the frontal cortex and in the amygdala (BDNF).

Panksepp therefore assumes that the dynamic changes of the brain evoked by the game facilitate brain growth and maturation, epigenetically creating cerebral prosocial circuits and refining the executive functions of the frontal lobe. There is an also sex difference in the neural networks mediating play. Measures of play in females were positively correlated with the number of double-labeled cells in the VTA, suggesting that play in females likely induces dopamine release from meso-corticolimbic neurons to reinforce play behaviors.

Neuromediators and endogenous activating or inhibiting substances	Interacting systems	Psychopathology	Drugs

No specific mediators are yet identified.
 	
Substances definitely involved are:
 	
a *endogenous opioids*, secreted during play from the pre-optic area and in the nucleus accumbens but not in the VTA.
b *dopamine* that mediates positive anticipation and euphoria in the brain (if secreted in a fluctuating way)
c *endocannabinoids,* which promote the other positive affective forms in the brain.
d *glutamate*
e *acetylcholine*
f *TRH (role against)*
  inhibitors:
 	
  a *Dopamine* (with tonic secretion and high levels)
  b *Testosterone* (the game turns into aggression)
  c oxytocine
  d *CRF*
	SEEKING: the dopaminergic rewards explain the pleasure of the exploratory game that takes the form of a predatory practice. The prodding and nibbling of younger animals is a product of the development of the seeking system.
	
	ANGER DOMINANCE: it is not clear whether the same dopaminergic networks are activated in the social game and in non-social exploration; it is possible that some dopamine activities activate the PLAY system while others like the exploratory SEEKING sector compete with motivation.
	
	High testosterone levels promote aggression while reducing play.
		ADHD: it can be considered in relation to a hungry or particularly developed game system, due to problems of social adaptation when the drives of the game are hindered. The use of psycho-stimulants could increase the craving towards drugs.
		
		Substance abuse
		
		Aggressiveness: Pathological aggression often follows a poor childhood of play, although there are no clear correlations with the game system.
		
		Tourette syndrome: Tics can represent aberrant and uncontrolled game impulses. Imaginary friends reduce feelings of suffering and loneliness in the child, joyful companionship fosters the development of the ability to feel happy and self-confident. Moreover, the little squeaking rat (equivalent to the man's
			Psycho-stimulants:
			
			amphetamine, methylphenidate and cocaine, which indirectly increase dopaminergic neurotransmission by inhibiting dopamine reuptake, suppress social play, but also inhibit the reuptake of noradrenaline and serotonin, so that neurotransmitters other than dopamine might underlie their effects on social play. Methylphenidate and similars reduce playfulness and hyperactivity, abolishing social play behavior, without altering general social interest that depend on noradrenergic neurotransmission.
			
			Low-dose opioids: opioids modulate the hedonic, rather than the motivational aspects of social play, through μ- and κ-opioid receptors, with opposite behavioral outcomes. Low doses of morphine, preferably acting on μ-opioid receptors, promote playfulness, dominance and social trust, reducing pain; activation of κ-opioid receptors decreases social play; δ-opioid receptor stimulation has no effects.
			
			Cannabinoids (direct cannabinoid receptor agonists reduce social

laughter) is more prone to depression.

Early-onset schizophrenia

Autism

Withdrawal/ Depression

Histrionic personality disorder

Borderline personality disorder

Schizotypal personality disorder

Schizoid personality disorder

Avoidant personality disorder

interaction; indirect cannabinoid agonists, which enhance endocannabinoid activity by interfering with endocannabinoid degradation or reuptake, increased social play).

Drugs that target noradrenergic neurotransmission: the non-selective adrenoceptor agonist ephedrine, the α-adrenoceptor antagonist phenoxy-benzamine, the β-adrenoceptor antagonist propranolol, the α-1 adrenoceptor antagonist prazosin and the α-2 adrenoceptor agonist clonidine strongly decreased social play. These findings should, however, be interpreted with caution

IGF-1: there is evidence for the role of IGF-1 in promoting positive affect

D-cycloserine and GLYX-13: molecules that act on the glycine site, modulators of the effects of glutamate as partial agonist of the glycine site on the NMDA receptor, with anti-depressant effects in treatment-resistant depressed humans.

Drugs or behaviors (rough and tumble) that increase or stimulate NMDA receptors in the medial prefrontal cortex.

Bibliography

Seeking system

Alcaro, A., Huber, R., & Panksepp, J. (2007). Behavioral functions of the mesolimbic dopaminergic system: an affective neuroethological perspective. *Brain Res Rev.* 56(2):283–321.

Alcaro, A., & Panksepp, J. (2011). The SEEKING mind: primal neuro-affective substrates for appetitive incentive states and their pathological dynamics in addictions and depression. *Neurosci Biobehav Rev.* 35(9):1805–1820.

Alcaro, A., Panksepp, J., & Huber, R. (2011). d-Amphetamine stimulates unconditioned exploration/approach behaviors in crayfish: towards a conserved evolutionary function of ancestral drug reward. *Pharmacol Biochem Behav.* 99(1):75–80.

Bazov, I., Sarkisyan, D., Kononenko, O., Watanabe, H., Yakovleva, T., Hansson, A. C., et al. (2018). Dynorphin and κ-opioid receptor dysregulation in the dopaminergic reward system of human alcoholics. *Mol Neurobiol* 55(8):7049–7061.

Berner, W., & Briken, P. (2012). Pleasure seeking and the aspect of longing for an object in perversion. A neuro- psychoanalytical perspective. *Am J Psychother.* 66(2):129–150.

Bodnar, R. J. (2018). Endogenous opiates and behavior: 2016. *Peptides.* 101:167–212.

Burgdorf, J., Colechio, E. M., Stanton, P., & Panksepp, J. (2017). Positive emotional learning induces resilience to depression: A role for NMDA receptor-mediated synaptic plasticity. *Curr Neuropharmacol.* 15(1):3–10.

Coenen, V. A, Panksepp, J, Hurwitz, T. A, Urbach, H., & Mädler, B. (2012). Human medial forebrain bundle (MFB) and anterior thalamic radiation (ATR): imaging of two major subcortical pathways and the dynamic balance of opposite affects in understanding depression. *J Neuropsychiatry Clin Neurosci.* 24(2):223–223.

Dai, X., Wang, N., Ai, S., Gong, L., Tao, W., Fan, J., et al. (2020). Decreased modulation of segregated SEEKING and selective attention systems in chronic insomnia. *Brain Imaging Behav* 15(1):430–443.

Farinelli, M., Panksepp, J., Gestieri, L., Leo, M. R., Agati, R., Northoff, G. et al. (2013). SEEKING and depression in stroke patients: an exploratory study. *J Clin Exp Neuropsychol.* 35(4):348–358.

Ferrari, L. L., Park, D., Zhu, L., Palmer, M. R., Broadhurst, R. Y., & Arrigoni, E. (2018). Regulation of lateral hypothalamic orexin activity by local GABAergic neurons. *J Neurosci.* 38(6):1588–1599.

Figueiredo, T., Segenreich, D., & Mattos, P. (2016). Fluoxetine adjunctive therapy for obsessive-compulsive symptoms associated with olanzapine in schizophrenic patients. *J Clin Psychopharmacol.* 36(4):389–391.

Hegde, A., Kalyani, B. G., Arumugham, S. S., Narayanaswamy, J. C., Math, S. B., & Reddy, Y. C. (2017). Aripiprazole augmentation in highly treatment-resistant obsessive-compulsive disorder – experience from a specialty clinic in India. *Int J Psychiatry Clin Pract.* 21(1):67–69.

Huber, R., Nathaniel, T. I., & Panksepp, J. (2009). Drug-seeking behavior in an invertebrate system: evidence of morphine-induced reward, extinction and reinstatement in crayfish. *Behav Brain Res.* 197(2):331–338.

Huber, R., Panksepp, J, B., Nathaniel, T., Alcaro, A, Panksepp, J. (2011). Drug-sensitive reward in crayfish: an invertebrate model system for the study of SEEKING, reward, addiction, and withdrawal. *Neurosci Biobehav Rev.* 35(9):1847–1853.

Ikemoto, S., & Panksepp, J. (1999). The role of nucleus accumbens dopamine in motivated behavior: a unifying interpretation with special reference to reward-seeking. *Brain Res Brain Res Rev.* 31(1):6–41.

Iliceto, P., D'Antuono, L., Bowden-Jones, H., Giovani, E., Giacolini, T., Panksepp, J. et al. (2016). Brain emotion systems, personality, hopelessness, self/other perception, and gambling cognition: a structural equation model. *J Gambl Stud.* 32(1):157–169.

Kang-Park, M., Kieffer, B. L., Roberts, A. J., Siggins, G. R., & Moore, S. D. (2015). Interaction of CRF and kappa opioid systems on GABAergic neurotransmission in the mouse central amygdala. *J Pharmacol Exp Ther.* 355(2):206–211.

Lv, Q., Wang, Z., Zhang, C., Fan, Q., Zhao, Q., Zeljic, K. et al. (2017). Divergent structural responses to pharmacological interventions in orbitofronto-striato-thalamic and premotor circuits in obsessive-compulsive disorder. *EBioMedicine.* 22:242–248.

MacLean, P. D. (1990). *The Triune Brain in Evolution. Role in Paleocerebral Functions.* New York: Plenum, xxiv, 672 pp., illus. [Science. 1990].

McLaughlin, S., Bonner, G., Mboche, C., & Fairlie, T. (2010). A pilot study to test an intervention for dealing with verbal aggression. *Br J Nurs.* 19(8):489–494.

Menchón, J. M., Bobes, J., & Saiz-Ruiz, J. (2016). Obsessive-compulsive disorder: the usefulness of a pharmacological practice guideline. *Rev Psiquiatr Salud Ment.* 9(3):131.

Montag, C., & Panksepp, J. (2017). Primary emotional systems and personality: an evolutionary perspective. *Front Psychol.* 8:464.

Montag, C., & Reuter, M. (2014). Review disentangling the molecular genetic basis of personality: from monoamines to neuropeptides. *Neurosci Biobehav Rev* 43:228–239.

Montag, C., Sindermann, C., Becker, B., & Panksepp, J. (2016). An Affective neuroscience framework for the molecular study of internet addiction. *Front Psychol.* 7:1906.

Olds, J., & Milner, P. (1954). Positive reinforcement produced by electrical stimulation of the septal area and other regions of rat brain. *J Comp Physiol Psychol* 47:419–427.

Ostrovskaia, R. U., Krupina, N. A., Gudasheva, T. A., Voronina, T. A., & Seredenin, S. B. (2009). Neurotensine dipeptide analog dilept decreases the deficiency of prestimulus startle reflex inhibition: a prognostic sign of antipsychotic activity. *Eksp Klin Farmakol.* 72(5):3–7.

Panksepp, J. (2005). *Affective neuroscience: the foundation of human and animal emotion.* New York: Oxford University Press.

Panksepp, J. (2011). Review cross-species affective neuroscience decoding of the primal affective experiences of humans and related animals. *PLoS 1* 6(9):e21236.

Panksepp, J. (2016). The cross-mammalian neurophenomenology of primal emotional affects: From animal feelings to human therapeutics. *J Comp Neurol.* 524(8):1624–1635.

Panksepp, J., & Biven, L. (2012). *The archeology of mind. Neuroevolutionary origins of human emotions.* New York: W.W. Norton & Company, pp. 103; 154.

Panksepp, J., & Moskal, J. (2008). Dopamine and SEEKING: subcortical "reward" systems and appetitive urges. In A. Elliot (Ed.), *Handbook of approach and avoidance motivation* (pp. 67–87). New York: Taylor & Francis.

Panksepp, J, & Watt, D. (2011). Why does depression hurt? Ancestral primary-process separation-distress (PANIC /GRIEF) and diminished brain reward (SEEKING) processes in the genesis of depressive affect. *Psychiatry.* 74(1):5–13.

Panksepp, J., & Yovell, Y. (2014). Preclinical modeling of primal emotional affects (Seeking, Panic and Play): gateways to the development of new treatments for depression. *Psychopathology.* 47(6):383–389.

Partridge, J. G., Forcelli, P. A., Luo, R., Cashdan, J. M., Schulkin, J., & Valentino, R. J., et al. (2016). Stress increases GABAergic neurotransmission in CRF neurons of the central amygdala and bed nucleus stria terminalis. *Neuropharmacology.* 107:239–250.

Skapinakis, P., Caldwell, D. M., Hollingworth, W., Bryden, P., Fineberg, N. A., Salkovskis, P., et al. (2016). Pharmacological and psychotherapeutic interventions for management of obsessive-compulsive disorder in adults: a systematic review and network meta-analysis. *Lancet Psychiatry.* 3(8):730–739.

Veale, D., Miles, S., Smallcombe, N., Ghezai, H., Goldacre, B., & Hodsoll, J. (2014). Atypical antipsychotic augmentation in SSRI treatment refractory obsessive-compulsive disorder: a systematic review and meta-analysis *BMC Psychiatry.* 14:317. Published online 2014 Nov 29.

Walker, B. M. (2017). Jaak Panksepp: pioneer of affective neuroscience. *Neuropsychopharmacology* 42(12):2470.

Xu, Q., Jia, Y. B., Zhang, B. Y., Zou, K., Tao, Y. B., Wang, Y. P., et al (2004). Chinese Schizophrenia consortium association study of an SNP combination pattern in the dopaminergico pathway in paranoid schizophrenia: a novel strategy for complex disorders. *Mol Psychiatry.* 9(5):510–521.

Żechowski, C. (2017). Theory of drives and emotions – from Sigmund Freud to Jaak Panksepp. *Psychiatr Pol.* 51(6):1181–1189.

Zellner, M. R, Watt, D. F, Solms, M., & Panksepp, J. (2011). Affective neuroscientific and neuropsychoanalytic approaches to two intractable psychiatric problems: why depression feels so bad and what addicts really want. *Neurosci Biobehav Rev.* 35(9):2000–2008.

Zherdev, V. P., Boĭko, S. S., Mesonzhnik, N. V., Appolonova, S. A., Rodchenkov, G. N, Ostrovskaia, R. U, et al. (2018). Experimental pharmacokinetics of the new neurotensine-derivedanti psychotic drug dilept. *Eksp Klin Farmakol.* 72(3):16–21.

Rage system

Asahina, K., Watanabe, K., Duistermars, B. J, Hoopfer, E., González, C. R., Eyjólfsdóttir, E. A., et al. (2014). Tachykinin -expressing neurons control male-specific aggressive arousal in Drosophila. *Cell.* 156(1–2):221–235.

Bassi, G. S., Carvalho, M. C., Almada, R. C, & Brandão, M. L. (2017). Inhibition of substance P-induced defensive behavior via neurokinin-1 receptor antagonism in the central and medial but not basolateral nuclei of the amygdala in male Wistar rats. *Prog Neuropsychopharmacol Biol Psychiatry.* 77:146–154.

Bhatt, S., & Siegel, A. (2006). Potentiating role of interleukin 2 (IL-2) receptors in the midbrain periaqueductal gray (PAG) upon defensive rage behavior in the cat: role of neurokinin NK (1) receptors. *Behav Brain Res.* 167(2):251–260.

Bhatt, S., Zalcman, S., Hassanain, M., & Siegel, A. (2005). Cytokine modulation of defensive rage behavior in the cat: role of GABAA and interleukin-2 receptors in the medial hypothalamus. *Neuroscience.* 133(1):17–28.

Burgdorf, J., Kroes, R. A., Moskal, J. R., Pfaus, J. G., Brudzynski, S. M., & Panksepp, J. (2008). Ultrasonic vocalizations of rats (Rattus norvegicus) during mating, play, and aggression: Behavioral concomitants, relationship to reward, and self-administration of playback. *J Comp Psychol.* 122(4):357–367.

Burgdorf, J., Panksepp, J., Beinfeld, M. C., Kroes, R. A., & Moskal, J. R. (2006). Regional brain cholecystokinin changes as a function of rough-and-tumble play behavior in adolescent rats. *Peptides.* 27(1):172–177. Epub 2005 Sep 6.

Cooper, S. E., Goings, S. P, Kim, J. Y., & Wood, R. I. (2014). Testosterone enhances risk tolerance without altering motor impulsivity in male rats. *Psychoneuroendocrinology.* 40:201–212.

de Sousa Gurgel, W., Dutra, P. E., Higa, R. A., da Costa, C. B., de Matos, E., & Souza, F. G. (2015). Hyperthyroid rage: when bipolar disorder hides the real disorder. *Clin Neuropharmacol.* 38(1):38–39.

de Zavala, A. G., Cichocka, A., Eidelson, R., & Jayawickreme, N. (2009). Collective narcissism and its social consequences. *J Pers Soc Psychol.* 97(6):1074–1096.

Gobbi, G., Gaudreau, P. O., & Leblanc, N. (2006). Efficacy of topiramate, valproate, and their combination on aggression /agitation behavior in patients with psychosis. *J Clin Psychopharmacol.* 26(5):467–473.

Graeff, F. G., Sant'Ana, A. B., Vilela-Costa, H. H, & Zangrossi, H., Jr. (2015). New Findings on the neurotransmitter modulation of defense in the dorsal periaqueductal gray. *CNS Neurol Disord Drug Targets.* 14(8):988–995.

Gregg, T. R., & Siegel, A. (2001). Brain structures and neurotransmitters regulating aggression in cats: implications for human aggression. *Prog Neuropsychopharmacol Biol Psychiatry.* 25(1):91–140.

Grotzinger, A. D., Mann, F. D., Patterson, M. W., Tackett, J. L., Tucker-Drob, E. M., & Harden, K. P. (2018). Hair and salivary testosterone, hair cortisol, and externalizing behaviors in adolescents. *Psychol Sci.* doi:10.1177/0956797617742981.

Haller, J. (2018). The role of central and medial amygdala in normal and abnormal aggression: a review of classical approaches. *Neurosci Biobehav Rev.* 85:34–43.

Herpfer, I., & Lieb, K. (2005). Substance P receptor antagonists in psychiatry: rationale for development and therapeutic potential. *CNS Drugs.* 19(4):275–293.

Ilchibaeva, T. V., Tsybko, A. S., Kozhemyakina, R. V., Kondaurova, E. M., Popova, N. K., & Naumenko, V. S. (2018). Genetically defined fear-induced aggression: Focus on BDNF and its receptors. *Behav Brain Res.* 343:102–110.

Johnson, S. L., Leedom, L. J., & Muhtadie, L. (2012). The dominance behavioral system and psychopathology: evidence from self-report, observational, and biological studies. *Psychol Bull.* 138(4):692–743.

Katsouni, E., Sakkas, P., Zarros, A., Skandali, N., & Liapi, C. (2009). The involvement of substance P in the induction of aggressivebehavior. *Peptides.* 30(8):1586–1591.

Krakowski, M. I., & Czobor, P. (2014). Depression and impulsivity as pathways to violence: implications for antiaggressive treatment. *Schizophr Bull.* 40(4):886–894.

Krakowski, M. I., Czobor, P., Citrome, L., Bark, N., & Cooper, T. B. (2006). Atypical antipsychotic agents in the treatment of violent patients with schizophrenia and schizoaffective disorder. *Arch Gen Psychiatry.* 63(6):622–629.

Meyer, J. M., Cummings, M. A., Proctor, G, & Stahl, S. M. (2016). Psychopharmacology of persistent violence and aggression. *Psychiatr Clin North Am.* 39(4):541–556.

Miczek, K. A., DeBold, J. F., Hwa, L. S., Newman, E. L., & de Almeida, R. M. M. (2015). Alcohol and violence: neuropeptidergic modulation of monoamine systems. *Ann N Y Acad Sci.* 1349(1):96–118.

Muñoz Centifanti, L. C., Kimonis, E. R., Frick, P. J, & Aucoin, K. J. (2013). Emotional reactivity and the association between psychopathy-linked narcissism and aggression in detained adolescent boys. *Dev Psychopathol.* 25(2):473–485.

Panksepp, J. (1971). Aggression elicited by electrical stimulation of the hypothalamus in albino rats. *Physiol Behav.* 6(4):321–329.

Panksepp, J. (2017). The psycho-neurology of cross-species affective/social neuroscience: understanding animal affective states as a guide to development of novel psychiatric treatments. *Curr Top Behav Neurosci.* 30:109–125.

Panksepp, J., Burgdorf, J., Beinfeld, M. C., Kroes, R. A., & Moskal, J. R. (2004). Regional brain cholecystokinin changes as a function of friendly and aggressive social interactions in rats. *Brain Res.* 1025(1–2):75–84.

Pompili, E., Carlone, C., Silvestrini, C., & Nicolò, G. (2016). Pathophysiology of aggressive behavior: evaluation and management of pathological aggression. *Clin Ter.* 167(2):e42–e48.

Reijntjes, A., Vermande, M., Thomaes, S, Goossens, F, Olthof, T, Aleva, L, & Van der Meulen, M. (2016). Narcissism, bullying, and social dominance in youth: a longitudinal analysis. *J Abnorm Child Psychol.* 44(1):63–74.

Riters, L. V., & Panksepp, J. (1997). Effects of vasotocin on aggressive behavior in male Japanese quail. *Ann N Y Acad Sci.* 807:478–480.

Sandweiss, A. J., McIntosh, M. I., Moutal, A, Davidson-Knapp, R, Hu, J, Giri, A. K, et al. (2017). Genetic and pharmacological antagonism of NK$_1$ receptor prevents opiate abuse potential. *Mol Psychiatry* 23(8):1745–1755.

Schank, J. R., & Heilig, M. (2017). Substance P and the Neurokinin-1 receptor: the new CRF. *Int Rev Neurobiol.* 136:151–175.

Siegel, A., Bhatt, S., Bhatt, R., & Zalcman, S. S. (2007). The neurobiological bases for development of pharmacological treatments of aggressive disorders. *Curr Neuropharmacol.* 5(2):135–147.

Siegel, A., Schubert, K. L., & Shaikh, M. B. (1997). Neurotransmitters regulating defensive rage behavior in the cat. *Neurosci Biobehav Rev* 21(6):733–742.

Van Der Westhuizen, D., & Solms, M. (2015). Social dominance and the affective neuroscience personality scales. *Conscious Cogn.* 33:90–111.

Vize, C. E., Collison, K. L., Crowe, M. L., Campbell, W. K., Miller, J. D., & Lynam, D. R. (2012). Using dominance analysis to decompose narcissism and its relation to aggression and externalizing outcomes. *Psychol Bull.* 138(4):692–743.

Wallin, K. G., Alves, J. M., & Wood, R. I. (2015). Anabolic-androgenic steroids and decision making: Probability and effort discounting in male rats. *Psychoneuroendocrinology.* 57:84–92.

Wrangham, R. W. (2018). Two types of aggression in human evolution. *Proc Natl Acad Sci U S A.* 115(2):245–253.

Wright, A. G. C., Stepp, S. D., Scott, L. N., Hallquist, M. N., Beeney, J. E., Lazarus, S. A., et al. (2015). The effect of pathological narcissism on interpersonal and affective processes in social interactions. *Abnorm Psychol.* 126(7):898–910.

Yang, C., Ba, H., Zhang, W., Zhang, S., Zhao, H., Yu, H., Gao, Z., & Wang, B. (2018). The association of 22 Y chromosome short tandem repeat loci with initiative-aggressive behavior. *Gene.* 18:30175–30176.

Zalcman, S. S., & Siegel, A. (2006). The neurobiology of aggression and rage: role of cytokines. *Brain Behav Immunity.* 20(6):507–514.

Fear system

Ammar, G., Naja, W. J., & Pelissolo, A. (2015). Treatment-resistant anxiety disorders: a literature review of drug therapy strategies. *Encephale.* 41(3):260–265.

Baldwin, D. S., den Boer, J. A., Lyndon, G., Emir, B., Schweizer, E., & Haswell, H. (2015). Efficacy and safety of pregabalin in generalised anxiety disorder: a critical review of the literature. *J Psychopharmacol.* 29(10):1047–1060.

Baraldi, M., Avallone, R., Corsi, L., Venturini, I., Baraldi, C., & Zeneroli, M. L. (2000). Endogenous benzodiazepines. *Therapie.* 55(1):143–146.

Blessing, E. M., Steenkamp, M. M., Manzanares, J., & Marma, C. R. (2015). Cannabidiol as a potential treatment for anxiety disorders. *Neurotherapeutics.* 12(4):825–836.

Burgdorf, J., Kroes, R. A., Disterhoft, J. F., Brudzynski, S. M., Panksepp, J., Moska, J. R., et al. (2011). Positive emotional learning is regulated in the medial prefrontal cortex by GluN2B-containing NMDA receptors. *Neuroscience.* 192:515–523.

Capehart, B. (2012). DaleBass, review: managing post-traumatic stress disorder in combat veterans with comorbid traumatic brain injury. *J Rehabil Res Dev.* 49(5):789–812.

Davis, M. L, Smits, J. A., & Hofmann, S. G. (2014). Update on the efficacy of pharmacotherapy for social anxiety disorder: a meta-analysis. *Expert Opin Pharmacother.* 5(16):2281–2291.

Farzampour, Z., Reimer, R. J., & Huguenard, J. (2014). Endozepines. *Adv Pharmacol.* 72:147–164.

Frampton, J. E. (2014). Pregabalin: a review of its use in adults with generalized anxiety disorder. *CNS Drugs.* 28(9):835–854.

Gehlert, D. R., Shekhar, A., Morin, S. M, Hipskind, P. A, Zink, C., Gackenheimer, S. L., et al. (2005). Stress and central Urocortin increase anxiety-like behavior in the social interaction test via the CRF1 receptor. *Eur J Pharmacol.* 509(2–3):145–153.

Grillon, C., Hale, E., Lieberman, L., Davis, A., Pine, D. S., & Ernst, M. (2015). The CRH$_1$ Antagonist GSK561679 increases human fear but not anxiety as assessed by startle. Neuropsychopharmacology. 40(5):1064–1071.

Haaker, J., Gaburro, S., Sah, A., Gartmann, N., Lonsdorf, T. B., Meier, K., et al. (2013). Single dose of L-dopa makes extinction memories context-independent and prevents the return of fear. *Proc Natl Acad Sci U S A.* 110(26):E2428–E2436.

Heldt, S. A., Davis, M., Ratti, E., Corsi, M., Trist, D., & Ressler, K. J. (2009). Anxiolytic-like effects of the neurokinin 1 receptor antagonist in the elevated plus maze and contextual fear-potentiated startle model of anxiety in gerbils. *Behav Pharmacol.* 20(7):584–595.

Hershenberg, R., Gros, D. F., & Brawman-Mintzer, O. (2014). Role of atypical antipsychotics in the treatment of generalized anxiety disorder. *CNS Drugs.* 28(6):519–533.

Hofmann, S. G. (2014). D-cycloserine for treating anxiety disorders: making good exposures better and bad exposures worse. *Depress Anxiety.* 31(3):175–177.

Ipser, J. C., Terburg, D., Solms, M., Panksepp, J., Malcolm-Smith, S., Thomas, K., et al. (2013). Reduced fear-recognition sensitivity following acute buprenorphine administration in healthy volunteers. *Psychoneuroendocrinology.* 38(1):166–170.

Jacobson, L. H., Hoyer, D., Fehlmann, D., Bettler, B., Kaupmann, K., & Cryan, J. F. (2017). Blunted 5-HT1A receptor-mediated responses and antidepressant-like behavior in mice lacking the GABABla but not GABABlb subunit isoforms. *Psychopharmacology. (Berl).* 234(9–10):1511–1523.

Janeček, M., & Dabrowska, J. (2019). Oxytocin facilitates adaptive fear and attenuates anxiety responses in animal models and human studies-potential interaction with the corticotropin-releasing factor (CRF) system in the bed nucleus of the stria terminalis (BNST). *Cell Tissue Res.* 375(1):143–172.

Jin, Z. L., Liu, J. X., Zhang, L. M, Ran, Y.H, Zheng, Y. Y., et al. (2016). Anxiolytic effects of GLYX-13 in animal models of posttraumatic stress disorder-like behavior. *J Psychopharmacol.* 30(9):913–921.

Keck, P. E., Jr., Strawn, J. R., & McElroy, S. L. (2007). Pharmacologic treatment considerations in co-occurring bipolar and anxiety disorders. *J Clin Psychopharmacol.* 27(3):263–272.

King, G., Graham, B. M. & Richardson, R. (2018). Effects of d-cycloserine on individual differences in relapse of fear. *Prog Neuropsychopharmacol Biol Psychiatry* 84(Pt A):115–121.

Ku, Y. H, Tan, L., Li, L. S., & Ding, X. (1998). Role of corticotrophin releasing factor and substance P in pressor responses of nuclei controlling emotion and stress. *Peptides.* 19(4):677–682.

Le Doux, J. (2014). Coming to terms with fear. *Proc Natl Acad Sci U S A.* 111(8):2871–2878.

Mandolini, G. M., Lazzaretti, M., Pigoni, A., Oldani, L., Delvecchio, G., & Brambilla, P. (2018). Pharmacological properties of cannabidiol in the treatment of psychiatric disorders: a critical overview. *Epidemiol Psychiatr Sci.* 27(4):327–335.

Massey, A. T., Lerner, D. K., Holmes, G. L., Scott, R. C., & Hernan, A. E. (2016). ACTH prevents deficits in fear extinction associated with early life seizures. *Front Neurol.* 7:65.

Mayer, S. E., Snodgrass, M., Liberzon, I., Briggs, H., Curtis, G. C., & Abelson, J. L. (2017). The psychology of HPA axis activation: examining subjective emotional distress and control in a phobic fear exposure model. Psychoneuroendocrinology. 82:189–198.

Möhler, H. (2014). Endogenous benzodiazepine site peptide ligands operating bidirectionally in vivo inneurogenesis and thalamic oscillations. *Neurochem Res.* 39(6):1032–1036.

Montgomery, S. A. (2006). Pregabalin for the treatment of generalised anxiety disorder. *Expert Opin Pharmacother.* 7(15):2139–2154.

Mula, M., Pini, S., & Cassano, G. B. (2007a). The role of anticonvulsant drugs in anxiety disorders: a critical review of the evidence. *J Clin Psychopharmacol.* 27(3):263–272.

Mula, M., Pini, S, & Cassano, G. B. (2007b). The neurobiology and clinical significance of depersonalization in mood and anxiety disorders: a critical reappraisal. *J Affect Disord.* 99(1–3):91–99. Epub 2006 Sep 25.

Mula, M., Pini, S., & Cassano, G. B. (2016). The role of anticonvulsant drugs in anxiety disorders: a critical review of the evidence. *Zwanzger P. Pharmacother Anxiety Disorders. Fortschr Neurol Psychiatr.* 84(5):306–314.

Murrough, J. W., Yaqubi, S., Sayed, S., & Charney, D. S. (2015). Emerging drugs for the treatment of anxiety. *Expert Opin Emerg Drugs.* 20(3):393–406.

Onat, S., & Büchel, C. (2015). The neuronal basis of fear generalization in humans. *Nat Neurosci.* 18(12):1811–1818.

Panksepp, J., & Abbot, B. B. (1990). Modulation of separation distress by alpha-MSH. *Peptides.* 11(4):647–653.

Panksepp, J., & Normansell, L. (1990). Effects of ACTH (1–24) and ACTH/MSH (4–10) on isolation-induced distress vocalization in domestic chicks. *Peptides.* 11(5):915–919.

Panksepp, J., & Watt, D. (2011). Why does depression hurt? Ancestral primary-process separation-distress (PANIC/GRIEF) and diminished brain reward (SEEKING) processes in the genesis of depressive affect. *Psychiatry,*J74(1):5–13.

Panksepp, J. B, & Lahvis, G. P. (2016). Differential influence of social versus isolate housing on vicarious fear learning in adolescent mice. *Behav Neurosci.* 130(2):206–211. Epub 2016 Feb 15.

Perez-Garcia, G., De Gasperi, R., GamaSosa, M. A, Perez, G. M, Otero-Pagan, A., Tschiffely, A., et al. (2018). PTSD-related behavioral traits in a rat model of blast-induced mTBI are reversed by the mGluR2/3 receptor antagonist BCI-838e. *Neuro* 5(15(1)).

Raskind, M. A., Peskind, E. R., Chow, B., Harris, C., Davis-Karim, A., Holmes, H. A., et al. (2018). Trial of Prazosin for post-traumatic stress disorder in military veterans. *N Engl J Med.* 378(6):507–517.

Rogóż, Z., & Skuza, G. (2011). Anxiolytic-like effects of olanzapine, risperidone and fluoxetine in the elevated plus-maze test in rats. *Pharmacol Rep.* 63(6):1547–1552.

Sarris, J., McIntyre, E., & Camfield, D. A. (2013). Plant-based medicines for anxiety disorders, Part 1: a review of preclinical studies. *CNS Drugs.* 27(3):207–219.

Sartori, S. B., & Singewald, N. (2019). Novel pharmacological targets in drug development for the treatment of anxiety and anxiety-related disorders. *Pharmacol Ther.* 204:107402.

Sepede, G., Gambi, F., Onofrj, M., DiGiannantonio, M., Salerno, R. M. (2011). Olanzapine enhances anxiety response to an SSRI in a woman with bipolar disorder. *Prog Neuropsychopharmacol Biol Psychiatry.* 35(1):303–304.

Shiner, B., Westgate, C. L, Bernardy, N. C., Schnurr, P.P, & Watts, B. V. (2017). Anticonvulsant medication use in veterans with post-traumatic stress disorder. *J Clin Psychiatry.* 78(5):e545–e552.

Terburg, D., Morgan, B. E, Montoya, E. R, Hooge, I. T., A. R, Panksepp, J., Stein, D. J, et al. (2012). Hypervigilance for fear after basolateral amygdala damage in humans. *J Transl Psychiatry.* 2:e115.

Van der Kolk, B. (2005). *The body keeps the score: Mind, brain and body in the transformation of trauma.* New York: Penguin Books, 2015, p. 464.

Lust system

Ågmo, A. (2014). Animal models of female sexual dysfunction: basic considerations on drugs, arousal, motivation and behavior. *Pharmacol Biochem Behav.* 121:3–15.

Banner, A., Frumin, I., & Shamay-Tsoory, S. G. (2018). Androstadienone, a chemosignal found in human sweat, increases individualistic behavior and decreases cooperative responses in men. *Chem Senses.* 43(3):189–196.

Berger, A., Tran, A. H., Dida, J., Minkin, S., Gerard, N. P., Yeomans, J., et al. (2012). Diminished pheromone-induced sexual behavior in neurokinin-1 receptor deficient (TACR1(-/-)) mice. *Genes Brain Behav.* 11(5):568–576.

Both, S., Laan, E., & Schultz, W. W. (2010). Disorders in sexual desire and sexual arousal in women, a 2010 state of the art. *J Psychosom Obstet Gynaecol.* 31(4):207–218.

Briken, P., & Kafka, M. P. (2007). Pharmacological treatments for paraphilic patients and sexual offenders. *Curr Opin Psychiatry.* 20(6):609–613.

Cernovsky, Z. Z. (2016). Fetishistic preferences of clients as ranked by a sex worker. *J Sex Marital Ther.* 42(6):481–483.

Coleman, E., Raymond, N., & McBean, A. (2003). Assessment and treatment of compulsive sexual behavior. *Minn Med.* 86(7):42–47.

Czerny, J. P., & Briken, P. (2002). Berner Antihormonal treatment of paraphilic patients in German forensic psychiatric clinics. *Eur Psychiatry.* 17(2):104–106.

Dennerstein, L., Lehert, P., Koochaki, P. E., Graziottin, A., Leiblum, S., & Leventhal Alexander, J. (2007). A symptomatic approach to understand women's health experiences: a cross-cultural comparison of women aged 20 to 70 years. *Menopause.* 14(4):688–696.

Fisher, H. E. (1998). Lust, attraction, and attachment in mammalian re production. *Hum Nat.* 9(1):23–52.

Graham, M. D., Gardner, G. J., Hussain, D., Brake, W. G., & Pfaus, J. G. (2015). Ovarian steroids alter dopamine receptor populations in the medial preoptic area of female rats: implications for sexual motivation, desire, and behavior. *Eur J Neurosci.* 42(12):3138–3148.

Graham, M. D., & Pfaus, J. G. (2012). Differential effects of dopamine antagonists infused to the medial preoptic area on the sexual behavior of female rats primed with estrogen and progesterone. *Pharmacol Biochem Behav.* 102(4):532–539.

Hill, A., Briken, P., Kraus, C., Strohm, K., & Berner, W. (2003). Differential pharmacological treatment of paraphilias and sex offenders. *Int J Offender Ther Comp Criminol.* 47(4):407–421.

Holder, M. K. & Mong, J. A. (2017). The role of ovarian hormones and the medial amygdala in sexual motivation. *Curr Sex Health Rep.* 9(4):262–270.

Holder, M. K., Veichweg, S. S., & Mong, J. (2015). A Methamphetamine-enhanced female sexual motivation is dependent on dopamine and progesterone signaling in the medial amygdala. *Horm Behav.* 67:1–11.

Hornung, J., Kogler, L., Wolpert, S., Freiherr, J., & Derntl, B. (2017). The human body odor compound androstadienone leads to anger-dependent effects in an emotional Stroop but not dot-probe task using human faces. *PLoS One.* 12(4):e0175055.

Javed, Z., Qamar, U., & Sathyapalan, T. (2015). The role of kisspeptin signalling in the hypothalamic-pituitary-gonadal axis current perspective. *Endokrynol Pol.* 66(6):534–547.

Khan, O., & Mashru, A. (2016). The efficacy, safety and ethics of the use of testosterone-suppressing agents in the management of sex offending. *Curr Opin Endocrinol Diabetes Obes.* 23(3):271–278.

Khera, M. (2015). Testosterone therapy for female sexual dysfunction. *Sex Med Rev.* 3(3):137–144.

Marazziti, D., Torri, P., Baroni, S., Catena Dell'Osso, M., Consoli, G., & Boncinelli, V. (2011). Is androstadienone a putative human pheromone? *Chem Curr Med.* 18(8):1213–1219.

Mick, T. M., & Hollander, E. (2006). Impulsive-compulsive sexual behavior. *CNS Spectr.* 11(12):944–955.

Miller, M. A., Kummerow, A. M., & Mgutshini, T. (2010). Othello syndrome. Preventing a tragedy when treating patients with delusional disorders. *J Psychosoc Nurs Ment Health Serv.* 48(8):20–27.

Myers, W. A. (1995). Addictive sexual behavior. *Am J Psychother.* 49(4):473–483.

Saleh, F. M., & Berlin, F. S. (2003). Sex hormones, neurotransmitters, and psychopharmacological treatments in men with paraphilic disorders. *J Child Sex Abus.* 12(3–4):233–253.

Samad, F. D. A, Sidi, H., Kumar, J., Das, S., Midin, M., & Hatta, N. H. (2017). Subduing the green-eyed monster: bridging the psychopharma-cological and psychosocial treatment perspective in understanding pathological jealousy. *Curr Drug Targets* 20(2):201–209.

Schöttle, D., Briken, P., Tüscher, O., & Turner, D. (2017). Sexuality in autism: hyper-sexual and paraphilic behavior in women and men with high-functioning autism spectrum disorder. *Dialogues Clin Neurosci.* 19(4):381–393.

Care system

Anagnostou, E., Soorya, L., Chaplin, W., Bartz, J., Halpern, D., & Wasserman, S., et al. (2012). Intranasal oxytocin versusplacebo in the treatment of adults with autism spectrum disorders: a random-ized controlled trial. *Mol Autism.* 3:16.

Boutet, C., Vercueil, L., Schelstraete, C., Buffin, A., & Legros, J. J. (2016). Oxytocin and maternal stress during the post-partumperiod. *Gynecol Obstet Biol Reprod.* 45(8):786–795.

Bouvard, M. P., Leboyer, M., Launay, J. M., Recasens, C., Plumet, M. H., & Waller-Perotte, D., et al. (1995). Low-dose naltrexone effects on plasma chemis-tries and clinical symptoms in autism: a double-blind, placebo-controlled study. *Psychiatry Res* 58(3):191–201.

Brown, R. S. E., Aoki, M., Ladyman, S. R., Phillipps, H. R., Wyatt, A., Boehm, U., et al. (2017). Prolactin action in the medial preoptic area is nec-essary for postpartum maternal nursing behavior. *Proc Natl Acad Sci U S A.* 114(40):10779–10784.

Catanese, M. C., & Vandenberg, L. N. (2017a). Low doses of 17α-ethinyl estradiol alter the maternal brain and induce stereotypies in CD-1 mice exposed during pregnancy and lactation. *Reprod Toxicol.* 73:20–29.

Catanese, M. C., & Vandenberg, L. N. (2017b). Developmental estrogen exposures and disruptions to maternal behavior and brain: effects of ethinyl estradiol, a common positive control. *Horm Behav* 101:113–124.

Clarici, A, Pellizzoni, S., Guaschino, S., Alberico, S., Bembich, S., Panksepp, J., et al. (2015). Intranasal administration of oxytocin in postnatal depression: impli-cations for psychodynamic psychotherapy from a randomized double-blind pilot study. *Front Psychol.* 6:426.

Cochran, D., Fallon, D., Hill, M., & Frazier, J. A., (2013). The role of oxytocin in psychiatric disorders: a review of biological and therapeutic research findings. *Harv Rev Psychiatry.* Author manuscript; available in PMC 2014 Sep 1. Published in final edited form as. *Harv Rev Psychiatry.* 21(5):219–247.

Coria-Avila, G. A., Manzo, J., Garcia, L. I, Carrillo, P., Miquel, M., & Pfaus, J. G. (2014). Neurobiology of social attachments. *Neurosci Biobehav Rev.* 43:173–182.

Cox, E. Q., Stuebe, A., Pearson, B., Grewen, K., Rubinow, D., & Meltzer-Brody, S. (2015). Oxytocin and HPA stress axis reactivity in postpartum women. *Psycho-neuroendocrinology.* 55:164–172.

Davies, W. (2017). Understanding the pathophysiology of postpartum psychosis: challenges and new approaches. *World J Psychiatry.* 7:77–88.

Davies, W. (2018). Sulfation pathways: the steroid sulfate axis and its relationship to maternal behavior and mental health. *J Mol Endocrinol.* 61(2):T199–T210.

De Waal, F., (2009). *The age of empathy.* Nature's lessons for a Kinder Society, New York, Broadway Books (tr. it. L'età dell'empatia. Lezioni dalla natura per una società più solidale, Milano, Garzanti, 2011).

Dowlati, Y., Segal, Z. V., Ravindran, A. V., Steiner, M., Stewart, D. E., & Meyer, J. H. (2014). Effect of dysfunctional attitudes and postpartum state on vulnerability to depressed mood. *J AffectDisord.* 161:16–20.

Feldman, R. (2017). The neurobiology of human attachments. *Trends Cogn Sci.* 21(2):80–99.

Gómora-Arrati, P., Dominguez, G., & Ågmo, A. (2016). GABA Receptors in the medial preoptic area modulate the onset of oestradiol-induced maternal behavior in hysterectomised-ovariectomised, pregnant rats. *J Neuroendocrinol* 28(11).

Jonas, W., Bisceglia, R., Meaney, M. J., Dudin, A., Fleming, A. S., & Steiner, M. (2018). The role of breastfeeding in the association between maternal and infant cortisol attunement in the first postpartum year. *Acta Paediatr* 107(7):1205–1217.

Lara-Cinisomo, S., Zhu, K., Fei, K., Bu, Y., Weston, A. P., & Ravat, U. (2018). Traumatic events: exploring associations with maternal depression, infant bonding, and oxytocin in Latina mothers. *BMC Womens Health.* 18(1):31.

Love, T. M. (2014). Oxytocin, motivation and the role of dopamine. *Pharmacol Biochem Behav.* 119:49–60.

Macrì, S., & Würbel, H. (2006). Developmental plasticity of HPA and fear responses in rats: a critical review of the maternal mediation hypothesis. *Horm Behav.* 50(5):667–680. Epub 2006 Aug 7.

McGregor, I. S., & Bowen, T. (2012). Breaking the loop: oxytocin as a potential treatment for drug addiction. *Horm Behav.* 61:331–339.

Nelson, E. E., & Panksepp, J. (1998). Brain substrates of infant-mother attachment: contributions of opioids, oxytocin, and norepinephrine. *Neurosci Biobehav Rev.* 22(3):437–452.

Saltzman, W., & Maestripieri, D. (2011). The neuroendocrinology of primate maternal behavior. *Prog Neuropsychopharmacol Biol Psychiatry.* 35(5):1192–1204.

Seth, S., Lewis, A. J., & Galbally, M. (2016). Perinatal maternal depression and cortisol function in pregnancy and the postpartum period: a systematic literature review. *BMC Pregnancy Childbirth.* 16(1):124.

Strathearn, L. (2011). Maternal neglect: oxytocin, dopamine and the neurobiology of attachment. *J Neuroendocrinol.* 23(11):1054–1065.

Swain, J. E., Lorberbaum, J. P., Kose, S., & Strathearn, L. (2007). Brain basis of early parent-infant interactions: psychology, physiology, and in vivo functional neuroimaging studies. *J Child Psychol Psychiatry.* 48(3–4):262–287.

Szymanska, M., Schneider, M., Chateau-Smith, C., Nezelof, S., & Vulliez-Coady, L. (2017). Psychophysiological effects of oxytocin on parent-child interactions: a literature review on oxytocin and parent-child interactions. *Psychiatry Clin Neurosci.* 71(10):690–705.

Yatawara, C. J., Einfeld, S. L., Hickie, I. B., Davenport, A., & Guastella, A. J. (2016). The effect of oxytocin nasal spray on social interaction deficits observed in young children with autism: a randomized clinical crossover trial. *Mol Psychiatry.* 21:1225–1231.

Panic system

Andrejew, R., Oliveira-Giacomelli, Á., Ribeiro, D. E., Glaser, T., Fernandes Arnaud-Sampaio, V., Lameu, C., et al. (2020). The P2X7 receptor: central hub of brain diseases. *Front Mol Neurosci.* 13:124.

Berrocoso, E., Ikeda, K., Sora, I., Uhl, G. R., Sánchez-Blázquez, P., & Mico, J. A. (2013). Active behaviors produced by antidepressants and opioids in the mouse tail suspension test. *Int J Neuropsychopharmacol.* 16(1):151–162.

Berrocoso, E., & Mico, J. A. (2009). Cooperative opioid and serotonergic mechanisms generate superior antidepressant-like effects in a mice model of depression. *Int J Neuropsychopharmacol.* 12(8):1033–1044.

Berrocoso, E., Micó, J. A., & Ugedo, L. (2006). In vivo effect of tramadol on locus coeruleus neurons is mediated by alpha-2-adrenoceptors and modulated by serotonin. *Neuropharmacology.* 51(1):146–153. Epub 2006 May 30.

Berrocoso, E., Rojas-Corrales, M. O., & Mico, J. A. (2006). Differential role of 5-HT1A and 5-HT1B receptors on the antinociceptive and antidepressant effect of tramadol in mice. *Psychopharmacology (Berl).* 188(1):111–118. Epub 2006 Jul 11.

Black, D. S., Cole, S. W., Irwin, M. R., Breen, E., St Cyr, N. M., Nazarian, N., et al. (2013). Yogic meditation reverses NF-κB and IRF-related transcriptome dynamics in leukocytes of family dementia caregivers in a randomized controlled trial. *Psychoneuroendocrinology.* 38:348–355.

Borges, G. P., Berrocoso, E., Mico, J. A., & Neto, F. (2015a). ERK1/2: function, signaling and implication in pain and pain-related anxio-depressive disorders. *Prog Neuropsychopharmacol Biol Psychiatry.* 60:77–92.

Borges, G. P., Berrocoso, E., Mico, J. A., & Neto, F. (2015b). Corticotropin-releasing factor mediates pain-induced anxiety through the ERK1/2 signaling cascade in locus coeruleus neurons. *Int J Neuropsychopharmacol* 18(8).

Borges, G. P., Miguelez, C., Neto, F., Mico, J. A., Ugedo, L., & Berrocoso, E., (2017). Activation of extracellular signal-regulated kinases (ERK 1/2) in the locus coeruleus contributes to pain-related anxiety in arthritic male rats. *Int J Neuropsychopharmacol.* 20(6):463.

Borges, G. P., Neto, F., Mico, J. A., & Berrocoso, E. (2014). Reversal of monoarthritis-induced affective disorders by diclofenac in rats. *Anesthesiology.* 120:1476–1490.

Boselli, C., Barbone, M. S., & Lucchelli, A. (2007). Older versus newer antidepressants: substance P or calcium antagonism? *Can J Physiol Pharmacol.* 85(10):1004–1011.

Boutet, C., Vercueil, L., Schelstraete, C., Buffin, A., & Legros, J. J. (2016). Oxytocin and maternal stress during the post-partum period. *Gynecol Obstet Biol Reprod.* 45(8):786–795.

Bower, J. E., Ganz, P. A., Irwin, M. R., Arevalo, J. M., & Cole, S. W. (2011). Fatigue and gene expression in human leukocytes: increased NF-κB and decreased glucocorticoid signaling in breast cancer survivors with persistent fatigue. *Brain Behav Immunity.* 25:147–150.

Brown, R. S. E., Aoki, M., Ladyman, S. R., Phillipps, H. R., Wyatt, A., Boehm, U. et al. (2017). Prolactin action in the medial preoptic area is necessary for postpartum maternal nursing behavior. *Proc Natl Acad Sci U S A.* 114(40):10779–10784.

Bufalino, C., Hepgul, N., Aguglia, E., & Pariante, C. M. (2013). The role of immune genes in the association between depression and inflammation: a review of recent clinical studies. *Brain Behav Immunity.* 31:31–47.

Capuron, L., & Miller, A. H. (2004). Cytokines and psychopathology: lessons from interferon-α. *BiolPsychiatry.* 56:819–824.

Carvalho, M. C, Santos, J. M., & Brandão, M. L. (2015). Dorsal periaqueductal gray post-stimulation freezing is counteracted by neurokinin-1 receptor antagonism in the central nucleus of the amygdala in rats. *Neurobiol Learn Mem.* 121:52–58.

Catanese, M. C., & Vandenberg, L. N. (2017a). Developmental estrogen exposures and disruptions to maternal behavior and brain: effects of ethinyl estradiol, a common positive control. *Horm Behav* 101:113–124.

Catanese, M. C., & Vandenberg, L. N. (2017b). Low doses of 17α-ethinyl estradiol alter the maternal brain and induce stereotypies in CD-1 mice exposed during pregnancy and lactation. *Reprod Toxicol.* 73:20–29.

Chen, J., Tsuchiya, M., Kawakami, N., Furukawa, & T. A. (2009). Non-fearful vs. fearful panic attacks: a general population study from the National Comorbidity Survey. *J Affect Disord.* 112(1–3):273–278.

Chiang, J. J., Eisenberger, N. I., Seeman, T. E., & Taylor, S. E. (2012). Negative and competitive social interactions are related to heightened proinflammatory cytokine activity. *Proc Natl Acad Sci U S A.* 109:1878–1882.

Clarici, A, Pellizzoni, S., Guaschino, S., Alberico, S., Bembich, S., Panksepp, J., et al. (2015). Intranasal administration of oxytocin in postnatal depression: implications for psychodynamic psychotherapy from a randomized double-blind pilot study. *Front Psychol.* 6:426.

Cochran, D., Fallon, D., Hill, M., & Frazier, J. A. (2013). The role of oxytocin in psychiatric disorders: a review of biological and therapeutic research findings. *Harv Rev Psychiatry Harv Rev Psychiatry.* 21(5):219–247.

Cohen, I. V., Makunts, T., Atayee, R., & Abagyan, R. (2017). Population scale data reveals the antidepressant effects of ketamine and other therapeutics approved for non-psychiatric indications. *Sci Rep.* 7:1450.

Cowley, D. S., Dager, S. R., & Dunner, D. L. (1987). Lactate infusions in major depression without panic attacks. *J Psychiatr Res.* 21(3):243–248.

Cox, E. Q., Stuebe, A., Pearson, B., Grewen, K., Rubinow, D., & Meltzer-Brody, S. (2015). Oxytocin and HPA stress axis reactivity in postpartum women. *Psychoneuroendocrinology.* 55:164–172.

Degnan, A. P., Tora, G. O., Han, Y., Rajamani, R., Bertekap, R., Krause, R., et al. (2015). Biaryls as potent, tunable dual neurokinin 1 receptor antagonists and serotonin transporter inhibitors. *Bioorg Med Chem Lett.* 25(15):3039–3043.

Degnan, A. P., Tora, G. O., Huang, H., Conlon, D. A., Davis, C. D., & Hanumegowda, U. M. (2016). Discovery of indazoles as potent, orally active dual neurokinin 1 receptor antagonists and serotonin transporter inhibitors for the treatment of depression. *ACS Chem Neurosci.* 7(12):1635–1640.

Di Fabio, R., Alvaro, G., Braggio, S., Carletti, R., Gerrard, P. A., Griffante, C., et al. (2013). Identification, biological characterization and pharmacophoric analysis of a new potent and selective NK1 receptor antagonist clinical candidate. *Bioorg Med Chem.* 21(21):6264–6273.

Dold, M., Bartova, L., Souery, D., Mendlewicz, J., Serretti, A., Porcelli, S., et al. (2017). Clinical characteristics and treatment outcomes of patients with major depressive disorder and comorbid anxiety disorders -*results from a European multicenter study. J Psychiatr Res.* 91:1–13.

Domingos, L. B., Hott, S. C., Terzian, A. L. B., Resstel, L. B. M. (2018). P2X7 purinergic receptors participate in the expression and extinction processes of contextual fear conditioning memory in mice. *Neuropharmacology.* 128:474–481.

Dowlati, Y., Segal, Z. V., Ravindran, A. V., Steiner, M., Stewart, D. E., & Meyer, J. H. (2014). Effect of dysfunctional attitudes and postpartum state on vulnerability to depressed mood. *J Affect Disord.* 161:16–20.

Duan, L., Gao, Y., Shao, X., Tian, C. S., Fu, C., & Zhu, G. (2020). Research on the development of theme trends and changes of knowledge structures of drug therapy studies on major depressive disorder since the 21st century: a bibliometric analysis. *Front Psychiatry.* 11:647.

Eisenberger, N. I. (2012). The pain of social disconnection: examining the shared neural underpinnings of physical and social pain. *Nat Rev Neurosci.* 13:421–434.

Eisenberger, N. I., Berkman, E. T., Inagaki, T. K., Rameson, L. T., Mashal, N. M., & Irwin, M. R. (2010). Inflammation-induced anhedonia: Endotoxin reduces ventral striatum responses to reward. *BiolPsychiatry.* 68:748–754.

Fava, M., Memisoglu, A., Thase, M. E., Bodkin, J. A., Trivedi, M. H., de Somer, M. et al. (2016). Opioid modulation with buprenorphine/samidorphan as adjunctive treatment for inadequate response to antidepressants: a randomized double-blind placebo-controlled trial. *Am J Psychiatry.* 173:499–508.

Feldman, R. (2017). The neurobiology of human attachments. *Trends Cogn Sci.* 21(2):80–99.

Gómora-Arrati, P., Dominguez, G., & Ågmo, A. (2016). GABA receptors in the medial preoptic area modulate the onset of oestradiol-induced maternal behavior in hysterectomised-ovariectomised, pregnant rats. *J Neuroendocrinol* 28(11).

Graeff, F. G., Sant'Ana, A. B., Vilela-Costa, H. H., & Zangrossi, H. Jr. (2015). New findings on the neurotransmitter modulation of defense in the dorsal periaqueductal. *CNS Neurol Disord Drug Targets.* 14(8):988–995.

Guiard, B. P, Guilloux, J. P, Reperant, C, Hunt, S. P, Toth, M, & Gardier, A. M. (2007). Substance P neurokinin 1 receptor activation within the dorsal raphe nucleus controls serotonin release in the mouse frontal cortex. *Mol Pharmacol.* 72(6):1411–1418. Epub 2007 Sep 21.

Johnson, P. L., Federici, L. M., & Shekhar, A. (2014). Etiology, triggers and neurochemical circuits associated with unexpected, expected, and laboratory-induced panic attacks. *Neurosci Biobehav Rev.* 46(Pt 3):429–454.

Johnson, P. L., Molosh, A., Fitz, S. D., Truitt, W. A., Shekhar, A. (2012). Orexin, stress, and anxiety/panic states. *Prog Brain Res.* 198:133–161.

Jonas, W., Bisceglia, R., Meaney, M. J., Dudin, A., Fleming, A. S., Steiner, M. et al. (2018). The role of breastfeeding in the association between maternal and infant cortisol attunement in the first postpartum year. *Acta Paediatr* 107(7):1205–1217.

Lara-Cinisomo, S., Zhu, K., Fei, K., Bu, Y., Weston, A. P., & Ravat, U. (2018). Traumatic events: exploring associations with maternal depression, infant bonding, and oxytocin in Latina mothers. *BMC Womens Health.* 18(1):31.

Layton, M. E., Friedman, S. D., & Dager, S. R. (2001). Brain metabolic changes during lactate-induced panic: effects of gabapentin treatment. *Depress Anxiety.* 14(4):251–254.

Liebowitz, M. R., Fyer, A. J., Gorman, J. M., Dillon, D., Davies, S., Stein, J. M., et al. (1985). Specificity of lactate infusions in social phobia versus panic disorders. *Am J Psychiatry.* 142(8):947–950.

Linge, R., Jiménez-Sánchez, L., Campa, L., Pilar-Cuéllar, F., Vidal, R., Pazos, A., et al. (2016). Cannabidiol induces rapid-acting antidepressant-like effects and enhances cortical 5-HT/glutamate neurotransmission: role of 5-HT1A receptors. *Neuropharmacology.* 103:16–26. Epub 2015 Dec 19.

Macrì, S., & Würbel, H. (2006). Developmental plasticity of HPA and fear responses in rats: a critical review of the maternal mediation hypothesis. *Horm Behav.* 50(5):667–680. Epub 2006 Aug 7.

Nelson, E. E., & Panksepp, J. (1998). Brain substrates of infant-mother attachment: contributions of opioids, oxytocin, and norepinephrine. *Neurosci Biobehav Rev.* 22(3):437–452.

Pereira, V. S., & Hiroaki-Sato, V. A. (2018). A brief history of antidepressant drug development: from tricyclics to beyond ketamine. *Acta Neuropsychiatr* 30(6):307–322.

Pick, C. G. (1996). Strain differences in mice antinociception: relationship between alprazolam and opioid receptor subtypes. *Eur Neuropsychopharmacol.* 6(3):201–205.

Price, R. B., Iosifescu, D. V., Murrough, J. W., Chang, L. C., Al Jurdi, R. K., Iqbal, S. Z., et al. (2014). Effects of ketamine on explicit and implicit suicidal cognition: a randomized controlled trial in treatment-resistant depression. *Depress Anxiety.* 31(4):335–343.

Rangel, M. P., Zangrossi, H., Jr., Roncon, C. M., Graeff, F. G., & Audi, E. A. (2014). Interaction between opioid and 5-HT1A receptors of panic-related defensive responses in the rat dorsal periaqueductal grey. 10a. *J Psychofarmacol.* 28(12):1155–1160.

Roncon, C. M., Biesdorf, C., Graeff, F. G., Audi, E. A., Zangrossi, H., Jr., & Coimbra, C. N. (2013). Cooperative regulation of anxiety and panic-related defensive behaviors in the rat periaqueductal grey matter by 5-HT1A and μ-receptors. *J Psychopharmacol.* 27(12):1141–1148.

Roncon, C. M., Biesdorf, C., Santana, R. G., Zangrossi, H., Jr., Graeff, F. G., & Audi, E. A. (2012). The panicolytic-like effect of fluoxetine in the elevated T-maze is mediated by serotonin-induced activation of endogenous opioids in the dorsal periaqueductal grey. *J Psychopharmacol.* 26(4):525–531.

Roncon, C. M., Graeff, F. G., Audi, E. A., Zangrossi, H., Jr., Coimbra, C. N., Maraschin, J. C., et al. (2015). Pharmacological evidence for the mediation of the panicolytic effect of fluoxetine by dorsal periaqueductal gray matter μ-opioid receptors. *Neuropharmacology.* 99:620–626.

Rooney, S., Sah, A., Unger, M. S., Kharitonova, M., Sartori, S. B., Schwarzer, C., et al. (2020). Neuroinflammatory alterations in trait anxiety: modulatory effects of minocycline. *Transl Psychiatry.* 10:256.

Ruan, X., Mancuso, K. F., & Kaye, A. D. (2016). Effects of ultra-low-dose Buprenorphine on suicidal ideation confounded by physical pain relief? *Am J Psychiatry.* 173(10):1043.

Seth, S., Lewis, A. J., & Galbally, M. (2016). Perinatal maternal depression and cortisol function in pregnancy and the postpartum period: a systematic literature review. *BMC Pregnancy Childbirth.* 16(1):124.

Shekhar, A., DiMicco, J. A. (1987). Defense reaction elicited by injection of GABA antagonists and synthesis inhibitors into the posterior hypothalamus in rats. *Neuropharmacology.* 26(5):407–417.

Shekhar, A., Johnson, P. L., Sajdyk, T. J., Fitz, S. D., Keim, S. R., Kelley, P. E., et al. (2006). Angiotensin-II is a putative neurotransmitter in lactate-induced panic-like responses in rats with disruption of GABAergic inhibition in the dorsomedial hypothalamus. *J Neurosci.* 26(36):9205–9215.

Slavich, G. M., & Irwin, M. R. (2014). From stress to inflammation and major depressive disorder: a social signal transduction theory of depression. *Psychol Bull.* 140(3):774–815.

Soares, V. P., & Campos, A. C. (2017). Evidence for the anti-panic actions of Cannabidiol. *Curr Neuropharmacol.* 15(2):291–299.

Strathearn, L. (2011). Maternal neglect: oxytocin, dopamine and the neurobiology of attachment. *J Neuroendocrinol.* 23(11):1054–1065.

Striebel, J. M., & Kalapatapu, R. K. (2014a). The anti-suicidal potential of buprenorphine: a case report. *Int J Psychiatry Med.* 47(2):169–174.

Szymanska, M., Schneide, M., Chateau-Smith, C., Nezelof, S., & Vulliez-Coady, L. (2017). Psychophysiological effects of oxytocin on parent-child interactions: a literature review on oxytocin and parent-child interactions. *Psychiatry Clin Neurosci.* 71(10):690–705.

Yovell, Y., & Bar, G. (2016). Ultra-low-dose Buprenorphine for mental pain: response to Ruan et al. *Am J Psychiatry.* 173(10):1043–1044.

Ziablintseva, E. A., & Pavlova, I. V. (2009). Influence of GABA agonist phenibut on the neuronal activity and interaction in hippocampus and neocortex in emotionally negative situations. *Ross Fiziol Zh Im I M Sechenova.* 95(9):907–918.

Play system

Aguilar, R. (2010). Infantile experience and play motivation. *Soc Neurosci.* 5(5–6):422–440.

Aguilar, R., Caramés, J. M., & Espinet, A. (2009). Effects of neonatal handling on playfulness by means of reversal of the desire to play in rats (Rattus norvegicus). *J Comp Psychol.* 123(4):347–356.

Beatty, W. W., Costello, K. B., & Berry, S. L. (1984). Suppression of play fighting by amphetamine: effects of catecholamine antagonists, agonists and synthesis inhibitors. *Pharmacol Biochem Behav.* 20(5):747–755.

Burgdorf, J., Colechio, E. M., Stanton, P., & Panksepp, J. (2017). Positive emotional learning induces resilience to depression: a role for NMDA receptor-mediated synaptic plasticity. *Curr Neuropharmacol.* 15(1):3–10.

Burgdorf, J., Kroes, R. A., Beinfeld, M. C., Panksepp, J. & Moskal, J. R. (2010). Uncovering the molecular basis of positive affect using rough-and-tumble play in rats: a role for insulin-like growth factor I. *Neuroscience.* 168(3):769–777.

Dai, X., Wang, N., Ai, S., Gong, L., Tao, W., Fan, J., et al. (2020). Decreased modulation of segregated SEEKING and selective attention systems in chronic insomnia. *Brain Imaging Behav* 15(1):430–443.

Gordon, N. S, Kollack-Walker, S., Akil, H., & Panksepp, J. (2002). Expression of c-fos gene activation during rough and tumble play in juvenile rats. *Brain Res Bull.* 57(5):651–659.

Ikemoto, S., & Panksepp, J. (1992). The effects of early social isolation on the motivation for social play in juvenile rats. *Dev Psychobiol.* 25(4):261–274.

Johnson, B. (2003). Psychoanalytic treatment of psychological addiction to alcohol (alcohol abuse). *Front Psychol.* 2:362.

Jordan, R. (2003). Social play and autistic spectrum disorders: a perspective on theory, implications and educational approaches. *Autism.* 7(4):347–360.

Møller, P., & Husby, R. (2000). The initial prodrome in schizophrenia: searching for naturalistic core dimensions of experience and behavior. *Schizophr Bull.* 26(1):217–232.

Moskal, J. R., Kuo, A. G., Weiss, C., Wood, P. L., O'Connor Hanson, A., Kelso, S., et al. (2005). Glix13: a monoclonal antibody-derived peptide that acts as an N-methyl-D-aspartate receptor modulator. *Neuropharmacology.* 49(7):1077–1087.

Nocjar, C., Zhang, J., Feng, P., & Panksepp, J. (2012). The social defeat animal model of depression shows diminished levels of orexin in mesocortical regions of the dopamine system, and of dynorphin and orexin in the hypothalamus. *Neuroscience.* 218:138–153.

Normansell, L. & Panksepp, J. (1985). Effects of clonidine and yohimbine on the social play of juvenile rats. *Pharmacol Biochem Behav.* 22(5):881–883.

Northcutt, K. V., & Nguyen, J. M. K. (2014). Female juvenile play elicits Fos expression in dopaminergic neurons of the VTA. *Behav Neurosci.* 128(2):178–186.

Panksepp, J. (2016). The cross-mammalian neurophenomenology of primal emotional affects: from animal feelings to human therapeutics. *J Comp Neurol.* 524(8):1624–1635.

Panksepp, J., & Moskal, J. (2008). Dopamine and SEEKING: subcortical "reward" systems and appetitive urges. In A. Elliot (Ed.), *Handbook of approach and avoidance motivation* (pp. 67–87). New York: Taylor & Francis.

Pellis, S. M., Field, E. F., Smith, L. K., & Pellis, V. C. (1997). Multiple differences in the play fighting of male and female rats. Implications for the causes and functions of play. *Neurosci Biobehav.* 21(1):105–120.

Santini, A. C., Pierantoni, G. M., & Gerlini, R. (2014). Glix13, a new drug acting on glutamatergic pathways in children and animal models of autism spectrum disorders. *BioMed Res Int.* 2014:234295.

Siviy, S. M. (2019). Basal ganglia involvement in the playfulness of juvenile rats. *J Neurosci Res.* 97(12):1521–1527.

Siviy, S. M., Fleischhauer, A. E., Kuhlman, S. J. & Atrens, D. M. (1994). Effects of alpha-2 adrenoceptor antagonists on rough-and-tumble play in juvenile rats: evidence for a site of action independent of non-adrenoceptor imidazoline binding sites. *Psychopharmacology (Berl).* 113(3–4):493–499.

Trezza, V., Baarendse, P. J. & Vanderschuren, L. J. (2010). The pleasures of play: pharmacological insights into social reward mechanisms. *Trends Pharmacol Sci.* 31(10):463–469.

Trezza, V., Damsteegt, R. & Vanderschuren, L. J. (2009). Conditioned place preference induced by social play behavior: parametrics, extinction, reinstatement and disruption by methylphenidate. *Eur Neuropsychopharmacol.* 19(9):659–669.

Trezza, V., & Vanderschuren, L. J. (2008). Cannabinoid and opioid modulation of social play behavior in adolescent rats: differential behavioral mechanisms. *Eur Neuropsychopharmacol.* 18(7):519–530.

Vanderschuren, L. J., Trezza, V., Griffioen-Roose, S., Schiepers, O. J. G., Van Leeuwen, N., De Vries, T. J. et al. (2008). Methylphenidate disrupts social play behavior in adolescent rats. *Neuropsychopharmacology.* 33(12):2946–2956.

Żechowski, C. (2017). Theory of drives and emotions – from Sigmund Freud to Jaak Panksepp. *Psychiatr Pol.* 51(6):1181–1189.

2 The evolutionary roots of Neuropsychoanalysis

The Instinct in Darwin and Freud

Teodosio Giacolini

> *The theory of the instincts is so to say our mythology.*
> *Instincts are mythical entities, magnificent in their indefiniteness*
>
> *Freud 1933, p. 95*

Introduction

Sigmund Freud's cultural and professional evolution was marked by his encounter with Charles Robert Darwin's evolutionist thought. Freud was born in 1856 and three years later Darwin published a book destined to be the most famous work of the nineteenth century, *On the Origin of Species* (Darwin, 1859). Darwin's first work was followed by two other volumes equally destined to arouse strong interest and controversy, namely *The Descent of Man, and Selection in Relation to Sex* (Darwin, 1871) and *The Expression of the Emotions in Man and Animals* (Darwin, 1872). In 1873, the young Freud enrolled at the Faculty of Medicine and the first optional seminar he attended was on the topic 'General Biology and Darwinism' taught by zoologist Carl Claus (1835–1899) (Jones, 1953; Sulloway, 1979). The evolutionist thought, whether more closely related to Darwin or to his disciples, as well as to his predecessors such as Jean-Baptiste de Lamarck (1744–1828), constituted the backbone of the epistemological construction of psychoanalysis.

Freud's interest in the clinical treatment of mental suffering, pursued through a psychological methodology, has always been intimately connected to study the 'physiological' functioning of the psyche. This objective was initially pursued through a neurobiological model, soon replaced by an electively psychological model rooted within a historical-evolutionary epistemology. Both models were united by underlying evolutionary thought and by placing the instinct/drive at the centre of the subjective mental dynamics, thereby taking up the topical interests of Darwin's studies on human mental functioning (Darwin, 1872). Freud used the term *trieb* (translated as *drive* in modern psychoanalysis) to treat instinct in the

DOI: 10.4324/9781003198741-3

human species – as the Germanic linguistic tradition indicated – defining it in this citation as:

> *If now we apply ourselves to considering mental life from a **biological** point of view, an 'instinct' appears to us as a concept on the frontier between the mental and the somatic, as the psychical representative of the stimuli originating from within the organism and reaching the mind, as a measure of the demand made upon the mind for work in consequence of its connection with the body.*
>
> (Freud, 1915a, p. 120)

In the subsequent development of psychoanalytic thinking, this led direct attention to be paid almost exclusively to the psychic/representational component. Recall that *trieb* is the German term that specifically refers to human instinct – in which the meaning of motivational drive prevails – and the object most exposed to cultural and environmental variations. Freud not only highlighted the *trieb* energetic component, but also its *source* and its *aim*, which are biologically identifiable. The other term *instinkt* (translated as *instinct*) is reserved by the Germanic tradition and by Freud to designate instincts in animals. The use of the term *trieb* contributed to a misunderstanding among Freud's followers, who interpreted it as evidence of the complete diversity of human mental/instinctual functioning from the animal one. For these reasons, in the present work, I will use the dual expression *instinct/drive* to emphasize its biological identity and: "[...] the derivation in man of drives from instincts" (Laplanche, 1976, p. 10; see for an exhaustive discussion Solms, 2018). As highlighted in this paper, psychoanalysis has progressively lost contact with its evolutionary biological roots; it has led to a broad reflection on this problem, partly within the International Psychoanalytic Society (IPA) and through the development of the *Neuropsychoanalysis* research paradigm (Johnson & Flores Mosri, 2016). The latter, bringing together psychoanalysts and scholars of neuroscientific disciplines, seeks to pursue the thread of evolutionary epistemology either in a more electively neurophysiological dimension or connected to a comparative biology, through which to study the subject as an expression of the *BrainMind* unit.

Sigmund Freud: evolutionist, biologist, neurologist

It is of particular interest that the young Freud aspired to become a research biologist rather than a professional doctor, first attending Claus' teaching class; Claus was a zoologist and full professor of Comparative Biology. It was thanks to Claus that he obtained a two-year (1875 and 1876) scholarship at the Zoological Station of Trieste, founded by Claus (Jones, 1953, p. 41). There, Freud studied the procreative activity of eels, or the structure of the gonads, which had not yet been identified in that species. Freud's extensive account of his interest in biology appeared in his first scientific work, presented by Prof. Claus at the Academy of Sciences in 1877, entitled *Observation on the Finer Structure of the Lobular Organs of the Eel, Described as Testicles* (Freud, 1877–1897). After his second residency at the Zoological Station of Trieste and his third year of Medicine, Freud's interest in biology led him to be admitted as a *famulus* – or research student – in the Physiology laboratory directed by Ernst Wilhelm von Brücke (1819–1892), where he remained until 1882. In that laboratory, Freud conducted neuro-histological research on the spinal cord of the *Ammocoetes* (*Petromyzon*), a genus of fish belonging to primitive cyclostomes, highlighting how nerve cells and fibres form a morphological and functional unit (Jones, 1953, p. 241), which would later be called *neuron*. With this study, he demonstrated the phylogenetic derivation of bipolar cells from unipolar ones by demonstrating the evolutionary continuity of upper animals from lower ones. This research was reported in two important works: *On the Dorsal Nerve Roots in the Spinal Cord of Ammocoetes (Petromyzon Planeri)* (Freud, 1877) and *On the Spinal Ganglia and Spinal Cord of the Petromyzon* (Freud, 1878). These were followed by a work in 1879 entitled *Note on a Method for the Anatomical Preparation of the Nervous System* and another in 1882, *On the Structure of Nerve Fibres and Nerve Cells of the Crayfish* (Freud, 1877–1897). These studies brought significant neuroanatomical knowledge to what would soon be called *neuron* in the 1891 monograph written by Heinrich Wilhelm Gottfried von Waldeyer-Hartz (1836–1921).

Freud graduated in Medicine in March 1881, and in 1882 von Brücke explained that Freud's aspiration for an academic career in his laboratory would be impossible, because there were already two colleagues ten years his senior, Sigmund Exner (1846–1926) and Ernst Fleischl von Marxow (1846–1891), and his financial conditions were unfavourable. The frustration resulting from this awareness is recounted in his dream *'Non vixit'* from *The Interpretation of Dreams* (Freud, 1899), as a result of which he irrevocably turned to professional medicine as a neurologist. Despite his departure from von Brücke's laboratories and his medical profession, for the next 15 years, Freud had continued to study and write about neurology, having, however, directed his attention from the nervous system of animals to that of the human species. The three works on the structure of the *medulla oblongata* (Freud, 1877–1897) date back to the years 1885 and 1886, but the best-known works – six between 1884 and 1887 – are on the medical properties of cocaine and on cerebral palsy, with the latter culminating in a mighty monograph entitled *Infantile Cerebral Palsy* (Freud, 1877–1897). The conference of 1882, then published in 1884 with the title *The Structure of the Elements of the Nervous System* (Freud, 1877–1897), anticipates the description and denomination of the neuron made in 1991 by Waldeyer-Hartz. The work that marks and highlights the complex transition that Freud undertook from neurology to psychology is *The Project for a Scientific Psychology* (Freud, 1895a); it was left unfinished and then rejected and can be considered an acknowledgment of the impossibility of going towards neurology of psychological functioning due to the limits of the scientific instruments of the time. That work substantially contributes to directing him towards psychology, even if it is 'inner psychology'. The *Project*, however, is a melting pot of psychological concepts, even if examined with the neurophysiologist's approach, such as the mechanism of pathological repression, reality testing, the distinction between primary and secondary processes, and dream theory as the fulfilment of desires. Thus, the *Project* marks the transition from neurology to psychological functioning and phenomena, or – according to the interesting observation of Frank Jones Sulloway (1979) – the transition from neurophysiological reductionism, which has the physical-chemical sciences as a reference point, to a historical-evolutionist reductionism. These two models of reductionism recall the subdivision outlined by the biologist Ernst Mayr (1961), who divides life sciences into those that deal with *functional, proximate causes* (for example, neurophysiology) and those that deal with the *ultimate causes*, which involve explanations of an evolutionary matrix, such as evolutionary and comparative biology. So Freud distanced himself from the *Project* and then shortly after, with the 'discovery' of the *Oedipus Complex*, he simultaneously took both the psychological path and the evolutionary psychology as one, which had its conceptual fulcrum in the use of the works of biogenetics by Ernst Heinrich Haeckel (1834–1919). Biogenetics would provide Freud with a strategic tool, which he resorted to for the rest of his intellectual life. Haeckel's thought highlights the passage from evolutionism, towards which Freud had dedicated himself until 1897 and that can be defined as *comparative morphology,* to the physiology of psychic functioning. The ideas of the German biologist became the basis for the construction of the *psychosexual stages of development* (Freud, 1905) and later on for the elaboration of the *death drive* concept (Freud, 1923).

Freud's *evolutionary psychology* was profoundly influenced by a pre-Darwinian researcher who had also inspired the work of Haeckel, Jean-Baptiste Pierre Antoine de Monet, knight of Lamarck (1744–1829), whose thought constituted one of the main elements of Freudian theory. Lamarck's pre-Darwinian theories regarding the *inheritance of the characteristics acquired by experience*, influenced evolutionary culture for a long time, including Darwin. Based on Lamarck's work, Freud conceptualizes neuroses as a legacy or vestige of experiences lived by prehistoric generations (see, e.g., *Totem and Taboo*, 1912–1913). Lamarck's influence on Freud is one of the aspects that John Bowlby (1968) most emphasizes, underlining how Freud's evolutionism has remained closer to Lamarck's rather than Darwin's ideas based on *natural selection*. On the other hand, it should be noted that current research on epigenetics (see, e.g., Skinner et al., 2014) is causing a certain re-evaluation of Lamarck's work. Another central author in the framework of Freud's evolutionary psychology was George John Romanes (1848–1894), who can be considered, after Darwin, the one who gave the greatest boost to comparative psychology, postulating the similarity between human cognitive processes and those of other animal species.

Charles Darwin and *comparative psychology*

The influence of Darwin's thought (1809–1882) on Freud is certainly a central element in the evolution of his theoretical clinical construction, not only in the field of *comparative biology* but also above all regarding its influence on the psychological field, which constituted the real ground on which psychoanalysis was built. Darwin himself had dedicated particular attention and interest to psychology and developmental psychology. He was especially attracted to the evidence that showed continuity and homology not only between the anatomical structures of animals and those of the human species but also between those of their emotional and mental functioning. Darwin was very much motivated by *comparative psychology*, which led him to conduct studies on emotional expressions in humans and animals (Darwin, 1872). The study of emotions was the natural consequence of the similarity of body gestures and non-verbal communications that showed the behavioural continuity between animals and humans. On the other hand, the evidence that facial expressions in humans were a function of the same muscle groups that in animal species were responsible for similar manifestations was significant. This in turn contributed to the demonstration of continuity between body and mind (Sulloway, 1979). Along with the expression of emotions, and closely associated with them, are instincts to which Darwin dedicated particular interest in understanding their nature and origin.

Darwin's interest in psychology led him to become interested in child psychology, as Freud would have done, and in the study of intelligence. Many of the ideas that accompany his two late works, *The Descent of Man* and *The Expression of the Emotions in Man and Animals*, had been elaborated by Darwin in the years 1838–1839, immediately after his return from the five-year trip around the world as a naturalist on the ship of his British Majesty, the *Beagle*. Returning from the exploratory journey, Darwin began writing a series of notebooks, two of which, signed by him as M and N, report annotations of his reasoning and studies on the evolution of man's mind and behaviour. From the very start, Darwin had dealt with the more specifically human qualities as aspects intimately connected to the evolution of the species and that could be addressed with the same comparative instrument. In the *Notebook M*, Darwin states: "Metaphysic must flourish. He who understands baboon would do more towards metaphysics than Locke" (Darwin, 1838). It should be remembered that at that time Metaphysics meant Psychology. More than 30 years after writing this sentence, in *The Descent of Man, and Selection in Relation to Sex* (1871), Darwin inserted a chapter of the famous biologist, Thomas Henry Huxley (1825–1895), entitled 'Note on the Resemblances and Differences in the Structure and the Development of the Brain in Man and Apes' (by Professor Huxley, F.R.S.). One of Darwin's central merits and proof of his profound influence on nascent psychiatry was precisely his founding work on the study of behavioural and psychological functioning on an organic and comparative basis. Darwin writes: "*Experience shows the problem of the mind cannot be solved by attacking the citadel itself — the mind is function of body — we must bring some stable foundation to argue from [...]*" (Darwin, 1839, p. 5). This is the current perspective of Neuroscience and in particular of Affective Neuroscience – summarized by Jaak Panksepp's concept of *dual monism* (Panksepp & Biven, 2012) – which has the *BrainMind* as its object of study. The term Metaphysics in Darwin's time – as mentioned above – was still designated to that branch of philosophy that was interested in psychology, and M, as the abbreviation of one of the two notebooks, stood for Metaphysics. It should be remembered that only in 1879 did Wilhelm Maximilian Wundt (1832–1920) established the first laboratory dedicated to psychology in Leipzig to collect the empirical data of research and analyze its results according to the criteria of natural sciences. Still, in Freud's time, psychology was a young science, and to highlight all its links with philosophy, he used the term Metapsychology to name a series of his writings on the psychology of the unconscious (Freud, 1915b). Returning to Darwin and his influence on Freud, let's first look at the importance of instincts and the expression of emotions, as an expression of excess nervous discharge (Darwin, 1872). Freud writes about the motor symptoms of a hysterical patient:

> *She played restlessly with her fingers (1888) or rubbed her hands against one another (1889) so as to prevent herself from screaming. This reason reminds one forcibly of one of the principles laid down by Darwin to explain the expression of the emotions —the principle of the overflow of excitation [*Darwin, 1872, Chap. III*], which accounts, for instance, for dogs wagging their tails.*

> (Freud , 1895b, p. 91)

Darwin's interest in instinctual and emotional dynamics was early intertwined with his interest in psychology and especially in developmental psychology. After the birth of his first son, he began to take note of the child's psychic growth, to which he added the observations on the children born later, thus collecting a data comparison. Only in 1877 did Darwin publish these observations on Mind as *A Biographical Sketch of an Infant* (Darwin, 1877), showing how over the years he had maintained his interest in the study of child psychology already anticipated in 1838 in notebook M, where he affirmed the importance of a *Natural Science of Babies* (Lorch & Hellal, 2010), a link between the inferior species and the adult man. Hence, Darwin's interest in instinctual, emotional and language development, includes all aspects that would have substantiated biological and developmental psychology. In addition, the sexual instinct, like an instinct that already develops within the baby during his first weeks, was highlighted both by

Darwin (Darwin, 1877) and a growing number of post-Darwinian scholars. Among these scholars, Romanes emerges with his works *Mental Evolution in Animal* (1883), taking a comparativist perspective; it was published the year after Darwin's death, followed by *Mental Evolution in Man* (1888), with particular reference to developmental psychology. All these works were known and quoted by Freud. Romanes' work, which gives a great impetus to the biology-based psychology supported by Darwin and which is found in Freud's psychoanalysis, at least until the complete development of the *first drive theory*, between 1910 and 1915, was subsequently replaced in 1820 by the *second drive theory*. It is useful to remember that in the *first drive theory*, Freud had divided the drives into *ego-drives* or *self-preservation drives,* and *sexual drives* (Freud, 1915a), taking up the classically Darwinian bipartition (Darwin, 1871, p. 140). With the *second drive theory*, Freud introduced the *death drive* to which he opposed the *life drives*; the *id* now included both the *self-preservation* and *sexual drives*. This new drive theory, unlike the first, was not based on an instinctual theory shared by the evolutionary scientific world even if, the *death drive theory* can be considered the biogenetic Haeckel's theory summarized in his famous phrase: "Ontogenesis is the short and fast recapitulation of phylogenesis" (Haeckel, 1866, p. 300, cit. in Levit et al., 2010) brought to the extreme (Sulloway, 1979). *Beyond the Pleasure Principle* (Freud, 1920) marked a further turning point for Freud towards a 'psychologism' dimension of mental functioning based on deductions that have remained, in a self-referential way, internal to the psychoanalytic world.

In the *first drive theory*, Darwin's presence is also traceable in some central concepts in the Freudian construction of psychoanalysis, such as the concept of *fixation*, that of r*egression* and the *importance of first impressions*. In the evolutionist and medical biology of Freud's time, the concept of *anatomical fixation* relating to inhibitions or arrests of physiological development existed. It was possible to study this in both embryology and subsequent development. These arrests or fixations that led to clinical pictures were attributed either to congenital causes or to damage suffered by the immature organism (Sulloway, 1979). To these latter causes, the inhibition of the development of brain tissue, Freud traced back part of the infantile paralysis with which he had dealt between 1877 and 1897. But the *fixations* that Freud continued to deal with, enough to make it a pivot of the etiopathogenesis on which psychoanalysis was called to operate, were the drive/instincts. Darwin had shown how instincts in animals were subjected to even severe changes in their evolution when repeatedly exposed to certain environmental conditions (Darwin, 1859, Chapter I). Following Darwin's work, scholars such as Douglas Spalding (1841–1877) and Romanes discovered various forms of instinctual fixations. The best known physiological instinctual fixation was the one identified by Spalding, who, in two short works in *On Instinct* (1872) and *Instinct: With Original Observations on Young Animals* (1873), described both the *instinct of pursuit* – later renamed by Konrad Lorenz as *Imprinting* – and the time windows within which an instinct must find a suitable environment to be able to develop properly. The discoveries of these European researchers were used by William James to support the two laws of sexual perversion, *Inhibition of instincts by habit* and the *Transitoriness of instincts* (Sulloway, 1979), which influenced European sexologists and psychiatrists. Starting from the *Three Essays on Sexuality* (1905), Freud made it a central concept of the etiopathogenesis of mental suffering, connected to the altered development of psychosexual phases. On the other hand, in the paragraph from *The Descent of Man* entitled "Arrests of development" (Darwin, 1871, p. 121), Darwin identified the cause of both physical and mental aberrations in the arrest of development, the echo of which can be found 30 years later in *Three Essays on Sexuality* (Freud, 1905).

Freud's concept of *fixation* is functionally related to that of *regression*, which Freud always elaborates within an evolutionary context, through the work of the English neurologist John Hughlings Jackson (1835–1911), who described the development of the nervous system as *evolution* of a hierarchical structure, which in the case of pathology tended to *dissolution* (Hughlings Jackson, 1884). This conception had been suggested to Jackson by the contents of Herbert Spencer's evolutionary philosophy (Smith, 1982a, 1982b). Freud, who knew Jackson thoroughly for his studies *On Aphasia* (Freud, 1891/1953; Fullinwider, 1983), used the word *regression* instead of *dissolution*. Another key concept of the Freudian theory of the genesis of psychoneuroses is that of *adhesiveness* of the first sexual impressions in those who will subsequently be neurotic. Also within this concept, it is possible to find one of the central concepts of Darwin's work concerning the construction of behavioural and emotional habits based on repeated experiences in past eras, where the presence of Lamarck's thought is evident. He wrote in one of his *Notebooks*: "Expression (of an emotion), is an heredetary habitual movement consequent on some action, which the progenitor did, when excited or disturbed by the same cause, which now excites the expression" (Darwin, 1838, p. 107).

In later works, especially *Totem and Taboo* (1912–1913), Freud will highlight how neuroses should be understood as emotional expressions of a phylogenetic heritage, brought up to date by early or traumatic experiences that cannot find conscious expression due to the development of the current social morality. The wealth of knowledge in the field of instinctual and emotional vicissitudes that Freud could draw from Darwin was enormous. First of all, there is the extremely modern vision of instincts as an expression of brain functioning. Darwin wrote: "Definite instincts begin acquired is most important argument, to show that they result from organization of brain [...] thought, however unintelligible it may be seems as much function of organ, as bile of liver" (Darwin, 1838–1840, pp. 36–37).

Furthermore, instincts became central elements in the regulation or dysregulation of individuals. "If the judgment persists, while the reason is forgotten, this judgment is consciousness or instinct" (Darwin, 1838–1839, p. 28). Here, Darwin proposes an extremely current concept of consciousness: that labelled as *simple* or *primary* consciousness (Damasio, 2010;

Edelman, 2004; Panksepp & Biven, 2012), whose characteristic is the transitive property – consciousness of an external object – to which self-reflection is still not united. This concept of *instinctual consciousness* will constitute a cornerstone of the Freudian construction of the unconscious, which has at its centre the desire or the instinctual intentionality to which self-reflexivity has not yet been added. Hence also the socially negative or dangerous component of *instinctual consciousness*, as indicated even before Freud by Darwin "[...] our descent, then, is the origin of our evil passions!! The devil under form of Baboon is grandfather" (Darwin, 1838, p. 124). Darwin therefore recognizes and proposes a double consciousness, the instinctual, implicit one, and the explicit one given by self-awareness. In this regard, the next passage from the *Notebook M* is impressive, in which, quoting the work of the physiologist Herbert Mayo (1796–1852), Darwin states:

> *In same book [...] wonderful case of perfect double consciousness Mayo compares it with Somnambulism. – the young lady almost equally in her senses in either state. – does this throw light on instinct, showing what trains of action may be done unconsciously as far as the ordinary state is concerned?*
>
> *(Darwin, 1838, p. 110)*

It is almost impossible not to find the echo of Freud's subsequent *Studies on Hysteria (1895b)*. And a little further on he continues:

> *But now in Mayo's [...] case of double consciousness, one would pity suffering in one state almost as much as in the other, though she when well did not recollect it anything [...]. Insanity is* ~~much~~ *somewhat the same as double consciousness, as shown in the tendency to forget the insane idea; & ones expression of double self, though as in Dr Ashe's case, one here was conscious of the two states.*
>
> *(Darwin, 1838, pp. 116–117)*

Here, it is possible to find Freud's unconscious world that expresses itself through symptoms or dreams. Darwin, therefore, identified instinct – as mentioned above – as the central element of the evolution of the brain, mental and cultural capacities. He writes:

> *[...] the instinct (or conscience) is always present (which is indeed, often felt at very time it is disobeyed) & is sure guide. – Hence conscience is improved by attending & reasoning on its action, & on the results following our conduct [...].*
>
> (Darwin, 1838–1840, p. 45)

Here, too, it is possible to find the Freudian echo of what will be conceptualized as an unconscious conflict between the various parts or *instances* of the personality and the various instincts/drives.

To end this brief exploration of Darwin's presence in Freud, which is useful for reconstructing the ideas and concepts present in the *Weltanschauung* in which the father of psychoanalysis was born and raised, we see how the study of the human mind – alongside the presence of instincts – was inextricably connected to the recognition of culture and therefore of society. Freud wrote

> *[…] In the individual's mental life someone else is invariably involved, as a model, as an object, as a helper, as an opponent; and so from the very first individual psychology, in this extended but entirely justifiable sense of the words, is at the same time social psychology as well.*

(Freud, 1921, p. 69)

Now we come to Darwin and to the instincts considered above all as the learning of the species:

> *the instinct of sociability & sociability, doubtless grow together […] the having received pleasure from some one/person/in early infancy, during many generations giving love of mother: the having received some advantage from man during many generations giving the social feeling […]. Although I cannot pretend to say how far & minutely our instincts extend, † yet as they are acquired by social animals, living under certain conditions, in this world […].*

(Darwin, 1838–1840, p. 50)

So Darwin identifies the dynamics of instincts in a cultural/social learning framework determined by group living, as in almost all animal and vegetable species to which he devoted much attention. Darwin, unlike Freud, considers the instinctive dimension connected to group living not as a renunciation of the rules of social living, as the second one expressed widely in *Civilization and its Discontents* (Freud, 1930), but as a store of knowledge – today we would say implicit – handed down through the hereditary result of positive experiences and therefore settled, because it is beneficial to the species. Shortly after the above passage, Darwin made a fulminating statement worthy of a current neuroscientist: "Reason can never lead to action" (Darwin, 1838–1840, p. 50), in which it reaffirms full confidence in the instinct as a guide to action.

From the death drive to the decline of Darwinian psychoanalysis

As deliberated above, a turning point in Freud's thought was the publication, in 1920, of *Beyond the Pleasure Principle*. This work elaborated a theory of instincts/drives of a teleological type, which was totally opposed to Darwin's evolutionist epistemology. The ultimate goal of all that is organic, as Freud pointed out, is to inevitably tend towards the inorganic, from which only transiently there can be liberation for the vitalizing presence of libido. This teleological approach allowed Freud to give a logical explanation to phenomena that had not hitherto found sufficient positioning in his theory. These problems were the *repetition compulsion, trauma fixity* and the transversal problem of *regression*. It has already been mentioned that the tendency to inorganic is the extreme consequence of the Haeckelian biogenetic theory of *ontogenesis that recapitulates the phylogeny*, based on his studies of comparative embryology. In Freud, the recapitulation would re-actualize the primary and primitive return of the living to the non-living. Freud wrote:

> *The instincts rule [...] reveal an effort to restore an earlier state of things. We may suppose that from the moment at which a state of things that has once been attained is upset, an instinct arises to create it afresh and brings about phenomena which we can describe as a 'compulsion to repeat'. Thus the whole of embryology is an example of the compulsion to repeat [...] which expresses the conservative nature of the instincts.*
>
> (Freud, 1933, p. 104)

The biogenetic theory at the centre of the *second drive theory* highlights a central factor in Freud's thought, which is his *Psycho-Lamarckism* conception (Sulloway, 1979). So Haeckel was at the same time deeply close to Darwin – his youngest follower – and to the Lamarckian ideas of settling the experience acquired in the biological memory, hence the biogenetic law so dear to Freud. Darwin also recognized the Lamarckian laws, *Law of use and disuse* and *Inheritance of acquired traits*, as important factors of evolution to add to natural selection. But Darwin did not share the presence of a teleological tendency towards a progressive evolution determined by the individual's internal needs as a subjective drive to adaptation, transmissible to subsequent generations through a biological memory that allowed the accumulation of progressive individual adaptations. Darwin considered Lamarck's approach as:

> *Heaven forfend me from Lamarck nonsense of a "tendency to progression" "adaptations from the slow willing of animals" &c, – but the conclusions I am led to are not widely different from his—though the means of change are wholly so – I think I have found out (here's presumption!) the simple way by which species become exquisitely adapted to various ends [...].*
>
> (Darwin to Joseph Dalton Hooker, January 11, 1844)

Therefore, Freud supported – with the biogenetic theory combined with Lamarck's teleological evolutionism –evolution as an expression of individual unconscious efforts. The letter addressed to Karl Abraham on November 11, 1917 is extremely clear in this regard:

> The idea is to put Lamarck entirely on our ground and to show that his "need", which creates and transforms organs, is nothing but the power of Ucs. Ideas over one's own body, of which we see remnants in hysteria, in short the "omnipotence of thoughts". This would actually supply a Ψα [psychoanalysis] explanation of expediency; it would put the coping stone on Ψα. [psychoanalysis].
>
> (letter to Karl Abraham on November 11, 1917a)

And again he wrote: "[...] a consistent application of Lamarck's theories of evolution turns into a conclusion of psychoanalytic thought" (Letter from Freud to Georg Groddeck, June 5, 1917b). Freud's evolutionary biology rested on a solid and shared Darwinian approach, on which a Lamarckian perspective increasingly suited to accompany Freud on the resolutely psychological path following the impossibility of continuing the one taken with the *Project for a Scientific Psychology* (Freud, 1895a). This allowed him to support the *omnipotence of thoughts* (see Freud, 1912–1913) as the fulcrum of the psychological interest in psychoanalysis.

The twofold detachment of psychoanalysis from (evolutionist) biology

The Lamarckian component of Freudian thought can therefore be considered the basis of the gradual detachment of psychoanalytic thought from dialogue with the biological sciences, and of the increasingly convincing epistemological autonomy. The consequence of both Freud's sharing of the Lamarckian conception and the *death drive* theory, as an endogenous aggressive and disruptive force, was a disinterest among the second generation of psychoanalysts to dialogue with the biological sciences to verify the congruity of their statements and find *humus* to increase their knowledge of mental functioning. It is known that although the drive/instinctual fulcrum of the Freudian system remained untouchable, there was a double reaction to it. Melanie Klein (1882–1960) placed the *death drive* at the centre of her theory, but had no interest in verifying its congruity, foundation and sharing with the natural sciences; rather, she continued and strengthened that part of the Freudian thought that elected the analytical session as the only source of scientific experience. Klein had, however, the undeniable merit of having promoted and supported, precisely through the Freudian conceptualization of the *death drive*, the exploration and dialogue with the world of psychosis connected to the disruptive/aggressive force present in an endogenous way in the human mind. In this way, Klein helped to project psychoanalysis into frontier psychiatry at the beginning of the Second World War. Structurally connected to this ability to have given meaning to the psychotic world,

Klein and followers particularly emphasized the *omnipotence of thoughts*, qualifying both the adult's unconscious functioning and the mental functioning of childhood. Hence the analogy between the adult's dreams, "The interpretation of dreams is the royal road to a knowledge of the unconscious activities of the mind" (Freud, 1899, p. 608) and her psychoanalytic play technique, the royal road to the child's mental functioning (see for example *Personification in the Play of Children*, 1929).

Shortly after Klein, some psychoanalysts who accepted Freud's drive theory, continued to ignore biological questions, adopting the relational reading of psychological and experiential order as the only practicable and useful referent. Among them, the most well-known names include Harry Guntrip, William Ronald Dodds Fairbairn, Donald Winnicott and a large army of disciples of the so-called relational psychoanalysis on both sides of the ocean.

At the same time, critical and innovative contributions to Freudian theory came precisely from psychoanalysts who, starting at the end of the fifties, went on to criticize or consider completely superfluous any interest in the instinctual/drive system of the Freudian theory of mental functioning; such was the case with the serious and refined George Klein who claimed that a theory for clinical practice assumes that the symbol and the motor-appetitive aspects (learned within a psychosocial process) are more important than the purely instinctual aspect of sexual capacity (Klein, 1976). This psychoanalyst and research psychologist at the Menninger Foundation in Topeka (Kansas) engaged in the empirical validation of metapsychological constructs, as did other colleagues such as David Rapaport and Robert R. Holt. George Klein highlighted how the instinctual energetic apparatus of psychoanalytic theory was a kind of body alien dropped into Freud's clinical experience. More recently, in the eighties, another American psychoanalyst, Joseph D. Lichtenberg, who was also engaged in the work of revising and modernizing the theoretical framework of psychoanalysis, wrote in his book *Psychoanalysis and Motivation* (1989): "A psychoanalytic theory of adaptive and maladaptive motivational functioning is about lived experience throughout life" (Lichtenberg, 1989, p. 2), which also privileged the experiential component of the structure motivating the Self. Lichtenberg – in his review of Freud's drive theory – made use of the fundamental contribution of *Infant Research* (Lichtenberg, 1991), just as G. Klein had previously made use of the contribution of experimental psychology. The gradual shift of the centre of gravity of psychoanalysis towards a *psychological* dimension, increasingly interested in the relational/experiential dimension of the subject (symbolized by the concept of Self) and less interested in the instinctual dimension was also the consequence of another cause completely external to the psychoanalytic movement. This cause was the lack of interest in evolutionary theory in biology itself as a privileged point of view from which to study the organic, behavioural and developmental processes of the individual as mutually interacting aspects, following the Darwinian lesson.

The paradigm shift in the biological sciences occurred – as Myron A. Hofer (2014) documents – in the years between 1900 and 1910, caused by the rediscovery of the work of Gregor Johann Mendel (1822–1884), father of genetics, whose work up to that date had been totally unrecognized. In 1906, his rediscovery led the British biologist and geneticist William Bateson (1861–1926), to coin the term *genetics* to define Mendel's research field. In 1909, the Danish botanist and geneticist Wilhelm Ludwig Johannsen (1857–1927) first used the word *gene* to describe the units of hereditary information, and then in 1911, he coined the terms *genotype* and *phenotype* to indicate the hereditary units that make up the chromosomes. In this new framework, the biology of instincts or motivations and development processes remained confined to the study of *genetics*, which contributed to reducing the interest in *Comparative Psychology* and in the study of the *phylogeny* of mental processes.

Conclusions

In 1935, the famous article by zoologist Konrad Zacharias Lorenz (1903–1989), *Der Kumpan in der Umwelt des Vogels (Der Artgenosse Als Auslösendes Moment sozialer Verhaltensweisen)* [The Companion in the bird's world; the fellow-member of the species as a releasing factor of social behaviour] (Lorenz, 1935/1937), began to revive the interest in instinctual behaviour and Comparative Psychology within the biological sciences. Lorenz was certainly the most significant author of this revival of interest in instinct, not only through his field research on animal behaviours, but also, since 1937, through his teachings of Animal Psychology and Comparative Anatomy at the University of Vienna and three years later, becoming professor of Psychology at the University of Königsberg, Germany. Through Lorenz's work, the comparative study of behaviour and the interest in understanding human mental functioning, evoking Darwin, revived in biology, currently named *Ethology*. In the first aforementioned work by Lorenz (1935/1937), two of the fundamental concepts that we will find in John Bowlby's later work are the concept of *releaser*, or stimulus triggering instinctive behaviour, and the even-more famous one of *imprinting*, a milestone in evolving the concept of attachment. During approximately the same years that saw the birth and development of Ethology in Europe, a similar discipline was emerging on the other side of the ocean: *comparative psychology in the laboratory*. The leading exponents of this experimental system were the psychologists who are listed as follows: Frank Ambrose Beach, Jr. (1911–1988); Donald Olding Hebb (1904–1985); Daniel S. Lehrman (1919–1972); developmental psychobiologist Jay Seth Rosenblatt (1923–2014); Karl Spencer Lashley (1890–1958); and Harry Frederick Harlow (1905–1981). Ethology and Comparative Psychology had and have areas of overlap and specific differences. One favoured the naturalistic observation of behaviour in the adaptation environment, with the particular ambition to explain the 'why', or 'the ultimate causes' (Mayer, 1961) of behaviours; the other, the laboratory-controlled study, mainly aimed at describing the 'how' or 'proximate causes' (Mayer, 1961) of an operation/functioning. However, both disciplines contributed to reconstitute that link of interest between the ontogenetic development of the individual and the phylogenetic development of the species.

In this scientific and cultural panorama – which blossomed between the two great wars and reached maturity in the post-war period – the work of John Bowlby came to light; it constituted a profound reinterpretation of the Freudian epistemological system precisely at the central point of psychoanalytic theory, instinct/drive, no longer denied or misunderstood, but re-founded from the inside.

References

Bowlby, J. (1968). *Effects on behaviour of disruption of an affectional bond.* Eugenics Society Symposia, 94–108.

Damasio, A. R. (2010). *Self comes to mind: Constructing the conscious brain.* London: Heinemann.

Darwin, C. R. (1838). *Notebook M: Metaphysics on morals and speculations on expression.* (K. Rookmaaker, Trad.) (http://darwin-online.org.uk/)

Darwin, C. R. (1839). *Notebook N: [Metaphysics and expression (1838–1839)].* CUL-DAR126.-Transcribed by K. Rookmaaker, edited by P. Barrett. (Darwin Online, http://darwin-online.org.uk/)

Darwin, C. R. (1838–1840). *Old & useless notes about the moral sense & some metaphysical points.* (P. H. Barrett, Trad.) (http://darwin-online.org.uk/)

Darwin, C. R. (1844) Correspondence Project, *"Letter no. 729".* Cambridge, MA: Cambridge University Library https://www.darwinproject.ac.uk/letter/DCP-LETT-729.xml. Also published in The Correspondence of Charles Darwin, vol. 3. Images of original letters from the Cambridge University Library collection are courtesy of Cambridge University Digital Library (cudl.lib.cam.ac.uk).

Darwin, C. R. (1859). *On the origin of species by means of natural selection, or, the preservation of favoured races in the struggle for life.* London: J. Murray. [1st edition]. Text prepared by John van Wyhe and Sue Asscher 2002, advertizements added 9.2006. Scanned by van Wyhe. Proofread and corrected by Asscher 8.2008. RN6.

Darwin, C. R. (1871). *The descent of man, and selection in relation to sex.* London: J. Murray. Volume 1. 1st edition. Scanned by John van Wyhe 1.2006; transcribed (double key) by AEL Data 4.2006, corrections by van Wyhe 2.2011, 2.2014. RN9.

Darwin, C. R. (1872). *The expression of the emotions in man and animals.* London: J. Murray. 1st edition. Transcribed for John van Wyhe 2002, corrections 2003, 8.2006. Proofread and corrected by Sue Asscher, 2.2008. RN5.

Edelman, G. M. (2004). *Wider than the sky. The phenomenal gift of consciousness.* New Haven, CT: Yale University Press.

Freud, S. (1877–1897). *Abstracts of the scientific writings of Dr. Sigmund Freud.* In J. Strachey (Ed. and Trans.), The Standard Edition of the Complete Psychological Works of Sigmund Freud, Volume III (1893–1899): Early Psychoanalytic

Publications (pp. 223–257). London: The Hogarth Press and the Institute of Psycho-analysis, 1962.

Freud, S. (1891). *On aphasia: A critical study.* (E. Stengel, Trad.) London: Imago. 1953.

Freud, S. (1895a). *Project for a scientific psychology.* In J. Strachey (Ed. and Trans.), The Standard Edition of the Complete Psychological Works of Sigmund Freud. Volume I (1886–1899): Pre-Psycho-Analytic Publications and Unpublished Drafts (pp. 281–391). London: The Hogarth Press and the Institute of Psychoanalysis, 1966.

Freud, S. (1895b). *Studies on hysteria.* In J. Strachey (Ed. and Trans.), The Standard edition of the Complete Psychological Works of Sigmund Freud, Volume II (pp. 1–323). London: The Hogarth Press and the Institute of Psycho-Analysis, 1953.

Freud, S. (1900). *The interpretation of dreams.* In J. Strachey The Standard Edition of the Complete Psychological Works of Sigmund Freud, Volume IV (1900) (pp. 1–310). London: The Hogarth Press and the Institute of Psycho-analysis. 1953.

Freud, S. (1905). *Three essays on sexuality and other works.* In J. Strachey (Ed. and Trans.), The Standard Edition of the Complete Psychological Works of Sigmund Freud, Volume VII (1901–1905) (pp. 125–321). London: The Hogarth Press and the Institute of Psychoanalysis, 1953.

Freud, S. (1912–1913). *Totem and taboo.* In J. Strachey (Ed. and Trans.), The Standard Edition of the Complete Psychological Works of Sigmund Freud, Volume XIII (1913–1914) (pp. vii–162). London: The Hogarth Press and the Institute of Psycho-analysis, 1953.

Freud, S. (1915a). *Instincts and their vicissitudes.* In J. Strachey (Ed. and Trans.), The Standard Edition of the Complete Psychological Works of Sigmund Freud, Volume XIV (1914–1916) (pp. 109–140). London: The Hogarth Press and the Institute of Psycho-analysis, 1957.

Freud, S. (1915b). *Papers on metapsychology and other works.* In J. Strachey (Ed. and Trans.), The Standard Edition of the Complete Psychological Works of Sigmund Freud. Volume XIV (1914–1916) (pp. 159–215). London: The Hogarth Press and the Institute of Psycho-analysis, 1957.

Freud, S. (1917a). *Letter from Sigmund Freud to Karl Abraham*, November 11, 1917. In E. Falzeder (Ed. and Trans.), The Complete Correspondence of Sigmund Freud and Karl Abraham 1907–1925 (pp. 361–362). London/New York: Karnac, 2002.

Freud, S. (1917b). *Letter from Sigmund Freud to Georg Groddeck*, June 5, 1917. Letters of Sigmund Freud (1873–1939) Classic Books, 1917, (51) pp. 316–318. Psychoanalytic Electronic Publishing, ISSN 2472-6982

Freud, S. (1920). *Beyond the pleasure principle.* In J. Strachey (Ed. and Trans.), The Standard Edition of the Complete Psychological Works of Sigmund Freud, Volume XVIII (1920–1922) (pp. 1–64). London: The Hogarth Press and the Institute of Psycho-analysis, 1953.

Freud, S. (1921). *Group psychology and the analysis of the ego.* In J. Strachey (Ed. and Trans.), The Standard Edition of the Complete Psychological Works of Sigmund Freud, Volume XVIII (1920–1922) (pp. 65–143). London: The Hogarth Press and the Institute of Psychoanalysis, 1953.

Freud, S. (1930). *Civilization and its discontents.* In J. Strachey (Ed. and Trans.), The Standard Edition of the Complete Psychological Works of Sigmund Freud, Volume XXI (1927–1931) (pp. 58–145). London: The Hogarth Press and the Institute of Psycho-analysis, 1961.

Freud, S. (1933). *New introductory lectures on psycho-analysis.* The Standard Edition of the Complete Psychological Works of Sigmund Freud, Volume XXII (1932–1936) (pp. 1–182). London: The Hogarth Press and the Institute of Psychoanalysis, 1961.

Fullinwider, S. P. (1983). Sigmund Freud, John Hughlings Jackson, and speech. *Journal of the History of Ideas*, 44(1), 151–158.

Haeckel, E. (1866). *Generelle morphologie der organismen.* Berlin: G. Reimer. cit in Levit, G. S., Hoßfeld, U., Naumann, B., Lukas, P., Olsson, L. (2021). The biogenetic law and the Gastraea theory: From Ernst Haeckel's discoveries to contemporary views. *Journal of Experimental Zoology (Molecular and Developmental Evolution).* doi: 10.1002/jez.b.23039. Epub ahead of print. PMID: 33724681.

Hofer, M. A. (2014). The emerging synthesis of development and evolution: A new biology for psychoanalysis. *Neuropsychoanalysis*, 16(1), 3–22.

Hughlings Jackson, J. (1884). The Croonian lectures on evolution and dissolution of the nervous system. *The British Medical Journal*, 5(1), 660–663.

Johnson, B., & Flores Mosri, D. (2016). The neuropsychoanalytic approach: using neuroscience as the basic science of psychoanalysis. *Frontiers in Psychology*, 7(1459). doi:10.3389/fpsyg.2016.01459

Jones, E. (1953). *Sigmund Freud. Life and work. The young Freud 1856–1900.* London: Hogarth Press.

Klein, M. (1929). Personification in the play of children. *The International Journal of Psychoanalysis*, 10, 193–204.

Klein, G. S. (1976). *Psychoanalytic theory: an exploration of essentials.* New York, NY: International Universities Press.

Laplanche, J. (1976). *Life and death in psychoanalysis.* Baltimore, MD: Johns Hopkins University Press.

Levit, G. S., Hoßfeld, U., Naumann, B., Lukas, P., & Olsson, L. (2020). The biogenetic law and the gastraea theory: From Ernst Haeckel's discoveries to contemporary views. *Preprints.* doi:10.20944/preprints202006.0215.v1

Lichtenberg, J. (1989). *Psychoanalysis and motivation.* Hillsdale, NJ: Analytic Press.

Lichtenberg, J. (1991). *Psychoanalysis and infant research.* New York: Taylor & Francis Ltd.Lorch, M., & Hellal, P. (2010). Darwin's "natural science of babies". *Journal of the History of the Neurosciences*, 19(2), 140–157. doi:10.1080/09647040903504823

Lorenz, K. Z. (1937). The companion in the Bird's world. *The Auk*, 54(3), 245–273. doi:10.1007/BF01905355 (Original work published 1935)

Mayr, R. (1961). Cause and effect in biology. *Science*, 134(3489), 1501–1506.

Panksepp, J. (1998). *Affective neuroscience. The foundations of human and animal emotions.* New York: Oxford University Press.

Panksepp, J., & Biven, L. (2012). *The archaeology of mind.* New York, NY: W. W. Norton & Company.

Romanes, G. J. (1883). *Mental evolution in animals.* New York, NY: D. Appleton, 1884.

Romanes, G. J. (1888). *Mental evolution in man: Origin of human faculty.* London: Kegan Paul and Trench & Co., 1888.

Skinner, M. K., Haque, M. M., Nilsson, E. E., Koop, J. A., Knutie, S., & Clayton, D. (2014). Epigenetics and the evolution of Darwin's finches. *Genome Biology and Evolution*, 6(8), 1972–1989. doi:10.1093/gbe/evu158.

Smith, C. U. (1982a). Evolution and the problem of mind: Part I. Herbert Spencer. *Journal of the History of Biology*, 15(1), 55–88.

Smith, C. U. (1982b). Evolution and the problem of mind: Part II. John Hughlings Jackson. *Journal of the History of Biology*, 15(2), 241–262. doi:10.1007/BF00233016

Solms, M. (2018). Extracts from the Revised Standard Edition of Freud's complete psychological works. *The International Journal of Psychoanalysis*, 99(1), 11–57. doi:1080/00207578.2017.1408306

Sulloway, F. J. (1979). *Freud, biologist of the mind: Beyond the psychoanalytic legend.* New York, NY: Burnett Books.

3 John Bowlby

From attachment to affective neuroscience

Teodosio Giacolini

Introduction

John Bowlby is universally recognized as the researcher who identified and initiated research on attachment behaviour. Relatively less known is his epistemological work that created an ideal bridge between the "sciences" of subjectivity – *in primis* psychoanalysis – and those of mental functioning that can be objectified through neuroscience. In this way, Bowlby laid the foundation for the integration of psychotherapeutic approaches that research on the brain and on *motivational/emotional* systems (Panksepp, 1998) are making possible. The cultural and scientific world in which J. Bowlby was trained and began to practice was profoundly different from the current one. Sigmund Freud was at the height of his productivity, as developmental psychiatry was taking its first steps, and evolutionary biology was beginning an exciting period with the founding of the new discipline of *ethology*. All this happened between the two world wars, a period during which Bowlby's training to become a psychoanalyst exposed him to Freudian thought, through which he absorbed the evolutionist point of view and recognized instincts/drives as a central factor in mental dynamics. The study of these two aspects had characterized the dialogue between phylogeny and ontogenesis, the supporting structure of Freud's work. In this dialectic, Bowlby identified the focal point from which to continue the study and exploration of human mental functioning. In his endeavour, he was "favoured" by the historical-social period which called for a particular attention to children and adolescents, who were finding it difficult to adapt themselves to an industrial world that was changing the characteristics of social coexistence. We shall see that during these years, there were three factors that coexisted, which influenced Bowlby's thought and work: initiatives to support the care and study of children and adolescents to make them adapt well to their own society; the emergence of ethology and comparative experimental psychology; and the enormous diffusion and penetration of psychoanalytic thought in the world of mental care.

DOI: 10.4324/9781003198741-4

John Bowlby and the developmental age

Edward John Mostyn Bowlby (1907–1990) – son of the royal surgeon Sir Anthony Bowlby (1855–1929) – undertook his medical studies, specializing in psychiatry and developmental psychiatry. At the same time, he qualified as a psychoanalyst and psychoanalyst of the developmental age. Bowlby, spent his early childhood with his family, and later at the age of seven, he was sent to *Preparatory school* and then to the *Royal Naval College* in Dartmouth. In 1925, he enrolled as a medical student at *Trinity College* in Cambridge, where he earned a first-class degree in preclinical studies and psychology. (Holmes, 1991). After graduating from Cambridge, Bowlby spent a few months working in a branch of *Summerhill*, a school for misfit boys founded by A. S. Neill (1883–1973) based on the *pedagogy of freedom* (Neill, 1960) and psychoanalytic ideas. Bowlby was deeply impressed by this experience, which influenced his future choices when in 1929 he enrolled at the *University College Hospital* in London. At the same time, he began his training at the *Institute of Psychoanalysis* founded by Ernest Jones. After graduating from medical school in 1933, he began his training as an adult psychiatrist at the *Maudsley Hospital* and then in 1936 moved to the *Child Guidance Clinic* to work with children and adolescents, where he remained until 1940. Meanwhile, in 1937 he joined the *British Psychoanalytic Association* (BPA) as an analyst, subsequently starting training as a child analyst with M. Klein.

The years between the two world wars saw the real development of the child and adolescent psychiatry in both academic and clinical fields. Its advance is intertwined with mental health movements through the *Child Guidance Movement*. Bowlby's professional training took place during these important social and health initiatives, within which psychoanalytic theory and clinical practice were a constant, as we will see below. The history of child and adolescent psychiatry certainly has a shorter and more complex history than that of adults. Interest in the child's mental suffering and physiological development grew during the first half of the nineteenth century (see for example Darwin's interest in the study of child and adolescent psychology and Giacolini, 2018 in this volume). At that time, mental suffering in childhood and adolescence was attributed to cognitive deficits. It was thus diagnosed as a mental disorder during the developmental age, assuming however a form of deviant behaviour, due to the limited knowledge about the physiology of mental processes in that period of life (Migone, 2014; Rey *et al.*, 2015). From the early twentieth century, journals in the medical area dealing with mental disorders, cognitive functioning, and learning skills of children and adolescents (Migone, 2014), began to appear in Europe and the USA. The sudden development of child and adolescent psychiatry, especially in the Anglo-Saxon world, came from the need related to the treatment and prevention of juvenile delinquency, which was the expression of a social unease connected to the new production contexts and massive immigration to the USA. In this context, movements for the promotion of mental health began through the *Child Guidance Movement*, founded in 1909 by neurologist William Healy in Chicago. It brought together doctors, lawyers and psychologists interested in preventing the risk of deviance in young people(Rey *et al.*, 2015). Thus the *Child Guidance Clinics* began to be organized in 1919, aimed at both children and their families, first in the USA, then – by the *Commonwealth Fund* – in Great Britain and subsequently also in India, Australia and Scandinavia, etc. The work of the *Child Guidance Clinics* was organized for the first time in the form of a *équipe*, in which three different professional figures participated: psychiatrists, psychologists and psychiatric social workers. The objective of the *Child Guidance Clinic* was not only in the interest of treatment but also in the research and study of the intervening factors involved in the adaptation processes between the individual and the environment. Both these objectives of the *Child Guidance Clinic* were influenced by two clinical theoretical models that would be the subject of strong opposition from the USA. The psychoanalytic one was the first; its founding moment was the invitation in 1909 from the American psychologist Stanley Hall (1844–1924) to Freud and some of his followers (C.G. Jung, A.A. Brill, E. Jones, S. Ferenczi) for a cycle of seminars in the USA. It should be remembered that in 1904 Hall, deeply interested in *developmental psychology* and at the same time in the evolutionary thought of Darwin and Haeckel, had published the monumental textbook *Adolescence: Its Psychology and Its Relations to Physiology, Anthropology, Sociology, Sex, Crime, Religion and Education*. A few years after Freud visited America, John B. Watson (1878–1958) published his landmark paper *Psychology as the Behaviorist Views* (1913), in which – from the point of view of *comparative psychology* – he proposed psychology as natural science. For this reason, psychology had to be characterized by the *observation* of behaviour, as opposed to the method based on *introspection*, prevalent in the experimental psychology of the time but also, in a different way, in psychoanalysis. In Watson's work, *learning* as an observable aspect of the formation of both animal and human behaviours was closely connected to the study of behaviour. At the time of the publication of his manifesto on behaviourism, Watson was in contact with the psychiatrist Adolf Meyer (1866–1950). Meyer – a leading exponent of US psychiatry – had an important role in guiding the theoretical and clinical research of psychiatry from a psychobiological and psychosocial point of view, coining the term "mental hygiene" (understood as the ability to achieve and maintain a state of mental health). Both Mayer – from 1910 to 1941 – and Watson – from 1908 to 1920 – were professors at *John Hopkins University*, where the former headed the psychiatric hospital and school of psychiatry and the latter was teaching as full professor of *comparative psychology*. Their presence not only constituted a cultural factor of mutual influence but also of differentiation. Mayer was influenced by psychoanalytic theories that recognize the importance of the environment on development, learning and mental functioning. Under Mayer's direction, in 1930 Leo Kanner (1894–1981) founded the first *Child Psychiatry Clinic* at the *Johns Hopkins Hospital Harriet Lane Home for Invalid Children* and published the first child and adolescent psychiatry textbook entitled *Child Psychiatry* (Rey *et al.*, 2015). The social features of the *Child Guidance Movement* became combined with psychoanalytic and behaviourist theoretical clinical models. The latter was particularly interested in the influence of the environment on adaptive and maladaptive learning. In the *Child Guidance Clinic*, the psychologist assessed the cognitive functioning of the children and adolescents – and the psychiatrist, who is also responsible for case management, assessed the emotional functioning. The family, the primary source of both functional and dysfunctional emotional and behavioural learned patterns, was observed by *psychiatric social workers.* It should be remembered that A. Mayer's wife, Mary Brooks, is considered to be the first social worker in history because she visited the families of young patients in their homes (Migone, 2014). In 1926, the *Child Guidance Council* was founded in Great Britain; in 1927 it organized *the East London Child Guidance Clinic* and in 1928, the *London Child Guidance Training Centre* was founded in Islington as the head school for the subsequent *Child Guidance Clinics.* Like the American predecessors, the latter was founded on a multidisciplinary model in which both the psychoanalytic and learning models were present with an *équipe* made up of a psychologist, psychiatrist and social worker. The clinics functioned not only for prevention and treatment but also for scientific research and to train the various specialized professionals who were called to work there. The history of *Child Guidance Clinics* (both in the USA but even more so in England) coincides with the development of *child and adolescent psychiatry* (Stewart, 2009), a consequence of an era in which science held considerable social, cultural and intellectual status (Stewart, 2009). Indicative of the interest in the study and care of children and adolescents are two magazines published in the 1920s; one in the USA, *Children: The Magazine for Parents*, and the other in Great Britain, *Mother and Child*, which collected the clinical and theoretical works of the three professions involved in the *Child Guidance Clinics.* This was the cultural and scientific climate in which Bowlby was trained professionally. Before resuming an account of the events more closely connected with Bowlby, it is necessary to dwell briefly on an institution which, shortly before the *Child Guidance Clinics*, would become intimately connected with them: The *Maudsley Hospital* in Camberwell, London. The *Maudsley*, initially opened as a military hospital in 1915, had since become a psychiatric hospital in 1923 and a centre for the training of future psychiatrists in collaboration with the *Institute of Psychiatry* at *King's College London*. It was at the *Maudsley* that Bowlby began his specialization training to become a psychiatrist in 1933. When the *Maudsley* opened, Britain's first child psychiatry ward was established there under the direction of Dr. D. W. Dawson (Evans *et al.*, 2008). At the beginning of his activity, only a few children had been followed, but by the end of the 1920s, he admitted hundreds of patients every year who were sent from education offices, juvenile courts and general practitioners (Evans *et al.*,

2008). Dawson's clinical theoretical model was psychoanalytic in that it conceived of mental development and, when necessary, his treatment was based on the possibility of gradually keeping instinctual drives and behaviours under the control of consciousness. In children, the latter tended to express themselves without the regulation and control of consciousness, as Dawson stated in his 1924 book *Aids of Psychiatry*. Therapeutic treatments were aimed primarily at children over the age of ten and adolescents were treated with a psychoanalytic method (such as dream analysis and free associations) (Evans *et al.*, 2008). In 1925, Dawson spent a few months of professional development in the USA, where there was a psychosocial approach to the mental disorders of the developmental age. In this approach, the goal was to take social adaptation into account, rather than be limited only to the management of hospitalization places. So when he returned from the USA, Dawson promoted the training of psychiatric social workers, also finding fertile ground for the influence the work of C. Lloyd Morgan (1852–1936) was exerting on Anglo-Saxon culture. The latter was a zoologist and comparative psychologist whowas interested in the study of instinctsand so advocated the need to stick to observed behaviours. His behaviourism had influenced the thinking of J. Watson (Evans *et al.*, 2008), who shared the so-called *Lloyd Morgan Canon* or the *Canon of Thrift*, used to counter a tendency in comparative psychology to anthropomorphize the behaviour of animals, and which stated: *"In no case may we interpret an action as the outcome of the exercise of a higher psychical faculty, if it can be interpreted as the outcome of the exercise of one which stands lower in the psychological scale."* (Morgan, 1894, p. 53).

Dawson's return from the USA led to an increase in psychological work with the parents of children at the *Maudsley* and had a profound influence on the *East London Child Guidance Clinic*, which would soon be operational. In 1927, Dawson left the head of the *Childhood Department* at *Maudsley*, which was since headed by Dr. Thomas Tennent who introduced the diagnosis of *Behavioural Disorder* in 1928, after being in the USA (Evans *et al.*, 2008). From 1930, the categories of behavioural disorders began to be defined by terms that described possible criminal activities (such as thieves) and their being treatable or untreatable by psychiatrists, teachers, educators, etc. (Evans *et al.*, 2008).

In 1936, Bowlby began attending the *Child Guidance Clinic* in London. Shortly after – in 1937 – he qualified as an associate member of the *British Psychoanalytic Society* and began training to become an expert in child analysis under the supervision of M. Klein. During these years, Bowlby came into contact with two different approaches to the mental suffering of children in developmental age, although they had common roots. While there was the possibility of following young patients in psychoanalytic psychotherapy at the *Child Guidance Clinic*, attention was mainly focused on highlighting the relational environmental issues that had contributed to the maladaptive behaviour of the child or adolescent. In the Kleinian view, however, attention was mainly focused on the patient's internal world: an expression of conflictual instincts/drives. The latter was expressed through unconscious representations that formed the grid through which the subject interpreted and endowed the real world with which he meaningfully interacted. At the *Child Guidance Clinic*, the patient was not only the child or adolescent, but also the child's or adolescent's relational environmental context (usually the parents and specifically the mother). These two clinical theoretical models were to be reconciled with the spirit of research and study present in the *Child Guidance Clinic*. The result of these multiple influences is visible in Bowlby's paper written in order to become an ordinary member of the B.P.A. (British Psychoanalytic Association) and then published in 1940 in the *International Journal of Psychoanalysis* with the title "*The Influence of Early Environment in the Development of Neurosis and Neurotic Character*" (Bowlby, 1940).

Bowlby's vision of etiopathogenesis of mental suffering is already evident in the title of this work, which is the interaction between the subject and the relational environment in the early years of development. Even more significant was the casuistry described by Bowlby and his clinical work. The casuistry was that of neurotic children and adolescents or with the neurosis of the character (today we would refer to them as personality disorders). Bowlby was particularly interested in those young patients the school or judicial authorities brought in for a consultation for problems of theft or aggression. Among these young thieves, a group of subjects particularly struck Bowlby: 14 young affectionless thieves. The issues of theft were in line with the objectives of the *Child Guidance Clinic* and the small group of young anaffective thieves all had a history of severe separation from their mothers. This element of their biographies was extracted by Bowlby as a fundamental fact in the formation of their peculiar character and became the element that would constitute the guiding star of his subsequent clinical theoretical work. In the three years of his presence at the *Child Guidance Clinic*, Bowlby consulted with about 150 children and adolescents, in collaboration with social workers and psychologists who assessed the cognitive endowment of all subjects through tests. Many of these young patients were followed up with a psychoanalytic approach once a week, in parallel with sessions conducted with parents (especially with the mothers). Bowlby shows how the interaction between the relational environment and the subject is the pivot of their mental suffering. This element can only be studied by a psychiatrist or psychoanalyst who works with children in an institution such as the *Child Guidance Clinic*.

In the context of the *Child Guidance Clinic*, work "on the ground" could be conducted, which allowed an understanding of both the character of the parents (or their substitutes), and the way that the children adapt to them. The following is Bowlby's effective description:

> *My own approach to the role of environment in the causation of neurosis has of course been from the analytic angle. For this reason I have ignored*

many aspects of the child's environment such as economic conditions, housing conditions, the school situation, diet and religious teaching, which some psychiatrists have thought important. Instead I have concentrated my attention upon the emotional atmosphere of the home and the personal environment of the child.

(Bowlby, 1940, pp. 155–156)

The environment to which Bowlby refers is therefore the relational and psychic environment of those who take care of the child: above all the character of the mother. An objective factor must then be added to these components of the emotional atmosphere and personality of the family's relational environment: the possible separation from the caregiver, which in itself constitutes a potential pathogenic factor. Bowlby writes:

Because of my belief that the early environment is of vital importance I make careful inquiries into the history of the child's relations to his mother and whether and in what circumstances there have been separations between mother and child.

(Bowlby, 1940, p. 156)

In this "general theory of the genesis of neuroses" (Holmes, 1991) that Bowlby proposes, he highlights how it is necessary to always keep in mind two factors: the quality of the breeding environment and the hereditary component (Bowlby, 1940, p. 157). The hereditary component is highlighted by the intensity of the instincts, especially of aggression, found in the young subjects during consultation. While the hereditary instinctual endowment is largely responsible for the intensity of emotional and behavioural manifestations, anxiety and guilt are also always visible; they are the result of interactive processes with the environment.

In his 1940 work, in addition to the 14 anaffective thieves with stories of early separations, Bowlby examines another group of children who exhibit neurotic traits, such as anxiety and guilt, together with behaviours that showed an intensity of both aggressive and sexual instincts. This group included children who had not experienced separation trauma or neglect. Bowlby links these emotional difficulties to the character and personality of their mothers, who excessively stimulated anxiety and guilt or aggressive or sexual fantasies and impulses.

While the influence of mothers on the emotional characteristics of their children can be observed, the same thing is not possible for fathers, who usually did not participate in the consultations. This aspect of the consultations also reveals the social characteristics of the time, in which the care of children was the responsibility of mothers (while the fathers had to go to work). However, with indirect material, Bowlby found that the function of fathers was not secondary, due to their ability either to make wives more anxious and guilty about their caring duties or to be supportive and share in the care of their offspring.

Bowlby proposes that children's neuroses (anxiety, guilt towards their own aggression, masturbation and excessive aggressive or sexual drives) are the result, in large part, of the internalization of the mother's character. The hostility and unconscious aggression of these mothers towards their children in turn developed in the childhood years through interaction with the primary environment. In these mothers, the unconscious hostility towards their offspring (in this we hear an echo of the Kleinian approach) coexisted with the anxiety for the children's protection, activated by the mother's perception of her own aggression. Hence the need – repeatedly underlined by Bowlby in his article – to work with parents, especially with mothers. Bowlby refers to the position of M. Klein who advised against giving advice when working with mothers to avoid increasing their sense of guilt and aggression. Bowlby proposes an alternative way of working: rather than giving advice, use the analytical tool to explore relational events during the mother's own childhood and thus recover her own relational sufferings and allow her to recognize them in her child. This was totally psychoanalytic work, rooted in the study of the identifying processes that caused the transgenerational passage of pathogenic mental organizations. At the same time, knowing the personalities of the parents allowed Bowlby to better understand the projective processes of young patients: *"Much has been written about the introjection of phantastically severe parents, an imaginary severity being itself the product of projection. Less perhaps has been written recently about the introjection of the parents' real characters."* (Bowlby, 1940, p. 173).

At the end of the article, Bowlby regrets that he was not being able to compare the groups of children described above with a normative sample, but still decides to draw some general conclusions:

> *Much more work needs to be done before either the observations or the theories advanced here can be accepted. For instance until a careful statistical comparison is made between the environment of neurotic children and that of normal children, definite scientific conclusions are impossible. I am hoping to undertake some such research. Meanwhile we must be content with clinical impressions.*

(Bowlby, 1940, p. 174)

Bowlby already lays the foundations for a psychoanalytic clinic of the child and adolescent based on the possibility of studying *"clinical impressions"* in a controlled manner. This attempt has always run up against classical psychoanalytic thought. Only recently this attempt has been taken up by the theoretical paradigm of *Neuropsychoanalysis*.

Bowlby's publication *"The influence of early environment in the development of neurosis and neurotic character"* (1940) coincided with the beginning of World War II and his enlistment as a medical officer in the *Royal Army Medical Corps*. The outbreak of war led to the implementation of the evacuation plan from London – *Air Raid Precautions* (ARP) – of children over the age of two in order to protect them from the bombing. Thousands of children (734, 883) were moved to the countryside and separated from their parents on the 1st of September 1939 (Van Der Horst, 2009, p. 24). Bowlby went several times to the lodgings where these children were housed to observe the effects of parental separation. Together with other colleagues, he pointed out the potential dangers of separation on mental health (Bowlby *et al.*, 1939, pp. 1202–1203). During the first winter of World War II, Bowlby started to work at *Forty-four juvenile thieves: their characters and home-life* (Bowlby, 1944) published in the *International Journal of Psychoanalysis* in 1944. This paper too is based on the population of children and adolescents in consultation at the *Child Guidance Clinic* from 1936 to 1938 and the casuistry is largely the same as his previous work. Bowlby specifically takes into account those found guilty of being thieves or had engaged in some illegal embezzlement. Bowlby points out that in the 1930s about half of those found guilty of being thieves were under the age of 21, one-sixth of them were under the age of 14 and the vast majority were 13 years old. From the consultations with these young patients, the great incidence both of maternal separation (in the years preceding the consultation) and of relational problems due to their mother's personality appears. The latter was characterized by ambivalent emotions (love and hate), which influenced the mothers in their relationship with the child. Bowlby describes the way of working at the *Child Guidance Clinic*: attention was mostly paid to the emotional state of the young patient during the cognitive test administration. The latter was then followed by a clinical interview. In parallel, the interview with the mother highlighted the primary environment to which the child had to adapt. The interviews, both with the child or adolescent, and with the mother, continued for months on a weekly basis. With this method, there was a better understanding of the mental functioning of both of them. At the same time, a psychotherapeutic intervention was planned. According to Bowlby, this specific clinical approach allows a better understanding of the psychopathology and emotional environment that had influenced the development of the child's object relations. It allows also a quantifiable data collection, which can subsequently be used in a statistical survey – something that psychoanalytic research lacks. In this regard, Bowlby points out that the works on delinquency until then didn't consider it as a symptom that could appear in different psychopathological conditions. Even if many subjects were taken into consideration and the statistical analyses were sophisticated, it wouldn't be possible to understand the object of study if each of these aspects weren't considered as separate and studied in depth.

In order to study human behaviour, Bowlby emphasizes the centrality of two points already formulated by Freud: the source of behaviour lies in the unconscious and within the early parent-child relationships. It is necessary to verify these hypotheses supported by careful and in-depth psychoanalytic analyses, with empirical and systematized research. The sample that Bowlby describes is made up of subjects aged between 5 and 16 years (of whom he specifies both the IQ and the psychiatric diagnosis). Among these, there are also the 14 cases of anaffective thieves that he already spoke of in 1940. The young thieves' character features are described within six categories: *normal, depressed, cyclothymic, hyperthymic, anaffective* and *schizoid.* Bowlby points out that, – due to age, it's difficult to establish whether those features will be part of the future personality. However, for many of these subjects, it was difficult to make a diagnosis because they hid a lot of themselves. The method followed was to rely on the parent's descriptions and on those people who shared a lot of time with them (such as teachers).

About ten years after writing *The influence of early environment in the development of neurosis and neurotic character,* Bowlby writes another historical work, *The study and reduction of group tensions in the family* (1949). Bowlby no longer refers to the clinical population who attended *the Child Guidance Clinic* in East London, but to the one at the *Tavistock Clinic.* This institution founded in 1920 by the psychiatrist Hugh Crichton-Miller had the objective to treat mental suffering, considering the patient as a result of his environment and his history. There too, clinical work was led by a team that was made up ofpsychiatrists, psychologists and social workers. The first patient of the *Tavistock Clinic* was a child. That happened a few years before the opening of the first *Child Guidance Clinic* in London (Stewart, 2014). The article *The study and reduction of group tensions in the family* was written after World War II. During the war, Bowlby had the chance to meet some fellow psychoanalysts who already worked at the *Tavistock Clinic,* including Wilfred Bion (1961) who had applied psychoanalysis to groups. This experience of clinical psychoanalysis applied to the group raised the interest of Bowlby, as evidenced in his 1949 article. In this article, Bowlby maintains his idea that the mental functioning of children and adolescents is a function of their adaptation to the family environment. He now considers the family (including also the father) as a group, and it's recognized as "the patient" to treat, in its multiple interactions. Bowlby underlines the experimental aspect of these joint family sessions – the first to be so-called – directly influenced by the works of W. Bion and P. Rickman with groups and of E. Jaques with groups of industrial workers (Bowlby, 1949). The family group is considered analogous to the body that needs to be stimulated in order to activate its natural self-healing resources. In his article, Bowlby also cites the works of the anthropologist Margaret Mead, to highlight the interconnections between the individual, the family and society. The real patient brought to consultation – Bowlby states – is not the child or the adolescent, but the *family tensions* (the child's suffering is the emerging element). Psychotherapeutic work is aimed at promoting the resources and cooperative drive of the family group participants. Bowlby thus highlights the motivation for cooperation, on which he will return later, even if not in-depth. In his study on mental functioning, he will describe the *complementarity of behavioural systems,* a concept of great utility without which it wouldn't be possible to understand the evolutionary functionality of a group/population.

The three works considered above – from the pre-ethological period – underline an aspect that will remain the central organizer of Bowlby's thought: the mind functioning can be studied only by considering the individual as an expression of the adaptation process to an environment, whether it is the mother, the family context or the human group to which he belongs. The *Child Guidance Clinic* framework had given Bowlby a theoretical and clinical model that was undoubtedly suitable to him. Furthermore, it provided him with the empirical presuppositions to make him critical towards psychoanalysis, prompting him to seek and find in other disciplines the methodological and content answers on which he could redevelop the "building foundations" composed by Freud.

From psychoanalytic psychiatry to ethology

We have reached the threshold of Bowlby's encounter with the ethological thought which will qualify his subsequent work. By the end of the 1940s, Bowlby had developed his precise model on the factors that influence the normal development of the subject, as well as his psychopathology. The discovery of ethology will provide him with that interface between the biological and mental dimensions that would allow him to move from clinical to basic research.

Bowlby began working at the *Tavistock Clinic* in 1946, and he was involved in its reorganization known as *Operation Phoenix* (Van Dijken, 1998), to structure the department of child and adolescent in a perspective where clinical practice and research were intertwined. In this reorganization Bowlby – enriched by his previous experience at the *Child Guidance Clinic* – maintained the focus on the individual-environment interaction. In 1949 Bowlby was commissioned by the *World Health Organization* (WHO) to draw up a report on the effects of family breakdown on childhood development, hence the essay *Maternal care and mental health* (1951). During the preparation of his report – which will allow him to collect further material to support his theories – he travelled to many European countries, spending five weeks in the USA. Here he met René Arpad Spitz (1887–1974), psychiatrist and psychoanalyst, who had already been interested in the effects of hospitalization and of separation between the child and the mother (see the articles he wrote in 1945 and 1946 and his famous film from 1947 *Grief: A peril in infancy*). In 1951 the psychologist N. Hotoph communicated to Bowlby Lorenz's discovery of the Imprinting described in Der Kumpan in der Umwelt des Vogels [*The Companion in the Bird's World*]. (Lorenz, 1935, p. 37). The following summer, the biologist J. Huxly – a family friend – suggested him to read Lorernz's *King Solomon's Ring* (Lorenz, 1952) and Tinbergen's *The study of instinct* (1951) (Van der Horst *et al.*, 2007). Soon Bowlby met Lorenz personally and then again at the four interdisciplinary study meetings on the psychobiological development of the child, which was organized by the WHO from 1953 to 1956. Bowlby also visited Lorenz in

Altenberg in 1954 and Lorenz returned Bowlby's visit at the *Tavistock Clinic* in October 1957, where they had the opportunity to speak at the weekly clinical theoretical meetings, organized within a multidisciplinary spirit.

At the 1954 conference on *Ethology and Psychiatry* organized by the *Royal Medico-Psychological Association* (RMPA) in London, Bowlby met on Lorenz's advice, Robert Hinde (1923–2016), a biologist and ethologist. The collaboration and friendship between Bowlby and Hinde did play a major role in the evolution of their ideas (Van der Horst *et al.*, 2007). Bowlby accepted from Hinde the suggestion to replace the word *instinct* with the expressions "*environmentally stable*" to qualify both the behaviours and other biological characteristics scarcely influenced by the environment, and "*environmentally labile*" for those that are influenced by the environment (Bowlby, 1969; Van der Horst *et al.*, 2007). With this new terminology, Hinde emphasised his critique towards the concept of *instinct* which implied the meaning of force (endogenous energy) – a conceptualization particularly present in Lorenz's work as a "*psycho-hydraulic model*" (see Lorenz, 1978). Another important concept whose authorship remains uncertain between Hinde and Bowlby is the *Environment of Evolutionary Adaptation* (EEA). Bowlby (1969; Van der Horst *et al.*, 2007) used it to explain how the human species had adopted attachment behaviour as a survival strategy.

In 1957 Bowlby presented one of his works to the *British Psychoanalytic Society* – published in 1958 in the *International Journal of Psychoanalysis* – entitled *The Nature of the Child's Tie to his Mother* (1958). This article collected seven years of study and observation, i.e. since Bowlby had been commissioned by the WHO to study the problem of abandonment and separation in childhood. It is an important work, in which the influence of ethology is now primarily present. But this work has its own particular significance because, between his reading at the *British Psychoanalytic Society* and his publication, Bowlby encountered *experimental and comparative psychology* through the acquaintance of Harry Harlow (1905–1981). In his research on the effects of separation in rhesus monkeys, Harlow was demonstrating that the clinging reaction was primary, compared to that related to nutrition in the relationship between pups and mothers. His findings were cited by Bowlby in the printed version of *The nature of the child's tie to his mother* (1958).

Let us then dwell on some aspects of Harlow's work that would be useful when we read Bowlby's work. In 1957 R. Hinde went to the USA to attend a month-long meeting at the *Center for the Advanced Study in the Behavioral Sciences* in Palo Alto. This meeting was organized by Frank Beach (1911–1988), one of the first psychobiologists. Hinde was studying mating and parental behaviour from a neuronal and endocrine point of view, within a dynamic interaction with the environment (Dewsbery, 1998). Beach wanted to bring together European ethologists – including Niko Tinbergen and Robert Hinde – and psychologists who had been working within the experimental and comparative fields in North America – including Donald Hebb,

Daniel Lehrman, Jay Rosenblatt, Karl Lashley and Harry Harlow (Dewsbury, 1985; Rosenblatt, 1995). In the USA, *ethology* wasn't widespread yet while *comparative and experimental psychology* – under the hegemony of *behaviourism* inaugurated by John B. Watson – was dominated by the learning paradigm. The brain was considered a *black box* whose contents and functionality was formed through learning, a privileged object of study. This approach was opposed to the ethological approach, focused on studying the behaviour in its natural environment through the observational method (Van der Horst, 2009). Harlow began his academic career studying learning processes in rats and then moved on to monkeys once he transferred to the University of Wisconsin. He studied learning processes in monkeys at the city zoo and developed the *Wisconsin General Test Apparatus*. The transition from rats to primates pointed out to Harlow the limits of the experimental method based on the *stimulus-response paradigm*. Therefore, in the early 1950s, he began to study the motivation and ontogenesis of learning (Van der Horst, 2009). He had then to raise a colony of 50 monkeys – the first one for scientific purposes in the U.S.A. – which would have allowed him longitudinal observations. It was at this point that his attention began to be drawn to affective processes. To raise the monkeys, he decided to isolate them in order to prevent the possibility that frequent diseases, such as tuberculosis, could spread within the colony. This led to healthy monkeys but incapable of social life. Harlow also noticed that the isolated monkeys grew fond of the pads and diapers of the cage and reacted desperately when they were periodically changed for cleaning (Van der Horst, 2009). At the same time to study how primates learn to learn, Harlow began in 1956 (Van der Horst & Van der Veer, 2008) to isolate the new-borns from their mothers, thus adopting the model of separation from the parents of hospitalized children used in hospitals of the old and new continent at that time. Several authors had highlighted the pathogenic effects of separation on the infantile psyche. Among these, R. Spitz's research in the USA significantly influenced Harlow, as he himself acknowledged in a letter:

> *[L]et me assure you that you research has been a great inspiration and that your friendship has been a relationship of great meaning. I have vast faith in the research area that you have established and I will do my very best to forward it.* (Harlow in a letter to Spitz dated January 22, 1963).
> (in Van der Horst & Van der Veer, 2008)

Thus between 1956 and 1957 Harlow also began to take an interest in the problems related to deprivation, separation and isolation. At that moment, he met R. Hinde at the 1957 congress, with whom he discussed the problems of breeding and interactions in monkeys. Harlow through Hinde became acquainted with Bowlby's studies on the mother-child bond and separation. At the same time, Hinde let Bowlby know about Harlow's research. Then Bowlby sent to Harlow a draft of his work *Nature of the Child's Tie to his*

Mother which he had read at the *B. P. A.* In June 1958, after a correspondence, Bowlby visited Harlow's laboratories in America. In the summer of 1958, Harlow read during his inauguration speech as president of the *American Psychologic Association* (1958–1959) *The nature of love* (later published in the *American Psychologist*, 1958), citing Bowlby's work. He underlined the importance of mother-child interaction in the dynamics of development, in which a prominent place was reserved "for the primary object of clinging" (Harlow, 1958, p. 676). Bowlby writes: *"It may be worth mentioning that this paper deals neither with ego nor superego. By confining itself to the instinctual roots of the child's tie, it is concerned only with an examination of certain parts of the id."* (Bowlby, 1958, p. 351).

Bowlby therefore remains both terminologically and conceptually within the psychoanalytic tradition: the *Id* as the seat of drives according to the Freudian model, and the centrality of the first year of life in the formation of object relations in the Kleinian model. Bowlby differs from classical psychoanalytic thinking by not considering the need for food experience as primary in the formation of the child's bond to his mother. Instead, he highlights the process that involves the progressive activation of various instinctual responses in the infant. Their synergy will determine the formation of the child' bond to his mother, the *Attachment*. This happens between the seventh and ninth months when – taking up the indication of J. Piaget – the constancy of the object is stabilized. These instinctual responses are: *sucking, clinging, following, crying* and *smiling*. They are all part of *Component Instinctual Responses* theory (Bowlby, 1958). In this article, Bowlby already uses the term *instinctual responses*, to underline pre-learned (instinctual) patterns of behaviours activated by specific signals, the so-called *releasers* (Lorenz, 1935/1937). Previously Lorenz, in his article of 1935/1937, had highlighted that in the animal world learning doesn't play a primary role in the processes of adaptation to the environment, but instinctive, pre-learned behavioural models are rather activated. These behavioural patterns have been selected by evolution because of their adaptive value to both the material and relational environment. With these concepts Lorenz connected external stimuli with the internal and innate behavioural patterns of the animal (Van der Horst, 2009). In the same article, Lorenz had described a behaviour that is neither learned nor instinctive. This behaviour involves the *following* response that birds have towards a moving object immediately after their birth. The effect of that response was named *imprinting* by Lorenz. Through *imprinting*, animals – that do not recognize members of their own species at birth – establish a preference for members of their own species, the *companions* (Lorenz, 1935/1937). Bowlby was struck by Lorenz's article and by the phenomenon of *imprinting*, which will be the central organizer of his attachment theory. In his 1958 article, Bowlby doesn't use the term *imprinting* but only *following*. This term – used by Hinde – was more flexible in tracing it in more advanced species. In this article – a fundamental act in the construction of his theory – Bowlby highlights that to ensure the survival of the individual and the species, the organism must be provided with a repertoire of instinctual responses at each stage of development. In the description of this ethological modelling of the instinct, Bowlby identifies a line of analogy and continuity with Freud's treatment of the drive-in works such as *The Three essays on the theory of sexuality* (Freud, 1905) and *Drives and their vicissitudes* (Freud, 1915). A factor that Bowlby emphasises is the *reciprocity* between behavioural systems (Bowlby, op. cit., p. 67), for example the crying of a child is a specific *social releaser* that has the power to activate complementary care behaviour in the mother. Bowlby takes up the ontogenesis-phylogeny dialectic and highlights how the instinctive responses – starting from simple behavioural models – have gradually been integrated into more complex and hierarchically defined behavioural sequences. A complexity that will gradually appear during development. Those sequences are articulated in a species-specific way with learning processes. Imitation, identification and the use of symbols were added in humans as behaviours resulting from extreme variability and plasticity. Finally, Bowlby learnt another lesson from Lorenz that makes it a significant link with current *Affective Neuroscience*. In the human being, the activation of an instinctual response system determines emotions and feelings that are peculiar to the individual systems:

> *When the system is active and free to reach termination, it seems, we experience an urge to action accompanied, as Lorenz (1950) has suggested, by an emotional state peculiar to each response. There is an emotional experience peculiar to smiling and laughing, another peculiar to weeping, yet another to sexual foreplay, another again to temper. When, however, the response is not free to reach termination, our experience may be very different: we experience tension, unease and anxiety.*

> (Bowlby, 1958, p. 365)

This passage underlines the complexity of the human ethology approach through which Bowlby wanted to re-establish the theory of the psychoanalytic *Id*. He will extensively develop it in the trilogy of *Attachment and Loss* (1969, 1973, 1980). Each instinctive response implies a neurophysiological and behavioural counterpart that is articulated through specific emotions and feelings connected to either the goal achievement or the impossibility to reach it. Bowlby writes:

> *If the view taken here is on the right lines, feeling is a phase of an appraisal process, in a way analogous to that in which redness is a phase of iron when heated. In considering our problem, therefore, we must first distinguish between feeling and the processes of which it is a phase.*

> (Bowlby, 1969, p. 116)

The *feeling* is a central phenomenon in the social behavioural systems that regulate relational life. Through the determination of an emotion and of a subjectively perceived *feeling*, the subject will understand the motivational structure characterizing the other member of his group. Bowlby again writes:

> *That the feeling states an individual perceives in his companions are pre-dictive of their behaviour is, of course, made use of when he decede how to behave towards them. The same is true for members of other species, especially primates. Only if an animal, human or sub-human, is reason-ably accurate at assessing the mood of another is he able to participate in social life: otherwise he might treat a friendly animal as likely to attack or an angry animal as unlikely to.*

(Bowlby, 1969, p. 122)

The trilogy *Attachment and Loss* – the sum of Bowlby's thought and clinical theoretical work – was preceded by two significant works: the report presented at the *Symposium* "Psychoanalysis and Ethology" of the *21st Congress of International Psychoanalytic Association* in Copenhagen on the 26 July 1959, then published in the *International Journal of Psychoanalysis* under the title of *Ethology and the development of object relation* (Bowlby, 1960a). In this article, Bowlby points out that his primary interests are *instinct* and *conflict*, as it was for Freud. But he distinguishes himself from Freud because he has a different conception of instinct. According to Bowlby, the instinct is no longer based on a "psycho-hydraulic" assumption – as it was also for Lorenz – but it's based on the concept of *instinctual response* to both internal and external stimuli (Lorenz's and Tinbergen's *releasers*).

During the same year, Bowlby publishes another fundamental work in *the International Journal of Psychoanalysis* entitled *Separation anxiety* (Bowlby, 1960b), where he leads back the dynamics of anxiety to the concept of *secure base* taken from Harlow: *"One function of the real mother, human or subhu-man, and presumably of a mother surrogate, is to provide ahaven of safety for the infant in times of fear and danger."* (Harlow, 1958, p. 678).

The separation from the attachment figure generates anxiety. Harlow's experiments were now providing Bowlby with experimental material.

In September 1959 Bowlby inaugurated the first of four interdisciplinary conferences organized by the study group on the mother-child relationship that led to the *Tavistock Clinic*. In addition to psychiatrists and psychoana-lysts, ethologists such as Hinde, experimental psychologists such as Harlow, and developmental psychologists such as Mary Ainsworth participated in the conferences held in 1959, 1961, 1963, and 1965.

Four years after the last conference, Bowlby published *Attachment and loss* (1969) where he systematically presented what he had largely antici-pated in his previous article. Instinct is the central pivot of its construction, or the behavioural window that allows you to understand the *comparative psychology* point of view launched by Darwin. Through comparison, it is possible to intercept the *ultimate cause* of a certain behaviour.

A reference author of its trilogy was Paul D. MacLean (1913–2007) – a forefather of neuroethology – who was particularly interested in instinctual behavioural dynamics with an eminently subcortical site. Jaak Panksepp was the one who picked up the baton and found the *Affective Neuroscience* (Panksepp, 1998) and then contributed to the creation of *Neuropsychoanalysis*.

Conclusions

Bowlby's modernization of psychoanalytic epistemology was made possible by the interaction of multiple variables that characterized the *Weltanschauung* of the historical period in which he trained and practiced. His psychoanalytic training on one side and his clinical experience at the *Child Guidance Clinic* and then at the *Tavistock Clinic* on the other side – together with the interdisciplinary climate that characterized the world of mental health after World War II – had a strong influence on him. These experiences created a fertile ground in Bowlby for the integration of *ethology* and *comparative experimental psychology* – two sciences in full development – and *cognitivist sciences* within his clinical theoretical framework of psychoanalytic psychiatry. In this panorama, Bowlby's papers and books were addressed primarily to his psychoanalyst colleagues, as it shows from all his publications in the *International Journal of Psychoanalysis*, the official organ of the IPA (*International Psychoanalytic Association*). Alongside the research on the mother-child ties and the effects of separation, Bowlby constantly pursued the same goal that is to study the instinctual systems, namely the fulcrum of the psychoanalytic edifice and of Freud's evolutionist thought.

Bowlby did always recognize the immense scope of Freud's work, which had brought subjective human mental functioning to attention in a coherent and clinically useful way. Therefore, it became necessary to consider also what is an expression of the individual *implicit, unconscious* functioning, which is rooted in our constitutive biology. To understand that unconscious functioning, Freud pointed out that ontogenetic acquisitions must constantly be understood by connecting them with the phylogenetic history of the species. Bowlby took up this path, which involved resuming an interdisciplinary study within an evolutionary frame of reference. It is therefore no coincidence that the last book written by Bowlby was the biography of C. Darwin (Bowlby, 1991). Through Darwin's ideas, the study of the mind was able to take its biological seat.

It is following this common thread that *The International Neuropsychoanalysis Society* was founded in 2000 (see the Foreword of M. Solms in this book). This society that bears in its name the "psychoanalysis" also recognizes the organic basis of our mental functioning. *Neuropsychoanalysis* was founded as a discipline by scholars who – whether or not they were practicing as psychoanalysts – recognize psychoanalysis as a fundamental heuristic acquisition for studying the human mind that requires to be conjugated with both the study of the brain and the comparative study of *motivational/emotional systems* (Panksepp, 1998).

References

Bion, W. (1961). *Experiences in Groups and Other Papers*. London: Tavistock.

Bowlby, J. (1940). The influence of early environment in the development of neurosis and neurotic character. *International Journal of Psycho-Analysis, 21*, 154–178.

Bowlby, J. (1944). Forty-four juvenile thieves: Their characters and home-life. *International Journal of Psycho-Analysis, 25*, 19–53.

Bowlby, J. (1949). The study and reduction of group tensions in the family. *Human Relations, 2* (2), 123–128.

Bowlby, J. (1951). *Maternal Care and Mental Health* (Vol. 2). Geneva: World Health Organization.

Bowlby, J. (1958). The nature of the child's tie to his mother. *International Journal of Psycho-Analysis, 39*, 350–373.

Bowlby, J. (1960a). Symposium on 'Psycho-analysis and ethology'. Ethology and the development of object relations. *International Journal of Psycho-Analysis, 41*, 313–317.

Bowlby, J. (1960b). Separation anxiety. *International Journal of Psycho-Analysis, 41*, 89–113.

Bowlby, J. (1969). *Attachment and Loss (Vol. 1): Attachment*. London: PIMLICO.

Bowlby, J. (1973). *Attachment and Loss (Vol. 2): Separation*. New York: Basic Books.

Bowlby, J. (1980). *Attachment and Loss (Vol. 3): Loss, Sadness and Depression*. New York: Basic Books.

Bowlby, J. (1991). *Charles Darwin: A New Life*. New York: W.W. Norton.

Bowlby, J., Miller, E., & Winnicott, D.W. (1939). Evacuation of small children. *British Medical Journal, 2* (4119), 1202–1203.

Dawson, W. S. (1924). *Aids to Psychiatry*. London: Bailliere, Tindall and Cox.

Dewsbury, D. A. (Ed.). (1985). *Leaders in the Study of Animal Behavior: Autobiographical Perspectives*. Lewisburg: Bucknell University Press.

Dewsbery, D. A. (1998). *Frank Ambrose Beach 1911–1988: A Biographical Memoir*. Washington: National Academies Press.

Evans, B., Rahman, S., & Jones, E. (2008). Managing the 'unmanageable': Interwar child psychiatry at the Maudsley Hospital, London. *History of Psychiatry, 19* (4), 454–475.

Freud, S. (1905). Three essays on the theory of sexuality. In J. Strachey (Trans.), *The Standard Edition of the Complete Psychological Works of Sigmund Freud* (Vol. 7), 123–246. London: Hogarth Press.

Freud, S. (1915). Instincts and their vicissitudes. In J. Strachey (Trans.), *The Standard Edition of the Complete Psychological Works of Sigmund Freud* (Vol. 14), 109–140. London: Hogarth Press.

Hall, G. S. (1904). *Adolescence: Its Psychology and Its Relations to Physiology, Anthropology, Sociology, Sex, Crime, Religion And Education* (Vol. 1). New York: D. Appleton & Company.

Harlow, H. F. (1958). The nature of love. *American Psychologist, 13* (12), 673–685.

Holmes, J. (1993). *John Bowlby and Attachment Theory*. London: Routledge.

Lorenz, K. Z. (1935). The companion in the bird's world: The fellow-member of the species as releasing factor of social behavior. *Journal fur Ornithologie Beiblatt (Leipzig)*, *83*, 137–213.

Lorenz, K. Z. (1950). The comparative method in studying innate behaviours patterns. *Symposia of the Society for Experimental Biology, 4*, 221–268.

Lorenz, K. Z. (1952). *King Solomon's Ring.* London: Methuen.

Lorenz, K. Z. (1978). *Vergleichende Verhaltensforschung: Grundlagen der Etholgie.* Wien: Springer Verlag GmbH (trad. it. L'etologia: Fondamenti e metodi, Bollati Boringhieri, Torino, 1980).

Migone, P. (2014). Storia della neuropsichiatria infantile (in tre parti). *Il Ruolo Terapeutico, 125*, 55–70; *126*, 55–72; *127*, 63–79.

Morgan, C. L. (1894). *An Introduction to Comparative Psychology.* London: Walter Scott.

Neill, A. S. (1960). *Summerhill.* New York: Hart.

Panksepp, J. (1998). *Series in Affective Science. Affective Neuroscience: The Foundations of Human and Animal Emotions.* New York: Oxford University Press.

Rey, J. M., Assumpção, F. B., Bernad, C. A., Çuhadaroğlu, F. C., Evans, B., Fung, D., Harper, G., Loidreau, L., Ono, Y., Pūras, D., Remschmidt, H., Robertson, B., Rusakoskaya, O. A., & Schleimer, K. (2015). History of child and adolescent psychiatry. In J. M. Rey (ed), *IACAPAP e-Textbook of Child and Adolescent Mental Health.* Geneva: International Association for Child and Adolescent Psychiatry and Allied Professions, 3–72.

Rosenblatt, J. S. (1995). *Daniel Sanford Lehrman, Biographical Memories* (Vol. 66). Washington: National Academy Press.

Spitz, R. A. (1945). Hospitalism: An inquiry into the genesis of psychiatry conditions in early childhood. *The Psychoanalytic Study of the Child, 1* (1), 53–74.

Spitz, R. A. (1947). *Grief, a Peril in Infancy* [Film]. New York: The Research Project.

Stewart, J. (2009). The scientific claims of British child guidance, 1918–45. *The British Journal for the History of Science, 42* (3), 407–432.

Stewart, J. (2014). *Child Guidance in Britain, 1918–1955: The Dangerous Age of Childhood.* London: Pickering & Chatto.

Tinbergen, N. (1951). *The Study of Instinct.* New York: Oxford University Press.

Van der Horst, F. C. P. (2009). *John Bowlby and Ethology: A Study of Cross-Fertilization.* Doctoral Thesis, Faculty of Social and Behavioural Sciences, Leiden University, Leiden, Netherlands.

Van der Horst, F. C. P., & Van der Veer, R. (2008). Loneliness in infancy: Harry Harlow, John Bowlby and issues of separation. *Integrative Psychological and Behavioral Science, 42* (4), 325–335.

Van der Horst, F. C. P., Van der Veer, R., & Van Ijzendoorn, M. H. (2007). John Bowlby and ethology: An annotated interview with Robert Hinde. *Attachment & Human Development, 9* (4), 321–335.

Van Dijken, S. (1998). *John Bowlby: His Early Life. A Biographical Journey into the Roots of Attachment Theory.* London: Free Association Books.

Watson, J. B. (1913). Psychology as the behaviorist views it. *Psychological Review, 20* (2), 158–177.

4 'What's left of sex'

A critical review of psychosexuality in the light of neurobiological research and affective neuroscience

Amedeo Falci

Introduction

Psychosexuality has always been one of the founding distinctive characters of Freudian psychoanalysis (Freud, S., 1892, 1892–1897, 1895, 1905, 1915a, 1915b, 1915c, 1916–1917, 1920a, 1920b, 1923b, 1925, 1933, 1938). Psychosexuality, as a direct promanation of one of his fundamental theoretical postulates—*energia sexualis*—represented the grounds for theorizing an evolutionary line based on the succession of certain stages of drive development.

The innovative relevance of psychosexual concepts in early psychoanalysis was pioneering compared to the other sciences of its time and was one of the decisive factors by which this new science gained the respect of the scientific communities and of the public opinion in the Western world.

However, the historical crisis of psychosexual concepts does not seem to be due not only to their marginalization in the extremely fertile field of the present research in psychological sciences but also to a crisis *within* psychoanalysis, which affected the psychosexual paradigm in the vast archipelago of contemporary models and theories. Such crisis was caused by the proliferation of new theories, the development of the models and the changes in the clinical approach.

Fictional: other possible worlds

The separation that occurred between psychoanalytic psychosexuality and modern research on sexuality was not caused by the separation of psychoanalysis from modern scientific knowledge alone, especially in the field of neurosciences and biological sciences. While it tried to be accredited in the field of natural science, psychoanalysis as a new science also represented a kind of *secession* from the paths, criteria and scientific methods of medicine, a collateral yet separate universe in respect of the universe of *scientific knowledge about the human body* that had been developing from the eighteenth century onwards.

DOI: 10.4324/9781003198741-5

The key step in this secession was the institution of the fictional concept, examples of which are found in the following quotations by S. Freud. *"We will picture the mental apparatus..."* (1899, SE, Vol. 5, p. 536) [*"Wir stellen uns also den seelischen Apparat..."*, G.W., II/III, p. 542]; *"We have already explored the fiction of a primitive psychical apparatus whose activities are regulated by an effort to avoid an accumulation of excitation and to maintain itself so far as possible without excitation"* (1899, SE, Vol. 5, p. 598.); *"It will, however, be useful to remind ourselves that as things stand our hypotheses set out to be no more than graphic illustrations"* (1915c, SE, Vol. 14, p. 175).

> *[...] the mental apparatus [...] not to ask what material it is constructed of. That is not a subject of psychological interest. Psychology can be as indifferent to it. [...] It is a hypothesis like so many others in the sciences: the very earliest ones have always been rather rough. 'Open to revision' [...]. It seems to me unnecessary for me to appeal here to the 'as if' which has become so popular. The value of a 'fiction' of this kind (as the philosopher Vaihinger would call it) depends on how much one can achieve with its help.*
>
> (1926a, SE, Vol. 20, p. 194)

Freud unknowingly preceded the philosophical concepts of *fictionalism* and *ersatzism*, which will be better explained further in this paper.

There is a difference between affirming that something *is*, or affirming that something *might* be, or *imagining that it is*. The affirmation of the possibility of an event is a *modal expression*, one of the *modalities*, studied by the modal logic (Borghini, 2009), which expresses the *modes of existence* of the predicate entities. The sentence (1), 'the eye *is* the sensory organ of the visual system', is not the precise equivalent of the sentence (2), 'the eye *might be* the sensory organ of the visual system', nor of the sentence (3), 'we *imagine* that the eye is the sensory organ of the visual system'. In fact, sentence (1) is ruled by a logic of necessity, dictated by data and operating laws of nature, and meets the true/false logic criteria without any margin of uncertainty. On the other hand, sentences (2) and (3) are *modal expressions*, as they indicate modes of existence of an entity. In Freud's sentence cited above—*"We will picture the mental apparatus..."* [*"Wir stellen uns also den seelischen Apparat"*]—the German verb *stellen* means *to imagine,* but also *to put, to position, to establish*. These are *epistemic doxastic modal expressions* relating to the expression of opinions, of how *we believe, we suppose, we picture* enunciations that do not predicate factual reality or natural data but that consist of an attribution of truth based on an opinion or belief, a cognitive cultural attribution (Kahan, Jenkins-Smith, Braman, 2011).

These sentences indicate a universal, permanent, general, non-specific, metaphysical conception of the psychic apparatus. The opposite happens, far example, in the sentence:

[*we* know] that the most active areas in the mirror neurons system are the front portion of the lower parietal lobe, the lower sector of the precentral gyrus, the opercular part of the inferior frontal gyrus, the dorsal premotor cortex.

(Rizzolatti and Sinigaglia, 2006, pp. 20–21)

This sentence refers to local, variable, partial, delimited and specific events, as in the method of scientific research. Enunciations implying modal logics of non-factual, belief-related or imaginary events fail to reach a satisfactory degree of conceptual and scientific truth, exactly because they deny or bypass the truth verification obligation applicable to events occurring in the reality, and, above all, because these modes are presented as postulates[1] and not as assumptions that require empirical testing.

Starting from his studies on modal logic, the philosopher Kripke (1980) introduced the idea that modal enunciations may be regarded as assumptions in other possible worlds (echoing Leibnitz's *infinite possible worlds*, 1710). Of course, we should have clear what we intend by possible alternative worlds. The notion of possible worlds was born in the modal metaphysics environment (Castellani, 1990), which deals with the metaphysical meaning of enunciations that lack realistic truth and that may be acceptable in worlds that do not coincide with the *actuality* of realism.

Therefore, the reference to possible worlds establishes a wider logical field where it is permitted to *play* with and to manipulate enunciations compatible with another existing reality, separate from *actuality*, where our senses, our cognitive abilities, our concepts and the scientific laws must match, somehow, in an irreversible time dimension. The main logic/philosophic approaches that have dealt with the ampliation of modal theories (notions of possibility, necessity, belief, and imagination) within the framework of the theories of possible worlds are *fictionalism* and *ersatzism*.

Fictionalism, or, better said, all a series of positions capable of being included under such 'umbrella' theory, has received ample consent in various specialized fields of philosophy and mathematics (Eklund, 2007). Fictionalism purports the existence of a series of alternative but unreal worlds that should be regarded as fictional worlds, whose utility is to explain and to create settings where the *possibilia* may be staged. If we then connect Fiction with literary Representation, we obtain a close relationship between fictionalism and literary or narrative fiction, or narrative/scientific world. Can we indeed admit that Ulysses never existed? His state of possibility, and hence of life, find a place within a given alternative literary world, coordinated and consistent but fictional, yet not lacking, as such, emotional expressions, character, power, anthropological value, and more intensely representative than in the real world, the one which is the actuality to ourselves.

On the other hand, *Ersatzism* (Brogaard, 2006) [*ersatz*, from the German *Ersatz*, 'units of the army reserve', literally 'compensation', 'replacement', 'substitute'[2]] that we might translate as 'substitutism', denies (like fictionalism) the status of real entities to possible worlds. However, it affirms that possible, or imaginary, or belief-based states should be intended as *substitute ideas* of the states of the real, actual world that we live in. It justifies the representational power of languages, models, artistic expressions as substitute representations of particular events or states of the world. Painting is a form of *ersatzism* of aspects of the world. In what world are Chagall's *Lovers* flying? Literature is *ersatz*, and even when it is about reality, it is about *another* reality. Last but not least, even scientific knowledge can be made of narrations of fictional substitutes of the natural world, a knowledge that pretends to be *realistic* even *without being real*.

Metapsychological fiction

The concept of *Fiktion* has been rarely used by Freud. It appears, however, prior to citations reported above, in his letter to Fliess dated 21 September 1897, where he says that "*there are no indications of reality in the unconscious, so that one cannot distinguish between truth and fiction [Wahrheit und Fiktion] that has been cathected with affect*" (Freud, S. 1897, pp. 264–267). Here the relationship between *Psyche* and *Fiktion*—or, more specifically the impossibility to differentiate what is the psychic from reality—is a pre-theoretical assumption, a postulate if you will, one of those '*abstract ideas*' (*abstracte Ideen*) (Freud S., 1915a, SE, Vol. 14, p. 117) that guided and shaped Freud's theoretical construction. What is real? Freud asks himself. "*The unconscious is the true psychical reality; in its innermost nature it is as much unknown to us as the reality of the external world*" (Freud S., 1899, SE, Vol. 5, p. 613). ["*Das Unbewußte ist das eigentlich reale Psychische, uns nach seiner inneren Natur so unbekannt wie das Reale der Außenwelt.*", G.W., II.III, p. 617] intending that "*psychical reality is a particular form of existence not to be confused with material reality*" (Freud S., 1899, SE, Vol. V, p. 620) ["*die psychische Realität eine besondere Existenzform ist, welche mit der materiellen Realität nicht verwechselt werden soll*", G.W., II.III, p. 625]. This philosophical upturning implemented by Freud marked the construction of psychoanalysis: unconscious psychism was transformed into *true reality*, more real than the contingent and actual reality. This is an interesting and paradoxical reversion to a dematerialized, disembodied psychism, to the primacy of *die Vorstellung* (idea) over *der Körper* (body). A second thought, compared to young Freud's enthusiastic participation in the materialistic and mechanistic research programme of von Helmholtz. Unable to continue scientific research, Freud moved his clinical approach to the observational sphere, building a theory of his own that articulated clinical experience and imaginative conjecturalism into a new terminological and conceptual language, imbued with its unwitting implicit assumptions and philosophical options. To the *epistemic question of psychic processes*, i.e. how individuals form their memories, ideas and affections (both conscious and unconscious) Freud answers in an innovative, conjectural, imaginative and hypothetical way, using a metaphysical language that *substitutes—ersatz—*the place of neurobiological physical reality. He makes use of rhetorically compelling but vaguely formulated terms that call to mind Descartes' *esprits animaux* in the way he describes forces, energies, cathexis, flows of excitement through hypothetical and never anatomical innervations (1892–1897, SE, Vol. 1, pp. 200–206), in a system that works like a hydraulic machine, with pressure ups and downs, governed by metempirical entities, such as systems, instances, unconscious, preconscious, conscious, barriers, all unknown to neurophisiology. Freud's metaphysical solution lies in separating the psychic from any contamination with Descartes' *res extensa*:

> I shall entirely disregard the fact that the mental apparatus with which we are here concerned is also known to us in the form of an anatomical preparation, and I shall carefully avoid the temptation to determine psychical locality in any anatomical fashion.
>
> (1899, SE, Vol. 5, p. 536)

Yet this brilliant *philosophical invention*, far from being taken as a separation from the methods and knowledge of the medical sciences of the time, was celebrated by the same term, *fictional*, as the gold standard for the representation of the new knowledge. "*Metapsychology, therefore, belongs to 'fiction', or more precisely to 'convention': it is only a way to portray the psychic event 'in image', i.e. in terms of psychic systems*" (De Mijolla and De Mijolla Mellor, 1996, trad.it. p. 252).

Exactly because this new knowledge pattern aims at understanding the unconscious, it was conceived by Freud not based on the already established medical/scientific knowledge—which he regarded as an obstacle to the new science—but based on the definition [*aufzustellen*] of a new series of *suppositions* [*Annahmen*] (1899, SE, Vol. V, p. 511; G.W., II–III, p. 516).

Freud's radical and secessionist idea, compared to the scientific research of the day, is not the unconscious, but the way in which he conjecturably describes the unconscious. In lieu of the logic of scientific enunciations, he presents the enunciations of another world, parallel and *fictional*, or populated with substitutes of the reality, where what is true is not true by the inevitable action of universal laws, but *it is true because it is possible*, and *it is possible because it is imagined* [*Wir stellen*], *fantasized, interpreted and guessed*.[3] This placed the construction of psychoanalysis in another parallel dimension of the universe, where *we imagine* a psychic system related to a body that has apparently material substance, but that is entirely speculative, having lost its connections with the body of biomedical knowledge.

This philosophical standing prevents psychoanalysis from any effective and reciprocal exchange with the other sciences about the data assumed from the empirical research about *this* real world. For example, let us suppose that psychoanalytic psychosexual theories were to be confronted with the present research on sexuality. It would be a difficult dialogue because psychoanalysis places itself in an epistemic and argumentative sphere where the *actual* and the *fictitious,* the *real* and the *fictional*, overlap and blur into one another. In fact, through the hard balance between natural science (*Naturwissenschaften*) (1914, 1915a, 1920b, 1923a, 1925, 1933, 1938) and the humanities (*Geisteswissenschaften*) (1926b) Freud could maintain a dual level of guarantee of the validity of his fictional constructions.

Now, we cannot exclude that these constructions may gather elements of *intuitive truth* (theoretical or clinical) having factual correspondence in the reality; the simple problem is that these *truths* cannot be supported with the methods and data of scientifically oriented research. Likewise, imaginary and fictional conjectures lead to many inaccuracies and many logic errors in the psychoanalytic theories, due to the ambiguous placement of their premises somewhere between empirical science and metaphysics. Take, for example, the *circular logic* on which psychoanalytic evidence is grounded: is it the *a priori* postulate, the premise, that *dictates* the criteria for clinical observations? Or is it the clinical work that generates retroactively the premises (on which the clinical activities themselves are based)? These logic distortions stand in the way of an effective confrontation between the logics of psychoanalysis and those of the current scientific research, while the fluctuation between fictionalism and realism gives rise to a certain degree of *epistemologic duplicity* in most part of psychoanalysis—which may be a value as well as a disvalue—, that consists of cultivating the *possibilia*, the founding *suppositions of possible events*, in the convincement of being in the *realia*, i.e. in the proven events of empirical science.

The discovery of psychosexuality in Freud

Freud rewrote human sexuality and translated it into psychosexuality starting from two strong core argumentations. One is his intuition about infantile sexuality, based on the erogenic power of body areas and mucosae (1905). The other is hysteria, taken as a uterine/sexual disorder, a leitmotif that had travelled along with the story of the Western world (Paracelsus' *Chorea Lasciva*). By connecting hysteria to sexuality, Freud makes of it the field of his essential clinical observations.

Therefore, psychosexuality, as it was conceived, is not only the psychological correlate of real events—human sexual activities—or an attempt to give a materialist guise to sexual psychology: it is above all a Freudian postulate, a founding presupposition of the psychoanalytic theory. A drive-based philosophy founded on the ontologic values of a naturalist *active substantialism*—in Aristotle *substance* is the category of what survives accidental change and in whom inhere the essential properties that define those universals—found in the notion of man as an active being, an efficient cause of motion, an active procreator, juxtaposed to *passive substantialism* in the woman. The psychosexual difference does not lie solely in the contingent and natural opposition of the organs and their physiology (as the bio-psychological-medical sciences would say), but, more profoundly, in the opposition of the philosophical and psychical categories of *active* and *passive*.

The discovery of psychosexuality was then the answer to the need to give theoretical classification to certain clinical observations (states of hysteria) and to certain assumptions on infantile psychosexuality, but also to certain essential philosophical needs that pushed Freud beyond the research on psychopathology and therapy, towards the construction of a system of universal knowledge on the human being.

Energy and drives as fouding concepts and myths of psychoanalysis

The cornerstones of Freud's understanding of sex are the notions of *energia sexualis* and drive, but what data or premises constitute the grounds for it?

The term *libido,* or *energia sexualis,* appears rather early in Freud's works (1982–1997, pp. 189–195), according to a physicalist approach in the wake of von Helmotz and in argumentative connection with the principle of constance (Freud S., 1895), within a mostly organic and physiochemical conception where energy bursts from the stimulation of erogenous areas and follows the neural pathways. This concept is not easily explained in Freud's works and has trouble in finding its place in neurobiological explanations. Where the *libido* is located in the cells and tissues, or how it flows in the '*innervations*' and pathways of the central and peripheral nervous system, is unclear. *Libido* is therefore a concept that is difficult to define in epistemically up-to-date scientific knowledge. In a sense, it is a claim based on an absolute truth that does not come from empirical data and does not require evidence. It might however be also a sort of postulate, a temporary statement that is not necessarily true but that is assumed to be true in order to follow the argumentations deriving from it. The *libido* is never presented as an assumption to be verified. It is rather an ontologic cornerstone of the Freudian science, existing *a priori* and not obtained from data, that does not come—neither conceptually nor empirically—from those neurologic sciences in which Freud, though, had been educated. If, on the one hand, *libido* relates to the notion of affects as energetic quantity [*Erregungsgrößen*] and energetic cathexis [*Energiebesetzung*] (1895), gaining credit as a *possible* neurophysical concept, on the other hand, its ambiguous position between a postulate and a natural datum poses the vexed question of scientific vs. metaphysical Freudian epistemology.

While it is at least apparently true that psychosexuality presents itself as having a somatic/organic and physiochemical matrix, it also shows between the lines a clear discrepancy between the laws of biology and the fictional world of ideational representations. The concept of drive [*Trieb*], presented as a bridge cast across the body/mind dichotomy, as a seam binding the somatic and the psychic, actually reveals its transboundary condition that fails to unify Freud's essential dualism based on the cartesian concept of *res extensa* concomitant but separate from *res cogitans* (Falci, 2015). While *die Vorstellung* is ideational representation, *die Repräsentanz* takes instead, in Freud's works, a juridical value of delegation[4] that has not been commented enough as being a representative, a diplomatic delegation between two different realms, between two heterogeneous *substantiae*, a *delegation-representation* that is needed so that something of the somatic may be *introduced* to the psychic. The delegation, however, implies a dualism that undermines the Freudian invoked unification Psyche/*Körper*.

Que reste-t-il de nos pulsions?

Even without getting into the detail of the vast scientific literature, we can draw a few guidelines from confronting the historical model of psychoanalytic psychosexuality with the models of scientific knowledge promoted by certain trends of the current research on affective neurobiology.

Human sexuality, especially psychical sexuality, is thought to be placed within a *continuum* at the two ends of which there are full enough female and male typologies—showing certain correspondence between somatic sexuality, psychical and gender identity—, with many other different degrees of combined typologies in between. This confirms, if need be, not only Freud's intuition of bisexuality but also how much human nature is also potentially multisexual.

The intersection of the genetically determined programmes of sexual organization with psychological and cultural environment gives rise to different combinations of anatomic and somatic sexuality and gender identity. This explains the high polymorphism of sexual identities and practices in contemporary social life and the broad spectrum of gender-related issues.

The sexual organizations relating to the body and to copulating activities, and the organization of gender identity in the mind, run on parallel but separate tracks. These elements do not deny the biological unicity of body and mind, but at the same time, they also find divergent organizational paths.

Lust, sexual attraction, copulating activities, not solely, but also affective relationships between partners, are triggered by the joint action of multiple neuromodulators and neuropeptides, among which the main roles lie with dopamine, serotonin, noradrenalin, oxytocin, vasopressin and endogenous opioid as endorphins. All these molecules have a very rapid action and determine immediate effects on the nervous system and on the mind. This is epistemologically important because gives evidence to a monistic stance of the mind embedded in the body without any *delegation-representation* between two substances, and furthermore belies the assumption of a not better identified somatic libido.

The relevance of the role of oxytocin, as well as of vasopressin and vasotocin, having different effects but all affecting the social cohesiveness of animal groups, finally gives some neurobiological grounds to the feelings of love ties, closeness, tenderness, but also to the competitiveness among males, the ability to defend the territory, and to social motivation, in other words to those pro-social emotions and behaviours that remained totally unexplained in the libido energy theory, unless as deflections and transformations of sexual drives.

It is rather clear that sexual and gender differentiations take place precociously already at intra-uterine stages, which confirms the genetic foundations of certain baseline programmes for the specification of human sexuality.

Then, overcoming the old (and obsolete) conflict between nature and culture due to an up-to-date paradigm about a close entanglement between nature and culture (Music, 2017), research data suggest that psychic typification appears to be a continuous intersection of innate biological devices and anthropological environment. Therefore, the organization of lust, of the orientation towards the love and/or sexual partner, the sensibility towards the various messages and the responses of approach to the sexual object appear to be determined early in the foetus by the interaction of genetic factors and biochemical processes embedded in emotional and cultural life inside and around us. Similarly, the *love map* (Money, 1988) *of the sexual and love relationships* that take place along the course of one's existence continues to depend on the personal and cultural background of each individual.

More specifically, given the complex network of interactions and retroactive regulations of body and mind biochemistry, the function of biochemical regulations is to lead us back in the world of natural processes, studied by scientific methods, that belie the vague and misleading *quantitative* characterization of organic energies flowing within the human body as it is described in metaphysical statements.

In conclusion, the primacy of *energia sexualis* as the main organizer of psychical life cannot explain, in itself, the evolutionary benefits that it can bring to animal species and to man in particular, nor can it explain the evidence of an evolutionary selection of different basic emotional systems capable of guaranteeing survival and adaptation.

Conclusions

Such complex issues as those that this paper attempts to argue cannot obviously reach a conclusion and remain absolutely in progress. I would like however to borrow a poignant tagline from the ethologist Barnett (1981): the more we succeed in explaining animal behaviour in terms of physiology, biology and biochemistry, the more the mentions of undetermined forces, drives and energies will fade out. And I might add: the more scientific data do appear, the more entities and substances disappear. In other words, the frequency of the references to indefinite forces, energies, instances and principles is only inversely proportional to the degree of development of our scientific knowledge.

Yet, it is equally true that we need imagination, dreams and alternative worlds where to place our *possibilia*. However, don't these fictitious worlds have to do with our innate need for creativity, imagination, and, above all, literature? And isn't any way the *reality* the subject of all this fiction? Or nearly that.

Notes

1 *Postulate*: an intuitive, arbitrary, untestable, unprovable, non-falsifiable assumption that is assumed to be true without need for further proof.
2 https://www.etymonline.com/word/ersatz.
3 Freud, S. 1897:

> a man like me cannot live without a hobbyhorse, without a consuming passion, without — in Schiller's words — a tyrant. [...] I have spent the hours of the night from eleven to two with such fantasizing, interpreting, and guessing, and invariably stopped only when somewhere I came up against an absurdity or when I actually and seriously overworked.
>
> (p. 129)

4 In contract law and administrative law, delegation is the act of giving another person the responsibility of carrying out the performance agreed to in a contract. The party who had incurred the obligation to perform under the contract is called the delegator; the party who assumes the responsibility of performing this duty is called the delegatee.

References

Barnett, S.A. (1981). *Modern ethology. The science of animal behavior*. New York: Oxford University Press.

Borghini, A. (2009). *Che cos'è la possibilità*. Roma: Carocci.

Brogaard, B. (2006). Two modal-isms: Fictionalism and ersatzism. *Philosophical Perspectives*, 20 (1), 77–94.

Castellani, F. (1990). *Intenzioni e mondi possibili*. Milano: FrancoAngeli.

De Mijolla, A., & De Mijolla Mellor, S. (1996). *Psychanalyse*. Paris: Presses Universitaries de France (trad.it. Psicoanalisi, Borla Roma, 1998).

Eklund, M. (2007). Fictionalism. *Stanford Encyclopedia of Philosophy*. https://plato.stanford.edu/entries/fictionalism/

Falci, A. (2015). Il reale e il rappresentato: Una disambiguazione di "rappresentazione mentale". *Rivista di Psicoanalisi*, 61 (3): 703–722.

Freud, S. (1892–1897). Draft E. How anxiety originates. In J. Strachey (Ed. and Trans.), *The Standard Edition of the Complete Psychological Works of Sigmund Freud* (Vol. 1, pp. 189–1959). London: Hogarth Press.

Freud, S. (1892). Draft G. Melancholia. In J. Strachey (Ed. and Trans.), *The Standard Edition of the Complete Psychological Works of Sigmund Freud* (Vol. 1, pp. 200–206). London: Hogarth Press.

Freud, S. (1895). Entwurf einer Psychologie. In *Gesammelte Werke: Texte aus den Jahren 1885 bis 1938* (pp. 375–486). Frankfurt am Main: S. Fischer Verlag, 1950.

Freud, S. (1897). The complete letters of Sigmund Freud to Wilhelm Fliess, 1887–1904. In J.M. Masson, *The Complete Letters of Sigmund Freud to Wilhelm Fliess,*

1887–1904 (p. 505). Cambridge, and London: The Belknap Press of Harvard University Press, 1985.

Freud, S. (1899). The interpretation of dreams (Second Part). In J. Strachey (Ed. and Trans.), *The Standard Edition of the Complete Psychological Works of Sigmund Freud* (Vol. 5, pp. 339–628). London: Hogarth Press.

Freud, S. (1900). Die Traumdeutung über den Traum. In *Gesammelte Werke: II/III* (pp. i–701). Frankfurt am Main: S. Fischer Verlag.

Freud, S. (1905). Three essays on the theory of sexuality. In J. Strachey (Ed. and Trans.), *The Standard Edition of the Complete Psychological Works of Sigmund Freud* (Vol. 7, pp. 123–246). London: Hogarth Press.

Freud, S. (1914). On Narcissism: An introduction. In J. Strachey (Ed. and Trans.), *The Standard Edition of the Complete Psychological Works of Sigmund Freud* (Vol. 14, pp. 67–102). London: Hogarth Press.

Freud, S. (1915a). Instincts and their vicissitudes. In J. Strachey (Ed. and Trans.), *The Standard Edition of the Complete Psychological Works of Sigmund Freud* (Vol. 14, pp. 109–140). London: Hogarth Press.

Freud, S (1915b). Repression. In J. Strachey (Ed. and Trans.), *The Standard Edition of the Complete Psychological Works of Sigmund Freud* (Vol. 14, pp. 141–158). London: Hogarth Press.

Freud, S. (1915c). The unconscious. In J. Strachey (Ed. and Trans.), *The Standard Edition of the Complete Psychological Works of Sigmund Freud* (Vol. 14, pp. 159–204). London: Hogarth Press.

Freud, S. (1916–1917). Introductory lectures on psycho-analysis (Parts I and II). In J. Strachey (Ed. and Trans.), *The Standard Edition of the Complete Psychological Works of Sigmund Freud* (Vol. 15, pp. 3–483). London: Hogarth Press.

Freud, S. (1920a). The psychogenesis of a case of homosexuality in a woman. In J. Strachey (Ed. and Trans.), *The Standard Edition of the Complete Psychological Works of Sigmund Freud* (Vol. 18, pp. 145–172). London: Hogarth Press.

Freud, S. (1920b). Beyond the pleasure principle. In J. Strachey (Ed. and Trans.), *The Standard Edition of the Complete Psychological Works of Sigmund Freud* (Vol. 18, pp. 1–64). London: Hogarth Press.

Freud, S. (1923a). Two encyclopaedia articles. A. Psychoanalysis. In J. Strachey (Ed. and Trans.), *The Standard Edition of the Complete Psychological Works of Sigmund Freud* (Vol. 18, pp. 233–254). London: Hogarth Press.

Freud, S. (1923b). Two encyclopaedia articles. B. The libido theory. In J. Strachey (Ed. and Trans.), *The Standard Edition of the Complete Psychological Works of Sigmund Freud* (Vol. 18, pp. 255–260). London: Hogarth Press.

Freud, S. (1925). An autobiographical study. In J. Strachey (Ed. and Trans.), *The Standard Edition of the Complete Psychological Works of Sigmund Freud* (Vol. 20, pp. 1–74). London: Hogarth Press.

Freud, S. (1926a). The question of lay analysis. In J. Strachey (Ed. and Trans.), *The Standard Edition of the Complete Psychological Works of Sigmund Freud* (Vol. 20, pp. 179–258). London: Hogarth Press.

Freud, S. (1926b). Psycho-analysis. In J. Strachey (Ed. and Trans.), *The Standard Edition of the Complete Psychological Works of Sigmund Freud* (Vol. 20, pp. 259–270). London: Hogarth Press.

Freud, S. (1933). New introductory lectures on psycho-analysis. In J. Strachey (Ed. and Trans.), *The Standard Edition of the Complete Psychological Works of Sigmund Freud* (Vol. 22, pp. 1–182). London: Hogarth Press.

Freud, S. (1938). An outline of psycho-analysis. In J. Strachey (Ed. and Trans.), *The Standard Edition of the Complete Psychological Works of Sigmund Freud* (Vol. 23, pp. 141–208). London: Hogarth Press.

Kahan, D.M., Jenkins-Smith, H., & Braman, D. (2011). Cultural cognition of scientific consensus. *Journal of Risk Research*, 14, 147–74.

Kripke, S.A. (1980). *Naming and necessity*. Oxford: Basil Blackwell.

Leibniz, G.W. (1710). *Saggi di teodicea sulla bontà di Dio, sulla libertà dell'uomo, sull'origine del male*. Milano: Feltrinelli, 1993.

Money, J. (1988). *Gay, straight, and in-between: The sexology of erotic orientation*. New York: Oxford University Press,

Music, G. (2017). *Nurturing natures* (2nd ed.). London: Routledge.

Rizzolatti, G., & Sinigaglia, C. (2006). *So quel che fai. Il cervello che agisce e i neuroni specchio*. Milano: Cortina.

5 Pornography, psychoanalysis and Affective Neuroscience

Claudia Spadazzi

Introduction

Since its invasion of the Western world, pornography has pervaded our culture, our lives as well as our analysis rooms. But it is not an "alien" invasion: created and transformed along with the evolution of mankind, pornography has existed since the dawn of civilization. However, the era of technology has triggered some radical changes in this phenomenon. Copper's "triple A" concept (2009) – "availability, affordability, anonymity" – explains in a very synthetic way the relentless progression of the use of pornography. Although of unthinkable proportions, the progression can be measured through the following data:

- 12% of all websites have pornographic content
- MindGeek, the world leader of internet pornography, has 100 million viewers per day and 80 billion videos screened per year (The Economist, September 26, 2015).
- about 30% of words typed on the Internet are related to pornography
- the US is the country with the highest number of pornography users with an estimated 40 million regular consumers
- 30% of internet traffic is dedicated to pornography

The culture of pornography

Our modern-day society is facing a process which can be defined as "pornographication". This term, introduced by Brian McNair in 1996 (1996, 2002), explains how the concept of pornography is related to the democratization of access to pornography and the enormous increase in the availability of hard-core material. This increase and its fruition are having a huge impact on trends, opinions, practices and moral behaviours. Even if secretly consumed, pornography has an open, public and profound influence on individuals through the media. Moreover, pornography has reached a "status" of normality in the common acceptance of it by all Western countries.

DOI: 10.4324/9781003198741-6

The term 'pornographication' is not only related to the quantity of videos, images, photos and stories which are offered by the Internet's enormous content, it also defines the transformations which pornographic canons have operated on visual culture and media practices.

(Stella, 2011)

A vast number of publications on this phenomenon (approximately 300 books with Anglo-American and European editions) run alongside the quarterly review "Porn Studies", edited by F. Attwood, one of the major scholars on this subject.

From J. Baudrillard's concept of "ob/scenity" (1979) to L. Williams' "on/scenity" (1989) we can see the transformation from private and intimate to progressive overexposure. This process trivializes and massifies not only sexuality and the body, but also and most of all, feelings, functions and life events. Talk shows, social networks, advertising, YouTube, viral videos: the border between privacy and exhibition fades in the unstoppable flow of images which pervade our everyday lives.

Parallel to the recent debate on the influence of social phenomena on theories and clinical practices with regard to sexuality, contemporary psychoanalysis does not seem to take enough into account the profoundly transformative effects of pornography (Ahumada, 2016; Paul, 2016). Obviously many clinical cases refer to pornography, however, albeit some publications within the field of psychodynamics (Galatzer-Levy, 2012; Janin, 2015; Kalman, 2008; Wood, 2013), pornography remains limited to studies in sociology/philosophy/audiovisual studies (Biasin, Maina and Zecca, 2011; Dines, 2010; Giddens, 1992; Marzano, 2003; Stella, 2011) and behavioural psychology/sexology (Attwood, 2006; Cooper, 1998; Cooper et al., 2004; Smith, 2010).

Anglo-American Cultural Studies, Women's Studies, Gender Studies, Film and Media Studies represent a vast, combined multidisciplinary area of research. Other models originated within these disciplines and, more specifically, the Porn Studies subsystem, with pornography remains as its main object of research and analysis.

Most behavioural psychology and neurobiology studies relating to the use of pornography are centred on young men and male adolescents. Viewings of pornographic content trigger an increasingly sexual excitement which culminates in masturbation. During puberty and adolescence, a period of life which features a rise in the sexual drive due to the sudden increase in hormonal activity, masturbation offers a cognitive function of one's own body and discovery. However, if, in adulthood, masturbation becomes a compulsive behaviour, it takes on the outlines of a sexual object-less activity, a surrogate of the encounter with the Other. This, in turn, encourages a narcissistic form of satisfaction which enables the subject to avoid searching for a partner, courtship and the establishing of a relationship. Obviously, from a species point of view, the goal of sexual activity is copulation. In both sexes, this goal is the result of the combination of both the SEEK-ING/REWARD system – partner research and favourable conditions – and the LUST system – excitement, copulation and orgasm. Before the onset of PMA(Medically Assisted Procreation) the continuity of the human species was necessarily founded on the sexuality-reproduction duo.

Pornography, psychoanalysis and neuroscience

According to Freudian drive dualism, drives are divided into sexual drives, necessary for the species, and those of self-preservation, necessary for survival. In his first drive theory, Freud (1910) details how sexual and self-preservation drives act in opposition to one another, however, within the context of his second drive theory (Freud, 1920), he specifies how they instead act jointly as life drives. What happens when the use of pornography on the Internet begins to replace one's "natural" interest in searching for a sexual partner? When the need for visual stimulation becomes a compulsion and replaces the ancestral desire to meet a possible sexual partner?

In a publication on the time spent on porn websites, Cooper and Delmonico (2000) differentiate between the "recreational" and "compulsive" use of pornography, where the compulsive use is quantified by an average of 11 hours per week. Whether, from a clinical point of view, pornography via the Internet combined with masturbation can be defined as an addiction, is controversial. Internet Addiction Disorder (IAD) is increasingly being studied from a clinical as well as a social point of view, in particular among adolescents and young males. Although confirming the neurobiological similarities between IAD and drug abuse, the DSM V has restricted Internet addiction to gambling.

From the affective neuroscience point of view, "addiction" features the alteration of psychic dynamics which are mostly related to three systems. All these become intertwined and determine an unbalance within the neurotransmitters which regulate the functioning of the three systems. In particular, the dopaminergic SEEKING/REWARD system is altered by all kinds of substances, such as drugs, opioids, alcohol and psychostimulants. This alteration triggers a progressive reduction of all appetite affects unrelated to each specific substance. In particular, D2 receptors are reduced by addiction (Volkow et al., 2007). The accumulation of a transcription genetic factor ΔfosB, (Nestler, 2001, 2004) remains at length within the neurons (6–8 weeks) and seems to provoke neuroplastic changes within the dopaminergic system. These changes determine neural and behavioural alterations which underpin the transition from acute consequences of substance assumption to a condition of chronic addiction. The accumulation of ΔfosB occurs also in addictions unrelated to drugs, such as IAD, food and intense sports activity. Two main features trigger the progression from use to abuse, and consequently to addiction. The first is a limitless offer, in terms of quality and quantity, which strengthens the subject's phantasmatic omnipotence.

Unlike in a real relationship, the pornography user can choose whatever representation he wishes from within the vast amounts of content on offer. This brings to mind the narcissistic gratification of Mozart's Don Giovanni: "Here is a list".

The second feature is based on the viewing of increasingly more hardcore content, similar to the consumption of stronger doses of drugs or alcohol. The grasping for an unreachable internal pacification forces the subject to a compulsive search for increasingly more explicit, more violent, more perverse images. In the majority of cases, masturbation follows the viewing of porn videos, allowing a temporary decrease in the tensions triggered by the viewing of the contents selected by the subject.

But we must underline the fact that sexuality is only marginally relevant within the context of pornography. Panksepp conceptualizes a three-way distinction between bodily-homeostatic affects, sensory affects and emotional affects. The LUST system regards a synergy between sensorial and homeostatic elements, in which perceptions through the five senses have a major role. Sexual desire originates from subcortical circuits, guided and supported by sexual hormones produced by genital organs (testes and ovaries), along with the hypothalamus and hypophysis axis. The combined activation of the medial regions of the anterior hypothalamus (interstitial nuclei) and cortical sensorial perceptions, determines the onset of sexual desire and excitement, through the release of vasopressin, oxytocin and other neurotransmitters. The LUST system, strictly connected to the SEEKING system, strongly pushes the subject towards courtship, copulation and orgasm. With orgasm representing the acme of sexual pleasure, it brings about the release of endorphins and especially vasopressin. Vasopressin has a feedback function towards the CNS (Central Nervous System) with regards to all neurobiologic aspects related to sexual drive and the behaviour linked to such drive. In the orgasmic experience, the trans-hypothalamic emotional systems are activated, as can be seen in MRI imaging. During the viewing of pornography, however, the LUST system remains secondary compared to the SEEKING system, with desire activation being provoked by the visual perception, namely in the cortical visual areas. The excitement from a video is deprived of the tactile, olfactory and taste components, relying solely on a visual hyper investment. Orgasms obtained through masturbation while viewing a video have an evacuative aim in relation to the tension awakened by the selected images.

With regards to the involvement of erogenous areas, Panksepp wonders whether the cortical specialized areas have direct access to subcortical emotional systems. Consequently, he underlines the irrelevance of sexual feelings in the absence of activation of the cortical specialized areas. In other words, the push towards pornography seems to be mostly based within the SEEKING system, with only a secondary involvement of the LUST system. So, through a top-down mechanism (cortical → subcortical) instead of the physiological down-top mechanism (subcortical→cortical).

Zellner, Watts, Solms, Panksepp's publication on neurobiological aspects of depression and addiction (2011) outlines a parallel mechanism between masturbation and addiction. The similarity between hedonistic pleasure induced by opiates and narcissistic pleasure derived by masturbation are self-evident. According to the Authors, all kinds of addictions are initially determined by the appetite SEEKING system; followed by the LUST/PLEASURE system, which brings about gratification; and, in parallel, by the PANIC/GRIEF system, which intervenes in the attachment process. As though the dependence inducing substance could have the function of an attachment object. The Authors differ from Berridge's classical addiction model (Berridge, 2007) – based on "incentive salience" –, and underline the importance of psychic pain induced by the PANIC/GRIEF system. They conclude: "In other words, drug addicts, as well as onanists, don't look for a sensorial gratification; the drug is also a self care which replaces the attachment experience they really need". The self-care aspects mentioned above underpin compulsion and are related to the psychodynamic process which, in turn, determines a compulsory behaviour.

Both Stoller's and Masud Khan's important contributions on pornography date back to the 1970s, and are related to the use/abuse of pornographic comics and magazines, adult movies and Video Home System (VHS) Masud Kahn conceptualizes the use of pornography as a form of alienation of Oneself and of the Other, in an increasing annihilation of phantasy and object relation. Sexual drive is mutilated and converted into a particular form of violence and eroticized in order to become bearable. Masud Khan declares: "Pornography is the stealer of dreams" (1979). At that time, he couldn't foresee the enormous impact of contemporary technology, and pornography, on the mind.

Following Winnicott, Masud Khan conceptualizes pornography as a denial of Self and of the Object, in the compulsive attempt to reconnect the sexual drive to aggressiveness. Rage is a dominant affect, which develops into a somatic event, excitement and finally orgasm. Masud Khan underlines the fact one cannot access sublimation or work through processes, and the tendency to isolation which derives from renouncing the Object. Hypermentalization and hyperrealism trap the mind in a perverse game which progressively reduces the subject's imagination and sensibility.

Throughout his vast work on sexuality, Robert Stoller (1985) has widely explored the world of pornography, both from a theoretical and clinical point of view. His rich contributions have investigated the innumerable aspects of pornography, and include a series of interesting interviews with porn stars. According to Stoller, pornography is a "published daydream", whilst perversion is an "acted daydream". Stoller's thought highlights the strong link between perversion as an "erotic form of hatred" and pornography, and the fact both lead to one's impossibility to tolerate intimacy. This impossibility is strictly connected to a process of dehumanization and a desire to humiliate, hurt, damage and be cruel to one's own sexual object.

In clinical practice, the approach to pornography is more consistent in contemporary psychoanalysis than it was in the Seventies. First, exposure to pornography is more and more precocious due to the vastness of its diffusion. The results of such a massive exposure in adolescence or even in pre-puberty have not been explored, though it seems the possible traumatic effects have been widely underestimated. (Woods, 2015). The comparison between one's own body, whose adolescent identity is still to be defined, and the body and the genitals of porn actors, can generate frustration and a narcissistic wound bearing significant consequences. Expectations related to the performances screened necessarily cause disillusionment and the gap between this disillusionment and omnipotent phantasies can bring to an increasing detachment from real, interpersonal relationships. Furthermore, omnipotent phantasy underpins this virtual particular object relation: all it takes is a click for it to be cancelled. The feeling of omnipotence favours anxiety containment related to becoming involved in a real, intimate relationship. The relationship is therefore confined to a virtual area where, thanks to a feeling of omnipotence, anything is possible.

Furthermore, the web itself guarantees impersonality and impunity. Alongside the decrease in superegoic disapproval for a practice which, nowadays, is considered part of contemporary culture, social irresponsibility is growing, strengthened by anonymity and a growing identity diffusion among Internet users. One doesn't feel responsible when watching scenes that are detrimental to human dignity, violent or perverse, and contents which are illegal and unethical. The borders of ethical principles tend to fade into the magma of the web. In the analytic room, pornography finds a place where a subject is allowed an open mental space of comprehension – whether the use of pornographic content is occasional or its frequency and need indicate a compulsive feature. The opportunity for a subject who is granted to choose a topic closest to his unconscious needs is linked to the self-healing theme proposed by Zellner, Watts, Solms and Panksepp (2011), mediated by the involvement of the PANIC/GRIEF system. Pornography enters the analysis room directly when the patients talk about it, or indirectly when it concerns people close to the patient. Pornography is often a traumatic element which breaks in through an iphone or a computer of a significant Other. Surprise is common as if pornography offered the Other's hidden side: when parents who find out about an adolescent, or a son/daughter about his/her parent (generally father or stepfather), a partner about his/her companion. In a couple, either hetero or homosexual, one partner can sometimes ask the other to share in viewing the content. This condivision can lead to an opening of the Other's inner world that can become intolerable. S., a patient in psychoanalysis for several years, recalls:

I thought seeing YouPorn together with A. would be a transgressive, exciting experience... In time, I realized that A. was more and more attracted to scenes of submission, with increasingly violent content... I felt uneasy and asked myself if he desired this from me.....

Sometimes the inner world appears directly when the patient introduces his/ her personal experience. A patient in analysis recalls how watching porn videos is his way of overcoming depressive states deriving from professional or sentimental frustrations. The search, and the choice of the "right" video, sometimes appear directly in the session, when the patient talks about his/ her personal experience. Searching and finding the video brings about an immediate and short-lived well-being, followed, shortly after, by a depressive relapse, together with feelings of uneasiness and irritability. For this patient, the exasperated search through porn websites reduces the time he could dedicate to productive activities and is perceived as an ego-dystonic, painful and unavoidable detachment from reality.

To me, pornography is a low-cost gratification: the problem is that it is never enough.

In this concise comment, all the narcissistic features, object relationship avoidance and repetition compulsion are brought into one; as well as the prevalence of the SEEKING/REWARD system over the LUST/PLEASURE system. The substitute attachment aspects – pain and healing attempts – are underpinned by the PANIC-GRIEF system. In clinical practice, communication about pornography is often embarrassing, because of the compulsion, as well as the fatigue that comes with feeling the need to explain in detail about the urge to watch that particular representation, within a precise setting and situation. The favourite representation corresponds to traumatic areas which have not been worked through and need a repetitive representation.

The relationship with phantasies and in particular with the "central masturbatory phantasy", as conceptualized by M. Laufer (1976), is crucial. Laufer's concept is particularly relevant in the understanding of normal and pathological adolescent developments. The unconscious drive which pushes a person towards choosing a certain representation is linked to each individual subjectivity, to the specific dynamic interactions of numerous elements which are intertwined and derive fundamentally from early relational traumatic experiences. Nevertheless, while the phantasy – as well as the dream – is able to provide a working through function, the spectator's passive attitude watching the screen determines that the representation – Stoller's "published daydream" – is prepackaged. Directed by an external hand, all the scene can offer is a solipsistic tension being released through an act of masturbation. The innumerable sexual scenes and the vast choice of representations of polymorphic perversions available on the web, do not create new phantasies or new needs. Easy access to all these representations seems to create a potential fast-track built on the weak points of an individual's childhood development.

In describing the path which leads to addiction, N. Doidge, of the Canadian Psychoanalytic Society and neuroscientist, writes how hardcore pornography reveals some of the neural networks established during critical periods of sexual development. According to this Author (2008), these forgotten or repressed primitive elements continue to establish new networks, in which all the features of the above-mentioned elements are interconnected. When a special image combination triggers sexual excitement, the subject watches them repeatedly, while masturbating and releasing dopamine. So, his libido is somehow reconstructed and deeply rooted in his hidden sexual tendencies. This kind of "neosexuality" becomes a sort of addiction, where satisfaction is mixed with aggressiveness. The combination of violent and sexual images increases the spread of sadomasochistic content on the web. The perverse aspect underlined by Doidge highlights the neurobiological dynamics triggered by the need for more and more violent and hardcore images, aimed at provoking an exciting response (2008, p. 125). This is linked to Stoller's thought about the mortiferous side of pornography, in which erotization is featured as a repetitive defence, often with manic characteristics.

Conclusions

Building a bridge between neurosciences and psychoanalysis constitutes a stimulating challenge which is enriching both fields as well as creating a constructive integration (Merciai and Cannella, 2009; Yovell et al., 2015). With regards to pornography abusers, thanks to the understanding of psychic dynamics and recent neurobiological findings in the field of addiction, some hypothesis can be elaborated and researched. But it is important to underline that recent studies are mostly related to male subjects, who represent 70–80% of pornography users. The feminine equivalent remains, to this day, within the mysterious "dark continent" which, since Freud's time, is still obscure. Nevertheless, pornography has raised a vast debate regarding the role of women, represented as sexually passive and exploited objects. These representations might lead to sadism, violence and submission. The anti-porn appeals of the 1970s came together around A. Dworkin's position and gave rise to the neo-feminist movement, which in Europe is represented today by M. Marzano, author of two books on pornography: "Pornographie ou l'Epuisement du désir" (2003) and "Malaise dans la sexualité. Le piège de la pornographie" (2006). Psychic and neurobiological dynamics which support amateur pornographic productions and distribution phenomena still remain very uncertain. Since the end of the 1990s, with the expansion of social networks, selfies, digital generations and the increase in Internet usage, these phenomena are globally known as Neoporn (Stella, 2011): a complex and elusive reality, a narcissistic "appearing to exist": the disquieting future of pornography.

References

Ahumada, J. L. (2016). Is the Nature of Psychoanalytic Thinking and Practice (E.g., in Regard to Sexuality) Determined by Extra-Analytic, Social and Cultural Developments?: Insight under Siege: Psychoanalysis in the 'Autistoid Age'. *International Journal of Psycho-Analysis*, 97(3): 839–851.

Attwood, F. (2006). Sexed Up: Theorizing the Sexualitaton of Culture. *Sexualities*, 9(1): 77–94.

Baudrillard, J. (1979). *Seduction*. London: Palgrave Macmillan.

Berridge, K. C. (2007). The Debate Over Dopamine's Role in Reward: The Case for Incentive Salience? *Psychopharmacology*, 191: 391–431.

Biasin, E., Maina, G., Zecca, F. (2011). *Il porno espanso: dal cinema ai nuovi media*. Sesto S. Giovanni: Mimesis.

Cooper, A. (1998). Sexuality and the Internet: Surfing into the New Millennium. *CyberPsychology & Behavior*, 1(2): 187–193.

Cooper, A., Delmonico, D. (2000). Cybersex Users, Abusers, and Compulsives: New Findings and Implications. *Sexual Addiction & Compulsivity the Journal of Treatment & Prevention*, 7 (1–2): 135–135.

Cooper, A., Delmonico, D. L., Griffin-Shelley, E., Mathy, R. M. (2004). Online Sexual Activity: An Examination of Potentially Problematic Behaviors. *Sexual Addiction & Compulsivity: The Journal of Treatment and Prevention*, 11: 129–143.

Dines, G. (2010). *Pornland: How Porn Has Hijacked Our Sexuality*. Boston: Beacon Press.

Doidge, N. (2008). *The Brain that Changes Itself*. London: Penguin.

Dworkin, A. (1989). *Pornography: Men Possessing Women*. New York: Dutton.

Freud, S. (1910). Vol. 11, SE.

Freud, S. (1920). Vol. 18, SE.

Galatzer-Levy, R. M. (2012). Obscuring Desire: A Special Pattern of Male Adolescent Masturbation, Internet Pornography, and the Flight from Meaning. *Psychoanalytic Inquiry*, 32(5): 480–495.

Giddens, A. (1992). *The Transformation of Intimacy: Sexuality, Love and Eroticism in Modern Societies*. Stanford: SUP.

Janin, C. (2015). Shame, Hatred, and Pornography: Variations on an Aspect of Current Times. *International Journal of Psychoanalysis*, 96(6): 1603–1614.

Kahn, M. M. R. (1979). *Alienation in Perversion*. London: Karnac.

Kalman, T. P. (2008). Frontline: Clinical Encounters with Internet Pornography. *The Journal of the American Academy of Psychoanalysis*, 36(4): 593–618.

Laufer, M. (1976). The Central Masturbation Fantasy, the Final Sexual Organization, and Adolescence. *Psychoanalytic Study of the Child*, 31: 297–316.

Love, T., Laier, C., Brand, M., Hatch, L., Hajela, R. (2015). Neuroscience of Internet Pornography Addiction: A Review and Update. *Behavioral Science*, 5(3): 388–433.

Marzano, M. (2003). *Pornographie ou l'Epuisment du Désir*. Paris: Buchet Chastel.

Marzano, M. (2006). *Malaise dans la sexualitè: le piège de la pornographie*. Paris: JC Lattes.

McNair, B. (1996). *Mediated Sex: Pornography and Postmodern Culture*. New York: St. Martin's Press.

McNair, B. (2002). *Striptease Culture: Sex, Media and the Democratisation of Desire*. London: Routledge.

Merciai, S. A., Cannella, B. (2009). *La psicoanalisi nelle terre di confine*. Milano: Cortina.

Nestler, E. J. (2001). Molecular Basis of Long-Term Plasticity Underlying Addiction. *Nature Reviews Neuroscience*, 2: 119–128.

Nestler, E. J. (2004). Molecular Mechanisms of Drug Addiction. *Neuropharmacology*, 47(Suppl 1): 24–32.

Paul, R. A. (2016). Is the Nature of Psychoanalytic Thinking and Practice (E.g., in Regard to Sexuality) Determined by Extra-Analytic, Social Cultural

Developments?: Sexuality: Biological Fact or Cultural Developments?: Sexuality: Biological Fact or Cultural Construction? The View from Dual Inheritance Theory. *International Journal of Psycho-Analysis*, 97(3): 823–837.

Panksepp, J. (2004). *Affective Neuroscience: The Foundations of Human and Animal Emotions*. Oxford: Oxford University Press, pp 53–70.

Smith, C. (2010). Pornographication: A Discourse for All Seasons. *International Journal of Media and Cultural Politics*, 6(1): 103–108.

Stella, R. (2011). *Eros, Cybersex, Neoporn*. Milano: Francoangeli.

Stoller, R. (1985). *Observing the Erotic Imagination*. New Haven: Yale University Press.

Volkow, N. D., et al. (2007). Dopamine in Drug Abuse and Addiction: Results of Imaging Studies and Treatment Implications. *Archives of Neurology*, 64(11): 1575–1579.

Wood, H. (2013). Internet Pornography and Paedophilia. *Psychoanalytic Psychotherapy*, 27(4): 319–338.

Woods, J. (2015). Seeing and Being Seen: The Psychodynamics of Pornography Through the Lens of Winnicott's Thought. In: *The Winnicott Tradition*. Edited by M. Boyle Spelman, F.Thomson-Sal, London: Karnac, pp 163–174.

Yovell, Y., Solms, M., Fotopoulou, A. (2015). The Case for Neuropsychoanalysis: Why a Dialogue with Neuroscience Is Necessary But Not Sufficient for Psychoanalysis. *International Journal of Psychoanalysis*, 96: 1515–1553.

Zellner, M. R., Watt, D. F., Solms, M., Panksepp, J. (2011). Affective Neuroscientific and Neuropsychoanalytic Approaches to Two Intractable Psychiatric Problems: Why Depression Feels So Bad and What Addicts Really Want. *Neuroscience and Biobehavioral Reviews*, 35: 2000–2008.

6 Applied affective neuroscience and psychoanalytic practice

Francesco Castellet Y Ballarà

If the main goal of psychoanalysis is to help patients question their malad-aptative views of reality, like those ideas that make them suffer and get them stuck in life, then why is it so difficult for psychoanalysis itself to acquire a similar stance towards its own beliefs?

(Luyten, 2015, p. 5)

"The search for knowledge does not feed on certitudes.
It feeds on a radical lack of them."

(Rovelli, 2014, p. 4)

Introduction

During the past decades between Psychoanalysis and Neuroscience, we have seen a progressive convergence of interests in common areas, such as subjectivity, consciousness, the unconscious, memory and dreams.

The contribution of neuroscientists, with their advanced neuro-physiological and neuro-imaging techniques, have for the first time been permitted to produce in vivo experimental studies on the physiology of superior mind functions and to offer further contributions to mind models in the philosophical area, and, potentially in our psychoanalytical models (Gerber & Peterson, 2006).

Moreover, the latest developments in Evolutionary and Developmental Biology have brought some biological concepts closer to psychoanalytical principles and praxis. These concepts concern the key role of early experience in the long-term development of the individual, especially the early relationships between infants and their caregivers.

In this respect, the contributions of Infant Research, Attachment Theory, Mentalization theory (Fonagy et al., 2002) in addition to that of the affective neurosciences have been essential.

The concept of drive from the viewpoint of affective neurosciences

As Solms and Turnbull write: "For some students of psychoanalysis, drive theory has been rejected as outmoded and inappropriate.........(but) there is

DOI: 10.4324/9781003198741-7

now abundant evidence in neurobiology of the existence of what we refer to as 'drives'" (Solms & Turnbull, 2011, p. 141).

After all, Freud himself believed that:

> The theory of the instincts is, so to speak, our mythology, Instincts are mythical entities, magnificent in their indefiniteness. In our work we cannot for a moment disregard them, yet we are never sure that we are seeing them clearly. [...] We have always been moved by a suspicion that behind all these little ad hoc instincts there lay concealed something serious and powerful which we should like to approach cautiously. [...] here we stand under the influence of an unshakable biological fact: each individual living organism is at the command of two intentions, self-preservation and the preservation of the species, which seem to be independent of each other, and which, as far as we know until now, have no common origin, and their interests are often in conflict in animal life. Actually what we are talking about now is biological psychology, we are studying the psychic equivalent of biological processes.
>
> (Freud, 1933, p. 95)

Actually, the concept of drive, as theorized by Freud remains a paradoxical concept:

> Trieb ist so einer der Begriffe der Abgrenzung des Seelischen von Kérperlichen.
>
> (Freud, 1905, p. 67)

This can be literally translated (my translation) as "Drive is, then, one of the concepts of boundary between the psychic and the somatic".

The official translation is that drive is "a boundary/concept between the mental and the somatic", therefore an obscure concept, "magnificent in its indeterminate nature".

So, Freud, admitting ignorance about "the mysterious leap from the mind to the body", puts the definition off to a probably better definition in light of future developments in biological psychology.

Weigel, a philosopher, argues that:

> When Freud states that the drive determines the amount of required work that is imposed on the soul because of its relation to corporeality [...], this means that the idea of drive consequently determines the amount of involvement with physiology and biology that is required by Psychoanalysis.
>
> (Weigel, 2016, p. 8)

Biological sciences are consequently at the core of classical psychoanalytical drive theory and great progress has taken place since Freud's definition.

It is enough to consider the discovery of the DNA, discoveries in immunology and the recent epigenetic revolution. Precisely, with the neurosciences, we can experimentally analyze the "psychical accompaniments of biological processes" the way Freud tried to do in 1932 from a theoretical point of view.

In this branch of biological and evolutionary psychology, including comparative findings on different species, Jaak Panksepp's work about basic emotional/motivational systems has been revolutionary.

These motivational forces have a subcortical origin, so we have them in common with mammals and birds, according to neurobiology (Panksepp & Biven, 2012).

Furthermore, the distinction between merely genetic instincts and drives, (a concept which borders between the psychic and the somatic) has been overcome by the epigenetic revolution, which shows the deep connection and influence between nature and environment\culture.

Recent translational studies on the effects of culture on genetic evolution point to how cultural change shapes human ecological niches that have had a reversal effect on our biology. For some aspects, we may say, that culture shapes the human genome (Laland et al., 2010).

We can say that if the DNA is purely genetic and relatively static and immutable, its final expression is changeable and influenced by relationships, i.e. the human environment.

Everything is Trieb, as Freud meant it, but it would not be based on just two drives (Eros and Thanatos), there would be at least seven or eight ones: the so-called basic emotions, which are genetically transmitted and active since birth, distinct but interacting amongst each other continually and with a long evolutionary history, which we share with other animal species.

"These emotional command systems are ancient and exist in all mammals and birds. More importantly, they exist in all humans" (Yovell, 2016, p. 134).

In most of the neuro-scientific and neuro-psychological realms, a true change of paradigm is taking place, which transfers the focus of research from cognition to emotion and body, in order to arrive at understanding the human being more accurately, both as an individual and as part of cultural groups.

Coming from a branch of cognitive research based on the exclusion of emotions and the subjective as potential "biases", we now recognize the enormous importance that emotions have on our learning mechanisms at a deep level, on memory and even more paradoxically on our capacity to think.

I would in fact propose, with the aim of overcoming excessively dualistic thinking, an "emotion-thought paradigm" along with the body-mind or mind-body paradigm, which reflects more accurately the reality of the phenomena we are analyzing, as, after all, Bion (1970) had already imagined and theorized.

We can therefore consider emotions amongst the most complex of mental states since they are present in all the other mental processes in very specific ways which depend on the quality of the emotions per se.

To be sure, emotions, as well as drives according to Freud, are ever-present in our clinical work and they are a specific object of our attention: "In our work, we cannot ignore them not even for a moment, and yet we are never sure to be observing them clearly" (Freud, op.cit. p. 95).

Emotions are also probably crucial for the establishment and maintenance of consciousness, and they are probably a mental state that we share – even if at different levels – with mammals, reptiles, birds, and also fish and insects.

Basic emotions originate in the subcortical and median structures of our brain and they can be defined as the mind's subcortical source (Panksepp & Biven, 2012, p. 514).

Any kind of damage to these ancient phylogenetic structures that we share with mammals causes in fact a loss or an alteration of consciousness and of the superior cognitive processes.

The brain-mind "is clearly an evolutionary stratified organ based upon affects" (Panksepp & Biven, 2012, p. 516), which plays a key role in the development of language.

But the problem of a clear linguistic and operative definition of the terms we use when we talk about affects in science for the purpose of experimental research, and, in parallel, of psychoanalytic practice, is very important and is reminiscent in fact of the difficulties and confusion related to the use of the term "drive", as we mentioned above.

I believe that it may be useful to define "affects" as the general category of these endo-perceptions of the inner psycho-physical state of body-mind which include emotions and feelings as sub-categories.

Emotions and feelings are different from each other and also linguistically: emotions are linked to action, or aiming at it, and therefore can also be non-conscious, as Le Doux states (Le Doux & Brown, 2017); whereas feelings are linked to perception and therefore to consciousness.

For a taxonomy of affects

The upper-level emotions, better known as feelings, are the most complex of mental states. They can reach such a level of sophistication that only poetic words can describe them, through their ability to communicate with the non-verbal dimension of the mind and the body.

The most obvious hypothesis is that feelings are a blend of basic emotions. We can metaphorically compare them to the theory of fundamental colors: starting with pure colors it is possible to obtain the whole range of colors, by mixing them in different proportions. In the same way, we can mix basic emotions to give birth to feelings.

In fact, concerning the a-modal perception (Stern, 1985) present in newborns and which is peculiar of mind at its early stage, we are predisposed towards using all of our sensorial channels at the same time and therefore associate various received inputs in a synesthetic way. Consequently, we could guess the existence of an ability to unify our basic emotions in more complex units. These complex units fit the inner regulation systems that are a function of the exchanges with the outside world, that is with other mind-bodies with whom we have a significant relationship.

To sum up, a feeling or a group of more feelings experienced in a precise moment of our conscious perception would be the description of the state of our relationships with our significant others.

A sort of MRI (Magnetic Resonance Imaging) or scan of what and who defines us as existent in our web of meaningful relationships.

It is therefore heuristically useful to think of a taxonomy of affects, starting from the simplest ones, such as the survival instincts present in the brain stem, our reptilian brain, to the most complex ones present in the neocortex, extremely developed in our species.

We could thus distinguish the affects as:

- *Primal emotions* (Danton, 2005) or Primal Affects, according to Hill (Hill, 2015) that are caused by interoceptors giving information concerning the inside of the body in order to ensure its survival: hunger, thirst, need to breathe, sensitivity to cold, lack of sleep, orgasm, etc. Damasio calls them "basic emotions" which have an intimate relationship with drives, but also with the arousal states of vital organs, i.e. the activation of the Autonomic Nervous System.
- *Basic or categorial emotions* (Darwin, 1872, Panksepp & Biven, 2012) are caused by exteroceptors (eyes, ears, nose, skin, etc.) that give information from the outside of the body, from the world: fear, anger, surprise, disgust, joy, sadness. These are the most powerful means of communication, common to humans and mammals.
- *Secondary, social, or complex emotions* (feelings): shame, guilt, pride, longing, jealousy, envy, remorse, hate, love, etc. These are probably biologically based on primary emotions but they are learned and set up in the midst of highly meaningful and precocious relational experiences, such as the socialization through shame induced by the caregiver when the child is around 2 years old (Panksepp, 2015).

Moreover, specialized literature (Tracy & Randles, 2011) provides some standards to define a "basic" emotion:

a   A basic emotion must be distinguishable from other emotions;
b   It must possess a set of typical neural and subcortical structures, and body expressions;
c   It must have an emotional or behavioral component with a distinct adaptive and cross-cultural function;
d   It must be observable in other species, at least in primates.

In conclusion, could we guess that basic emotions are the current biological concept that corresponds most closely to drives?

It seems useful at this point to briefly expose the opinions of the main scholars in affective neuroscience such as A. Shore, J. Panksepp, A. Damasio and J. Le Doux, on the fundamental nature of affects.

I would begin with Le Doux's position, which has been expressed and restated also in some recent articles (Le Doux & Brown, 2017).

In Le Doux's opinion, basic emotions, and specifically fear, are non-conscious, implicit processes, genetically programmed, even if modifiable with learning. They can be more aptly defined as defensive survival circuits belonging to the prefrontal cortex which, interacting with the working memory, give birth to the feeling of fear. Ledoux believes that only if the cortex is involved are we conscious of emotion, which he defines as emotional awareness, or feeling.

His critique of Panskepp's and partially of Damasios' positions is that even though everybody agrees on the presence of subcortical representations in both animals and humans, that are capable of feeling basic and rough emotions, this is only based on the similarity of intra-species subcortical circuitry, but is not a direct evidence of the existence of consciousness and therefore feelings in animals.

In an article he wrote with a mind philosopher he affirms: "In our opinion, the subcortical circuits proposed by Panksepp and Damasio are better interpreted as non-conscious first-order representations that contribute and indirectly influence the higher-order assembly of conscious feelings by the GNC (General Network of Cognition)" (Le Doux & Brown, 2017).

According to Damasio (Damasio, 2010), proto-self maps store information about the body, while another map stores information about the environment. Both then merge into a third map which he calls Core-Self or Nuclear Self which marks the environment map through the reactions of the proto-Self. To sum up, this is the theory of the Somatic Marker, which does not correspond to feelings, which remain a neocortical achievement, since they require self-consciousness and autobiographical memory. Later, Damasio himself recognized that animals nearest to us, such as primates, are probably equipped with emotional feelings and therefore consciousness, thanks to the notable contribution of the subcortical areas. According to Panksepp, who is no doubt the author who has considerably elaborated and extended McLean's tripartite brain theory (MacLean, 1973), emotions are divided into three groups (apart from homeostatic and sensory emotions such as hunger, thirst, cold, sexual desire, which do not create theoretical problems regarding the question of consciousness):

- The seven basic/primary process emotions occur due to the neural basic activity of the brain's deep and median subcortical structures. They are ancient from an evolutionary point of view, and we share them with other animal species.
- Secondary process emotions correspond to basic emotions that have been modified by the learning process while in contact with the environment, starting at birth. These emotions are located in the most recent part of the limbic system, from an evolutionary point of view.

- Tertiary process or neocortical emotions occur, when secondary and primary process emotions meet cognitive and reflexive processes found in the frontal cortex, leading to the conscious elaboration of feelings related to verbalization.

Therefore for Panksepp, basic or primary process emotions are ancestral instruments, innate, provided by evolution for survival, and they correspond to "intrinsic evolutionary values" (Panksepp & Biven, 2012, p. 69; Panksepp, 2014). According to this author, the theories of the so-called affect peripheral feedback, which affirm that these affects would only be cortical secondary evaluations in reaction to the environment, and lack the necessary data to back them up. Through tertiary processes, the cortex, and the cognitive functions active in it, are able to name and elaborate primary and secondary emotions of subcortical origin.

In support of his theory, he exposes experiments on decortication, quadriplegia, studies on brain stem injuries, locked-in syndrome, and complete cortical agenesia, where affects would be stored and would be communicable through non-verbal modality.

According to Shore (Shore, 2015), neuroscientist and clinical psychologist, the body language of emotions is a non-verbal implicit communication resulting from the activity of the right hemisphere.

This author makes no distinction between different groups of affects, but he affirms that emotions are basically non-cortical and not linked to verbal language, as opposed to Le Doux's theory. In his books, he continually underlines the importance of memories and embodied affects, which he defines "affective unconscious" and of affective interchanges between human beings, where words have a minimal impact. He theorizes, in fact, how, on the basis of experimental evidence, direct communication from the left brain to the right brain through the body and the non-verbal language of mimic, gestures and tone of voice is possible. This is not different from the rich affective interaction between infant and caregiver in the first year of life. Unconscious affects are such, according to Schore, not because of repression, but because of dissociation following relational traumas. We owe to this author, in fact, the theory of emotional regulation, which is one of the most stimulating theories from a clinical point of view since it has its roots in infant research and attachment theory.

Unconscious affects should be experienced on a corporeal level and accepted by the therapist before being symbolized through verbalization.

Affective regulation is based on the fact, often underestimated, that affects reflect the inner state of an individual and they have two dimensions: a hedonistic one (pleasant or unpleasant) and one related to the arousal or activation,which is their energetic intensity.

The intensity (arousal) of an emotion is extremely changeable and can be so high so as to completely shut off our mind, as is the case of anger and panic. A window of tolerance (Ogden et al., 2006) of moderate arousal corresponds to the verbal function in a neutral or pleasant state of the right hemisphere, whereas above and below this arousal level we have, on the one hand, emotions such as anger, fear and pain that are connected to the sympathetic hyperarousal, and on the other hand we have shame, disgust, discouragement, and depression that are connected to the parasympathetic hyperarousal. The latter ones are more difficult to regulate with verbalization.

To sum up, Shore and Panskepp agree on the subcortical and non-verbal nature (limbic system) of affects and they both agree on the importance of comparative psychological studies involving also other species with which we probably share the experience of basic emotions. The only aspect all authors agree on is the acceptance of the existence of robust subcortical contributions to emotional feelings and consciousness.

In a way, affects are still an enigma for the affective neurosciences, but now we know they are crucial for the development and the functioning of the mind.

As a consequence, we may say that the dichotomy emotion-reason is intrinsically false.

The central role of attachment

Amongst the basic emotions, Panksepp singles out the special role of the care system in which we can find the attachment, which amply satisfies all the criteria listed before for the inclusion in this group.

In fact, during childhood, as we well know, the bond between the infant and the caregiver is vital for the neurological development of the infant, and it is under the control of the panic\pain and care systems which regulate the attachment behavior discovered by Bowlby (Bowlby, 1977) and investigated by Main and associates (Main, 1990).

The sheer size of experimental and clinical evidence of attachment in the first years of life and later in adult life as a relational style cannot be ignored and must be integrated into a modern and scientific psychoanalytical theory willing to face the knot of affects in clinical practice.

Polan and Hofer (Polan & Hofer, 2008) underline how basic research on neural development in animals and on newborn humans are both inspired by evolutional principles where "the historic nature of both development and evolution closes the gap between the reductionist emphasis of molecular/cellular neurosciences and the holistic emphasis on meaning, which is the central focus of Psychoanalysis-oriented clinicians" (Polan & Hofer, op.cit.).

In newborns as well as in children and adults, attachment regulates needs and basic emotions, which are, therefore, in reality, recognition of need, absence of self-sufficiency (Nussbaum, 2001).

A typical example is the attachment response to the caregiver in dangerous situations (Coan, 2008, p. 274).

> Many neural structures are involved in a way or another in attachment, to the point that it is possible to think of the entire human brain as a neural attachment system... in particular, it is the Anterior Cingulate Cortex (Limbic System) that monitors conflicts that concern attachment.
>
> (Coan, op.cit, p. 277)

In the case of the child, the filial attachment bond can precede birth. The fetus can recognize the voice and odor of the mother; in particular, the mother's odor can elicit orientation responses and can have a calming effect on human babies who cry.

> In addition, in the newborn, it is the Locus Coeruleus that consolidates the memory of the aspect, sound and odor of the caregiver while the amygdala is not yet sufficiently functioning, so an aversive conditioning is difficult or impossible... so that... almost all stimuli are simply codified as familiar.
>
> (Coan, op.cit., 282–283)

Therefore the filial bond or attachment of the newborn happens rapidly and unconditionally also towards mistreating caregivers, both in the case of abuse and neglect, even if the second has more serious consequences. This bond is created during a temporal window of postnatal brain development (brain growth spur, from the third trimester of pregnancy to the second year of life) when the amygdala and the pre-frontal cortex are not yet sufficiently active nor capable of regulating the filial bond. Probably this early bond (within the first 6 months of life) creates a rough pre-operational model of interdependence and regulation of attachment that is going to be changed and reinforced during childhood and the teenage years. Therefore, this filial bond would be one of our procedural memories, implicit and corporeal, shaping the capacity of separating the familiar from the foreign on a relational and social level.

The attachment bond to multiple caregivers allows the passage from a physiological need regulation through affect (hunger, thirst, sleep, warmness-closeness, contact, etc.) to a regulation of affect per se. In fact, the functionality of the Prefrontal Cortex (PFC) and the emotional self-regulation in adults depend on the precocity and quality of compensating activity of the right PFC of the caregivers towards that of the newborn, not yet activated (Hofer, 2006; Schore, 2012).

Affect regulation or social-emotional regulation (regulation through another human or at least another living being) is the most efficient and convenient of all self-regulating strategies. One might say that we are born and survive thanks to our belonging to a social group that molds us and that we constantly model also through specific emotions such as shame, guilt, disapproval, pride.

From a clinical point of view, the theoretical opening towards an inter-species comparison of those basic emotions that are common at least among mammals, makes us more aware of the importance of exploring the relationship between our patients and their pets, As soon as these animals enter the analytic setting figuratively, they stand as a precious source of information concerning the mode of our patients' attachment styles, as well as their personalities and their defensive mechanisms. Their presence in the life of these people often acts as a predictive factor for positive relationships. As stated by Sable: "We now have convincing scientific evidence that pets have a positive effect on the physical and psychic wellbeing of people, helping them to regulate their emotions and manage stress, traumas and relationships with others" (Sable, 2016, p. 208).

Bridges between neurosciences and clinical psychoanalysis

The recent paradigm shifts in the field of neuroscience – from cognition to affects, from the Central Nervous System (CNS) to the Autonomous Nervous System (ANS), from the sympathetic system to the parasympathetic system and from affective self-regulation to dyadic co-regulation – have brought on some changes in the techniques adopted by some psychotherapies. This is particularly true of dynamic-oriented therapies that focus on non-verbal and emotional contents, and more specifically on the treatment for post-traumatic conditions such as PTSD (Post Traumatic Stress Disorder).

We shall focus on the Affect Regulation Theory (Hill, 2015; Schore, 2012), on the Sensory-Motor Psychotherapy (Ogden et al., 2006) and the Accelerated Experiential Dynamic Psychotherapy (Fosha, 2000, 2002).

Affect regulation theory according to Hill

According to this theory, affects can be classified into two categories:

> Primary affects are the body response (our first response) to salient stimuli in the inner and outer worlds. They are neurophysiological responses of our autonomic nervous system and the vital organs, especially the heart. They have two basic dimensions: the CNS manifests itself along a hyper or hypo-activation continuum and the hedonist tone as positive or negative'.
>
> (Hill, 2015, p. 106)

Secondary affects, on the other hand, are primary affects which have been transformed by the reflexive function or mentalization, which occurs by means of a verbalization process.

Mentalization is a conscious, cortical and voluntary affects-regulation system ruled by the left hemisphere that is based on verbal communication (Fonagy et al., 2002).

What is crucial to notice, though, is that a secure attachment style determines a state of optimal non-verbal regulation of primary emotions allowing mentalization to occur otherwise it would be deactivated into a state of primary affective dis-regulation, In other words, the first system – the non-verbal, implicit system of primary affective regulation enables the other system, the conscious one, based on verbalization, to function; but the opposite is not possible.

The communication of primary affects is in fact non-verbal and it happens by way of facial expressions, body movements, the tone and prosody of the voice – which serve as powerful activators of emotional response in relationships. From a neurobiological perspective, we are programmed to pair up with each other's affective states, which represent the state of arousal/activation of our internal vital organs and therefore the activation of the Self from a body-mind viewpoint.

This affective exchange happens within the duration of 30 ms (Hill, op.cit., p. 7), which is too rapid to be able to access consciousness, and thus remains implicit but still constitutes the neuro-physiological basis of intersubjectivity. The latter is fundamental because it supplies – albeit in a subliminal way –crucial information in order to read the internal state of the other and their intentions. This information conveys the meaning of a social interaction in terms of affects, which means whether or not one person acquires a particular importance for another at a specific time.

Naturally, affect regulation and interpersonal neurobiology are enmeshed, and they correspond to the limbic brain, which comprises cortical and sub-cortical structures, as part of the brain that is specialized in social behavior and cooperation. This cerebral area remains malleable and alterable throughout life, though there are certain temporal windows during childhood that are crucial for the connection between the different areas of the limbic system and especially between the PFC and the amygdala. It is upon these connections that the possibility of an emotional self-regulation and other regulations depends on adulthood as well.

In fact, one can define optimal emotional regulation as a balance between self-regulation and other-regulation abilities.

Regulation of primary affects in clinical psychoanalysis

The neurobiological model of affective regulation of primary affects provides a theoretical framework for those techniques that are primarily centered on the body and mostly aimed at post-traumatic states. It has played a leading role in Bromberg's Multiple Self theories and in the therapeutic use of enactment (Bromberg, 1998).

Once the primary affects regulation is accomplished, that is the regulation of the limbic control on the ANS, the corporeal, non-verbal dyadic relationship, regulation through mentalization and reflective function intervenes (Fonagy et al., 2002). In practice, what is crucial is that the mother, or the therapist, is capable of verbalizing with enough accuracy the mental states of the child/patient, an ability which is a direct consequence of the capacity to verbalize one's own mental states to oneself and to others.

In brief, both at a non-verbal and more reasonably at a verbal level, the mind is always shaped by the outside, namely by the relationship with the other. To name an emotion, a state of the mind, an intention, a need or a desire is the final milestone of an interaction process that is, at least, bipersonal and generates an affective dyadic or even multiple co-regulation, if we want to include group-level phenomena, as well.

In other words: the ability of mentalizing, particularly one's own affective states, implies communicating them to someone else in such a way that they may be represented, interpreted, modified and – through the act of sharing – regulated in an inter-subjective neurobiological sense.

Pat ogden's sensory motor therapy

According to these authors (Ogden et al., 2006), information in our brain is processed according to three different modalities: sensorimotor, emotional, and cognitive. In normal conditions, each one of these modalities interacts with the others, whereas in the case of pathology, notably in the case of traumatic conditions, the cognitive modality is deactivated and the other two predominate. Developmentally speaking, they correspond to the early stages of the child's mental development.

The sensory-motor level of functioning is the same as described by Piaget (1962) and it is typical of the newborn, in which tactile and kinesthetic as well as olfactory and gustatory perceptions guide attachment behavior and allow the physiological and behavioral regulation provided by the caregiver.

In such a level of functioning, people have often suffered a trauma, which later develops into PTSD. In these individuals, the emotional, sensory-motor self-regulation coming from the frontal-cortex is ineffective – even when faced with undemanding stimuli.

We can distinguish three main components in sensory-motor information processing:

- Internal bodily sensation as diffused by interoceptors,
- Perceptions deriving from the five senses due to the exteroceptors
- Movement, which originates initially in the pre-motor and motor areas of the cortex.

The discovery of mirror neurons (Rizzolatti et al., 2014) has further demonstrated how movement and emotions/thoughts are linked to each other, especially if we consider how mimic, posture, and gestures unconsciously continually communicate our internal world to others and how they influence our own emotional state.

One of the principles of sensory-motor therapy is actually that of working on movements and on repetitive chronic postures that contribute to the preservation of limiting, invalidating cognitive-emotional tendencies, which can be modified by engaging the body in a bottom-up modality, or rather from the movement towards emotions and cognition. The interesting thing is that, while top-down processes depend on the lower levels in order to function, sensory-motor processing can function independently from the top-down regulation.

Ultimately, being aware of one's own body under the empathic guide of the therapist as well as being conscious of its functioning in every punctual detail is likely to reinstate -or even provide for the first time – a containment function described by Bion and Winnicott, as indispensable for traumatic pathologies, especially in case of neglect.

The fact that the focus is on the body appears to be a necessary adjustment to the patient's level of functioning, avoiding the risk of distancing oneself too much or being too near to what is bearable for the other.

After all the body – as expression of the unconscious, procedural and implicit under-structure of the relationship – is the fruit of all the previous relationships from pre-birth onwards.

From a relational psychoanalytical point of view, one can hypothesize that the transferential components belonging to both participants may be essential, mostly because the capability for harmony at the body level cannot happen in the presence of traumatic experiences that have not been sufficiently elaborated by the therapist him/herself, regardless of the technique, no matter how accurate.

The corporeal affective resonance that is mediated by the right hemispheres of the analytic couple at work is in fact largely non-conscious, implicit and related to the sub-cortical affective memory.

Diane Foshas's accelerated experiential dynamic psychotherapy (AEDP)

The AEDP is an intervention model specifically intended for post-traumatic pathologies that combines relational and experiential elements in a psychodynamic theoretical framework focused on affects and affects dyadic regulation in the course of treatment.

Thus, a major role is conferred to the affects in the manner in which Darwin originally formulated them – therefore, as either basic or categorical emotions (Darwin, 1872) – followed by Tomkins (1963), Ekman (1992) and the above-mentioned Panksepp and Damasio.

In addition, the author adheres to a theoretical clinical tradition that supports the patient in focusing, moment by moment, on somatic and emotional experiences, omitting the rational and cognition experiences, with the aim of encouraging a natural process of emotional self-regulation, which has profound roots in the body, a sort of "body wisdom", which is aroused in the presence of intense and dyadic affective states.

Diane Fosha's method is based on attachment and neuro-developmental assumptions and, in particular, on the dissociation function seen from a neurobiological perspective (Lanius et al., 2011), as a surviving modality of the "core Self", or nuclear Self, also called "True Self" (Damasio, 2010, Northoff & Panksepp, 2008). Work done on dissociation is central and it is the most delicate part of the intervention, during which patient and analyst «walk on the fine line between healing and re-traumatizing» (Fosha, op.cit., p. 519).

While the patient is still immersed in his/her own dissociation, the therapist works on the identification of subtle but recognizable integrated aspects of Self – from the outside towards the inside-, This generates moments of matching that result in an outburst of energetic vitality, which launches the transformation process towards more integrated states of the Self (Lane et al., 2015).

Fosha's intervention model, in contrast with the sensory-motor therapy, better integrates the contribution of Infant Research and of the Attachment Theory. While on the technical side it seemingly overlaps with the sensory-motor theory, regarding the tracking of body emotions (Ogden et al., 2006), this model pays instead more attention to the profound transferal, relational dynamics, in line with the psychodynamic tradition.

Discussion

All of the previously discussed theoretical and therapeutic approaches have in common the fundamental and primary role of the unconscious, unrepressed, implicit, procedural and non-verbal processes of affects, as compared with the small portion of affects that can be verbalized.

The therapeutic approach aiming at the regulation of the hyper and hypo-arousal of the ANS, hence of the dissociation, in all circumstances operates as a bottom-up procedure since the desirable increasing of affects self-reflection and mentalization -namely, the actualization of the "talking cure" top-down processes- is only practicable when the autonomic emotional dis-regulation are kept within a certain range of tolerance.

If the co-regulation of primary affects or co-transference happens by definition in an implicit, embodied and non-verbal modality, it would require the acquisition of a specific sensitivity to body language.

Infant Observation is proved to be the most appropriate learning modality for it.

The usefulness of including this formative experience within the standard analytical training is already largely felt amongst the psychoanalytic community, and this body of knowledge reinforces its necessity, also for the increasing consensus towards the use of long-term analytical psychotherapies in the Borderline Disorder therapy, whose correlation with emotional regulation disorders resulting from early relational trauma has been confirmed authoritatively (Lyon-Ruth, 2003).

In addition, if the central role of early relational trauma in regulation disorders during childhood, and later adolescence and adulthood is accepted, then particular attention will have to be paid during therapy, at the risk of re-traumatizing the patient with out-of-sync interventions or inadequate settings and, to the primary necessity of favoring the re-establishment of basic trust, in other words of a co-regulation of primary affects,

Practically, it would be necessary to adopt a flexible setting, which would adapt to the patient's emerging demands and would not impose, for example, those standardized analytic settings however useful and reassuring for the analyst.

The flexibility of the setting, for example, can be a test of the therapist's ability to welcome the patient's defenses, before being able to modify them, since the patient should be left free to able to auto-regulate the distance and the intimacy from the therapist within his/her own window of tolerance. It is the case of errors or mismatch in attunement, which are somehow unavoidable and useful if adequately faced, towards the construction of a relationship that is truly adequate to the patient's needs.

Finally, since in this theoretical area the regulation of primary affects, first on the part of the therapist, followed by that of the patient, builds the emotional co-regulation as the goal of the therapeutic change through the reduction of the defensive dissociation. – The difficult question is posed of how to facilitate and sustain the analyst in this process generally, and more particularly in cases of de-enactment or enactment.

The objective would be to theoretically facilitate the therapist's affects co-regulation first, and then his/her mentalization. The tools at our disposal remain invariably, the same: individual or peer supervision, or still an individual or group relationship. I believe that in both cases, the level of emotional co-regulation is dependent obviously on the quality and duration of the relationship; and that it is not always guaranteed that the level thus achieved will be sufficient to prevent the risk of re-traumatizing both members of the analytic couple stuck in an impasse or in an intractable enactment.

For this reason, I would tend to prefer a supervision group that works intensely and long-term, which, if well-matched, will allow a much wider and varied vision of what is happening during the analysis and containment of dissociated emotions – which is theoretically better than a dual relationship.

We know that as far as borderline personality disorder is concerned, the severe emotional dis-regulation is one of the key issues to work on, but it seems clinically evident how internal working models and their corresponding identifications are multiple and continuously interacting with each other.

The multiplicity of attachment styles and of Selves that are activated depending on the ongoing relationship probably represents an essential factor that increases the complexity of these deceptively linear theories. Luckily enough, the attachment styles, as well as the transference types, are not infinite but classifiable into few clusters, based on the fundamental relationships and the basic emotions involved.

At the level of analytic technique, according to the emotion regulation theory, the patient should ideally be stimulated and aided in bringing his/her emotions into focus, particularly those that concern the body and that are less easily verbalized.

In lieu of the classic invitation to surrender to free associations – "What are you thinking about?

Would you freely describe to me what is coming to your mind?" – we should ask the following questions: "How do you feel? What are you feeling? Would you try and describe what you are experiencing deep inside, in your guts?".

In this way the attention of the analytic couple at work would be, not so much on the verbal and thus known and describable, but on the non-verbal, corporeal, vague, on the verge of awareness without assuming the meaning of the terms chosen in the description, but rather asking to better describe them, to provide examples and to narrate in detail: beyond the when, how, and with whom, also in which part of the body and with which sensations,

Profound visceral emotional experiences can then emerge; but in this case, too Pat Ogden's window of tolerance concept is essential in order to avoid that any overly intense, unmanageable emotions invade the analytic setting. I would say that the defining and limiting nature of linguistic thought here plays a rather reassuring and necessary role.

Naming the "demon" that internally controls the patient, giving it a noun and a predicate, being able to find the word that defines an internal state would enable transformation and then, in time, acceptance.

For instance, one of my women patients, who was in consultation, was extremely surprised and relieved from her chronic sense of oppression when, while describing her childhood and adolescence under the control of a narcissistic and denigrating father, I employed the term "sadistic" in response to her description. For years she had tried, in previous psychotherapy sessions, to define her father's behavior towards her, and the word I used now made everything a lot clearer in her mind.

Now she could understand the disquieting and detestable smile the father had when he used to make her feel ashamed in front of her peers.

Conclusions

Biology, with its stupefying expansion, stands more and more as a borderline science that fulfills the possibility of an encounter between culture and nature, between environment and genetics, between, man and the biosphere, between the individual and the group. The borders between the different sciences, as it is between human and animal, become mobile and porous with the increasing of our knowledge.

Affective neurosciences aim to re-integrate man in his original evolutionary-biological milieu even from a psychic and emotional point of view. The encounter – or collision – with psychoanalysis – a science, too, bordering between biology, psychology, philosophy and art, is inevitable.

It comes along with our common clinical experience as psychoanalysts that a structural, deep modification of the personality and its related symptoms are achievable only within intense and prolonged affective dynamics between the analyst and the patient- which correspond to what has been defined as the transference/counter-transference dynamic, and to what nowadays, in the language of interpersonal neurobiology, is known as affect co-regulation.

Furthermore, thanks to the clinical and research experience in the field of mental suffering within the analytic setting, we know and should always remember how each theoretical or research contribution could be used as a defense, moreover, how each theory or clinical or scientific evidence could function as a sophisticated defense system against the unknown that we face in our encounter with the other. This defensive reaction on the part of the analyst is decreased in the same measure as his/her ability to withstand the emotional and corporeal sharing of the other's suffering, without becoming overwhelmed to the point of having to rigidly adhere to a portion of knowledge that becomes idealized and no longer questionable.

Each analysis knows such impasses, which help the analyst to cultivate doubt, the paradoxical sort of Light House common to all sciences.

References

Bion W.R (1970) Attention and interpretation: A scientific approach to insight. In W. R. Bion (Ed.), *Psycho-analysis and groups* (pp. 1–130). London: Tavistock.

Bowlby J. (1977) The making and breaking of affectional bonds: I. Aetiology and psychopathology in the light of attachment theory. *British Journal of Psychiatry* 130: 201–210.

Bromberg P. (1998) *Standing in the spaces: Essays on clinical process, trauma, and dissociation.* Hillsdale: The Analytic Press.

Coan, J. A. (2008) Toward a neuroscience of attachment. In J. Cassidy & P. R. Shaver (Eds.), *Handbook of attachment: Theory, research, and clinical applications* (pp. 241–265). New York: The Guilford Press.

Damasio A. R. (2010) *Self comes to mind: Constructing the conscious brain.* New York: Pantheon Books.

Danton D. (2005) *Les emotiones primordiales et l'éveil de la conscience.* Paris: Flammarion.

Darwin C. (1872) *The expression of the emotions in man and animals.* New York: D. Appleton and Company.

Ekman P. (1992) An argument for basic emotions. *Cognition and Emotion* 6: 169–200.

Fonagy P., Gergely G., Jurist EL, Target M. (2002) *Affect regulation, mentalization and the development of the self.* New York: Other Press.

Fosha D. (2000) *The transforming power of affect: A model of accelerated change.* New York: Basic Books.

Fosha D. (2002) The activation of affective change processes in AEDP (accelerated experiential psychotherapy). In J. J. Magnavita (Ed.), *Comprehensive handbook of psychotherapy: Vol.1 psychodynamic and object relations psychotherapies* (pp. 309–344). New York: Wiley Ed.

Freud S. (1905) Three essays on the theory of sexuality (1905). *The Standard Edition of the Complete Psychological Works of Sigmund Freud, Volume VII (1901–1905): A Case of Hysteria, Three Essays on Sexuality and Other Works*, pp. 123–246.

Freud S. (1933) New introductory lectures on psycho-analysis. *The Standard Edition of the Complete Psychological Works of Sigmund Freud, Volume XXII (1932–1936).* New Introductory Lectures on Psycho-Analysis and Other Works, pp. 1–182.

Gerber A. J., Peterson B. S. (2006) Measuring transference phenomena with FMRI. *Journal of the American Psychoanalytic Association* 54: 1319–1325.

Hill D. (2015) *Affect regulation theory. A clinical model.* New York, London: WW Norton & Company.

Hofer M.A. (2006) Psychobiological roots of early attachment. *Current Directions in Psychological Science* 15(2):84–88. doi:10.1111%2Fj.0963-7214.2006.00412.x.

Laland K. N., Odling-Smee J., Myles S. (2010) How culture shaped the human genome: Bringing genetics and the human sciences together. *Nature Reviews Genetics* 11: 137–148; doi:10.1038/nrg2734.

Lane R. D., Ryan L., Nadel L., Greenberg L. (2015) Memory reconsolidation, emotional arousal, and the process of change in psychotherapy: New insights from brain science. *Behavioral and Brain Sciences* 38: 1–64; doi:10.1017/$0140525X 14000041.

Lanius R. A., Bluhm R. L., Frewen P. A. (2011) How understanding the neurobiology of complex post-traumatic stress disorder can inform clinical practice: A social cognitive and affective neuroscience approach. *Acta Psychiatrica Scandinavica* 124(5): 331–348; doi: 10.1111/j.1600-0447.2011.01755.x. 118–124.

Le Doux J. E., Brown R. (2017) A high order theory of emotional consciousness. *PNAS*; www.pnas.org/cgi/doi/10.1073/pnas.1619316114.

Luyten P. (2015) Unholy questions about five central tenets of psychoanalysis that need to be empirically verified. *Psychoanalytic Inquiry* 35(supl): 5–23.

Lyon-Ruth K. (2003) Dissociation and the parent infant dialogue: A longitudinal perspective from attachment research. *Journal of the American Psychoanalytic Association* 57: 883–911.

MacLean P. D. (1973) *A triune concept of the brain and behavior.* Toronto: University of Toronto Press.

Main M. (1990) Cross-cultural studies of attachment organization: Recent studies, changing methodologies, and the concept of conditional strategies. *Human Development* 33(1): 48–61.

Northoff G., Panksepp J. (2008) The trans-species concept of self and the subcortical-cortical midline system. *Trends in Cognitive Sciences* 12(7): 259–264; doi: 10.1016/j.tics.2008.04.007.

Nussbaum M. (2001) *Upheavals of thought. The intelligence of emotions.* Cambridge: Cambridge University Press.

Ogden P., Minton K., Pain C., Eds. (2006) *Trauma and the body. A sensorimotor approach to psychotherapy.* New York London: W.W. Norton Company.

Panksepp J. (2014) Crossing the brain-mind Rubicon: How might we scientifically understand basic human emotions and core affective feelings of other animals? *Neuropsychoanalsis* 16(1): 39–44; doi:10.1080/15294145.2014,900259.

Panksepp J. (2015) Toward the constitution of emotional feelings. *Emotion Review* 7(2): 110–115. ISSN 1754-0739; doi: 10.1177/1754073914554788 et.sagepub.com.

Panksepp J., Biven L. (2012) *The archaeology of mind.* New York: W. W. Norton & Company; doi:10.1016/j.tics.2011.11.005.

Piaget, J. (1962) The stages of the intellectual development of the child. *Bulletin of the Menninger Clinic* 26(3): 120–128.

Polan H., Hofer M. A. (2008) Psychobiological origins of infant attachment and its role in development. In J. Cassidy, P. R. Shaver (Eds.), *Handbook of attachment: Theory, research, and clinical applications* (2nd ed., pp. 158–172). New York: Guilford Press.

Rizzolatti G., Semi A. A., Fabbri-Destro, M. (2014) Linking psychoanalysis with neuroscience: The concept of ego. *Neuropsychologia* 55: 143–148.

Rovelli C. (2014) *The first scientist: Anaximander and his legacy.* Chicago: Westholme Publishing, 2016.

Sable P. (2016) The pet connection: An attachment perspective. *Attachment: New Directions in Psychotherapy and Relational Psychoanalysis* 10(3): 199–210.

Shore A. (2015) *Affect regulation and the origin of the self: The neurobiology of emotional development.* New York: Routledge.

Solms M., Turnbull O. H. (2011) What is neuropsychoanalysis? *Neuropsychoanalysis* 13(2): 1–11.

Stern, D.N. (1985) *The interpersonal world of the infant* (pp. 1–294). New York: Basic Books.

Tomkins S. (1963) *Affect, imagery, and consciousness: Vol. 1. The negative affects.* New York: Springer.

Tracy J. L., Randle D. (2011) Four models of basic emotions: A review of Ekman and Cordaro, Izard, Levenson, and Panksepp and Watt. *Emotion Review* 3(4): 397–405; ISSN 1754-0739; doi: 10.1177/1754073911410747 er.sagepub.com.

Weigel S. (2016) Introduction. In S. Weigel, G. Scharbert (Eds.), *A neuro-psychoanalytical dialogue for Bridging Freud and the neurosciences* (pp. 1–10). Switzerland: Springer International Publishing.

Yovell Y. (2016) Drive and love: Revisiting Freud's drive theory. In S. Weigel, G. Scharbert (Eds.) (a cura di) *A neuro-psychoanalytical dialogue for Bridging Freud and the neurosciences.* Switzerland: Springer International Publishing.

Part Two
Clinical aspects

7 The usefulness of the endo-psycho-phenotypic approach in diagnosis and treatment from a neuropsychoanalytic perspective

Cristiana Pirrongelli

Introduction

This article introduces the notion of psychophenotype as a useful semeiotic element in various psychopathological cases (Cannon & Keller, 2006; Gottesman & Gould, 2003; Gould & Gottesman, 2006; Miller & Rockstroh, 2013). Then the article discusses the concept of emotional endo-psycho-phenotypes according to Jaak Panksepp's theory, to develop a new taxonomic principle and examine its clinical usefulness.

Endophenotypes

The endophenotype is by definition "a measurable component, invisible to the naked eyes, located between the genotype and the phenotype of a disease. It is a mere hint of the genetic bases of the disease".

Sometimes the endophenotype is only a vulnerability trait, i.e. a biological or behavioural indicator that suggests the likeliness that a disease may develop or give precocious hints of itself. A good example is that of cardiovascular diseases in individuals who are apparently healthy but have a series of predisposing conditions, some of which are genetic while some others depend on life habits (smoke, sedentariness or excessive food intake, that lead to hypertension, hyperlipidemia, atheromatous plaques, etc.) causing underlying alterations that *per se* do not make a healthy individual, but an individual more likely than others to develop a cardiovascular disease. Hence not a monogenic disease tied to a "simple trait". In this latter case, in fact, either a subject has the disease or he hasn't it, there is no halfway. Conventional genetics essentially studies the so-called "simple Mendelian traits", i.e. those where a given phenotype trait is the direct outcome of the activity of a given gene, e.g. blue eyes genotype = blue eyes phenotype, or mutation of the CFTR gene = cystic fibrosis by Mendel's law, where the outcome depends exclusively on genetic action and is indifferent to any other influence. In the case of simple diseases, the phenotype is qualitative, according to the principle of all or nothing.

DOI: 10.4324/9781003198741-9

Endo-psycho-phenotype

The endo-psycho-phenotype trait is sometimes (but not always) an elementary, identifiable trait, similar to a conventional biomarker when it is strictly related to the physiological setting. A typical example in classic psychiatry are working memory deficits in schizophrenic subjects and in some of their family members (Apud & Weinberger, 2007; Bertolino, et al., 2017); oculomotor anomalies (Caldani et al., 2017), or altered evoked potential P50, (Potter, 2006). An endophenotype was identified in bipolar subjects and their family members in the deficit concerning the recognition of facial emotions (Brotman, 2008; Chen et al., 2006) thanks to fMRI, associated with a dysfunction in the prefrontal cortex and other brain areas (there is a polymorphism in the CACNAC gene tied to the functioning of calcium channels, Bhat, 2012; for more recent discoveries see, Kazour et al., 2020, Kim et al., 2020, Li et al., 2020, Lozupone et al., 2019, Winship et al., 2019). These small, distinct, detectable, discreet manifestations, with a more easily identifiable genetic origin, are easy to detect and helpful for clinical activities in a conventional psychiatric setting.

Complex traits in genetics

In behavioural genetics, which also covers psychopathological manifestations, clinical pictures are the outcome of "complex traits", i.e. characters deriving from the interaction of (most often multiple) genetic factors and environmental factors (Bodmer, 2008; Hartl & Jones, 2005; Lvovs, et al., 2012). These do not follow Mendel's law. The phenotype (i.e., the evident clinical manifestation, or picture) is quantitative as well as qualitative and becomes manifest in different ways: diagnosed cases, mere personality traits, "spectrum" traits, behavioural/response tendencies, but not necessarily a determined, defined and immutable syndrome or disease bound to progress towards a written fate. Certain genetic variants may even result protective and capable of reducing pathological risk (Fasano, et al., 2007)

In the case of "complex traits", there is no true genetic mutation nor loss of gene function: certain genes arrange themselves in a way that may turn out to be more or less efficient, without causing a total functional loss. Therefore, the cases will present themselves within a range from less serious to more serious, from present to absent, depending not only on genetic sequence fluidity but also on environmental factors.

To confirm such complexity, the studies on autistic endo-psycho-phenotypes (Losh, et al., 2017; Ruparelia, et al., 2017; Stickley, et al., 2017; Sucksmith, et al., 2011) have shed light on a necessary resizing of the diagnoses, showing that genetic alterations are distributed in a uniform pattern across the entire population but often without a high correlation between genetic traits and symptoms. By interacting with the environment, the same genomes (the entire DNA contained in one cell of a living organism) lead to the creation of different neurological structures, and an apparently identical behaviour may derive from different genes and neurological structures. The famous triad that is found in autism — serious alteration of social reciprocity, serious dysfunctions in verbal and nonverbal communication, a limited behavioural repertoire with motory stereotypes and persistent, excessive interest in parts of objects — (Happé et al., 2006) is distributed across the population in an almost entirely independent way. While a large percentage of subjects in the general population (about 3%) meets the diagnostic criteria for the autism spectrum (Kim et al., 2011; Wheelwright et al., 2010), only 0.8–1% has clinically significant difficulties. The consequence, for instance, is that the same drug given to two patients with a similar picture may have positive effects on one and negative effects on the other. Likewise, depression, which is observed in the autistic patient is often a bipolar disorder (Joshi et al., 2013; Munesue et al., 2010; Skokauskas & Frodl, 2015), and may not manifest itself clinically as such. Nevertheless, treating an ASD (Autism Spectrum Disorder) patient suffering from depression with an antidepressant is often a hazard. However, this is not true for all ASD patients. It is true on average. In the practice there is a huge dispersion of data, the brain of a subclinical subject may be more autistic than that of an autistic, and vice-versa. The same happens in all those cases of mental distress that can no longer be defined under a category-based descriptive approach, nor a syndrome-based approach, nor with a purely psychodynamic diagnosis.

Psychopathology according to Panksepp

According to Jaak Panksepp, the various psychopathological pictures always imply the seven basic subcortical emotional systems that were selected for survival as in all mammals. These systems have a behavioural correlate and a neurovegetative correlate in addition to the emotional one. Panksepp regards them as endophenotypes tied to complex traits, and therefore capable of predisposing an individual to the development of a complex clinical picture (or a genetic "trait"). These endophenotypes, which Panksepp calls endo-psycho-phenotypes, are dominant forms of neuroaffective organization that depend on both hereditary and learned factors.

On genetics and hereditariness, Panksepp affirmed: "No specific thought or behaviour is transmitted directly, but certainly the disposition to hear, think and act in various ways and situations is". "Certain psychologic tendencies may be represented within the intrinsic brain of the corporeal constructions that the organisms inherit". So, with regard to the genetic transmission of "complex traits", there is no direct transmission of behaviours and no predetermined fate; there are tendencies that "foster certain possibilities and reduce others" (Panksepp, 1998). Panksepp assumes that the ancient affective brain developed in order to anticipate the hardships of life through unconditional affective/instinctive reactions that contribute to guiding the behaviours learned and to act and think accordingly. Affective

Neuroscience has correlated the research data on subjective mental states (easier to obtain from human beings) with the brain functions (more easily studied in animals) and the instinctive behaviour of the other animals, in a triangulation that "renders the idea of the ancient fundamental plan for man's mental life and the deep neuronal sources of our primigenial feelings". In order to understand the fundamental nature of human feelings, we need to know the primary emotions of the BrainMind. These exist in human beings regardless of the huge complexity of the superior mental processes that climb various gradually ascending levels: the secondary processes tied to memory and learning, and the tertiary cortical processes peculiar to the human species.

Motivational/emotional systems as a basis for endo-psycho-phenotypes

This section describes very briefly (for more details see the synoptic tables at the beginning of this volume) the seven basic emotional command systems identified by Panksepp so far and the related emotions, also shown dimensionally from physiological to pathological. It is worth noting that the basic emotional system, in order to be regarded as such, must:

a   Be identifiable, recognizable and distinguishable from the other system;
b   Correspond to a genetic background;
c   Have a network of subcortical neural structures that give rise to typically motory and neurovegetative body expressions;
d   Allow its behavioural characteristics to be interpreted from an adaptation perspective;
e   Be present also in other species, at least in all mammal species.

SEEKING: Being eager to explore the world, striving to find solutions to problems and mysteries, anticipating new experiences positively and feeling able to achieve almost anything. (The Explorer)

CARE: Feeding, being attracted by little children and pets, feeling tenderness towards the animals and the needy, feeling empathy, being willing to taking care of the ill, feeling affection and sympathy in taking care of the others, wanting to feel oneself as necessary to the others. (The Nest Builder)

GRIEF: Feeling lonely, crying often, thinking about one's family members and past relationships and feeling anxiety when the loved ones are not close. (The Sad Poet)

FEAR: Being anxious, feeling tense, worrying, having difficulty in making decisions, pondering about past decisions and statements, being unable to sleep, and not being brave in general. (The Sentry)

RAGE: Being a hothead, being prone to irritation and frustration, express rage verbally or physically and remaining angry for long. (The Commander in Chief)

Table 7.1

Basic emotional system	Rising emotions	Linked emotional disorders
	Curiosity	Obsessive compulsive
SEEKING	Annoyance/Discomfort	Cluster B disorder
(+ and −)		Paranoid schizophrenia
	Craving/desire ⟶	Addictive personality
	Nurturance/Care	Dependency disorders
CARE (+)	Love/Kindness	Autistic aloofness
	Attraction/Infatuation	Attachment disorders
	Separation distress/Anxiety	Separation anxiety disorder
	Sadness/Grief	Panic attacks
PANIC (−)	Guilt/shame	Pathological grief
	Timidityness/Shyness	Depression
	Embarrassment	Agoraphobia
		Social phobias, autism
	Anger/Rage	Aggressiveness
	Irritability/Irascibility	Psychopathic tendencies
RAGE (− and +)	Competitiveness/Touchiness	Personality disorders
	Contempt/Disdain/Hostility	Intermittent Explosive Disorder
	Hatred/Malevolence	
	Simple anxiety/Apprehension	General anxiety disorders
FEAR (−)	Worry/Preoccupation	Phobias
	Psychic trauma/Shock/Scare ⟶	PTSD variants
	Erotic feelings/Desire	Fetishistic disorder
LUST (+ and −)	Jealousy/Possessiveness	Paraphilia
		Sexual addictions
PLAY (+)	Joy and glee/Euphoria/ecstatic reaction	Mania
	Happy playfulness ⟶	ADHD
SPIRITUALITY?	Yet to be fully explained	Yet to be fully explained

LUST: Feeling sexual desire, desire to copulate, being available to all courting rituals, with or without love feelings. (The Sensualist)

PLAY: Being playful versus being serious; doing games that imply physical contact, humour and laughter and being happy and joyful in general. (The Jester)

Temperaments, character, personality

Already Hippocrates believed that the different temperaments (choleric, sanguine, melancholic or phlegmatic) were related to body fluids or 'humours' (blood, yellow bile, black bile, and lung phlegm). Later on, Galen refined and completed Hippocrates' theory, which remained popular until the Middle Ages (Stelmack & Stalikas, 1991). The term has persisted in modern psychopathology to define a body-related innate component of the personality, as first affirmed by Kretschmer (1923) and then resumed by Kernberg (1984),

McWilliams (1994). In the psychoanalytic theory of Otto Kernberg (1994), a normal personality is thought to be formed by two essential components: temperament and character. While the character is how the individual has forged his temperament according to life events, temperament is intended as the whole of the innate, genetically determined tendencies by which the individual reacts to environmental stimuli in one way rather than another. According to Kernberg (1994), these innate tendencies (that are thought to correspond to the seven endo-psycho-phenotypic basic emotional systems) manifest themselves according to the intensity, frequency and threshold of each individual's typical affective response to the activation of each type of emotion, from positive ones to painful or aggressive ones, highlighting their innate and biological aspect, including in their balancement.

Even in psychodynamic diagnostics, there is an aspect called temperament that is thought to be rooted in the patient's genetics and biology. The word comes from Latin *temperare*, i.e. mixing the innate aspects of the individual. The theory of primary or basic emotional systems is presently the best studied and developed scientific basis available for the studies on temperament. (Davis & Panksepp, 2011; Karterud, et al., 2016; Montag & Panksepp, 2016, 2017; Montag & Reuter 2014).

The emotions in "the human"

Panksepp's research is aimed at understanding how primary emotional systems actually create feelings in the mammals' brain, and particularly in the human brain. Their cognitive processing in secondary processes (supralimbic system, memory and learning) and in tertiary processes (cortex) can give rise to multiple manifestations, including complex emotions such as courage, envy, guilt, jealousy, pride, shame, contempt. Individual defences, from the most primitive to the most sophisticated, contribute to outline the picture in a totally idiopathic way, which is unique for each individual. This would lead to discarding DSM (Diagnostic and Statistical Manual of Mental Disorders) criteria that are category-based, medicalizing and not dimensional enough: two patients with identical symptoms but different histopathologies treated according to the guidelines and with the same tools but with different outcomes. For example, the trigger of a depression syndrome should certainly be sought in the imbalance of various emotional systems, mostly the PANIC/GRIEF and also the SEEKING systems. A full endo-psycho-phenotypical observation (including on genetic and personal background) carried out for that specific depressive event, at that particular moment and on that particular individual, will allow us to understand what, how and how much, in that individual's genetic/personal *continuum*, has contributed to generating his/her clinical picture. Of course, there is still much research to do on the mechanisms of attachment and separation disorders (a peculiar form of anxiety different from conventional anxiety that gives rise to panic manifestations and does not respond to common anxiolytics but rather to antidepressants).

What is new according to Panksepp

The two emotional systems of anxiety that, according to Panksepp, might be activated in our patients can derive from two different systems, only partially overlapping, for quite different reasons and with emotional, behavioural and neurovegetative manifestations for which we should be able to differentiate the diagnosis — further evidence of the importance of semeiotics (Klein & Fink, 1962; Panksepp, 1998). Anxiety can be triggered by the fear that something negative may happen suddenly, causing fear, injuries or death to us, a sort of catastrophe. Or it can be triggered by the panic of isolation due to desertion or to the sudden loss of a safe reference point.

1 – The two systems are anatomically separate

2 – Different chemical substances have an effect on the two forms of anxiety (benzodiazepines in the former, opioids and antidepressants in the latter)

3 – In fear anxiety, all the alert signals tied to the activation of the sympathetic system are turned on (see the paragraph on Porges below)

4 – In isolation panic, vagal signals like weakness, lump in the throat, breathing difficulty, etc. are activated (Porges, below)

Panksepp notes that children learn more effectively when they are happy and engaged in playing and in interesting activities, and this is believed to depend on the mutual influence of the SEEKING and the PLAY systems. This led Panksepp to develop an unconventional theory and treatment guidelines for attention deficit hyperactivity disorder (ADHD). Panksepp firmly believes in the usefulness of introducing playful and positive emotions in the therapeutic relationship.

Such dimensional approach enables the fine-tuning of more targeted therapies, more consistent with the manifestations, in any form including drugs, psychotherapy or others, because each primary emotional system shows itself rather clearly in its functioning deficits or in the hyperactivation of the neurotransmitters concerned. Sometimes drugs homologous to natural neurotransmitters may be used (see the enormous work done on opiates or on oxytocin). New molecules are being synthesized, or already being tested, targeted to the single emotional system involved in the onset of a clinical case. The same is happening in psychotherapy, although Panksepp believes that psychoanalysis is the reference therapy, due to its detailed knowledge of the emotional contents of the relationships and their consequences. It is no coincidence that "The Archaeology of Mind" was written together with Lucy Biven, and with a foreword by Daniel Siegel.

The conscious/unconscious overturning

According to Panksepp, secondary processes corresponding to automatic learning and memory processes, must be considered unconscious. Basic emotional states instead, when intense enough, are accomplished in an affective, non-reflective, knowing way, and this also happens in human beings. Even anencephalic babies are capable of showing all range of basic emotions.

> We can now be certain that the other mammals draw experience from their emotional stimulations — although, like human babies, most of them may not have reflexive awareness of such experiences. They are raw affective experiences — special phenomenal states of mind, a unique category of *qualia* that arises from the very foundation of the conscious mind.

Primary affections, initially processed at the subcortical level, are gradually re-defined and re-processed by the superior and most 'recent' brain regions, forming complex ideas mixed with more sophisticated emotions that we might call feelings. However, there is no magic giving more awareness to these complex emotions, compared to primary emotions. To support his position, Panksepp points at the fact that, in both man and the animals, deep electric stimulation provokes much stronger feelings in the lower regions of the brain, especially in the periaqueductal gray (PAG) that is located at the centre of the midbrain.

Is a new taxonomy useful?

Panksepp then proposes renovating the BrainMind science, based on the "endophenotypic thought", i.e. the study of the objective and genetic traits of the disease. Emotional endo-psycho-phenotypes, which represent the basis of affective neurosciences, show the way for treating symptoms of true emotional imbalances, rather than vague nosological abstractions such as autism, depression and schizophrenia. In Panksepp's view, modern nosology is still largely "pre-neuroscientific" and the source of incorrect and reductive therapeutic approaches. Panksepp believes that the possibility to build a diagnostic taxonomy based on emotional endophenotypes is, for the time being, the best one for the future of the studies on the BrainMind from a diagnosis and treatment perspective.

At the subcortical level, body/visceral feelings and basic emotions already constitute a 'core self', a primeval representation of the self and especially of the body — the visceral body. A self that, giving consistency to the organism, lays the foundation on which the entire affective experience will be built — quite overlapping with the body at the beginning. It is something shared and universal that through the interaction with superior cognitive processes stimulates the creation of several "idiographic selfs", each unique and refined by experience, that increase their self-awareness ("extended self"). It is worth reminding that there are two body maps rooted in the midbrain: one relates to visceral functioning and the internal milieu, while the other maps the musculoskeletal system (the proprioceptive system that provides information on muscular tone, posture and movement). This latter map blueprints the body structure and is located in the periaqueductal gray (where the seven basic emotions are) and in the superior colliculus of the midbrain. Such proximity of these two maps, or *homunculi*, explains why the emotions have immediate access to the generation of actions (intents-in-action). According to Solms and Turnbull, in "The Brain and the Inner World" (one of the milestones of Neuropsychoanalysis (2002)), "the homunculus in the dorsal tegmentum provides a combined sensorimotor map of the body, which generates primitive action tendencies". At the same time, we can perceive an emotional experience that translates into emotional drive, and express it in our actions. It is from this morpho-functional proximity of homeostatic regulation, emotion generation and motility control systems, that Panksepp developed the idea of the emotional operating systems of the basic emotions (Panksepp, 1998). These are defined as emotional endo-psycho-phenotypes and are deemed to be the core of the temperament of each individual (Panksepp, 2006), leading to psychopathological cases when severely dysregulated.

Can the endo-psycho-phenotypic approach be useful in diagnoses and in psychoanalytic clinics?

All the work done by Panksepp is not aimed at creating a diagnostic taxonomy, as he believes that there is an enormous genetic variability (complex traits) and an endless quantity of experiential and epigenetic variables (from intrauterine life to the relationships with the environment throughout the course of the existence). For this reason, overcoming all classification attempts, Pankespp believes that each individual should be regarded as a *unicum* and observed with a neuropsychoanalytic eye, always taking into account what the genes can tell us, the early learning or the later interactions, the epigenetics, the background and the physical conditions of the patient. "For example, a good psychotherapist cannot do without knowing the biological mechanism underlying loss and separation, because every therapeutic relationship is first and foremost an affective relation with a cognitive component" (Panksepp & Biven, 2012). However, Panksepp warns that too high levels of suffering and danger might express an imbalance of one of the basic emotional systems that are in themselves less flexible than the superior regions of the brain and might not be reached easily, or at least not as fast as desired.

As a conclusion to this first part, I feel the need to mention a complementary theory to Panksepp's theory or to other studies on the emotional/motivational systems.

Stephen Porges (2011) like Panksepp studied the neurobiology of emotions from an evolutionary and adaptive perspective, i.e. how affections are regulated and, above all, how the autonomic nervous system has a decisive impact on our ability to relate to one another, accompanies and sometimes decides our emotions, our experiences, our self-regulation abilities and even our thoughts.

As all basic emotions have a correlation in the autonomic nervous system (parasympathetic and sympathetic), these studies, along with a more detailed knowledge of the way in which the peripheral nervous system accompanies emotional manifestations, may be extremely useful in clinical practice.

Stephen Porges's polyvagal theory

Stephen Porges resumed the theories and research of MacLean (1998), focusing in particular on the study of the physiology of the autonomic nervous system and developing the "polyvagal theory" (Porges, 2001) that connects the evolution of the autonomic nervous system with affective experience, emotional expression, facial expression, voice communication and social behaviour (Porges, 2011). This theory supports and adds to Panksepp's observations on the neurovegetative aspect of the expression of basic emotions, and may be useful in clinical practice. In an interview in 2011, Porges affirmed that in a phylogenetic framework the responses of the nervous system may be seen as an organization structured into different levels of hierarchy, according to the notion of dissolution that Jackson (Jackson, 1958) had used for nervous system diseases caused by brain damage. According to this principle, the most evolved circuits of the nervous system inhibit the most primitive ones, and the older ones are activated only when the newer circuits fail, following a hierarchical order, responding adaptively to challenges and always with safety as a goal. According to Porges, there are three neural circuits that correspond to three development stages and to three different defence strategies. The oldest circuit is the dorsal vagal one that is activated in situations of danger, causing stillness of the body and dulling of the emotions. In extreme cases, when danger to life is very high, unsurmountable or overwhelming, then freezing, collapse, thanatosis — and dissociative states in man — may occur. The sympathetic nervous system developed phylogenetically at a later stage, and its most important contribution to safety is that of preparing the animal or the human being for the fight-or-flight response. The ventral vagal circuit was developed last and is peculiar to superior mammals and man. It has a calming effect, allows us to stand still and relaxed without fear, disposes to listening and social exchange, to listening and thinking/mentalizing at the same time. This is the optimal condition that should be recreated in a good psychoanalytic setting.

New outlooks for the clinical practice

At the beginning of his clinical practice, Freud used hypnosis and needed a sofa for this (Freud, 1895). After discarding hypnosis, Freud sought a way to help patients recall the forgotten things that were at the origin of their symptoms. The couch allowed the patients to relax and focus on their thoughts, in order to facilitate free association. However, Freud himself said that "each case was to be taken as if it were the first", case by case (Freud, 1909, 1910).

The body talks, tells, sometimes in a subtle manner (a slight trembling, blushing, showing paleness), sometimes conspicuously (a sudden muscular contracture, a jerk, a stiffening). Van Der Kolk (2015) would say "The body sends a signal" speaking of traumatized patients. However, in less serious cases, it would be sufficient to use Panksepp's endo-psycho-phenotypes theory and Porges' poly-vagal theory in order to collect information about the basic emotional states of a given patient, that are activated in that given moment. For an in-depth review of the therapies that focus also on the body (Fosha, 2002, 2009; Ogden, et al., 2006, 2016), which I believe to be of great interest, I would refer to Castellet y Ballarà's contribution in this volume.

An important recommendation, that also applies to borderline patients, is to always monitor vagal activation signs during the therapy (see Porges), because if we succeed in creating an environment in which the patient feels safe, this will enlarge the window of pro-social trust and openness generated by the recovered balance of the myelinated ventral vagal nerve (Porges, 2003, 2004) and the tolerance window in respect of the therapy will be enlarged accordingly (Ogden & Fisher 2015), opening up to insight possibilities and social interactions in general. Special focus on "what to do with the body", and how, should be put when the patients are people who feel "uprooted" from the reality and the pleasure of living, who suffer from continuing unease and that often live, create and make plans only in their thoughts, going around in circles and probably nowhere. In her contribution to this volume, Dr Anatolia Salone describes accurately such "anhedonic" experiences, sometimes related to a hypoactive SEEKING system, sometimes to an activation of the GRIEF, suffering, loss, separation systems in their various components, e.g. *wanting*, *liking* and *learning*. This is essential to understand what to target and with which of our inner tools. We may refer to what psychoanalysts used to working with extreme states of the self, like Alvarez (2018), Beebe and Lachmann (2013, 2017), affirm in these cases. For example, cases of adults or children who never found an object interested or interesting and who therefore stopped seeking (de-activated SEEKING system). They present themselves as depressed, lifeless, dull, and dissociated. These states require a more intense and vital focus on the meaning that the therapist wants to communicate, a more lively relationship and a HEY. "In order for the Alpha function to operate, the object must first be seen as capable of taking action" (Alvarez et al., 2016). Anne Alvarez, a therapist who has used the approach of Pankespp's Affective Neurosciences for years when dealing with children, affirms that "Without dopamine (the neurotransmitter of the SEEKING, CURIOSITY system), only the strongest emotional messages can stimulate behaviour" (Alvarez et al., 2016).

> I have previously suggested that there are certain states of the mind (hence of the brain) that require insisting on a more intense and vital meaning, because this creates what some psychologists of the developmental age call 'intensified affective moment'.
>
> (Beebe & Lachman, 2013)

Three clinical cases viewed from a neuropsychoanalysis perspective

1   A 33-year-old patient, single, virgin, serious and composed, good look-ing but asexual, an intellectual like all her family members, whom she is tied to in an exclusive way. She never laughs, never raises her voice, has no sense of humour or strives not to show it, in order to frustrate the therapist and prevent any attempt of showing a relationship between herself and the therapist. She lives with her parents. After two years in therapy, she arrived at the session with a "mischievous" attitude and re-ported the following dream, pronouncing the first sentence with a firm voice and a sharp tone: *"I went to the bar for a coffee! The bar owner beat about the bush, she told me I had to prepare it myself, no, that I had to prepare coffee for all my family and bring it to them"*. Those who have some working experience with basic emotional systems will notice two new things in this sequence:

    a   The patient's "mischievous" attitude, perfectly aware that she is surprising me (her therapist) and has fun in PLAYING with me, with both her facial and voice expressions.

    b   The DESIRE TO GO OUT and HAVE A COFFEE, something that in the social dimension of the patient's life corresponds to an activa-tion of the exploration system and, in this case, also of the 'wanting' and the 'seeking independency' aspects of the SEEKING system (Pirrongelli, 2015).

2   A 35-year-old patient, very depressed, suffering from panic attacks, without any sexual experience and obsessed with this, reported the fol-lowing dream: *"The mouse of my computer was running in the street, with the cord resembling a tail. I was running after it. All of a sudden, a big she-rat appeared before me, standing on her hind legs, menacing. I fainted"*. In this case, the patient makes an association: in the Rome area dialect, the female rat is called by a name that is also the name of the female sexual organ. My comment was that the desire and the search for a woman are intact in the patient (SEEKING and LUST), and that the little mouse is brave, but still feeling small and frightened in front of what the patient sees as female aggressiveness, which takes the shape of a large, sexuated and threatening rat. In this exemplary case, the patient even faints in his dream. According to the poly-vagal theory (Porges, 2001) this appears to be a case of "extreme fear" and "feigned death" caused by the activa-tion of the dorsal part of the vagal nerve, the one that is phylogenetically the oldest. Thanatosis, here, protects the subject from the extreme fear of being killed.

3   Another 30-year-old patient, only daughter, with no friends, nerdy, four-eyed, but longing for a life with friends. She is a teacher and does well enough during the school year, but then as soon as summer holidays

arrive she gradually slides into an "experience of cold, silence, dulling and, in the end, recurring panic". The patient told me that, although she was born after a term pregnancy, she spent about one week in the family, breastfed, and then she was hospitalized again and put in an incubator for a few weeks. It is worth noting that this was a case that reached such a high level of suffering in the summer that I was tempted to prescribe drugs. As to the emotional systems into play, in the summer months, this patient had her SEEKING system (curiosity, seeking, will of action), social engagement system, and PLAYING system turned off and her PANIC system, linked to loss and bereavement, gradually activated. The patient felt and saw the lowering of her vital parameters (see Porges and the dorsal vagal nerve), desolation, sense of loneliness, all the way down to PANIC. We worked on the assumption that the early separation and isolation experienced at seven days from birth might have made her PANIC system more susceptible and activated a tendency towards panic caused by isolation and towards depression in situations of loneliness. This experience was so overwhelming that prevented the other vital systems (care, seeking, playing) from remaining active, just as it happens to a baby that is isolated again into an incubator.

The neuropsychoanalytic approach, in addition to the psychodynamic approach, allows the therapist to perceive the strength of the neurobiological and genetic substrate of each patient, understand to what extent it can be changed (if at all) with the therapy, and also develop new theories and techniques. We are certainly in a better position to understand disadaptative programmes, false convincements, defences built and expressed at superior cognitive levels, even if they interact with one another and are not easy to detect and differentiate. But we also have the basic emotional levels, easier to recognize because of following reasons: 1) they are behavioural, emotional and autonomic reactions clearly identifiable for having been accurately described by those who studied them (J. Panksepp in the first place), 2) they manifest themselves in a strong, continuing and repetitive form in both verbal and body expressions, and 3) they appear very clear in dreams.

The technical difficulty lies in learning to work with and "sensitize" these basic affections that show some genetic (and hence biologic, emotional and behavioural) rigidity. We are aided in this by the fact that emotional memories remain malleable forever (Alberini, 2010; Alberini & Kandel, 2014; Lewis, 2017; Nader & Einarsson, 2010) and can be modified by future events. While memories do not pertain to the genetic dimension, the subjectivity, in part, and the rigidity of the emotional endo-psycho-phenotypes, that belong to genetically complex traits, leaves the field open to a series of actions capable of changing the level of genic expression, epigenetics and memory reconsolidation — and therefore their subjective aspect.

As PLAY can have extraordinary effects on the cortex (Burgdorf, et al., 2010), Panksepp suggested that the findings on memory reconsolidation should accompany new methods of conceiving the psychotherapy session. "Much preclinic work [...] has now shown that the memories retrieved tend to return changed to the memory banks" and proposed that free access should be given to "shared laughter" and other positive emotions during the session (Fosha, 2013; Panksepp, 1985, 2012), with those patients that need them.

Children, for whom verbal interaction is not sufficient, are traditionally allowed to move and play during the session. Perhaps focusing on how the body should have a role in the psychoanalytic theory and practice might be an interesting perspective in the treatment of patients with major deficits in the regulation of the expression of positive basic emotions.

Conclusions

Emotional endo-psycho-phenotypes have confirmed their promising usefulness for the treatment of psychopathologies. Further research in the field of endo-psycho-phenotypes might lead to an increasingly better understanding of their operation in psychopathological settings and constitute a very important knowledge base for the development of competencies capable of enlightening and facilitating the therapist's work.

References

Alberini, C. M. (2010). Long-term memories: The good, the bad, and the ugly. *Cerebrum* 2010: 21.

Alberini, C. M, & Kandel, E. R. (2014). The regulation of transcription in memory consolidation. *Cold Spring Harbor Perspectives in Biology* 7(1): a021741, 1–18.

Alvarez, A. (2018). Paranoid/schizoid position or paranoid and schizoid position. In P. Garvey and K. Long (Eds.), *The Kleinian tradition: Lines of development: Evolution of theory and practice over the decades. Ch. 21* (pp. 301–316). London: Routledge.

Alvarez, V. A., Dobbs, L. K., Kaplan, A. R., Lemos, J. C., Matsui, A., & Rubinstein, M. (2016). *Dopamine* regulation of lateral inhibition between striatal neurons gates the stimulant actions of cocaine. *Neuron* 90: 1100–1113.

Apud, J. A., & Weinberger, D. R. (2007). Treatment of cognitive deficits associated with schizophrenia: Potential role of catechol-O-methyl transferase inhibitors. *CNS Drugs* 21: 535–557.

Beebe, B., & Lachmann, F. (2013). *The origins of attachment: Infant research and adult treatment.* New York and London: Routledge Taylor & Francis.

Beebe, B., & Lachmann, F. (2017). Maternal self-critical and dependent personality styles and mother-infant communication. *American Psychoanalytic Association* 65(3): 491–508.

Bertolino, A., Lo Bianco, L., Attrotto, M. T., Torretta, S., Masellis, R., Rampino, A., et al. (2017). Genetic variation is associated with RTN4R expression and working memory processing in healthy humans. *Research Bulletin* 134: 162–167.

Bhat, S., Dao, D. T., Terrillion, C. E., Arad, M., Smith, R. J., & Soldatov, N. M. (2012). *CACNA1C* (Ca$_v$1.2) in the pathophysiology of psychiatric disease. *Progress in Neurobiology* 99(1): 1–14.

Bodmer, W. F. (2008). The human genome sequence and the analysis of multifactorial traits. In *CIBA foundation symposium. Molecular approaches to human polygenic disease* (pp. 215–228), Amsterdam, NY: Associated Scientific Publishers.

Brotman, M. A., Guyer, A. E, Lawson, E. S., & Horsey, S. E. (2008). Facial emotion labeling deficits in children and adolescents at risk for bipolar disorder. *The American Journal of Psychiatry* 165(3): 385–389.

Burgdorf, J., Panksepp, J., & Moskal, J. R. (2010). Frequency-modulated 50 kHz ultrasonic vocalizations: A tool for uncovering the molecular substrates of positive affect. *Neuroscience & Biobehavioral Reviews* 35(9): 1831–1836.

Caldani, S., Amado, I., Bendjemaa, N., Vialatte, F., Mam-Lam-Fook, C., Gaillard, R., et al. (2017). Oculomotricity and neurological soft signs: can we refine the endophenotype? A study in subjects belonging to the spectrum of schizophrenia. *Psychiatry Research* 256: 490–497.

Cannon, T. D., & Keller, M. C. (2006). Endophenotypes in the genetic analyses of mental disorders. *Annual Review of Clinical Psychology* 2: 267–290.

Chen, C., Lennox, B., Jacob, R., Calder, A., Lupson, V., Bisbrown-Chippendale, R., et al. (2006). Explicit and implicit facial affect recognition in manic and depressed states of bipolar disorder: A functional magnetic resonance imaging study. *Biological Psychiatry* 59(1): 31–39.

Davis, K. L., & Panksepp, J. (2011). The brain's emotional foundations of human personality and the affective neuroscience personality scales. *Neuroscience & Biobehavioral Reviews* 35(9): 1946–1958.

Fasano, T., Cefalù, A. B., Di Leo, E., Noto, D., Pollaccia, D., Bocchi, L., et al. (2007). Atherosclerosis and lipoproteins. A novel loss of function mutation of PCSK9 gene in White subjects with low-plasma low-density lipoprotein cholesterol. *Arteriosclerosis, Thrombosis, and Vascular Biology* 27: 677–681. Originally published February 14.

Fosha, D. (2002). The activation of affective change processes in accelerated experiential-dynamic psychotherapy (AEDP). In F. W. Kaslow, & J. J. Magnavita (Eds.), *Comprehensive handbook of psychotherapy: Psychodynamic‐object relations*, Vol. 1 (pp. 309–343). New York: John Wiley & Sons ed.

Fosha, D. (2009). Positive affects and the transformation of suffering into flourishing. *Annals of the New York Academy of Sciences* 1172: 252–262. doi:10.1111/j.1749-6632.2009.04501.x. PMID: 19735249.

Fosha, D. (2013). Turbocharging the affects of healing and redressing the evolutionary Tilt. In D. J. Siegel, & M. F. Solomon (Eds.), *Healing moments in psychotherapy*, Chapter 8 (pp. 129–168). New York: Norton.

Freud, S. (1895). Project for a scientific psychology (1950 [1895]). *SSE Volume I* (1886–1899): Pre-Psycho-Analytic Publications and Unpublished Drafts, pp. 281–391.

Freud, S. (1910). 'Wild' psycho-analysis. *SSE, Volume XI* (1910): Five Lectures on Psycho-Analysis, Leonardo da Vinci and Other Works, 219–228.

Freud, S. (1910 [1909]). *Five lectures on psychoanalysis, Vol. 5.* Worcester: Clark University.

Gottesman, I. I., & Gould, T. D. (2003). The endophenotype concept in psychiatry: Etymology and strategic intentions. *American Journal of Psychiatry* 160(4): 636–645.

Gould, T. D., & Gottesman, I. I. (2006). Psychiatric endophenotypes and the development of valid animal models. *Genes, Brain, and Behavior* 5(2): 113–119.

Happé, F., Ronald, A., & Plomin, R. (2006). Time to give up on a single explanation for autism. *Nature Neuroscience* 9(10): 1218–1220.

Hartl, D. L., & Jones, E. W. (2005). *Genetic: Analysis of genes and genomes.* Sudbury: Jones and Bartlett Publishers.

Jackson, J. H. (1958). Evolution and dissolution of the nervous system. In J. Taylor (Ed.), *Selected writings of John Hughlings Jackson* (pp. 45–118). London: Stapes Press.

Joshi, G., Biederman, J., Petty, C., Goldin, R. L, Furtak, S. L, & Wozniak, J. (2013). Examining the comorbidity of bipolar disorder and autism spectrum disorders: a large controlled analysis of phenotypic and familial correlates in a referred population of youth with bipolar I disorder with and without autism spectrum disorders. *The Journal of Clinical Psychiatry* 74(6): 578–586.

Karterud, S., Panksepp, J., Pedersen, G., Johansen, M., Wilberg, T., & Davis, K. (2016). Primary emotional traits in patients with personality disorders. *Personal Mental Health* 10(4): 261–273.

Kazour, F., Richa, S., Abi Char, C., Surget, A., Elhage, W., & Atanasova, B. (2020). Olfactory markers for depression: Differences between bipolar and unipolar patients. *PLoS One* 15(8): e0237565. Published online 2020 Aug 13.

Kernberg, O. F. (1984). *Severe personality disorders. Psychotherapeutic strategies.* New Haven: Yale University Press.

Kernberg, O. F. (1994). Aggression, trauma, and hatred in the treatment of borderline patients. *Psychiatric Clinics of North America* 17(4): 701–714.

Kim, H. K., Blumberger, D. M., & Daskalakis, Z. J. (2020). Neurophysiological biomarkers in Schizophrenia—P50, mismatch negativity, and TMS-EMG and TMS-EEG. *Front Psychiatry* 11: 795.

Kim, Y. S., Leventhal, B. L, Koh, Y., Fombonne, E., Laska, E., Lim E., et al. (2011). Prevalence of autism spectrum disorders in a total population sample. *American Journal of Psychiatry* 168(9): 904–912.

Klein, D. F, & Fink, M. (1962). Psychiatric reaction patterns to imipramine. *American Journal of Psychiatry* 119: 432–438.

Kretschmer, E. (1923). *Hysterie reflex instinkt [Hysteria reflex instinct].* Leipzig: Thieme.

Lewis, S. (2017). Learning and memory: Holding the space. *Nature Reviews Neuroscience* 18(12): 711.

Li, X., Liu, S., Kapoor, K., & Xu, Y. (2020). PPARD may play a protective role against the development of Schizophrenia. *PPAR Research* 2020: 3480412.

Losh, M., Lee, M., Martin, G. E., & Berry-Kravis, E. (2017). Developmental markers of genetic liability to autism in parents: A longitudinal, multigenerational study. *Autism Research* 10(5): 852–865.

Lozupone, M., La Montagna, M., D'Urso, F., Daniele, A., Greco, A., Seripa, D., et al. (2019). The role of biomarkers in psychiatry. *Advances in Experimental Medicine and Biology* 1118: 135–162.

Lvovs, D., Favorova, O. O., & Favorov, A. V. (2012). A polygenic approach to the study of polygenic diseases. *Acta Naturae* 4(3): 59–71.

MacLean, P. (1998). *The history of neuroscience in autobiography,* Larry Squire (Ed.), Vol. 2 (pp. 244–275). San Diego: Academic Press.

McWilliams, N. (1994). *Psychoanalytic diagnosis: Understanding personality structure in the clinical process.* New York: Guilford Press.

Miller, G. A., & Rockstroh, B. (2013). Endophenotypes in psychopathology research: Where do we stand? *Annual Review of Clinical Psychology* 9: 177–213.

Montag, C., & Panksepp, J. (2016). Primal emotional-affective expressive foundations of human facial expression. *Motivation and Emotion* 40: 760–766.

Montag, C., & Reuter, M. (2014). Disentangling the molecular genetic basis of personality: From monoamines to neuropeptides. *Neuroscience & Biobehavioral Reviews* 43: 228–239.

Montag, C. J., & Panksepp, J. (2017). Primary emotional systems and personality: An evolutionary perspective. *Frontiers in Psychology* 8: 464.

Munesue, T., Ono, Y., Mutoh, K., & Shimoda, K. (2010). High prevalence of Bipolar Disorder comorbidity in adolescents and young adults with high-functioning autism spectrum disorder: A preliminary study of 44 outpatients. *Journal of Affective Disorders* 45(2): 79–88. Letter to the editor Affective Disord. 2008; 111:170-five.

Nader, K., & Einarsson, E. O. (2010). Update. *Annals of the New York Academy of Sciences* 1191: 27–41.

Ogden, P., & Fisher, J. (2015). *Sensorimotor psychotherapy: Interventions for trauma and attachment.* New York: W.W. Norton and Co.

Ogden, P., Minton, K., & Pain, C. (Eds.) (2006). *Trauma and the body. A sensorymotor approach to psychotherapy.* New York and London: W.W. Norton.

Panksepp, J. (1985). Mood changes. In P. J. Vinken, G. W. Bruyn, & H. L. Klawans (Eds.), *Handbook of clinical neurology*, Vol. 1, 45 (pp. 289–302). Amsterdam: Elsevier Science.

Panksepp, J. (1998). *Affective neuroscience: The foundations of human and animal emotion.* New York: Oxford University Press.

Panksepp, J. (2006). Emotional end phenotypes in evolutionary psychiatry. Progress in 581 *Neuro-Psychopharmacology and Biological Psychiatry* 30(5): 774–784.

Panksepp, J., & Biven, L. (2012). *The archeology of mind. Neuroevolutionary origins of human emotions.* New York: W. W. Norton & Company.

Pirrongelli, C. (2015). *Una relazione analitica nell'ottica neuro psicoanalitica* [An analytic relationship from a neuro-psychoanalytic perspective]. XLI Conference on Multiple Seminars of the Italian Psychoanalytic Society, Bologna, 23 May.

Porges, S. W. (2001). The polyvagal theory: Phylogenetic substrates of a social nervous system. *International Journal of Psychophysiology* 42(2): 123–146.

Porges, S. W. (2003). Social engagement and attachment: A phylogenetic perspective. *Annals of the New York Academy of Sciences* 1008: 31–47.

Porges, S. W. (2004). Neuroception: A subconscious system for detecting threats and safety. *Zero to Three* 24: 19–24.

Porges, S. W. (2011). *The Polyvagal theory: Neurophysiological foundations of emotions, attachment, communication, and self-regulation, first end.* New York: W.W. Norton & Co.

Potter, D., Summerfelt, A., Gold, J., & Buchanan, R. W. (2006). Review of clinical correlates of P50 sensory gating abnormalities in patients with Schizophrenia. *Schizophrenia Bulletin* 32(4): 692–700.

Ruparelia, K., Manji, K., Abubakar, A., & Newton, C. R. (2017). Investigating the evidence of behavioral, cognitive, and psychiatric endophenotypes in autism: A systematic review. *Autism Research and Treatment* 2017:6346912, pp 1–17, doi:10.1155/2017/6346912. Epub 2017 Jul 5. PMID: 28761767; PMCID: PMC5516739.

Skokauskas, N., & Frodl, T. (2015). Overlap between autism spectrum disorder and bipolar affective disorder. *Psychopathology* 48(4): 209–216.

Stelmack, R. M., & Stalikas, A. (1991). Galen and the Humour theory of temperament. *Personality and Individual Differences* 12(3): 255–263.

Stickley, A., Tachibana, Y., Hashimoto, K., Haraguchi, H., Miyake, A., Morokuma, S., et al. (2017). Assessment of autistic traits in children aged 2 to 4½ years with the preschool version of the Social Responsiveness Scale (SRS-P): Findings from Japan. *Autism Research* 10(5): 852–865.

Sucksmith, E., Roth, I., & Hoekstra, R. A. (2011). Autistic traits below the clinical threshold: Re-examining the broader autism phenotype in the 21st century. *Neuropsychology Review* 21(4): 360–389.

Van Der Kolk, B. (2015). *The body keeps the score: Brain, mind, and body in the healing of trauma*. New York: Penguin.

Wheelwright, S., Auyeung, B., Allison, C., & Baron-Cohen, S. (2010). Defining the broader, medium and narrow autism phenotype among parents using the Autism Spectrum Quotient (AQ). *Molecular Autism* 1: 10.

Winship, I. R., Dursun, S. M., Baker, G. B., Balista, P. A., Kandratavicius, L., Maia-de-Oliveira, J. P., et al. (2019). An overview of animal models related to Schizophrenia. *Canadian Journal of Psychiatry* 64(1): 5–17.

8 The experience of pleasure

A neuropsychoanalytic perspective

Lorenzo Moccia, Marianna Mazza,
Luigi Janiri

Introduction

Far from being a mere sensorial representation, pleasure can instead constitute a complex psychic experience entailing various processes, such as memory, motivation, homoeostasis, and, in some occurrences, pain. Furthermore, the hedonic marking of affects is the quality that, at a basic level, distinguishes emotions from other psychological processes (Damasio, 2004). The complexity of affects, as phenomena behind the mechanisms of the brain regulating the development of painful or gratifying experiences, explains why, from a biological point of view, these were understood only partially until recent years; since then, significant progress has been made by neuroscience in this field. Pleasure is the subjective hedonic quality linked to stimuli or objects defined in behavioural terms as incentivising or rewarding. The concept of reward, however, entails various neuropsychological components: first, the hedonic qualities linked to consumption (i.e., *liking*); second, the motivational/appetising properties that drive an individual to obtainment (i.e., *wanting*); finally, the mnestic representation and the subsequent associative learning that derive from the achievement of these gratifying experiences (i.e., *learning*). Each of these components plays a key role in predisposing the biological resources in the brain that are necessary for evolutionary survival, guaranteeing an essential contribution to the success of adaptive behaviour (Kringelbach & Berridge, 2010).

Similarly, the concept of pain entails both the hedonic aspect (i.e., suffering) and the motivational one (i.e., avoidance) of a painful experience. The search for pleasure and avoidance of pain are important concerning survival, and these two motivational elements compete with each other in various mechanisms that regulate the functioning of the brain. A determining factor is a subjective utility or individual motivation, termed *meaning*, which is conditioned by sensorial, homoeostatic and cultural characteristics (Leknes & Tracey, 2008). For instance, the motivational value of a stimulus increases if its effectiveness in restoring bodily homoeostasis is greater (Cabanac, 1979). This effect, known as *alliesthesia*, is particularly evident if we think of the incentivising/hedonic properties of food, which

DOI: 10.4324/9781003198741-10

increase when it has the function of alleviating hunger. Because also painful experiences are a deviation from homoeostatic equilibrium, the same principle can be applied to pain and, in particular, to the pleasure deriving from the alleviation of pain. Thus, when a threat to the internal equilibrium of an organism increases, unpleasant sensations grow stronger, and defence and avoidance mechanisms are immediately activated (Leknes & Tracey, 2008). Therefore, the alternating of pleasure and pain guarantees a constant optimisation of our homoeostatic equilibrium. The influence of homoeostatic imbalance generated by hunger or thirst can be assessed in physiological terms, for instance, by measuring glucose levels or blood volume, or from a behavioural point of view by looking at the increase in food and fluid consumption. However, research on animals has shown that the quantitative and qualitative characteristics of objects (i.e., incentivising properties) can influence behavioural reactions and learning to a much higher degree than homoeostatic modifications (Mook, 1989). Thus, the decrease in the homoeostatic drive alone is not always effective (Panksepp & Biven, 2012).

Pleasure and affects: current perspectives in neuroscience

Pleasure, therefore, cannot be defined simply as a sensation. Even the simplest sensorial pleasure, such as the one associated with something sweet, requires the contemporary involvement of other neuronal circuits aimed at adding a positive hedonic impact to the stimulus. Without this emotional nuance, even a feeling associated with something with a sweet taste may result in being neutral or even unpleasant (Kringelbach et al., 2012). Furthermore, the characteristics of pleasure are not only subjective but also objective. Although the subjective and conscious dimension associated with pleasure is the most evident, this dimension is underlain by objective neural systems that are selected and maintained in time by the same evolutionary metamorphoses that interest all the main psychological functions. Indeed, hedonic experience requires the contemporary activation of neuronal circuits situated in mesocorticolimbic areas (Damasio, 2010; LeDoux, 2012; Panksepp, 2011) which have undergone an extraordinary evolution in time, precisely because affective reactions guarantee a significant objective gain for the organism (Darwin, 1872). Biological systems of pleasure connote different experiences linked to the survival of the species in a positive hedonic sense, such as experiences deriving from relationships of attachment or sexual relationships, and have, for this reason, an adaptive function (Panksepp & Biven, 2012; Schore, 1994). However, some central issues relating to the nature of pleasure, and more in general the nature of affects, are still the subject of debate in the field of neuroscience today. Among the most pressing issues: is it possible to hypothesise the presence of unconscious affects? In other terms, is the origin of an affective experience located in the cortical or in the subcortical regions?

As observed by some authors, the subjective/conscious dimension of pleasure cannot be separated from the ancestral objective/unconscious dimension, linked to less sophisticated subcortical circuits. The translation of stereotypical behavioural reactions, normally associated with hedonic experience, into more complex subjective and conscious sensations, however, requires the activation in humans of additional cortical circuits specialised in the cognitive-experiential evaluation of stimuli (Berridge & Kringelbach, 2013). According to this approach, there is a marked difference between unconscious visceral-motor and behavioural manifestations associated with emotions, mediated by subcortical regions, and conscious affective experience, which is regulated by prefrontal cortex (PFC) and other cortical areas activity. Affects are thus constituted as a sort of cortical reading of physiological and automatic stimuli that are generated in the subcortical region (LeDoux, 2002). On the contrary, other authors propose a radically different conceptual model, according to which the origin of affective perception can be located in subcortical brain regions, the activation of which supposedly influences a form of embryonic consciousness, defined *affective protoconsciousness* (Alcaro et al., 2017; Solms & Panksepp, 2012). This is described as being a form of consciousness centred around particular emotional states lacking an explicit objectual representation, a sort of "affective disposition" that is, however, necessary for the subsequent idiographic representation of experience (Northoff & Panksepp, 2008). Despite there being no differentiation between subject and object, this diffused state of affective consciousness is supposedly limited by an implicit sense of identity and differentiation that is established starting from the relationship between the perception of one's own body (i.e., interoception) and that of the external environment (i.e., exteroception). Perception and regulation of interoceptive states are accompanied by affective states of pleasure or unpleasure according to whether the body state is of instinctive relaxation or tension or, in other words, depending on the degree of internal homoeostasis (Damasio & Carvalho, 2013). Accordingly, primordial exteroceptive sensations have an intrinsic affective connotation (Alcaro et al., 2017), as in the case of innate pleasure generated by a sweet taste or by the unpleasure caused by a bitter taste, and are always linked to the activation of motor sequences of active exploration mediated by emotional operating systems (Panksepp, 2010).

Neurobiological underpinnings of pleasure: brain hedonic systems

The sensation of pleasure linked to the consumption of tasty food differs from the pleasure deriving from sexual intercourse or from the pleasure deriving from substance abuse. Yet another different kind of pleasure is linked to experiences of socialisation or to the act of listening to music. Recent findings in the field of neuroscience have, however, demonstrated that a single functional circuit, incorporated inside the broader dopaminergic mesocorticolimbic system, seems to be involved in various experiences of pleasure (Georgiadis et al., 2012; Kringelbach et al., 2012; Salimpoor et al., 2011). Moreover, studies on animal models have recently identified a network for enhancing "liking" hedonic reactions, embedded as a set of small hedonic hot spots distributed among several limbic structures throughout the brain, ranging from the cortex to the brainstem (Berridge & Kringelbach, 2015). However, these hedonic hotspots are only partially overlapped with the so-called *brain reward system* (Berridge & Kringelbach, 2013), which was once thought to be at the origin of every sensation of pleasure, and which today some authors believe may mediate the enthusiastic drive to search and explore the environment in mammals (SEEKING System; Panksepp, 2010), while according to others, its function is to mediate the expectation of gratification or, in a broader sense, to mediate desire (Berridge & Robinson, 2016).

Neuroimaging studies indicate that a distinct group of cortical [e.g., orbitofrontal cortex (OFC), anterior cingulate cortex, insular cortex] and subcortical regions [e.g., nucleus accumbens (NAc), amygdala, ventral pallidum] are activated by diverse hedonic stimuli in humans. Cortical hedonic representations (i.e., *encoding*) seem to be regulated by the activity of OFC, particularly within the medial and anterior regions (Murray et al., 2007). These structures seem to be particularly active in the subjective attribution of pleasure in reaction to a hedonic stimulus; also, they seem to mediate variations in the subjectively perceived hedonic intensity. Similarly, additional medial PFC areas, along with regions of the anterior insular cortex, seem to be connected to monitoring and anticipating pleasant objects' reward value, as well as to the integration of perceptual stimuli with associated interoceptive states (Craig, 2009). However, it seems possible to trace in humans the origin (*i.e., causation*) of affective experience, including hedonic experience, in subcortical regions more than in cortical ones. Cortical affective representation would thus imply elements that are inherent in cognitive contextualisation of hedonic experience and second, the capacity of affective regulation and of decision-making. This aspect is demonstrated by the fact that relatively normal affective reactions continue to occur in humans when the PFC and other cortical areas have been severely damaged (Damasio et al., 2013). The neural circuits believed to be responsible for the actual origin of hedonic experiences, or at least of the sensorial pleasure that is associated with the consumption of tasty food, have been identified in brain stimulation experiments carried out on animals. The ability to experience pleasure in relation to sweet food is innate, just as expressive-facial manifestations associated with responses to these stimuli, which are extremely evident in mammals (Berridge & Kringelbach, 2013). Thus, the hedonic impact of specific food can be measured objectively in rats by carefully observing their facial expressions, in particular the movements of their tongue (Steiner et al., 2001). From a neurochemical point of view, the neural systems implicated in the development of sensorial pleasure are much more limited than what was previously believed. Indeed, it has been found that dopamine released in the mesocorticolimbic region, in no way mediates any hedonic manifestation linked to consumption (i.e., *liking*), but rather it mediates aspects linked to motivation or, in a broader sense, to desire (i.e., *wanting*) (Berridge, 2012). However, as some authors stress (Di Chiara, 2005; Panksepp, 2010), the release of dopamine within mesocorticolimbic regions may promote a behavioural state of appetite, intrinsically connected to positive affective states, even to hedonic ones (i.e., *state hedonia*; Di Chiara, 2005). Similarly, the neural centres responsible for the development of sensory pleasure are, from an anatomical point of view, much smaller than what was previously hypothesised, and that only the selective stimulation of μ opioid and endocannabinoid receptors located inside these centres can effectively amplify sensations of pleasure (Mahler et al., 2007; Smith et al., 2011). Specifically, opioid and endocannabinoid stimulation is able to amplify pleasure derived from consumption only in some specific sub-regions of the NAc and of the ventral pallidum, while in other limbic structures it only promotes an increase of appetitive motivation (Peciña & Berridge, 2005; Smith & Berridge, 2005).

Pain–pleasure interactions

A large quantity of neuroscientific evidence indicates that there is a high degree of superimposition, in anatomical and functional terms, between areas of the brain and the neurotransmitter systems responsible for the regulation of physical pain and those responsible for the regulation of affective states. For instance, endogenous opioids and dopamine seem to be involved in a series of processes that take place in central and peripheral regions, among which the regulation of the motivational and hedonic aspects of reward, nociception and modulation of physical pain and, in a broader sense, affective regulation (Leknes & Tracey, 2008). An increase in the activity of the μ and δ opioid receptors in the amygdala and in the anterior cingulate cortex (ACC), other than being associated with deep analgesic states, seems also to be associated with a decrease of subjective unpleasantness experienced in response to nociceptive stimuli (Zubieta et al., 2001). On the contrary, a reduction in the activity of the μ receptors in the ACC region, of the amygdala and of the ventral pallidum, has been recorded during the prolonged recollection of painful memories, whereas an increase in the activity of the κ opioid receptor is generally associated with states of fatigue, confusion, dysphoria and, at higher levels, with states of depersonalisation (Zubieta et al., 2003). In the region of the striate the dopaminergic system seems to carry out various functions depending on the level of activation: states of tonic dopaminergic stimulation have been associated with an increase in algesic response in relation to nociceptive stimuli, while phasic stimulation seems to have antinociceptive properties, perhaps involving the activation of μ opioid receptors (King et al., 2001; Zubieta et al., 2003). The fine neurobiological interactions between dopaminergic neurotransmitter systems and opioids may finally explain some maladaptive behaviours, such as self-harming, which apparently conflict with the principle that guides human beings towards maximisation of pleasure and avoidance of pain. As research on animals and humans has shown, self-harming could be associated with a substantial release of endogenous opioids such as β-endorphins and enkephalins. Similarly, it has been demonstrated that algesic stimuli can reduce, through opioid receptor stimulation, the subjectively perceived intensity of emotional states connoted by a negative affective value. Finally, numerous studies have highlighted a reduction in basal levels of endogenous opioids in individuals who self-harm or who are prone to suicide (Bresin & Gordon, 2013)

Pleasure, unpleasure and affect in psychoanalytic theory

The issue of pleasure and, more in general, of motivation and affects, has a fundamental importance in the psychoanalytical theory because it is able to explain aspirations, thoughts and behaviours of human beings from the point of view of subjective experience. Their role in psychoanalysis has been the object of debate for a century, a debate started with Freud's formulation of the concept of drive, which is itself a theory of motivation and affect (Yovell, 2008). Freud originally claimed that the guiding principle behind the functioning of human beings is the pleasure principle: that is the search for pleasure and avoidance of pain. The pleasure principle, as set out in the texts dating to 1900, is based on the idea that the psychic apparatus is constituted at the level of a reflex arc, the discharge of which is motility: the quantitative accumulation of excitement is indicated as unpleasure, its decrease as pleasure, while the fluctuation from one state to the other is desire, the only able to set the apparatus in motion because the course of excitement is regulated automatically by the perception of the quantum of pleasure and unpleasure (Le Guen, 2008). Later, at the time of his writings on metapsychology, Freud fully elaborated what has been defined as the "drive model of the mind" (Greenberg & Mitchell, 1983). According to this model, man has, from birth, a motivational system, "pushes" that are on the border between the psychic and the somatic, an inner source of stimuli that influences and even guides the dynamics of the mind. The concept of drive is central in this model, "a request of work put forward to the mind", a paraphysiological quantity of energy able to determine, from inside the psychic apparatus, the disturbance of a homoeostatic condition (Ammaniti & Dazzi, 1991).

Similarly, the aim of all drives is their satisfaction, achieved only through the suppression of the state of excitement that is present at the source. An affect, in this more complex explanation, is constituted again as the primary manifestation of a drive, equally elementary, and also grounded in biology, qualitative and subjective expressions of the quantity of drive energy. According to Freud:

> An affect includes in the first place particular motor innervations or discharges and secondly certain feelings; the latter are of two kinds—perceptions of the motor actions that have occurred and the direct feelings of pleasure and unpleasure which, as we say, give the affect its keynote.
>
> (Freud, 1917, p. 395)

Also:

> We have decided to relate pleasure and unpleasure to the quantity of
> excitement that is present in the mind but is not in any way 'bound';
> and to relate them in a such a manner that unpleasure corresponds to
> an *increase* in the quantity of excitement and pleasure to a *diminution*.
>
> (Freud, 1920, p. 8)

Probably, Freud's most original idea came from the fact that he intended
affects as conscious perceptive modalities, experienced subjectively in the
qualities of pleasure and unpleasure, and so relating to the Ego, whereas
the unconscious affect is only a potentiality, blocked by the mechanism of
repression. Previously, in his *Project for a Scientific Psychology* (1895), Freud
had started to describe in theoretical terms the way experiences of pleasure
and pain could interact with the issue of affects. In the chapter titled *The
Experience of Satisfaction*, Freud puts forward his hypothesis on the econ-
omy of the mind: the endogenous psychic excitement cannot be arrested if
not by a specific action brought on by an external object, an action a child,
initially, is not capable of. And again: "In this way this path of discharge acquires a secondary function of the highest importance, that of communication, and the initial helplessness of human beings is the primal source of all
moral motive" (Freud, 1895, p. 318). From now on, pleasure will be associated with the image of the object that provided it and with the motor image
of the movement of the reflex that allowed the discharge. Thus, according to
Freud, affects are linked on the one hand to the function of communication,
and so of language, and on the other to corporeal experience, by means of
the motor image of discharge (Green, 1973).

Neuropsychoanalytic formulation on the concept of drive

The area of the brain in which the requests of the body are supposedly men-
talised could be located, according to some authors, in the hypothalamic
region, and, more specifically, in the regions of the neural groupings specialised in the detection of homoeostatic physiological parameters and in the
control of the activity of both the autonomic and the neuroendocrine nervous systems (Panksepp 2010; Solms &Turnbull, 2002). The activity of these
neural groups, both from an electrophysiological and neurochemical point
of view, is able to evoke intense somatic, visceral sensations in human beings, at a subjective level, such as the ones linked to hunger, thirst and sexual
arousal. The Freudian concept of drive is deeply connected to energetic aspects, not only in terms of discharge but also in terms of energy necessary to
set the psychic apparatus in motion. As some authors have observed (Pfaff,
1999), such a mechanism predisposed to the generalised arousal of the
whole activity of the brain can be found in all vertebrates, including human
beings. This neural system, called Bilateral, Bipolar, Universal Response

Potentiating System (BBURB), is thought to originate at the level of the brainstem's medial and ventral reticular formations, which have projections to both superior and inferior anatomical areas. The ascending projections of the BBURB system are believed to enhance the sensorimotor response and the affective one in relation to stimuli that act with diverse modalities, while the descending ones enhance the autonomic response of the organism. The activity of the BBURB system thus guarantees the necessary quantity of energy for the promotion of all intrinsically motivated behaviours, from affective processes to cognitive ones, and, finally, also of the aspects linked to the emergence of individual consciousness. One of the branches of the BBURB system is thought to coincide with the ascending portions of the abovementioned mesocorticolimbic dopaminergic system (Panksepp, 1998). Thus, the latter constitutes the neuroanatomical substratum of what Panksepp has defined as the emotional SEEKING/desire System (SEEKING System; Panksepp, 1998). As some authors have observed in the field of neuropsychoanalysis (Pfaff et al., 2007; Solms & Turnbull, 2002; Yovell, 2008), the SEEKING emotional system displays a series of analogies with the Freudian concept of *libido*. The activity of the SEEKING system promotes an appetitive predisposition in individuals, a euphoric mental state that is itself gratifying, which is thought to allow individuals to enter into relation with the surroundings in positive affective terms. This predisposition activates specific behavioural patterns (increased motor energy, exploration and approach energy), and also affects the cognitive level, leading to associative reinforcement between gratifying experiences and the stimulus behind experience itself, through the creation of episodic memories. The activity of the SEEKING system thus predisposes the immediate organisation of specific behavioural assets, which are thought to confer a direction to the action also when the object is not represented as the final goal (i.e., *intention-in-action;* Panksepp & Biven, 2012). This aspect characterises the basic, unconditioned nature of the SEEKING system, in that the latter is able to unconditionally activate behavioural patterns (for instance of search, approach, removal, attack), the aim of which becomes increasingly clear with the interaction taking place between the processes initiated by the basic affective systems (so at the level of subcortical regions) and neocortical areas. Thanks to these feedbacks between subcortical and neocortical areas, it is possible to construct patterns of relationship with the external object, with its potential ability to offer gratification and with our capacity to experience it by acting (Panksepp & Biven, 2012). The affective pre-representational (lacking an object) disposition, mediated by the activity of the SEEKING system, seems thus to project the organism towards external space, pushing it to act in a specific way. Only through interaction with the surroundings this affective disposition is, however, able to achieve full realisation.

This characteristic, inherent in the functioning of the SEEKING system can be seen in relation not only to the concept of *libido*, but also to some conceptual formulations by Bion and, in particular, to the notion of *pre-conception*

(Bion, 1962). This is described by Bion as a sort of a priori knowledge, in psychoanalysis the equivalent of the Kantian concept of "empty thought", its main quality being that it can be "thought" but not "become known". In the mind of a newborn, there is a preconception of the breast, an innate presentiment of it, which is, so to speak, "preformed". What characterises preconceptions is essentially a sentiment of expectation that has the capacity to orient the newborn towards certain realisation. Bion claims that when an expectation meets its corresponding realisation, the psychological result is conception. In other words, when a newborn is breastfeeding, its preconception (or "idea") of the breast is connected with its corresponding realisation. Thus, conceptions (or "notions") must be connected to an experience of satisfaction: not only at a physical level but also at a cognitive one (Neri, 1987). Similarly, in the field of ethology, the theory of instinct says that the phenomenon of imprinting in a young animal is the encounter of a temporised predisposition and of an object present in its surrounding that realises it, though imprinting seems to not entail forms of rewarding (Lorenz, 1988).

To conclude: interactions or integrations?

What has been discussed concerns, on the one hand, the complexity and, conversely, the risk of reductionism that connote the concept of pleasure, and on the other, the neurobiological substratum that supports the view of such complexity. Pleasure is not only the mere absence of tension, a return to the central fluctuating state prescribed by homoeostasis. Indeed, pleasure is inextricably linked to its "negative", that is pain: the psychopathological and dynamic issue of masochism addressed by Freud (1924) in economic terms, reveals the drive interconnection of hedonic and anti-hedonic or destructive forces, which have potentially extreme consequences. Pleasure can become independent of libido and can include objects unrelated to sexuality or instinctual satisfaction: perception of self-efficiency, cultural signification, the propensity to communicate and form interpersonal relationships are telling examples of a type of "pleasure beyond the pleasure principle". The concept of pleasure is closely connected to other bordering concepts, such as affect, desire, motivation, drive, which are not always unequivocally definable and differentiable and belong to different epistemological domains, such as experimental and cognitive psychology and psychoanalysis. What we have attempted to do, by necessarily restricting the field of research, is to describe the neural structures and neurochemical systems involved in the functioning of pleasure, without giving into the paradigm of simple localisationism. The advancement of neuroscientific knowledge allows us to explain plurisemantic and sometimes paradoxical phenomena linked to pleasure and to the search of pleasure. The development of "bordering" or "bridging" disciplines, such as neuropsychoanalysis, that study conceptual methodologies of modelling of experimental data that can be understood with a theory of the functioning of the mind and that have possible clinical applications, seems to confirm the need for integrated knowledge. Writing about the border between psychoanalysis and neuroscience, already in 1996, Arnold Modell remarked that "unification of ideas derived from neurobiology and psychoanalysis can help to illuminate a very broad and diverse range of problems extending from traumatic memories to the repetition compulsion, the psychoanalytic theory of instinct and the concept of the self" (Modell, 1996). Because both psychoanalysis and neuroscience have distinct and separate objects, methods and types of knowledge, the objective of integration is complex and difficult to pursue in a clear way, that is, without running the risk of hyper-simplification or vagueness. Indeed, integration presupposes that two subjects, which are irreducible one to the other at a structural level, share or render compatible parts or functions of themselves. What parts or functions can psychoanalysis and neuroscience share? The issue forms the backdrop, as it were, or a challenge, for the emerging dialogue.

References

Alcaro, A., Carta, S., & Panksepp, J. (2017). The affective core of the self: a neuro-archetypical perspective on the foundations of human (and animal) subjectivity. *Frontiers in Psychology, 8,* 1424. doi:10.3389/fpsyg.2017.01424.

Ammaniti, M., & Dazzi, N. (1991). *Affetti. Natura e Sviluppo delle Relazioni Interpersonali.* Roma: Laterza.

Berridge, K. C. (2012). From prediction error to incentive salience: mesolimbic computation of reward motivation. *The European Journal of Neuroscience, 35*(7), 1124–1143. doi:10.1111/j.1460-9568.2012.07990.x.

Berridge, K. C., & Kringelbach, M. L. (2013). Neuroscience of affect: brain mechanisms of pleasure and displeasure. *Current Opinion in Neurobiology, 23*(3), 294–303. doi:10.1016/j.conb.2013.01.017.

Berridge, K. C., & Kringelbach, M. L. (2015). Pleasure systems in the brain. *Neuron, 86*(3), 646–664. doi:10.1016/j.neuron.2015.02.018.

Berridge, K. C., & Robinson, T. E. (2016). Liking, wanting, and the incentive-sensitization theory of addiction. *The American Psychologist, 71*(8), 670–679. doi:10.1037/amp0000059.

Bion, W. R. (1962). *Learning from Experience.* London: Tavistock.

Bresin, K., & Gordon, K. H. (2013). Endogenous opioids and nonsuicidal self-injury: a mechanism of affect regulation. *Neuroscience and Biobehavioral Reviews, 37*(3), 374–383. doi:10.1016/j.neubiorev.2013.01.020.

Cabanac, M. (1979). Sensory pleasure. *The Quarterly Review of Biology, 54*(1), 1–29. doi:10.1086/410981.

Craig, A. D. (2009). How do you feel—now? The anterior insula and human awareness. *Nature Reviews. Neuroscience, 10*(1), 59–70. doi:10.1038/nrn2555.

Damasio, A., & Carvalho, G. B. (2013). The nature of feelings: evolutionary and neurobiological origins. *Nature Reviews. Neuroscience, 14*(2), 143–152. doi:10.1038/nrn3403.

Damasio, A., Damasio, H., & Tranel, D. (2013). Persistence of feelings and sentience after bilateral damage of the insula. *Cerebral cortex (New York, NY: 1991), 23*(4), 833–846. doi:10.1093/cercor/bhs077.

Damasio, A. R. (2004). "Emotions and feelings: a neurobiological perspective," in *Feelings and Emotions: The Amsterdam Symposium*, eds. A. S. R. Manstead, N. Frijda, and A. Fischer, Cambridge: Cambridge University Press. doi:10.1017/CBO9780511806582.004.

Damasio, A. R. (2010). *Self Comes to Mind: Constructing the Conscious Brain*. New York: Pantheon Books.

Darwin, C. (1872). *The Expression of the Emotions in Man and Animals (1998 Edition: Revised and with Commentary by P. Ekman)*. Oxford: Oxford University Press.

Di Chiara, G. (2005). *Dopamine, Motivation and Reward*. New York: Elsevier.

Freud, S. (1895). *Project for a Scientific Psychology. The Standard Edition of the Complete Psychological Works of Sigmund Freud*, Vol. 1. London: Hogarth Press.

Freud, S. (1917). *Introductory Lectures on Psycho-Analysis. The Standard Edition of the Complete Psychological Works of Sigmund Freud*, Vol. 16. London: Hogarth Press.

Freud, S. (1920). *Beyond the Pleasure Principle, Group Psychology and Other Works. The Standard Edition of the Complete Psychological Works of Sigmund Freud*, Vol. 18. London: Vintage.

Freud, S. (1924). *The Economic Problem of Masochism. The Standard Edition of the Complete Psychological Works of Sigmund Freud, (1923–1925): The Ego and the Id and Other Works*, Vol. 19. London: The Hogarth Press and the Institute of Psychoanalysis.

Georgiadis, J. R., Kringelbach, M. L., & Pfaus, J. G. (2012). Sex for fun: a synthesis of human and animal neurobiology. *Nature Reviews. Urology, 9*(9), 486–498. doi:10.1038/nrurol.2012.151.

Green, A. (1973). *Le Discours vivant*. Paris: Presses Universitaires de France.

Greenberg, J. A., & Mitchell, S. A. (1983). *Object Relations in Psychoanalytic Theory*. London: Harvard University Press.

King, M. A., Bradshaw, S., Chang, A. H., Pintar, J. E., & Pasternak, G. W. (2001). Potentiation of opioid analgesia in dopamine2 receptor knock-out mice: evidence for a tonically active anti-opioid system. *The Journal of Neuroscience: The Official Journal of the Society for Neuroscience, 21*(19), 7788–7792. doi: 10.1523/JNEUROSCI.21-19-07788.2001.

Kringelbach, M. L., & Berridge, K. C. (2010). *Pleasures of the Brain*. Oxford: Oxford University Press.

Kringelbach, M. L., Stein, A., & van Hartevelt, T. J. (2012). The functional human neuroanatomy of food pleasure cycles. *Physiology & Behavior, 106*(3), 307–316. doi:10.1016/j.physbeh.2012.03.023.

LeDoux, J. (2002). *Synaptic Self: How Our Brains Become Who We Are*. London: Macmillan.

LeDoux, J. (2012). Rethinking the emotional brain. *Neuron, 73*(4), 653–676. doi:10.1016/j.neuron.2012.02.004.

Le Guen, C. (2008). *Dictionnaire Freudien*. Paris: Presses Universitaires de France.

Leknes, S., & Tracey, I. (2008). A common neurobiology for pain and pleasure. *Nature Reviews. Neuroscience, 9*(4), 314–320. doi:10.1038/nrn2333.

Lorenz, K. (1988). *Hier bin ich – wo bist du? Ethologie der Graugans*. Munich: Serie Piper.

Mahler, S. V., Smith, K. S., & Berridge, K. C. (2007). Endocannabinoid hedonic hotspot for sensory pleasure: anandamide in nucleus accumbens shell enhances 'liking' of a sweet reward. *Neuropsychopharmacology: Official Publication of the American College of Neuropsychopharmacology, 32*(11), 2267–2278. doi:10.1038/sj.npp.1301376.

Modell, A. H. (1996). "The interface of psychoanalysis and neurobiology," in *Paper Presentation – The Poles of Health: Biological and Social Approaches to Disordered Minds*. Boston, MA: Boston Colloquium for Philosophy of Science in *Psiche, 5*(2), 27–37.

Mook, D. G. (1989). Oral factors in appetite and satiety. *Annals of the New York Academy of Sciences (USA) 575*, 265–278; discussion 279–280. doi:10.1111/j.1749-6632.1989.tb53249.x.

Murray, E. A., O'Doherty, J. P., & Schoenbaum, G. (2007). What we know and do not know about the functions of the orbitofrontal cortex after 20 years of cross-species studies. *The Journal of Neuroscience: The Official Journal of the Society for Neuroscience, 27*(31), 8166–8169. doi:10.1523/JNEUROSCI.1556-07.2007.

Neri, C. (1987). *Letture Bioniane*. Roma: Borla.

Northoff, G., & Panksepp, J. (2008). The trans-species concept of self and the subcortical-cortical midline system. *Trends in Cognitive Sciences, 12*(7), 259–264. doi:10.1016/j.tics.2008.04.007.

Panksepp, J. (1998). *Affective Neuroscience: The Foundations of Human and Animal Emotions*. New York: Oxford University Press.

Panksepp, J. (2010). Affective neuroscience of the emotional BrainMind: evolutionary perspectives and implications for understanding depression. *Dialogues in Clinical Neuroscience, 12*(4), 533–545.

Panksepp, J. (2011). The basic emotional circuits of mammalian brains: do animals have affective lives? *Neuroscience and Biobehavioral Reviews, 35*(9), 1791–1804. doi:10.1016/j.neubiorev.2011.08.003.

Panksepp, J., & Biven, L. (2012). *The Archaeology of Mind: Neuroevolutionary Origins of Human Emotion*. New York: W. W. Norton & Company.

Peciña, S., & Berridge, K. C. (2005). Hedonic hot spot in nucleus accumbens shell: where do mu-opioids cause increased hedonic impact of sweetness? *The Journal of Neuroscience: The Official Journal of the Society for Neuroscience, 25*(50), 11777–11786. doi:10.1523/JNEUROSCI.2329-05.2005.

Pfaff, D., Martin, E. M., & Kow, L. M. (2007). Generalized brain arousal mechanisms contributing to libido. *Neuropsychoanalysis, 9*(2), 173–181.

Pfaff, D. W. (1999). *Drive: Neurobiological and Molecular Mechanisms of Sexual Motivation*. Cambridge: MIT Press.

Salimpoor, V. N., Benovoy, M., Larcher, K., Dagher, A., & Zatorre, R. J. (2011). Anatomically distinct dopamine release during anticipation and experience of peak emotion to music. *Nature Neuroscience, 14*(2), 257–262. doi:10.1038/nn.2726.

Schore, A. N. (1994). *Affect Regulation and the Origin of the Self: The Neurobiology of Emotional Development*. Hillsdale: Lawrence Erlbaum Associates, Inc.

Smith, K. S., & Berridge, K. C. (2005). The ventral pallidum and hedonic reward: neurochemical maps of sucrose "liking" and food intake. *The Journal of Neuroscience: The Official Journal of the Society for Neuroscience, 25*(38), 8637–8649. doi:10.1523/JNEUROSCI.1902-05.2005.

Smith, K. S., Berridge, K. C., & Aldridge, J. W. (2011). Disentangling pleasure from incentive salience and learning signals in brain reward circuitry. *Proceedings of the National Academy of Sciences of the United States of America*, *108*(27), E255–E264. doi:10.1073/pnas.1101920108.

Solms, M., & Panksepp, J. (2012). The "id" knows more than the "ego" admits: neuropsychoanalytic and primal consciousness perspectives on the interface between affective and cognitive neuroscience. *Brain Sciences*, *2*(2), 147–175. doi:10.3390/brainsci2020147.

Solms, M., & Turnbull, O. (2002). *The Brain and the Inner World: An Introduction to the Neuroscience of Subjective Experience*. London: Karnac.

Steiner, J. E., Glaser, D., Hawilo, M. E., & Berridge, K. C. (2001). Comparative expression of hedonic impact: affective reactions to taste by human infants and other primates. *Neuroscience and Biobehavioral Reviews*, *25*(1), 53–74. doi:10.1016/s0149-7634(00)00051-8.

Yovell, Y. (2008). Is there a drive to love? *Neuropsychoanalysis*, *10*(2), 117–144.

Zubieta, J. K., Ketter, T. A., Bueller, J. A., et al. (2003). Regulation of human affective responses by anterior cingulate and limbic mu-opioid neurotransmission. *Archives of General Psychiatry*, *60*(11), 1145–1153. doi:10.1001/archpsyc.60.11.1145.

Zubieta, J. K., Smith, Y. R., Bueller, J. A., Xu, Y., Kilbourn, M. R., Jewett, D. M., Meyer, C. R., Koeppe, R. A., & Stohler, C. S. (2001). Regional mu opioid receptor regulation of sensory and affective dimensions of pain. *Science (New York, N.Y.)*, *293*(5528), 311–315. doi:10.1126/science.1060952.

9 Anedonia and emotional-motivational systems

Anatolia Salone

Introduction

From an evolutionary point of view, the ability to experience pleasure can be considered the most important element of adaptation by living organisms to fight for the survival of the species, through the search for a reward (Kringelbach, 2005, Kringelbach & Berridge, 2009). Anhedonia, the reduced or absent ability to perform this important function, should be seen as a highly non-adaptive feature. However, it represents a very widespread experience, which has persisted over time and which has become part of many psychic disorders (Whybrow, 1998).

Historical background

The term anhedonia, from the Greek ἀν + ἡδονή, literally "absence of pleasure", was introduced in psychiatry by Théodule-Armand Ribot in 1896 (Ribot, 1896). He defined anhedonia as the inability to experience pleasure and, over time, this concept has been associated with the description of both specific symptomatology and a personality characteristic. At the end of the nineteenth century, it seemed quite clear that the loss of pleasure was an important feature of various psychopathological conditions, above all depression. However, anhedonia assumed a central role in classical psychopathology theories from the beginning of the twentieth century. Kraepelin was the first to identify in anhedonia a core aspect of what he called *dementia praecox* (1919). He described in his patients a typical state of inability to feel joy concerning life and considered the indifference to social interactions previously felt as a source of pleasure, the reduction of interpersonal skills and the loss of gratification for work or other playful activities as early symptoms of the disorder. These symptoms were so important that they were considered what we would call today "markers" of the pathology.

Similarly, Bleuler (1911), highlighting the typical indifference that many patients showed towards loved ones and towards life itself, defined anhedonia as a basic characteristic of their disorder, an objectively identifiable equivalent of their pathological condition.

DOI: 10.4324/9781003198741-11

What emerges from the works of Kraepelin and Bleuler is their interpretation of the loss of the experience of pleasure as an equivalent to the deterioration of the emotional life of the schizophrenic patient.

Over the course of the twentieth century, however, interest in anhedonia declined rapidly. Even Jaspers (1997) fails to mention it, merely referring in general terms to the severe and pervasive loss of emotional response present in psychosis. On the other hand, in the context of mood disorders, the presence of mood depression has started to be defined as a pathognomonic feature.

It was only in 1960 that the interest in anhedonia was rekindled, first of all in the field of psychosis, thanks to the work of Rado (1956, 1962), who attributed to anhedonia a more central role in the development of schizophrenia, considering it a crucial, genetically transmissible defect in both schizophrenia and compensated schizotypy without obvious psychotic symptoms. Rado considers anhedonia as a predisposing condition to the development of abnormal sexual functioning and to the reduction of interpersonal skills and perception of positive feelings. Meehl (1962, 1973), extending the theory of Rado, considers the reduction of hedonic capacity as a heritable trait predisposing to the development of schizophrenia and depression, and a causal factor of social withdrawal, inappropriate behaviour and deviant logic.

Subsequently, Klein (1974), introducing the concept of "endogenomorphic depression", rekindled interest in the concept of anhedonia, to such an extent that the DSM, in its third edition published in 1980, placed it at the centre of the diagnosis of major depressive disorder, considering it one of the two pathognomonic symptoms. Klein's definition, "a sharp, unreactive, pervasive impairment of the capacity to experience pleasure, or to respond affectively, to the anticipation of pleasure" was taken up and changed in the DSM into "a loss of interest or pleasure in all or almost all usual activities and pastimes" (DSM-III, 1983). Furthermore, the anhedonic experience was recognized as essential for the definition of melancholic depression.

In the phenomenological tradition, especially in the context of melancholia, the anhedonic dimension has been addressed by various authors, such as Tellenbach (1975), Heidegger, (1991). Weitbrecht (1979), and Callieri, (1995). In all these contributions, the anhedonic dimension represents the background of the melancholic universe and intersects with other depressive aspects. The phenomenological approach to anhedonia places depressive experiences in a temporal background of their development, which inevitably leads to considering anhedonia as an integral part of a depressive personality. Kurt Schneider (1955), therefore, speaks of the impossibility to experience pleasure as part of depressive psychopathy, which would reside in a personality characterized by fear of life and of the world.

According to the psychoanalytic perspective, the concept of anhedonia inevitably leads back to that of the death drive, introduced by Freud in *Beyond the Pleasure Principle* (1920) as a principle of disconnection from the vitality of Eros. In anhedonia, the death drive disconnects pleasure from its possible and multiple objects, having as a background the generalized loss of this function. Freud again, in *Mourning and Melancholia* (1917), clarifies the nature of melancholia, comparing it with the normal effect of mourning. Faced with the loss of the loved object, the individual may experience a loss of interest in the world, inhibition in the face of any type of activity and loss of the ability to love. This situation partly overlaps with the two conditions, but in melancholia, it takes the typical characteristic of self-deprivation, which is expressed through feelings of guilt and wait for punishment. Mourning is overcome after a certain period of time, which does not occur in melancholia. Like endless mourning, it tends instead to have pervasive and chronic characteristics. Freud explains that in conditions of normality the reality principle prevails so that the libido can be gradually withdrawn from the unconscious representation of the object and at the end of this process the ego can be free again. In melancholia, however, the lost object may not be real but may have a more ideal and phantasmic nature, a lost object removed from consciousness. The result is that the libido can't invest in another object; it is brought back into the ego, establishing identification of the ego with the object. It's as if splitting of the ego took place in the melanchonic subject, where one part turns against the other part, punishing it, blaming it and violently attacking it. Despite the developments in psychoanalytic theory, Freud's original theory of melancholia introduced a new element, the loss, which has remained central even in modern neuroscientific approaches to the anhedonic experience.

Anhedonia as a transnosographic dimension

Over time, apart from the controversial fortunes experienced by the concept of anhedonia, it appears evident that it was initially treated as a specific condition, which can be found in different psychopathological dimensions. In the present diagnostic systems, on the other hand, the concept of anhedonia appears to be used in a rather confusing way, even though it is considered a crucial feature for the diagnosis of depression and schizophrenia.

The International Classification of Diseases, 9th revision (ICD-9), for example, does not include anhedonia in the symptomatic description of the depressive phases of manic-depressive psychosis but rather defines it in terms of "widespread depressed mood of gloom and wretchedness with some degree of anxiety" (WHO, 1978).

According to the DSM, on the other hand, in addition to depressed mood, one of the two necessary symptoms for the diagnosis of depression is anhedonia; moreover, the lack of reactivity and anhedonia are the key symptoms for the definition of melancholic depression (DSM-IV, 2001). In the fifth edition of the DSM, the term anhedonia is not used explicitly in depression but is captured in the main criterion of lack of interest and pleasure in most daily activities (2013). However, this definition can be confusing, as it combines two important characteristics of pleasure, namely motivation and hedonic impact. Furthermore, as pointed out by Rush and Weissemburger (1994), only four of the nine major classification systems report anhedonia among the criteria for the diagnosis of endogenous melancholic depression. As further evidence of the complexity of the concept, Silverstone (1991) reported in a clinical study that anhedonia occurs significantly in over 50% of patients, regardless of their psychiatric diagnosis. These results appear to suggest that anhedonia does not constitute a pathognomonic trait of depressive disorders and that it should not be treated only in its definition as an objective symptom, but rather be considered more widely as a subjective experience that pervades the personality of the subject and therefore becomes a transnosographic entity.

As previously highlighted, anhedonia is historically one of the most important negative symptoms in schizophrenia (Ettemberg, 1993; Andreasen, 1982). However, beyond the classical psychopathological tradition, there are currently different views on this topic. For example, Blanchard and Cohen (2006) continue to consider anhedonia, together with diminished expression, one of the two main characteristics of the negative syndrome complex in schizophrenia. On the contrary, other authors, such as Myin-Germeys et al., (2003), based on specific studies, affirm that in schizophrenic patients the ability to feel pleasure is preserved. In the DSM-V, anhedonia is not directly included in the diagnostic criteria for schizophrenia, but some of its important characteristics are captured in some of the negative symptoms, such as avolition (understood as the inability to initiate and pursue specific purposes) and affective blunting (defined as the absence of signs of affective expression). Although there are clear similarities regarding the role of anhedonia in the two disorders, important differences should also be underlined. First of all, in depression, anhedonia represents a transitory state (except in extremely severe cases), which is described in the DSM as a "significant change from the past". Conversely, in schizophrenia, anhedonia seems to reflect a lasting and pervasive experience. These differences are also supported by longitudinal studies that show stability over time of self-reported anhedonic experiences by schizophrenic patients and a significant reduction in depressed patients, after 1 year of follow-up (Blanchard et al., 2001).

Furthermore, although anhedonia plays a fundamental role in depressive and schizophrenic spectrum disorders, it is not limited to such psychopathological conditions. Indeed, anhedonia has been linked to anxiety disorders, adaptation disorders, suicidal ideation and suicide (Oei et al., 1990; Fawcett, 1993; Robbins & Alessi, 1985). On the other hand, there is a model proposed by Loas (1996), according to which a genetically determined reduced hedonic capacity can be considered a specific trait (together with introversion, obsession, pessimism and passivity) and a risk factor for the development of the so-called "endogenomorphic" unipolar depression. Also, in Cloninger's descriptive personality system (1994), anhedonia could be considered as a basic trait of temperament, rooted as such in the biology of the subject and defined as reward dependence, i.e., a tendency to gratification that derives from acknowledgments and relations obtained in the social sphere. The spread of the anhedonic experience beyond its symptomatological definition and its categorical classification is confirmed by strong clinical and research evidence, which identifies the presence of anhedonia also in substance use disorders, as part of withdrawal symptoms (Gawin & Kleber, 1986). Anhedonia appears to be an important factor involved in relapses (Koob & Le Moal, 2001; Volkow et al., 2002) and in the transition from occasional and recreational use of a given substance to the assumption of larger quantities (Ahmed and Koob, 1998). In the context of various substance-related disorders, anhedonia is frequently present in the use of alcohol (Heinz, et al., 1994), cocaine, stimulants and cannabis (Gawin & Ellinwood, 1988; Miller, et al., 1993; Bovasso, 2001). Heinz (Heinz et al., 1994) has shown that anhedonia, dysphoria and avolition are common symptoms in relapses, regardless of whether they are comorbid with schizophrenia, depression or alcohol dependence. However, anhedonia and craving as symptoms predisposing to relapse occur independently of each other during drug abstinence, and their intensity, time of onset and response to treatments are not superimposable. In a condition of prolonged abstinence, what is described as a depressive syndrome is identified as anhedonia and should not be attributed simply to the psychological effect of abstinence (Jaffe et al., 1997). There are also correlations between anhedonia and other withdrawal symptoms that support the hypothesis of a clinical condition in which different aspects must be considered part of the same process (Janiri et al., 2005; Martinotti et al., 2008a, 2008b). To conclude the description of the wide panorama of clinical situations in which anhedonia may be present, some disorders with behavioural alterations should also be noted, such as Parkinson's disease (Isella et al., 2003), binge eating (Davis and Woodside, 2002) and risk behaviours in general (Franken et al., 2006).

Thus, on purely symptomatic level, anhedonia may be defined as a complex experience within a vast psychopathological framework that might be nosographically conceived as a pathology in itself, and that may remain constant or evolve in other psychopathological frameworks. The transversality and complexity of anhedonia should also be understood in the light of the experience of patients, who report that their lack of satisfaction of desire is due to the actual absence of desire itself: in other words, these subjects are unable to obtain pleasure because they are unable to desire (Snaith, 1993). In addition to the nosographic transversality of anhedonia, the recent progress in understanding the genetic basis of psychopathological syndromes and the identification of endophenotypes has brought the anhedonic dimension back to the centre of research interest. Endophenotypes are subclinical traits associated with the expression of a pathology and represent the genetic predisposition to the disease in unaffected subjects (Leboyer et al., 1998). Hasler et al. (2004) showed that anhedonia, together with the increased response to stress, can be considered as the most probable endophenotype of major depression.

The neurobiological alterations of the reward system in anhedonia... beyond dopamine

The growing recognition of the role of anhedonia in the main psychiatric and neurological disorders leads to the need for its reconceptualization, especially starting from a more precise definition of which aspects of the so-called "Pleasure System" are altered and on which cerebral networks such dysregulation is possibly based.

Despite numerous studies in the literature on major depression and schizophrenia, not enough space has been given to the specific assessment of the presence and severity of anhedonia, which is often evaluated starting from its behavioural correlation rather than through the patients' self-reported evaluation. In recent years, there has been a certain trend towards evaluating anhedonia as a specific symptom, regardless of the disorder in which it occurs, in an attempt to identify its neurobiological correlates (Hyman & Fenton, 2003; Insel et al., 2010; Der-Avakian and Markou, 2012).

Most neurobiological studies propose the rewarding system as a possible neural substrate of anhedonia, i.e. the mesolimbic and mesocortical dopaminergic reward circuit (Heinz et al., 1994; Isella et al., 2003; Markou & Koob, 1991; Willner et al., 2005). This is a set of structures dedicated to the regulation of behaviour through the induction of the experience of pleasure. Reward, from a psychological point of view, is a process that reinforces a certain behaviour. Situations that induce reward include the necessary stimuli for the survival of the species, such as food, water, sex, struggle and, in subordinate form, money, home, beauty, music, etc. Reward is generally considered more effective than punishment in reinforcing positive behaviour and induce learning. The research carried out in the context of the evaluation of anhedonia in addiction disorders mainly converges on the identification of a dopaminergic transmission deficit in the reward system. Of the two dopaminergic pathways involved in the rewarding system, the mesolimbic one (from the ventral tegmental area (VTA) to the ventral striatum, including the nucleus accumbens, the amygdala and the hippocampus) plays a more important role as it is involved in associative learning, motivation and reinforcement. Conversely, the mesocortical pathway projects towards cortical regions, including the anterior cingulate, orbitofrontal cortex, medial prefrontal and insula and appears to be involved in working memory, attention and inhibitory control (Treadway & Zald, 2010).

A central alteration of the dopaminergic circuits, therefore, has been widely proposed as a neurobiological correlate of anhedonia. This hypothesis is supported by a demonstrated reduction in the concentrations of homovanillic acid (a derivative of dopamine) in the cerebrospinal fluid in patients with major depression, as well as by genetic, neuroimaging and post-mortem studies. Drugs that increase dopamine transmission show antidepressant action (Willner, 1995; Boyer et al., 1995; Smeraldi, 1998; Brunello et al., 1999), while neuroleptic therapy can cause the onset of an anhedonic state (Wise, 1982). There is also strong evidence from neuroimaging techniques, such as transcranial stimulation (Salamone et al., 1997), PET and SPECT (Bannon, 1995), as well as from studies on animal models (Diana et al., 1996).

The assumption that the mesocortical and mesolimbic dopaminergic neuronal circuits play an important role in the mechanism of gratification, and therefore also in all clinical conditions with anhedonia, appears to be accepted today; however, the boundaries of this role appear still blurred at present. There is evidence in the literature of the involvement of other neurotransmitter systems in the reward mechanism, in particular, the GABAergic/BDZ system of the brainstem and the opioid system. In particular, endogenous opioids are certainly involved in the hedonic experience. They include a set of families of neuropeptides, called endorphins, enkephalins, dynorphins and orphanins, with a varied panorama of receptor subtypes characterizing their response (μ, δ, κ and ORL1) (Cooper et al., 2003). Overall, these peptides play a significant role in the subjective experience of euphoria. Opioid receptors (μ, δ and κ) are widely expressed in the ventral striatum; the stimulation of these receptors is considered the functional basis of the hedonic responses to food and other conditions that naturally stimulate the reward (Pecina et al., 2006). The two subcortical regions that are mostly implicated as central to affective responses to pleasure are the nucleus accumbens (NAcc) (Pecina & Berridge, 2005) and the ventral pallidum (VP) (Smith et al., 2009), as well as a number of other areas that respond to opioid stimulation, such as the ventromedial prefrontal cortex (vmPFC), orbitofrontal cortex (OFC) and anterior cingulate (ACC), involved in the complex processing of the hedonic impact of the rewarding stimulus. The OFC has excitatory projections towards the ventral striatum (Zald & Kim, 1996a, 1996b) and, overall, this system appears to play a key role in stimulus evaluation and its association with reward. Furthermore, the rostral part of the ACC possibly encodes the receipt of the reward (Knutson et al., 2001, 2005; Sanfey et al., 2003) and appears to be involved in rewarding choices, particularly in the case of complex decisions that require a cost–benefit assessment (Kennerley et al., 2006; 2009; Rushworth & Behrens, 2008; Walton et al., 2006). Finally, a fundamental role in the positive evaluation of the stimulus is played by the amygdala (Balleine & Killcross, 2006; Baxter & Murray, 2002; Murray, 2007).

The pleasure system

Despite the recognition of the transversal importance of the anhedonic experience in psychiatric disorders, the concept of anhedonia as "inability to feel pleasure" is still widely accepted, practically unchanged since Ribot's times. In recent years, thanks to new knowledge about neurobiological mechanisms, some authors have begun to make a clear distinction between motivation alterations and consummatory behaviour alterations in anhedonia (Tredway & Zald, 2010). The research carried out (not directly on anhedonia, but aimed at defining the anatomical-functional substrates of the hedonia) has led to important findings. In addition to the studies conducted on the sources of pleasure fundamental for survival, such as food and sex, the experiments that consider the gratification deriving from social interactions are very interesting (King-Casas et al., 2005; Kringelbach et al., 2008; Frith and Frith, 2010; Chelnokova et al., 2014). Of course, the full repertoire of social situations that can determine pleasure is difficult to investigate and control from an experimental point of view, since it was seen, for example, in neuroimaging studies on the role of facial expressions, that pleasantness is recorded in the same way as sensory pleasure (Kringelbach, 2003; Rømer Thomsen et al., 2011). Furthermore, human beings can experience a high level of gratification from music, art, altruistic and intellectual pleasures. Despite the relatively recent expansion of neuroscientific research on such complex types of pleasure, experimental evidence suggests that all types of gratification converge in a common hedonic system (Frijda, 2010; Leknes & Tracey, 2010; Salimpoor et al., 2011), which Kent Berridge and Terry Robinson have schematically divided into the sub-components of *wanting, liking* and *learning*, which are thought to represent different reward levels and processes. In particular, wanting is defined as the motivation for reward or the incentive for its salience, while liking represents the actual pleasure or the hedonic impact of the reward; as to learning, it determines the associations, representations and predictions of future rewards based on experience, i.e. ultimately the temporal perspective of wanting and liking. Each component plays a fundamental role, being at the basis of the appetitive, consummatory and satisfactory phases within the pleasure cycle (Robinson & Berridge, 1993; 2003; Berridge & Kringelbach, 2008). Another important feature of these psychological states is that they consist of both conscious and unconscious aspects (Berridge & Kringelbach, 2008). This theoretical framework has laid the foundations for scientific studies concerning pleasure that have made it possible to quantify, measure and evaluate the connections between the different psychological components and, therefore, to identify the underlying brain circuits. Starting from experiments on animal models, the different components have been tested with different stimulations. In rats, for example, the hedonic (liking) or aversive reactions are measured based on facial reactions (some of which are also observed in other animal species), while wanting is quantified by referring to the degree of motor activation that the subject is able to implement in order to obtain a reward. Thanks to these studies, designed based on a very precise *a priori* hypothesis and therefore of an open and dynamic reference theory, the demonstration of the presence of two distinct anatomical circuits was made possible (Berridge, 1996). In particular, wanting is thought to reside in the NAS-DA mesolimbic system and liking in the opioid system, which includes, among other things, the shell of the nucleus accumbens, the ventral pallidum and the pons. These circuits appear to function independently from each other, as was shown by targeted experiments where, for example, it was observed that an interference with the dopaminergic system does not alter the appetitive reactivity for sweet substances such as sucrose (Berridge & Robinson, 1998), as well as an increase in the dopamine release is not sufficient to produce pleasant subjective effects in humans (Rothman & Glowa, 1995). Dopamine, therefore, does not seem to mediate liking but is involved mainly in wanting, in the pursuit of natural pleasant rewards or through the drug use.

Another advantage of this theoretical approach lies in the methodological stage, which is no longer based only on self-reported evaluation tools, but mainly on behavioural and physiological pleasure evaluation procedures, that also permit to investigate the unconscious components of gratification.

Anhedonia might be the result of a dysregulation of any of the aforementioned components (wanting, liking, learning), rather than the mere absence of the ability to feel pleasure. Furthermore, it can be expressed both at a conscious and unconscious level (Rømer Thomsen et al., 2015), so such an extent that the use of self-referenced rating scales for its measurement is restrictive. In addition to the studies conducted on animals and to the contribution of translational neuroscience, the findings from behavioural and neuroimaging studies on humans support the hypothesis that various subtypes of anhedonia correspond to a dysregulation of the systems that underlie not only the ability to experience gratification but also the ability to pursue and/or learn it. All these considerations have direct implications for the diagnosis and treatment of anhedonia.

In a review work on anhedonia in depression, Treadway and Zald (2010) conclude that, despite decades of clinical investigation and research on the role of dopamine, the empirical evidence still remains confused and often contradictory, precisely due to the use of a non-specific view of anhedonia, without a differentiation between the consummatory and motivational aspects of behaviour aimed at rewarding. Taking into account that liking – hence anhedonia tied to the consummatory phase – is thought to be linked mostly to the opioid system, the ventromedial prefrontal cortex and the amygdala, while wanting – hence motivational anhedonia – to dopamine and basal ganglia, the concept of anhedonia needs to be redefined, especially by distinguishing between motivation deficits and pleasure experience deficits. There is also a theoretical gap between the preclinical and clinical models of anhedonia, which can only be filled by conceptualizing the anhedonia as a "background aspect", i.e. therefore in terms of process and then of phenomenon, not only of symptom.

Hedonic processes, therefore, occur in a heterogeneous and different way from one individual to another and in the context of different mental disorders, and their dysregulation is conceivable as an imbalance between the different components of the process itself. Normally, the subcomponents of the process (wanting, liking and learning) are balanced over the course of time, but a dysregulation affecting only one of them can lead to the manifestation of different symptoms or subtypes of anhedonia. More specific studies would be needed to evaluate the nuances, even at the subjective level, of such a complex mechanism, in order to better understand the psychic disorders in which anhedonia occurs. At present, the research data available support the idea that all the components of the hedonic process are altered at the same time in different disorders; however, these data are biased by the use of experimental models based on a theory that does not include the identification of the subcomponents of anhedonia. For example, it would not be surprising to verify that some aspects of conscious liking remain unchanged in such disorders as depression or schizophrenia, while the aspects of wanting and learning are more compromised. Some studies already support this idea, showing that in the aforementioned pathologies, there is rather a reduced willingness to seek gratification and a reduced ability to learn from punishment and reward, while all that is characterized as liking remains apparently intact (based on the example on taste reactivity evaluations).

Anhedonia in the framework of emotional/motivational systems

The neuroscientific hypothesis of a subdivision of the hedonic process into different components, correlated to distinct cerebral circuits, has the unquestionable merit of making the understanding of the anhedonic experience more complex and hopefully closer to subjective reality, which is extremely pervasive and invalidating in many psychopathological conditions, with consequent implications for diagnosis and therapy.

However, it is still evident that neuroscientific studies on hedonic processes are partly disconnected from other areas of interest potentially connected to it. In particular, many studies are strongly influenced by a theoretical framework, which includes the broader territory of investigation on emotions, burdened in recent decades by behaviourist conceptions that have not given any importance to the study of so-called emotional feelings (because of the affective aspects related to emotions), and by the cognitive theories that have instead considered them for a long time as a sub-category of cognitive processes.

Under this perspective, the four decades of studies by neuroscientist Jaak Panksepp, the founder of Affective Neuroscience, appear revolutionary. Starting from the evolutionist assumption that affective emotions are present even in lower animal species, Panksepp tried to demonstrate that our emotional feelings, or primitive emotional affects, arise from ancient neuronal circuits located at the subcortical level. This theoretical perspective also completely overturned the neuroscientific methodological approach necessary for the study of emotions.

Panksepp postulated the presence, in the ancient subcortical regions of the mammalians' brain, of at least seven emotional-affective systems, remaining however open to the possibility of identifying others. Each of the systems of SEARCH, FEAR, ANGER, LUST, CARE, PANIC/SUFFER-ING and PLAY control distinct but specific types of behaviour associated with superimposable psychological changes. Furthermore, such systems are thought to generate distinct types of affective awareness in humans (For a detailed review of this topic, see the beginning of this volume and Pank-sepp's work *The Archaeology of Mind,* 2014).

Anhedonia and the SEEKING system

In Panksepp's theoretical-experimental model, the SEEKING system is the most important, as it is involved in the correct functioning of all the other systems. It corresponds to what is traditionally called the Rewarding system, which has been extensively discussed in the previous paragraphs. However, the latter definition, in the light of the theoretical perspective of Affective Neuroscience, appears outdated and incomplete, albeit widespread. Speaking of reward presupposes that the pleasant experience derives from obtaining something, while this is only partially true, as the SEEKING system plays a crucial role in the state of desire (wanting), activation and persistence of a purposeful behaviour. These aspects of the research system that are independent from obtaining the reward are not taken into adequate consideration in many studies which, mostly conducted on animals, assume that these behave with a certain degree of intentionality; conventional studies on emotions exclude *a priori* the possibility of considering that the emotional abilities of "primary process", as Panksepp defines them, mediate in animals the so-called "intentions in action", i.e. their becoming active agents in their natural environment, and that these abilities, in humans, are precursors of the "intentions to act".

The anatomy of the SEEKING system includes the ascending pathway from the VTA and reaches three main destinations, namely the medial prosencephalic fascicle and the lateral hypothalamus (MFB-LH), the nucleus accumbens (NAS) and the medial prefrontal cortex via the mesolimbic and mesocortical dopaminergic pathways. The VTA dopaminergic neurons receive input from many other brain areas. In some mammals, the ascending dopaminergic pathways reach the frontal cortical regions, but in humans, they reach the sensory cortices, naturally in relation to the fact that in humans, the SEEKING system involves superior cognitive functions. The SEEKING system is mainly powered by dopamine, but it seems that glutamate also plays an essential role in the acquired functions of the system (what we may define appetitive learning). Overall, the SEEKING system is mostly responsible for our feelings of involvement and excitement in waiting and searching for the resources necessary for survival. In the human being, it is also activated in relation to the most variegated and mature desires and needs, such as aesthetic needs. However, if inactivated, it unequivocally produces (like in animals) a state that contains many of the characteristics of anhedonia, especially the lack of motivation. In Panksepp's formulation, the SEEKING system corresponds exclusively to the sub-component called *wanting* according to the Robinson and Berridge model previously described.

Anhedonia and the PANIC/GRIEF system

Based on the study of the hedonic processes and the identification of their different components, in addition to the parallelism between the *wanting* sub-component and the Research system, there is sufficient theoretical-experimental evidence to support the hypothesis of a correlation between the *liking* component and the so-called system of Suffering (PANIC/GRIEF system), which Affective Neuroscience is particularly focused on.

The PANIC/GRIEF system includes the cerebral areas of the anterior cingulus, the dorsomedial thalamus and the periaqueductal gray, and is mainly regulated by opioids and oxytocin. It has two faces as it can cause a depressive state resulting from separation but also return feelings of comfort and security when secure social bonds are restored. Several studies have shown that social bonding is part of an "addiction" process, which is partly promoted by some of the brain systems that account for pathological addiction to psychotropic substances. On the other hand, the research system contributes to the formation of social and sexual bonds in adults (Insel, 2003).

The endogenous substances that have so far proved to be able to reduce suffering, through an overall deactivation of this system, are opioids, oxytocin and prolactin, while glutamate and the release factor of corticotropin (CRF), neuropeptides generally implicated in stress reactions, activate it.

Overall, the activation of the PANIC/GRIEF system causes a state of psychic pain very different from what was previously defined as "lack of motivation and desire". Conversely, it is closer to the panic caused by separation anxiety and necessarily derived from the perception of the loss of something desired and already experienced as necessary for one's well-being. It is therefore a feeling of loss (grief) deeply rooted in social need and attachment processes. Beyond the parallelism between this specific aspect of "lack of pleasure" and liking, the theoretical-clinical consequences appear evident. First of all, unlike the liking subcomponent, this anhedonic aspect is not relegated exclusively to the symptomatic experience of the absence of pleasure, but is deeply rooted in the suffering from an emotional loss; second, the location of the system in the ancient subcortical structures of the brain and its connection with the SEEKING system give room to profound reflections on how the lack of desire and motivation partly determines the depressive response characterized mostly by the absence of pleasure, establishing a sort of interdependent hierarchy between experienced systems/effects. Further reflections on the difference and the psychopathological roles of the different aspects of anhedonia would be necessary.

Anhedonia and the dysregulation of self-related processing

Hedonic processes can be conceived as deriving from a complex and delicate balance of various components, corresponding to specific neuronal circuits that if altered, even partially, can lead to the development of different symptoms, and therefore different subtypes of anhedonia.

A very important implication of focusing mainly on the motivational-appetitive component that resides in the SEEKING system, therefore shifting the focus of the study of anhedonic experiences towards primitive emotional/affective aspects, is the insertion of real-life anhedonic experience within a more complex conception of the subjective experience.

One of the most relevant contributions of Affective Neuroscience and of the study of emotional/motivational systems comes from the wider research on the so-called Self-Related Processing.

Although the nature of the Self has been one of the crucial themes of philosophical thought, starting from Greek philosophy, in the neuroscientific field there is perhaps no more controversial and still the largely unexplored theme. Without being entangled in the different conceptions of the Self and the consequent different study approaches that have arisen, the experimental data suggest that the Self is not a prerogative of human beings only. Humans share with many animal species a *core self*, a basic self with related common neural substrates, which gives to an organism the ability to correlate interoceptive stimuli with exteroceptive stimuli deriving from the external world. From an evolutionary point of view, there seems to be a similarity gradient across the different mammal species in the basic emotional, cognitive and neural aspects, as several studies have shown.

Affective Neuroscience has given an enormous contribution to the development of this assumption, providing a picture clear and exhaustive enough of how the *core self* deals exactly with the activation of basic emotional/affective systems. The core self may be conceived as the 'operations centre' that caters for the body's most urgent needs by activating: i) the Search system to try and meet homeostatic needs first (food, water and thermoregulation) and then subtler needs (Denton, 2006); ii) the Anger and Fear systems to avoid risks and physical injury and to compete effectively for the available resources; iii) the Lust system, to guarantee the perpetuation of the species. The Care, Suffering and Play systems, strongly influenced by the Search system, were presumably integrated into the core self at a later stage of evolution.

While the theoretical/experimental framework of Affective Neuroscience constitutes a strong conceptual basis for the study of the processes related to self-perception, some authors combined the studies on subcortical levels with the study of the higher, more evolved aspects that are peculiar to the human species. Georg Northoff in particular, as an addition to the emotional/motivational systems theory, formulated the broader and more complex concept of *Self Related Processing*, conceived as the interaction between subcortical circuits and body representations, that are affective and emotional and cortical structures, whose prevailing function is cognitive, situated in the medial frontal regions. The existence of a specific neural network is assumed, in common to multiple species, having the function of integrating body and brain states with the surrounding environment, so as to coordinate and direct needs and desires. With regard to functional brain organization, subcortical networks regulate basic body processes of attentive, homeostatic, emotional and motivational nature (Northoff & Panksepp, 2008). Emotional/motivational systems, as they are postulated by Affective Neuroscience, are an integral part of this level. Their activation leads to a consistent form of self-representation, while their connection with fronto-medial regions first, and then with the dorsolateral prefrontal cortex (where the working memory resides) leads to the connection between external and internal world, and hence to the possibility to set up, with the other parts of the brain, an emotionally and psychologically meaningful world. Later on, superior cognitive functions contribute to the learning process.

Self-related processing is related to the activity of subcortical and cortical midline structures (SCMS) and other limbic structures, like the insula. In addition, in man, the PAG and the adjacent tectum, essential structures in the study of emotional/motivational systems, show the highest convergence of sensorimotor and emotional processing.

Within the framework of the studies on self-related processing, it also appears that the Search system plays a central role. Some studies have shown that the neural activity relating to self-relatedness is the same that takes place when a reward process is activated; reward and self-related processes seem to share the same evaluation processes. In addition, the connection between subcortical search regions with other subcortical regions (hypothalamus, amygdala and dorsomedial thalamus) and cortical reasons (medial prefrontal cortex) seems to be shared in both processes. The consequent hypothesis is that affective/emotional processes, especially those related to appetitive and search aspects, play a fundamental role and are an integral part of the core self, and therefore of a basic perception and representation of the self.

Considering that the most evolved social functions, like the Theory of Mind, are developed starting from the core self, and given the experimental evidence that neural circuits (SCMS) are recruited by self-relatedness processes and empathy-related processes together, the core self may be defined as a relational self, separate from other aspects of the self (i.e., narrative, autobiographic, conscious), although related to them. The assumption that emotional/motivational systems, and the Search system in particular, are part of the core self, and the evidence of their being in common to other species, leads to conceiving the most evolved aspects of the self as more species-specific and deriving from superior, mostly cortical brain functions, that are however anatomically and functionally related to the SCMS.

In the light of these considerations, it is self-evident that, if the anhedonic experience is thought to be caused, in part, by Seeking system alterations, this will inevitably lead to attributing a very important role to anhedonic clinical pictures as correlates of profound alterations of the perception of the self, especially of the bodily self. In this view, anhedonia would hardly lend itself to being regarded as a mere secondary symptom arising from an alteration of the cortical neurotransmission exchange, which would instead represent only one of the possible consequences of deeper and more complex self-structuring processes.

Towards a new notion of anhedonia

Based on the considerations formulated in the preceding paragraphs, it is clear that the concept of anhedonia, originally developed taking into account the complexity and heterogeneity of the experience related to it, has been downsized, in the course of time, to an objectifiable symptom. Its re-definition in terms of subcomponents has certainly the merit of having distinguished certain aspects (appetitive, consummatory and learning-related) that were confused at both theoretical and clinical level, and of having linked them empirically to separate neurobiological systems. However, studying anhedonia only by recovering its more definite aspects and categorizing the clinical pictures where they prevail is equally reductive, in respect of such a major psychic aspect as the hedonic experience.

Affective Neuroscience has partly resumed the need to find a better conceptual and neurobiological definition for various components of pleasure and has the unquestionable merit of having cast light on the evolutionary precocity of the appetitive/motivational aspect (related to the Seeking system, that is thought to be "primary" compared to the others from an evolutionary and also experiential perspective) and of the consummatory aspect (related to the Panic/Suffering system). Moreover, if the Suffering system is conceived as related to the Care system and, overall, closely linked to affective dependence, the focus may be brought on the role of separation experiences in certain clinical cases where the presence of an alteration of consummatory pleasure appears more evident. Such conceptual leap, made possible by Affective Neuroscience, relates above all to the theory of the earlier development of emotional/motivational systems, that not only promote and regulate bottom-up the functioning of the neural structures where the so-called "second-level and third-level" emotional processes are thought to reside (according to Panksepp) but are also essential for structuring the most precocious and basic sense of the Self, i.e. the core self.

In this conceptual scenario, anhedonia, in all its complexity, would be regarded as the direct expression of alterations of the self rather than as a symptom; as a consequence, the clinical pictures where it is present should be subject to a more exhaustive evaluation, based on a model intrinsically related to the structuring of the self in the early stages of life, in connection with precocious experiences.

Taking into account the cross-connection of subcortical structures where emotional/motivational systems reside, cortical midline structures [part of the Default Mode Network (DMN)] and other cortical networks, an imbalance of the various neural circuits towards an increase in the DMN and a reduction in the cortical inhibitory action may lead to an accentuation of the reflexive state and to a closure from the external world, a process that has already been experimentally shown in schizophrenia (Hoptman et al., 2010; Whitfield-Gabrieli et al., 2009). Given that the Seeking system is greatly involved in the general balance, it is reasonable to assume that such dysregulation might lead to a form of anhedonic experience characterized mostly by a reduction in motivation and appetitive drives and consequently by self-withdrawal, as observed in psychotic patients. Vice-versa, a situation without alterations in the Seeking system but with compromised Suffering and Care systems may be expected to engender an anhedonic experience characterized by a reduction in the consummatory behaviour but, at the same time, by a continuous drive towards seeking gratification. These experiences, which imply a lesser deterioration of relational abilities, are more typical of clinical conditions of substance dependence, but also of melancholia. It should be taken into account, however, that the impossibility to achieve the full severability of neuronal regulation mechanisms (as proved by Affective Neuroscience) implies an intersection of different facets of the anhedonic experience (possibly with one or more aspects prevailing over others). This would suggest, from a clinical perspective, that anhedonia should not be limited to the mere diagnostic sphere but rather used to evidence the precocity of, and the degree of damage suffered by the affective systems, in order to provide an evaluation of clinical seriousness.

References

Ahmed, S.H. & Koob, G.F. (1998). Transition from moderate to excessive drug intake: change in hedonic set point. *Science, 282*, 298–300.

American Psychiatric Association. (1983). *Diagnostic and statistical manual of mental disorders (3rd ed.)*. Washington: Author.

American Psychiatric Association. (2001). *Diagnostic and statistical manual of mental disorders (4th ed.)*. Washington: Author.

American Psychiatric Association. (2013). *Diagnostic and statistical manual of mental disorders (5th ed.)*. Washington: Author.

Andreasen, N.C. (1982). Negative symptoms in schizophrenia. Definition and reliability. *Archives of General Psychiatry, 39(7)*, 784–788.

Balleine, B.W. & Killcross, S. (2006). Parallel incentive processing: an integrated view of amygdala function. *Trends in Neuroscience, 29*, 272–279.

Bannon, M.J. (1995). The dopamine transporter: potential involvement in neuropsychiatric disorders. In: F.E. Bloom & D.J. Kupfer (eds.), *Psychopharmacology: The Fourth Generation of Progress* (179–188). New York: Raven Press.

Baxter, M.G. & Murray, E.A. (2002). The amygdala and reward. *Nature Review Neuroscience, 3*, 563–573.

Berridge, K. & Robinson, T.E. (1998). What is the role of dopamine in reward: hedonic impact, reward learning, or incentive salience? *Brain Research Reviews, 28,* 309–369.

Berridge, K.C. (1996). Food reward: brain substrates of wanting and liking. *Neuroscience and Biobehavioral Reviews, 20,* 1–25.

Berridge, K.C. & Kringelbach, M.L. (2008). Affective neuroscience of pleasure: reward in humans and animals. *Psychopharmacology, 199,* 457–480.

Blanchard, J.J. & Cohen, A.S. (2006). The structure of negative symptoms within schizophrenia: implications for assessment. *Schizophrenia Bulletin, 32,* 238–245.

Blanchard, J.J., Horan, W.P. & Brown, S.A. (2001). Diagnostic differences in social anhedonia: a longitudinal study of schizophrenia and major depressive disorder. *Journal of Abnormal Psychology, 110,* 363–371.

Bleuler, E. (1911). *Dementia Praecox oder Gruppe der Schizophrenien/Dementia Praecox or the Group of Schizophrenias.* New York: International Universities Press.

Bovasso, G.B. (2001). Cannabis abuse as a risk factor for depressive symptoms. *American Journal of Psychiatry, 158,* 2033–2037.

Brunello, N., Akiskal, H., Boyer, P., Gessa, G.L., Howland, R.H., Langer, S.Z., et al. (1999). Dysthymia: clinical picture, extent of overlap with chronic fatigue syndrome, neuropsychopharmacological considerations, and new therapeutic vistas. *Journal of Affective Disorders, 52,* 275–290.

Boyer, P., Lecrubier, Y., Puech, A.J., Dewailly, J. & Aubin, F. (1995). Treatment of negative symptoms in schizophrenia with amisulpride. *British Journal of Psychiatry, 166,* 68–72.

Callieri, B. (1995). "Dazione di senso nella psicosi melancolica". *NOOς, 1,* 61–70.

Chelnokova, O., Laeng, B., Eikemo, M., Riegels, J., Loseth, G., Maurud, H., et al. (2014). Rewards of beauty: the opioid system mediates social motivation in humans. *Molecular Psychiatry, 19,* 746–747.

Cloninger, C.R. (1994). *The Temperament and Character Inventory (TCI): A guide to its development and use.* St Louis: Washington University School of Medicine.

Cooper, J.C., Bloom, F.E. & Roth R.H. (2003). *The biochemical basis of neuropharmacology (8th edn.).* New York: Oxford University Press.

Davis, C. & Woodside, D.B. (2002). Sensitivity to the rewarding effects of food and exercise in the eating disorders. *Comprehensive Psychiatry, 43,* 189–194.

Denton, D. (2006). *The primordial emotions: the dawning of consciousness.* New York: Oxford University Press.

Der-Avakian, A. & Markou, A. (2012). The neurobiology of anhedonia and other reward-related deficits. *Trends in Neuroscience, 35,* 68–77.

Diana, M., Pistis, M., Muntoni, A. & Gessa, G. (1996). Mesolimbic dopaminergic reduction outlasts ethanol withdrawal syndrome: evidence of protracted abstinence. *Neuroscience, 71,* 411–415.

Ettemberg, A. (1993). Anhedonia. In: C.G. Costello (Ed.), *Symptoms of schizophrenia* (pp. 121–144). New York: Wiley.

Fawcett, J. (1993). The morbidity and mortality of clinical depression. Special Issue: affective disorders: current and future perspectives. *International Clinical Psychopharmacology, 8,* 217–220.

Franken, H.A., Zijlstra, C. & Muris, P. (2006). Are nonpharmacological induced rewards related to anhedonia? A study among skydivers. *Progress in Neuropsychopharmacology and Biological Psychiatry, 30,* 297–300.

Freud, S. (1920). *Beyond the pleasure principle.* SE *XIIX.* London: Karnac.

Freud, S. (1917). *Mourning and melancholia.* SE *XIV.* London: Karnac.

Frijda, N. (2010). On the nature and function of pleasure. In: M.L. Kringelbach & K.C. Berridge (Eds.), *Pleasures of the Brain* (pp. 99–112). New York: Oxford University Press.

Frith, U. & Frith, C. (2010). The social brain: allowing humans to boldly go where no other species has been. *Philosophical Transactions of the Royal Society London B: Biological Sciences, 365,* 165–176.

Gawin, F.H. & Ellinwood, E.H. Jr. (1988). Cocaine and other stimulants. Actions, abuse and treatment. *New England Journal of Medicine, 318,* 1173–1182.

Gawin, F.H. & Kleber, H.D. (1986). Abstinence symptomatology and psychiatric diagnosis in cocaine abusers. *Archives of General Psychiatry, 43,* 107–113.

Hasler, G., Drevets, W.C., Manji, H.K. & Charney, D.S. (2004). Discovering endophenotypes for major depression. *Neuropsychopharmacology, 29,* 1765–1781.

Heidegger, M. (1991). *Seminari di Zollikon.* Napoli: Guida.

Heinz, A., Schmidt, L.G. & Reischies, F.M. (1994). Anhedonia in schizophrenic, depressed, or alcohol dependent patients: neurobiological correlates. *Pharmacopsychiatry, 27,* 7–10.

Hoptman, M.J., Zuo, X.N., Butler, P.D., Javitt, D.C., D'angelo, D., Mauro, C.J., et al. (2010). Amplitude of low frequency oscillations in schizophrenia: a resting state fMRI study. *Schizophrenia Research, 117,* 13–20.

Hyman, S.E. & Fenton, W.S. (2003). Medicine. What are the right targets for psychopharmacology? *Science, 299,* 350–351.

Insel, T., Chuthbert, B., Garvey, M., Heinssen, R., Pine, D.S., Quinn, K. et al. (2010). Research domain criteria (RDoC): toward a new classification framework for research on mental disorders. *American Journal of Psychiatry, 167,* 748–751.

Insel, T.R. (2003). Is social attachment an addictive disorder? *Physiology and Behavior, 79,* 351–357.

Isella, V., Iurlaro, S., Piolti, R., Ferrarese, C., Frattola, L., Appollonio, I. et al. (2003). Physical anhedonia in Parkinson's disease. *Journal of Neurology, Neurosurgery, and Psychiatry, 74,* 1308–1311.

Jaffe, H. (1997). Opiates: clinical aspects. In: J.H. Lowinson, P. Ruiz, R.B. Millman & Langrod J.G. (Eds.), *Substance abuse – A comprehensive textbook, ed 3* (pp. 158–166). Baltimore: Williams & Wilkins.

Janiri, L., Martinotti, G., Dario, T., Reina, D., Paparello, F., Pozzi, G. et al. (2005). Anhedonia and substance-related symptoms in detoxified substance dependent subjects: a correlation study. *Neuropsychobiology, 52,* 37–44.

Jaspers, K. (1997). *General psychopathology.* Baltimore: Johns Hopkins University Press (Original work published 1911).

Kennerley, S.W., Dahmubed, A.F., Lara, A.H. & Wallis J.D (2009). Neurons in the frontal lobe encode the value of multiple decision variables. *Journal of Cognitive Neuroscience, 21,* 1162–1178.

Kennerley, S.W., Walton, M.E., Behrens, T.E., Buckley, M.J. & Rushworth, M.F. (2006). Optimal decision making and the anterior cingulate cortex. *Nature Neuroscience, 9,* 940–947.

King-Casas, B., Tomlin, D., Anen, C., Camerer, C.F., Quartz, S.R. & Montague, P.R. (2005). Getting to know you: reputation and trust in a two-person economic exchange. *Science, 308,* 78–83.

Klein, D. (1974). Endogenomorphic depression. A conceptual and terminological revision. *Archives of General Psychiatry, 31,* 447–454.

Knutson, B., Fong, G.W., Adams, C.M., Varner, J.L. & Hommer, D. (2001). Dissociation of reward anticipation and outcome with event-related fMRI. *Neuroreport, 12*, 3683–3687.

Knutson, B., Taylor, J., Kaufman, M., Peterson, R. & Glover, G. (2005). Distributed neural representation of expected value. *Journal of Neuroscience, 25*, 4806–4812.

Koob, G.F. & Le Moal, M. (2001). Drug addiction, dysregulation of reward, and allostasis. *Neuropsychopharmacology, 24*, 97–129.

Kraepelin, E. (1919). *Dementia praecox and paraphrenia*. Edimburgh: Livingstone. (Original Work Published 1913).

Kringelbach, M.L. (2005). The human orbitofrontal cortex: linking reward to hedonic experience. *Nature Review Neuroscience, 6*, 691–702.

Kringelbach, M.L. & Berridge, K.C. (2009). Towards a functional neuroanatomy of pleasure and happiness. *Trends in Cognitive Science, 13*, 479–487.

Kringelbach, M.L., Lehtonen, A., Squire, S., Harvey, A.G., Craske, M.G., Holliday, I.E., et al. (2008). A specific and rapid neural signature for parental instinct. *PLoS One, 3*, e1664.

Kringelbach, M.L. & Rolls, E.T. (2003). Neural correlates of rapid reversal learning in a simple model of human social interaction. *Neuroimage, 20*, 1371–1383.

Leboyer, M., Bellivier, F., Nosten-Bertrand, M., Jouvent, R, & Mallet, J. (1998). Psychiatric genetics: search for phenotypes. *Trends in Neuroscience, 21*, 102–105.

Leknes, S. & Tracey, I. (2010). Pleasure and pain: masters of mankind. In: L. Kringelbach & K.C. Berridge (Eds.), *Pleasures of the Brain* (pp. 320–335). New York: Oxford University Press.

Loas, G. (1996). Vulnerability to depression: a model centered on Anhedonia. *Journal of Affective Disorders, 41*, 39–53.

Markou, A. & Koob, G.F. (1991). Postcocaine anhedonia. An animal model of cocaine withdrawal. *Neuropsychopharmacology, 4*, 17–26.

Martinotti, G., Cloninger, C.R. & Janiri, L. (2008b). Temperament and character inventory dimensions and Anhedonia in detoxified substance-dependent subjects. *American Journal of Drug and Alcohol Abuse, 34*, 177–183.

Martinotti, G., Di Nicola, M., Reina, D., Andreoli, S., Focà, F., Cunniff, A., et al. (2008a). Alcohol protracted withdrawal syndrome: the role of anhedonia. *Substance Use and Misuse, 43*, 271–284.

Meehl, P.E. (1962). Schizotaxia, schizotypy, schizophrenia. *American Psychologist, 17*, 827–838.

Meehl, P.E. (1973). *Psychodiagnosis. Selected papers*. Minneapolis: University of Minnesota Press.

Miller, N.S., Summers, G.L. & Gold, M.S. (1993). Cocaine dependence: alcohol and other drug dependence and withdrawal characteristics. *Journal of Addiction Disorders, 12*, 25–35.

Murray, E.A. (2007). The amygdala, reward and emotion. *Trends in Cognitive Science, 11*, 489–497.

Myin-Germeys, I., Peeters, F., Havermans, R., Nicolson, N.A., DeVries, M.V., Delespaul, P., et al. (2003). Emotional reactivity to daily life stress in psychosis and affective disorder: an experience sampling study. *Acta Psychiatrica Scandinavica, 107*, 124–131.

Northoff, G. & Panksepp, J. (2008). The trans-species concept of self and subcortical-cortical midline system. *Trends in Cognitive Sciences, 12(7)*, 259–264.

Oei, T.I., Verhoeven, W.M., Westenberg, H.G., Zwart, F.M. & van Ree, J.M. (1990). Anhedonia, suicide ideation and dexamethasone nonsuppression in depressed patients. *Journal of Psychiatry Research, 24,* 25–35.

Panksepp, J. & Biven, L. (2014). *The archaeology of mind: neuroevolutionary origins of human emotions.* New York: Norton & co.

Pecina, S. & Berridge, K.C. (2005). Hedonic hot spot in nucleus accumbens shell: where do mu-opioids cause increased hedonic impact of sweetness? *Journal of Neuroscience, 25,* 11777–11786.

Pecina, S., Smith, K.S. & Berridge, K.C. (2006). Hedonic hot spots in the brain. *Neuroscientist, 12,* 500–511.

Rado, S. (1956). *Psychoanalysis of behavior: collected papers (Vol.1).* New York: Grune & Stratton.

Rado, S. (1962). *Psychoanalysis of behavior: collected papers (Vol. 2).* New York: Grune & Stratton.

Ribot, T. (1896). *La Psychologie Des Sentiments.* Paris: Felix Alcan.

Robbins, D.R. & Alessi, N.E. (1985). Depressive symptoms and suicidal behavior in adolescents. *American Journal of Psychiatry, 151,* 249–498.

Robinson, T.E. & Berridge, K.C. (1993). The neural basis of drug craving: an incentive-sensitization theory of addiction. *Brain Research Reviews, 18,* 247–291.

Robinson, T.E. & Berridge, K.C. (2003). Addiction. *Annual Review of Psychology, 54,* 25–53.

Rømer Thomsen, K., Lou, H.C., Joensson, M., Hyam, J.A., Holland, P., Parsons, C.E., et al. (2011). Impact of emotion on consciousness: positive stimuli enhance conscious reportability. *PLoS One, 6,* e18686.

Rømer Thomsen, K., Whybrow, P.C. & Kringelbach, M.L. (2015). Reconceptualizing anhedonia: novel perspectives on balancing the pleasure networks in human brain. *Frontiers in Behavioral Neuroscience, 9,* 49.

Rothman, R.B. & Glowa, J.R. (1995). A review of the effect of dopaminergic agents on humans, animals, and drug-seeking behavior, and its implications for medication development. Focus on GBR 12909. *Molecular Neurobiology, 11,* 1–19.

Rush, A.J. & Weissenburger, J.E. (1994). Melancholic symptom features and DSM IV. *American Journal of Psychiatry, 151*(4), 489–498.

Rushworth, M.F. & Behrens T.E. (2008). Choice, uncertainty and value in prefrontal and cingulate cortex. *Nature Neuroscience, 11,* 389–397.

Salamone, J.D., Cousins, M.S. & Snyder, B.J. (1997). Behavioral functions of nucleus accumbens dopamine: empirical and conceptual problems with the Anhedonia hypothesis. *Neuroscience and Biobehavioral Reviews, 21,* 341–359.

Salimpoor, V.N., Benovoy, M., Larcher, K., Dagher, A. & Zatorre, R.J. (2011). Anatomically distinct dopamine release during anticipation and experience of peak emotion to music. *Nature Neuroscience, 14,* 257–262.

Sanfey, A.G., Rilling, J.K., Aronson, J.A., Nystrom, L.E. & Cohen, J.D. (2003). The neural basis of economic decision-making in the Ultimatum Game. *Science, 300,* 1755–1758.

Schneider, K. (1955). *Les Personalities psychopathiques.* Paris: P.U.F.

Silverstone, P.H. (1991). Is anhedonia a good measure of depression? *Acta Psychiatrica Scandinavica, 83,* 249–250.

Smeraldi, E. (1998). Amisulpride versus fluoxetine in patients with dysthymia or major depression in partial remission: a double-blind, comparative study. *Journal of Affective Disorders, 48,* 47–56.

Smith, K.S., Tindell, A.J., Aldridge, J.W. & Berridge, K.C. (2009). Ventral pallidum roles in reward and motivation. *Behavioral Brain Research, 196,* 155–167.

Snaith, P. (1993). Anhedonia: a neglected symptom of psychopatology. *Psychological Medicine, 23,* 957–966.

Tellembach, H. (1975). *Melanconia: Storia del problema, Endogeneità, Tipologia, Patogenesi, Clinica.* Roma: Il Pensiero Scientifico Editore.

Treadway, M.T. & Zald, D.H. (2010). Reconsidering anhedonia in depression: lessons from translational neuroscience. *Neuroscience & Biobehavioral Reviews, 35,* 537–555.

Volkow, N.D., Fowler, J.S., Wang, G.J. & Goldstein, R.Z. (2002). Role of dopamine, the frontal cortex and memory circuits in drug addiction: insight from imaging studies. *Neurobiology of Learning and Memory, 78,* 610–624.

Walton, M.E., Kennerley, S.W., Bannerman, D.M., Phillips, P.E. & Rushworth, M.F. (2006). Weighing up the benefits of work: behavioral and neural analyses of effort-related decision making. *Neural Networks, 19,* 1302–1314.

Weitbrecht, H.J. & Glatzel, J. (1979). *Psychiatrie in Grundriss.* Berlin: Springer.

Whitfield-Gabrieli, S., Thermenos, H.W., Milanovic, S., Tsuang, M.T., Faraone, S.V., McCarley, R.W., et al. (2009). Hyperactivity and hyperconnectivity of the default network in schizophrenia and in first degree relatives of persons with schizophrenia. *Proceedings of National Academy of Science U.S.A., 106,* 1279–1284.

Whybrow, P.C. (1998). *A Mood Apart; The Thinkers Guide to Emotion and its Disorder.* New York: Harper Perennial.

Willner, P. (1995). Dopaminergic mechanism in depression and mania. In: F.E. Bloom & D.J. Kupfer (Eds.), *Psychopharmacology: The Fourth Generation of Progress* (921–931). New York: Raven Press.

Willner, P., Hale, A.S. & Argyropoulos, S. (2005). Dopaminergic mechanism of antidepressant action in depressed patients. *Journal of Affective Disorders, 86,* 37–45.

Wise, R.A. (1982). Neuroleptics and operant behaviour: the anhedonia hypothesis. *Behavioral and Brain Sciences, 5,* 39–88.

World Health Organisation. (1978). *Mental Disorders: Glossary and Guide to Their Classification with the Ninth Revision of the International Classification of Diseases.* Genève: WHO.

Zald, D.H. & Kim, S.W. (1996a). Anatomy and function of the orbital frontal cortex. I. Anatomy, neurocircuitry; and obsessive-compulsive disorder. *Journal of Neuropsychiatry and Clinical Neuroscience, 8,* 125–138.

Zald, D.H. & Kim, S.W. (1996b). Anatomy and function of the orbital frontal cortex. II. Function and relevance to obsessive–compulsive disorder. *Journal of Neuropsychiatry and Clinical Neuroscience, 8,* 249–261.

10 Motivational systems in child development

A neuropsychoanalytic perspective on disorders of attention and learning

Andrea Clarici, Andrea Zanettovich, Antonio Alcaro

Introduction

What is the role of emotional processes in the so-called developmental learning disorders (DLD) of child development? In what way is learning and attention in children influenced by emotional processes and relational experiences? Contemporary neuropsychology underestimates the relevance of emotional and especially relational factors in DLD (Miller, 2015). In the past, a child who did not learn was considered either stupid (unable to learn) or lazy (doesn't want to learn). Today, these two categories have been replaced by other terms which, although seemingly more charitable and understanding, are disguised variants of the same: "stupidity"[1] corresponds to a set of well-defined *deficit disorders* (the dyslexic child is an example), while the lazy and insubordinate child is diagnosed with *Oppositional Defiant Disorder* (ODD, American Psychiatric Association, 2013). Both of these two diagnoses are matched by corresponding precise therapeutic "protocols" linked to the different ways of interpreting these "clinical pictures": (1) stimulation or (2) "bringing back into line" (an approach that might include medical-pharmacological treatment).

Each of these points of view rules out the possibility that the child might be displaying an adaptive reaction encompassing a complex situation, from the relational (intrapsychic or interpersonal) standpoint – a condition requiring an equally complex diagnostic and therapeutic response. Fortunately, nowadays, even those who view learning from a cognitive and neuroscientific perspective (Immordino-Yang and Damasio, 2007) feel more inclined to include the *motivational variable* in cases where a conflict, an inhibition or a psycho-relational behavior disturbance can be found underlying a child's learning problem (Immordino-Yang, 2015). This is because even in the field of cognitive psychology, there is now a general awareness that learning processes are complex and connected. They occur at different levels (see, e.g., the distinction made between the various memory systems:

DOI: 10.4324/9781003198741-12

implicit, procedural, semantic, explicit, working, autobiographical, etc.) and it is now universally recognized that learning is also supported by affective and relational dynamics. Further, these dynamics include the basic neurobiological processes common to both man and other animal species. From this point of view, we believe the description of emotional processes that Jaak Panksepp gives in his important research (Panksepp, 1998 and 2014 for a summary) is particularly enlightening with regard to these issues and can help create increasingly cogent and verifiable hypotheses in the field of child neuropsychological development.

The neuro-ethological studies carried out by Panksepp in the past 50 years show that affectivity is located at the heart of individual neuropsychic organization and that it is the missing link between the primary processes of animal instinct and the more advanced functions of the human mind (Alcaro and Panksepp, 2014; Panksepp, 2011).

His research focuses on a very ancient part of the brain, the source of instinctive behavior and the site of homeostatic and visceral control functions, which Paul MacLean (1990) referred to as the "reptilian brain". From the anatomic standpoint, the area includes a number of deep subcortical regions extending along the brain stem and the diencephalon (Figure 10.1). Panksepp identifies this area of the brain, located between the spinal cord and the two cerebral hemispheres, as the locus of the core-self, because it houses the instinctual and archetypal nucleus of the personality. Indeed, not only is it the seat of all the body's vital functions, it is also the place where some of the brain circuits responsible for generating the seven primary

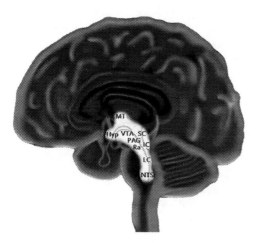

Figure 10.1 The figure shows a median section of the brain. The area highlighted in blue represents the set of medial subcortical structures that make up the core-Self region. [Abbreviations: Hyp = hypothalamus; IC = inferior colliculus; LC = locus coeruleus; MT = mid-dorsal thalamus; NTS = nucleus of the solitary tract; PAG = periaqueductal gray area; Ra = rafe nuclei; SC = superior colliculus; VTA = ventral tegmental area.].

emotional systems[2] and an ancestral form of affective consciousness are located (Alcaro and Panksepp, 2014; Panksepp and Biven, 2012).

The seven basic emotional systems "define a series of common biological values that unite us all in the face of the various conflicts that life obliges us to face" (Solms and Turnbull 2002 pp. 130–131). The basic emotions channel the whole bundle of our behaviors and learning along certain "adaptive paths". In this chapter, we therefore aim to use an approach based on neuropsychoanalysis (Kaplan-Solms and Solms, 2002) to combine the contributions of the affective neurosciences and psychoanalysis to try to describe how emotions influence learning in children from birth and how affective dynamics dovetail with cognitive ones in the development of the mind and nervous system in relational life.

It is precisely starting from basic emotional promptings that the child begins to develop the primal feelings that draw the Self into contact with the outside world and thus, through learning, to build an increasingly sophisticated network of representations of the world and of the objects therein (initially based on "affections," feelings or motivational states emerging from the visceral component of the bodily Self, then through representations of perceptible and concrete "things," including the body's musculoskeletal and proprioceptive element). In a landmark article on child development, Panksepp himself (2001, p. 132) outlines his scientific approach thus:

> One aim of healthy development is to generate harmonious, well-integrated layers of emotional and higher mental processes, as opposed to conflicts between emotional and cognitive experiences. To understand such processes scientifically, we need to conceptualize the deep nature of the emotional brain and the psychiatric difficulties that can emerge from underlying imbalances.

The seeking system and the other primary process emotional systems

Today, it is universally recognized that children do not passively absorb salient information from the environment but are active and interested "seekers" (as will be considered in the last paragraph of this chapter, the analogies between the child, a "researcher" from the first days of life, and the scientist are very close); they are driven to learn primarily based on innate motivational forces. Although the vast number of behaviorist and neuro-cognitive studies have emphasized the role of external reinforcements (positive and negative) in learning, the truly decisive element in all learning appears to be an instinctive, emotional disposition common to both humans and animals, which urges the individual to actively explore and interact with the world; this instinctual disposition leads to frustrating as well as gratifying experiences. Without this endogenous drive, it would not be possible to remain open to novelty and to allow the input and assimilation of external reality, of "the new," of "unfamiliar" and "the foreign" within the individual's psycho-behavioral structure.

The neuro-ethological studies of Jaak Panksepp and his numerous collaborators have identified a neurodynamic circuit in the brain that controls, organizes and integrates the set of orientation, exploration, search and approach behaviors, and has therefore been called the *seeking* system[3] (Alcaro, et al., 2007; Alcaro and Panksepp, 2011; Ikemoto and Panksepp, 1999, Figure 10.2).

This primary emotional system, many of whose neuroanatomical, neurochemical and neurodynamic aspects are known, is expressed subjectively in the form of feelings of desire, curiosity and enthusiasm, through which individuals express interest in the world, directing them towards sources of gratification of their basic survival and reproductive needs. Furthermore, clinical studies confirm that the learning capacity is strongly influenced by the emotional disposition to *seek* and by the way in which the environment is able to support it. For example, when this system is not very active, as in the case of anhedonic depressive symptoms, the individual is emotionally uninterested in the surrounding environment and is unable to learn from it (Panksepp and Watt, 2011). In contrast, when this system is too reactive to stimuli from the outside world, as in the case of *Attention Deficit Hyperactivity Disorders* (ADHD; see Section 10 below), the individual becomes extremely easily distracted and his/her ability to concentrate (and think) is compromised (Badgaiyan, et al., 2015; Panksepp, 2007). For long wrongly considered merely a pleasure or reward system, the emotional *seeking* system does not provide post-consumption satisfaction, but rather an appetitive activation that stimulates our interest in the world, generating the expectation that something "good" will happen, but only if we explore the environment and interact

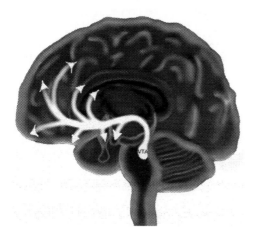

Figure 10.2 The SEEKING system: **The median** section of the brain schematically represents the ascending projections of the mesolimbic dopaminergic system which constitute the main activating component of the system that process our affective thrusts to approach or avoid a source of a bodily or mental need. The SEEKING system stems mainly from the Ventral Tegmental Area (VTA) of the mesencephalus.

with its objects. This is why the *seeking* system has been compared to the neurodynamic counterpart of the psychoanalytic concept of libido (Kaplan-Solms and Solms, 2002). Usually, this system is activated by specific biological drives (needs) that perform a fundamental function in the survival of the individual and the species, such as hunger, thirst, sex, etc. However, the emotional disposition activated by this system is non-specific and non-objective (without specific goals): it "does not know" what it is looking for, limiting itself to "energetic exploration" and approaching everything based on perceived need. Therefore, to satisfy an animal's adaptive needs, the *seeking* system must inevitably interact with perceptual and memory systems, with which it is closely connected and which represent the "thing," object, sexual partner, prey or nourishment that can fulfill that particular need. The representative systems (mainly cortical) are the structures that provide the information (memory traces of past perceptual interactions between the subject and these objects) that guarantees the individual learns from experience. Although the *seeking* system has been studied mainly with reference to the behavior of laboratory animals, neurobiological evidence suggests that the evolutionarily more recent ramifications of this system at the level of the ventral and orbitofrontal areas of the human forebrain plays an essential role in thought processes in humans too (Alcaro and Panksepp, 2011). Put more simply, we are talking about a system capable of triggering not only the motor exploration of the external physical environment but also the mental exploration of the internal psychological, emotional, cognitive, and even conceptual environment (Depue and Collins, 1999; Passamonti, et al., 2015; see Clarici, 2014, pp. 36–42, for the definition of *examination of conceptual reality*). For example, recent studies show that dream activity depends directly on the neuroanatomical integrity of this system (Malcolm-Smith, et al., 2012; Solms, 2000) and on its neurochemical functionality (Dahan, et al., 2007). More generally, it is plausible that the *seeking* system's activity constitutes the emotional background or *milieu* that is indispensable for all thought processes, acting as the emotional vector of our imaginative activity. Borrowing from psychoanalytical theory, we could say that the ability to give form to our thoughts (to invest them with affective cathexis), i.e., to explore and manipulate them mentally (Bion, 1967), depends on this system, in order to then generate (or inhibit) a plan of action best able to fulfill our most pressing survival and reproductive needs.

The *seeking* system functions as a "compass," orienting all the other basic motivational systems: it is closely linked to the evolution of three other basic emotional systems, which tend to be linked to experiences of gratification: *lust* (Figure 10.3), that of *play* (Figure 10.4) and that of *care* (Figure 10.5; Panksepp and Biven, 2012). These are three social-emotional systems, which constitute an evolutionary extension of the *seeking* system, to the extent that it is co-opted in the search for stimuli and environmental conditions associated respectively with sexual behavior (finding the object that will satisfy sexual desire), playful interaction with peers (offering contact with

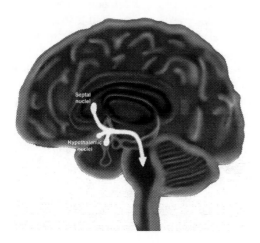

Figure 10.3 The **"positive" motivational systems** (Figures 10.3.4.5) are those that aim
to obtain a gratification and tend to the approach to the source of a
specific need: Figure 10.3 the **system of SEXUAL DESIRE (LUST)**
is the first (and more classically "Freudian") of the three systems underlying the gratification or satisfaction of a specific need. The central
anatomical-functional structures around which the motivational system of desire and sexual satisfaction are organized around the hypothalamus and the pellucid septum.

"objects" that enable the child to try to do what grown-ups do), and relationships of attachment and love. All three of these social-emotional systems, and especially the *seeking* system, obviously play a fundamental role
in learning processes, providing the primary motivational urge to have new
experiences and explore reality.

While the *seeking* disposition and its social derivatives constitute the primary thrust for the exploration and assimilation of novelty, other emotional
dispositions instead act in the opposite direction, that is, to distance the
child from the experiences of contact and knowledge, generating subjective
experiences of sorrow and suffering to prevent sources of greater frustration. The main control system for emotions related to potential frustration
(which therefore mediates the avoidance of psychic pain) and the one most
thoroughly studied among the so-called "negative emotional systems" is
probably the *fear* system (for a review, see LeDoux, 1998, 2015). From the
subjective point of view, this system generates feelings of fear-anxiety, and
from a behavioral point of view, it triggers active avoidance (flight) and passive avoidance (immobilization or motor freezing) responses (Figure 10.6).

The *rage (or* ANGER) system (Figure 10.7) is also activated by states of
frustration which occur when the child's actions aimed at a biologically significant goal are hindered. When triggered, it produces a subjective state of
anger and actions aimed at attacking and eliminating the obstacle thwarting

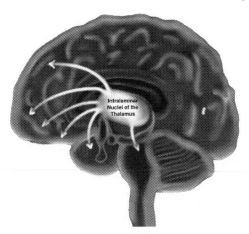

Figure 10.4 The **PLAY system** is another important system underlying gratification, whose primary structures are the intralaminar nuclei of the thalamus which regulate and modulate the functional organization of the frontal orbito-frontal regions and dorso-lateral prefrontal regions.

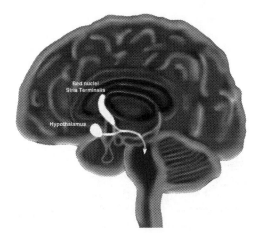

Figure 10.5 The CARE system is the third of the three systems to appease and obtain satisfaction on innate needs. The centre of this system is located in the regions of the bed nucleus of the stria terminalis, in the pre-optic area of the hypothalamus. These zones inform the medial hypothalamus which mediates the autonomic responses and the dorsal tegmental area (which regulate musculoskeletal motor responses) linked to feelings of attachment, as well as the periaqueductal gray (PAG) which confers the emotional sensations connected to these feelings. The habenula, on the other hand, seems connected to the inhibition of harmful behaviours for the offspring.

its well-being. The *sadness* system (separation, distress, and panic; Figure 10.8) is initially associated with feelings of anguish and panic due to the distancing of social support and is expressed with active beckoning behavior (vocalizations) whose purpose is to draw the caregiver closer. If this action fails to draw the caregiver back, after a while the state of agitation and anguish changes to sadness and the child gives up calling and shuts itself away from the outside world and prepares to give up hope of obtaining the object, experiencing this with a sense of grief, that is, with sorrow at its separation from the caregiver. For reasons identifiable in its neurochemistry and in the way it is designed to function, the *sadness* (separation, anxiety) system is intimately connected with the processes of socialization and parental care (for anatomical localization of the *panic* and *care* systems, see Figure 10.9).

Motivational and consciousness systems: their role in learning

Motivational systems signal to us our homeostatic state, that is they process information about our primary, bodily needs and send it to us, suggesting how and where to fulfill them in the outside world.

Mark Solms (2018) puts forward in *The Conscious Id*, a revolutionary hypothesis connecting psychoanalysis and affective neuroscience. Freud (1900) considered consciousness to be "a sensory organ for the perception of psychic qualities". Today, however, we know that consciousness is not perceptive; it is fundamentally affective. Consciousness is not primarily a perception, but an affective excitement (*arousal*). The function of consciousness is to inform the mind, "arousing it," on the state of the bodily needs essential for survival and invites one to take action to try to satisfy them. Our body is represented in two different ways (Solms, 2013): on the one hand, we have a representation of our exteroceptive body (or external body) and on the other an image relating to our interoceptive body (internal body; Fotopoulou and Tsakiris, 2017). These two aspects of the body are associated with different aspects of consciousness: thanks to the basic motivational systems, the brain stem (in the loci associated with the above-mentioned core-Self), supports the affective consciousness, while the cerebral cortex supports the cognitive component in consciousness. The latter can be conceptually superimposed on what in neuropsychology is called working memory (Baddeley and Hitch, 1974), the component in short-term memory that allows us to be aware of our current perceptions and the stimuli that come to us from the outside world, from inside our body and from our mind. This part of the short-term memory regarding our "present" is limited to only about seven audio-verbal memories and about five visual-spatial memories at a time, before being consolidated as long-term memory (Alberini, 2009).

The upper brain stem and the related motivational components are therefore the main source of affective consciousness, while the cerebral cortex is unconscious and derives its own, cognitive consciousness via a second route, from the brain stem (Solms, 2018). By transposing these concepts to the psychodynamic field, we could therefore say that the Id, the aspect of the mind from which instincts and drives derive and which functions according to the "pleasure principle," is fundamentally conscious and originates in these subcortical structures, while the Ego is made up of unconscious cortical memories and representations that can only secondarily become conscious thanks to the activation of the affective consciousness in response to certain needs. The cerebral cortex is therefore not the primary seat of conscious awareness. It is known that hydro-anencephalic children, who are born or develop without the cerebral cortex, are conscious, have the capacity for emotional learning, and respond to external stimuli (Merker, 2007).

Furthermore, it was believed that the insula (a portion of the cerebral cortex "hidden" within the convolutions of the other cerebral lobes) was the cortical seat of conscious awareness (Craig, 2009), but bilateral destruction of the cortex of the insula does not involve substantial loss of self-consciousness (Damasio, Damasio and Tranel, 2012). No cortical lesion leads to the definitive loss of consciousness: only damage to the subcortical areas leads to the cessation of consciousness (i.e. persistent coma) and the most localized area where damage leads to a persistent vegetative state is precisely the periaqueductal gray (the neural fulcrum of the core SELF). Using the analogy (so dear to Freud as regards psychic energy) of physical hydraulic systems, we could say that the cortex transforms the ephemeral and shapeless "liquid" states of activation of the brain stem into "mental solids" of memory traces stored in the neocortex (Solms, 2013). The cortex provides a representational (almost unlimited) memory space, which allows perceptive images to stabilize, consolidating them in the synaptic patterns of its circuits: only the cortex is therefore able to generate the mental objects that make up our conscious perceptions, the daydreams, our thoughts and fantasies. These representations are in themselves unconscious and the site of their elaboration is cortical; however, when consciousness is extended onto these representations by means of attention (see Section 10 below regarding child attention disorders), they are transformed into something conscious and stable, which can be thought of in cognitive consciousness or working memory.

Even the Self is the product of learning: the Self is that particular "mental solid" given by the sum of the representations of our external body (the body as an object) and internal (the body as a subject) that represents ourselves; it is a "stabilized representation of the subject of consciousness, an object experienced by the subject itself and acquired through learning" (Solms, 2013, p. 15). Some experiments have shown that it is easy to deceive our senses into perceiving foreign "objects" as belonging to our own body. In the 'rubber hand illusion' (Botvinick and Cohen, 1998) by synchronously touching a visible rubber hand and, at the same time, the subjects' own hand (hidden from view), it is possible in a very simple way to trick the subject into believing that the fake hand belongs to him or herself. Furthermore, it has been observed that the real hand undergoes a sharp drop in temperature at the moment in which this illusion prevails, demonstrating that both the external body and the internal body (and therefore our entire Self) are representations susceptible to continuous mental reworking (Tsakiris, 2010). Even the whole body can be deceived into feeling it belongs to another person, as in the 'body transfer illusion' (Petkova and Ehrsson, 2008): this involves placing a visor in front of the subject's eyes transmitting images from a camera placed on the forehead of another person who is in front of the subject (a "screen of consciousness" which shows the subject to him or herself). Again, the visual sensation is that of being in the other's body (dislocation of one's external body), but if the person is exposed to a sudden threat, the person is only frightened when the other's body is attacked (where he "feels" to be), not his own (which he sees threatened from "outside" as if he were threatened by a stranger; dislocation of his own internal body). We must therefore conclude that not only our representation of worldly things, internal and external objects (and we will also see words that can represent them), and even the representation of our Self (which includes our external and internal body) are constructs, learned experiences, representations that can become conscious (or remain unconscious) through activation by the affective consciousness.

The generative models of prediction in learning in childhood

Computational neuroscience (Friston, 2010) supports us in these hypotheses on the role of the cerebral cortex as a large reservoir of learned memories: the main task of the hierarchical structures of the central nervous system that culminates in the cortical organization is therefore not so much to produce a register of fixed and permanent memories of the external world as to generate predictive models to satisfy our basic needs and best guarantee our survival. The principal role of the cortical Ego is therefore to generate predictions based on the memories of our relationship with the external world so that what we find "outside" coincides as much as possible with what we feel are our "inside" needs: when this perceptual concordance is not reached, the Ego (with its stable and stratified tertiary processes) registers a predictive error (Friston, 2005). One sees in this a particular similarity with the psychoanalytic concepts of the identity of perception (Freud, 1900; Sandler, 1976). We can speculate, along the lines of computational neuroscience, that the Ego is regulated by predictive errors that represent psycho-neural events which cause the updating of predictive capabilities whenever they are contradicted by reality: when predictions (of the Ego) fail to reach their main goal (which is to reduce arousal and activation from feelings) this generates predictive errors that inform (the id) of the pressing need for an adjustment of the predictive model.

Prediction errors generate what Friston (2010) has called "free energy," a state of entropy, a tendency to chaos and disorder that can potentially lead the individual to the risk of survival. In our opinion, this concept appears very close to Sandler's (1960) idea of an intrapsychic safety principle as a fundamental regulator of mental functioning. The Bayesian model of the brain (Friston, 2012) is a probabilistic explanatory abstraction, based on mathematical theories of information applied to brain functions, which seeks to explain how these predictive models are generated to solve individual existential problems. According to this model, problems in the external world (such as intrapsychic conflicts) can be addressed (a) through perceptual inferences, which require the updating of one's predictions based on sensory feedback (and based on predictive errors); they lead to a bottom-up adjustment of the examination of reality which becomes more and more accurate or (b) through active inferences, implemented through the motor system of the planned action, which allow to select (according to a top-down modality) the perceptual afferents, "sampling" only those stimuli that are "pleasant" and avoiding the "unpleasant ones" To reconstitute and maintain our current generative model of internal and external reality, avoiding the predictive errors signaled by our feelings.

Free energy is measured by the brain's probability computational systems as "surprise" (Schwartenbeck, et al., 2013), a parameter that translates as an increase in the degree of uncertainty and insecurity, secondary to the unpredictability of the events we perceive or put in place to supply our basic needs for survival. The concept of surprise is taken from information theory and corresponds to what we could subjectively perceive as a feeling of being at the mercy of unpredictable forces, to a drastic decrease in our feelings of safety: here too we can find important references to the psychoanalytic concept of the background of safety suggested by Sandler (1960) and also with that of a secure base in infant development advanced by attachment theorists (Bowlby, 1988).

It is a major evolutionary advantage to have a system in one's mind/brain that measures one's entropy (i.e., any imbalance or deviation from the optimal range in our physical and psychic homeostasis). The motivational mechanisms underlying affective consciousness are our tool to measure these imbalances: any persistent homeostatic deviation runs the risk of being translated as a risk to the survival of the individual (from thermoregulation, hunger, sleep, to the loss of caregiver). All of these imbalances are immediately signaled by areas in the subcortical regions of the motivational systems highlighted by Panksepp (1998): each system registers, for the specific need it processes, any deviation from the optimal homeostatic range as *unpleasant affect*, while progressive restoration of homeostasis gives rise to *pleasant affect*. The achievement of homeostatic equilibrium corresponds to the reduction of the affective signal. In this way, confirmed predictions are increasingly automated: *the Ego becomes temporarily conscious due to the onset of a need and then returns to being unconscious.* Most of the Ego's predictions are repeated automatically: even cognitive psychology now recognizes that 95% of the brain's finalized activities are unconscious; only predictions falsified by reality generate predictive errors that arouse "surprise". This feeling leads to an increase in attentional salience and arouses the affective awareness of the conflict, we could say, between our expectations and reality. For our discussion, therefore, what we call attention is nothing other than the afferent, or perceptual component of the motivational systems; that part of the motivational process that continuously monitors and records the significant variations to our needs and which in turn informs the efferent, or active component to "seek" and which thereby creates a "thrust" to find the source of that specific need to be appeased. The conscious affective attentional activation allows us to reconsolidate (update) our predictive models, actually bringing about the temporary deconstruction of the synaptic connections at the basis of our memory processes and then reorganizing them in a new generative memory model (*i.e.*, the reconsolidation/consolidation cycle of declarative memories; Alberini, 2005).

The brain systems of memory and learning

Understanding the emotional basis of learning allows us to better understand how this may be disrupted in child development. Learning processes constitute the fundamental juncture for understanding the underlying properties and the adaptive function of our neuropsychic apparatus. As implicitly affirmed by the work of neuroscientists: *"We are our memory"* (Alberini, 2005). Research in neuropsychology has shown that memory processes are encoded in different ways, layered into systems organized hierarchically in our mind/brain. Affective neuroscience has contributed more and more evidence to this statement: from the neuronal and molecular level to that of the more sophisticated higher memory functions of the brain. Affective neuroscience has allowed us to clarify the complex picture of cerebral processes at the basis of conscious awareness, directed to our present, to our past and to the planning of our future, they are organized in elements which, in temporal and spatial continuity, between them, constitute the subjective "we". The contribution of affective neuroscience has been fundamental in focusing attention on some essential elements in the reconstruction of the complex mosaic of child learning and assimilation of experience.

All personal memories that accumulate in the mind/brain of the child are not only influenced by basic emotions but are also organized around the affective states characteristic of each emotion, so as to form a complex of actions and representations that incline towards an emotion. Janet (1889) had expressed this idea by speaking of "autonomous personality complexes". The personality complexes constitute sets of memory traces with a common objective-emotional value that can be well integrated both into the conscious aspects of the Ego, or that may act independently of our conscious will.

The memory traces formed by the processes of classical and operant conditioning, which we described in the previous paragraph, can act in a completely automatic way when they are not represented at the level of subjective consciousness. This is what cognitive psychologists define with as "implicit memory," or cognitive unconscious and psychoanalysts as *unrepressed unconscious* (Kandel, 1999; Kihlstrom, 1987; Schacter, 1996; Schore, 2011), to distinguish it from the *dynamic unconscious* (which we will discuss in Section 9 of this chapter). We all know the effects of these memories on behavior or on our subjective states, but we cannot have any perception of the memory link that is at its origin. Let us give some examples to illustrate: little Albert, as widely known, was conditioned by Watson (1930) to associate fear to the sight of a rabbit using the intense sound of a gong sound. The child was unable to understand rationally why the animal frightened him so. Similarly, an adult who has experienced a traumatic event may feel terrified at the sight of the stimuli that were present during the event, even if all conscious memories of that event have vanished. In other words, in these types of memories, the perceptual experiences that were present during the traumatic event establish a connection with a particular emotional disposition (in these cases, fear) and are able to trigger the fear response again, at a later time, in a completely automated fashion. Equally, motor habits or operant procedural memories that are established after one or many repetitions (depending on the level of the memorial process) also end up conditioning the individual's attitude and behavior in a unconscious way that is beyond voluntary control. For example, when our expectations are organized in such a way as to predict the failure of any attempt to cope with and overcome a stressful situation, the resulting depressive reaction is due to the unconscious action of these inner operating models (Seligman, 2006).

If we were entirely guided by unconscious memory, our past would be imposed upon us in a rather dictatorial way, leaving little room for subjective intentionality, and the external environment would condition us in an overly consistent fashion. This is what happens to animals with simpler and less evolved nervous systems such as the invertebrates, but also of many vertebrates, such as reptiles and fish. However, at some point in evolutionary history, there has been a qualitative leap of considerable importance (Alcaro and Panksepp, 2014): in parallel with the ability to thermo regulate, the brains of mammals and birds show intense metabolic activity when they are resting (resting-state activity). This can reach levels typical of active wakefulness, even exceeding it, in certain brain regions, such as the cortical midline structures (see Figure 10.1). This phenomenon is very evident in a specific phase of sleep, the REM phase, generally associated in humans with the occurrence of dreams (Hobson, 2009). Furthermore, the same phenomenon can also be found in conditions of inactive and relaxed wakefulness (Lu, et al., 2012; Mantini, et al., 2011). Human studies indicate that the intense brain activity during REM sleep and during inactive wakefulness is associated with the production of images and conscious thoughts, through which virtual scenarios are constructed using information accumulated throughout past experiences (Schacter, et al., 2012). We believe that the same processes may also occur in birds and other mammals, which exhibit surprising and unexpected cognitive abilities, perhaps very close to what we call imagination in humans (Crystal, 2012; Roberts, 2012). From our point of view, this activity forms the (phylogenetic and ontogenetic) basis of the acquisition of what Bion (1962, 1967) defined as "the capacity to think," or what he termed "the alpha function," meaning not so much the automatic processing of information (as happens in a computer) but the ability to creatively combine and recombine stored information, infinitely multiplying the creative and transformative potential of the individual mind. Through the experimentation of virtual scenarios, the individual is no longer mechanically conditioned by experiences but becomes capable of devising innovative solutions that can then be tested and verified when the actual opportunity arises (Cai, et al., 2009; Schacter, et al., 2012).

The SEEKING system not only actively sets in motion the child to search in the external environment for an object suitable of satisfying its impulses, but also constitutes the primary thrust of its thought processes. The SEEKING system acts as an essential energizing input to the mid-line cortical areas which remain active in conditions of rest and which therefore allow that libidinal energy to be transferred within a neuropsychic apparatus capable of containing it (Alcaro and Panksepp, 2014). In this way, the desired object can be perceived through imagination and thought, taking the form of a mental object. It is the phase of infantile omnipotence or magical thinking, in which the child can mentally recreate what it needs to survive. If a caregiver is able to understand the wishes of the child, there is a correspondence between the desired object and the real object, an essential condition for the child to develop a sense of trust in itself and in the surrounding world and to create, a "transitional space" preceding any later distinction between the internal and the external world. If this correspondence is not present in early childhood experiences, the premature separation between the internal and external world may lead to a narcissistic and omnipotent condition, or alternatively, a tendency to conform to the demands of the external world (see the concept false self; Winnicott, 1974). However, it must also be stressed that satisfaction or gratification alone is not enough for the thinking process. To develop the capacity to think, the child must endure the experience diametrically opposite to satisfaction, that is, *frustration.* The experiences of frustration are associated with the operational modes of the negative emotional dispositions, such as FEAR, ANGER and SEPARATION ANXIETY/SADNESS.

These emotions are activated if the caregiver does not satisfy the child's instinctive desires for fulfillment and its search for protection and care. Furthermore, these emotions end up inhibiting the SEEKING system (which would cause the child to continue to the search satisfy its needs), eliciting instead a withdrawal from the external world or even aggression towards its own needs. Even more relevant and as we have previously outlined, from a psychological point of view, these negative emotions can disturb brain activity at rest, presenting a serious risk to the child's imagination and its capacity to think, which is fuelled by the SEEKING system. Fortunately, however, if the caregiver is able to stay in touch with and contain these negative emotions, mirroring and modulating them, then the child's imagination and capacity for thought can develop to accommodate or tolerate them. Otherwise, however, its mental activity will suffer an important sense of discontinuity, and some fragments of emotional memories may be lost or excluded from thought. The fundamental factor in tolerance to frustration is a reflection of how much a child tends to resort to repression or other even more primitive defenses that arise from magical thinking and infantile omnipotence: it is on this basis that we may also understand the highly specific disturbances to learning on which all secondary and tertiary acquisition is structured; spoken language and the abilities to read or write, the so-called *developmental learning disorders* (DLD, see Section 9). Following the research on Panksepp's motivational systems we may assume that in many developmental disorders of symbolic processing, including specific disorders such as dyslexia, dysphasia and dyscalculia, a primary motivational dysfunction should be at least be considered.

From primary to the secondary process: the path towards thinking

Historically, psychoanalysis has identified a central developmental point in the thinking of children as the transition between primary thought processes, dominated by the pleasure principle, and secondary processes, dominated by the reality principle. According to Freud (Freud, 1911, 1920) the primary process is a particular mode of psychic functioning, which involves forming a mental representation of the desired object of an emotional drive to satisfy the desire for that object. It operates without regard for logic or reality, is dominated by the pleasure principle, and provides hallucinatory fulfillment of wishes as often happens in dreams. The secondary (Freudian) process (subsequent in order of psychological development) is generated as a way of thinking when the child experiences frustration and delay of gratification of a need as dictated by reality.[4] In *Formulations Regarding the Two Principles in Mental Functioning*, Freud (1911) states that the fundamental step for the child to learn from experience is given by the progressive detachment of the pleasure principle to adapt to the conflicts imposed by reality. He argues that the individual remains subject to regression or a return to functioning according to the primary process, and primitive defensive modalities such as denial and infantile omnipotence may come to prevail again.

A large amount of neuroscientific data indicates that the upper cortical and limbic areas, in particular of the right hemisphere, are fundamental in allowing the transition from the primary to the secondary process, that is, in favoring an organization of the memory traces cantered on the constancy of the external object (or thing), rather than being oriented exclusively to the hallucinatory "discharge" of drive energy. Psychological analysis of neurological patients with lesions of the perisylvian area of the right cerebral hemisphere has shown that they suffer much more profound personality disorders than those of patients with similar lesions of the left "linguistic" hemisphere (Kaplan-Solms and Solms, 2002). For example, patients with injuries of the right hemisphere have a tendency not only to deny the dysfunctions caused by the injury (anosognosia), but they often have severe psychiatric symptoms, such as melancholic depression or paranoid ideation. Even more severe symptoms have been observed in patients with lesions of the mesial frontal regions of the right hemisphere, who show a complete collapse of ego functions, as observed in florid psychotic episodes. The Solms, therefore, conclude that the cortico-limbic regions of the right hemisphere are involved in the spatial-temporal organization of mental life necessary for the "object cathexis" of the libido. If this function is damaged by brain injury, mental life reverts to being dominated by the primary thought process and by the hallucinatory fulfillment of wishes.

The acquisition of the secondary thought process, therefore, linked to the formation of mnestic systems of representation of the total object, depends directly on the action and fluctuations of a basic emotion, which Panksepp (1998) recognized in the functions of the system of the SEPARATION ANXIETY/ SADNESS (Figure 10.8), central to mammalian behavior. The elaboration and integration of this emotion at the level of subjective consciousness, and in particular within the imagery/thought elaborated in the medial cortical structures, seems to provide the child with a fundamental drive in its process of separation from the object and, therefore, in the possibility of forming representations of external objects that are not invested narcissistically or, at least, not solely narcissistically. Narcissistic attitudes are predominantly dominated by the SEEKING, ANGER, and FEAR emotions, while the development of the capacity for object love is primarily sustained by the prevalence of the emotion of SEPARATION ANXIETY/SADNESS, which transforms the child's frustrations into an acceptance of the inevitable discrepancies between its desires and the actual opportunities present in the external world to satisfy them, an important prerequisite for accepting one's dependence needs.[5]

The cortical representation of words

A child's ability to learn can be affected by many factors (genetic, congenital, or acquired) which can result in the persistence of the infantile processes that can interfere with the submission of narcissistic thinking, that is necessary, in order to allow the updating of its internal and external perception. This tendency is not only the prerogative of the child: in the history of humankind there have been many instances of omnipotent, narcissistic beliefs. Just think that until Copernicus and Galileo we thought we were at the center of the universe until Darwin that we were special and unique animals, quite distinct from the animal world and, obviously, until Freud that we could consciously dominate our actions and our intentions, to painfully discover that we are not "masters even in our own house" due to the predominance of the unconscious mechanisms of the mind.

One narcissistic aspect of the human Ego that, until very recently, has withstood the challenge of scientific investigation is that of Language. This has long been seen as a unique faculty of man that represents the collective grandiosity of humankind. In particular, the main spokesman for this orientation is Noam Chomsky who in his main works (Chomsky, 1968) has always supported the theory that the development of language in children is determined by genetic factors, a genetic peculiarity, which distinguishes human beings from all other animals. This "genetic theory" of the origin language has given rise to the idea of a unique human congenital component that allows the development of what is called *universal grammar*. These ideas have also influenced psychoanalysis. It is a known fact, that for a long time, the so-called American Ego school of psychoanalysis, with Hartmann and Rapaport (1958) as its most influential figure, supported the concept of mental functions exempt from conflict (*autonomous Ego functions*), with language as one of those functions. This psychoanalytic theory argued that these autonomous functions (*i.e.*, not subject to conflict) are innate, present from birth, develop independently and are immune to drive "pressure" and related defenses. The position of these psychoanalysts appears to be in line with that of Chomsky and holds that the development of functions such as perception, memory and learning, intelligence, language, thought, complex motor skills and many other cognitive functions develop in the child based on innate factors. Nevertheless, advocates of this viewpoint also admitted that each of these cognitive processes (and the related aspects of the Ego free from conflict) may be susceptible to secondary dynamic developmental interference.

Chomsky (1988) has revised his theories on language extensively over the years, without, however, revising his main thesis, namely that it in its syntactic and semantic complexity, language remains a prerogative of only human beings. Today, this thesis has been vigorously refuted based on the demonstration that even the most symbolic components of our cognitive function *par excellence*, language, originate from basic and more elementary cognitive processes (such as object manipulation), which are also present in other animals and which constitute the evolutionary foundations for human symbolic function and speech. Tommasello (2003) has suggested a complete revision of the concept of language as innate, based on the fact that (1) language functions have evolved from more general cognitive processes, such as mental manipulation of objects (e.g., visuo-spatial and visuo-motor imagery). These have also been shown to be present in other mammals (and even birds can accomplish some simple tasks of purposeful manipulation), and (2) secondary – but of extreme importance in our argument, all cognitive functions have motivational processes at their basis, in particular, they derive from the functions of coding and decoding the intentions of others and the interactions of others with us.

Freud described the linguistic organization of the brain in particular in his pre-psychoanalytic study of aphasias (Freud, 1891). Freud, at the time a neurologist and not yet a psychologist or psychoanalyst, took a deep interest in the problem of the development of language in man, linking it to the formation of memories and their cataloging (a process that could be compared to the development of symbolic capacity and ultimately of thinking skills). In his early studies on aphasia, (Freud 1891; see also Saling and Solms, 1986), attempted to describe the functioning of language based on evidence of deficits due to cortical neurological lesions as well as the higher functions of the brain-mind of the intact brain (Luria, 1976). In Freud's neurolinguistic theory there is (1) a more ancient system of representation of *a thing* (in German *dingvorstellung, sachvorstellung* or, in certain passages, *objectvorstellung*) and (2) a more recently evolved system of symbolic representation of the same object, *a word* (in German, *wortvorstellung*). He conceived of a relationship between object-representations and word-representations as a double-layered network where there is an initial set of memory images *things* in association with each other but which constitute a relatively "open" system (in the sense that there are an infinite set of declinations of the representation of that "thing" – for example, the many perceptual images of a mother) which is connected (through the learning process of language in the child) to a "closed" system of words (in our example the word "mother"), which expresses all those representations within a single symbolic concept (Figure 10.6). The semantic system of language is thereby linked to the corresponding representations of the thing. The system of representation of the things, or objects is according to Freud "open" in the sense that it can be connected to a network of countless other "objects," each composed of traces of memory deriving from the perception of that object (the visual images of the mother, her physical appearance, physiognomy of the face, the sound of her voice, etc.). The maternal images are then linked to the image of other "objects" (such as the image of the father and then to the image of other mothers) and thus semantic categories are created (fathers, grown-ups, and so on). According to Freud, parallel to this "open" plane of association between images of things (which is infinitely expandable), there is the "closed" plane of the representation of the corresponding word.

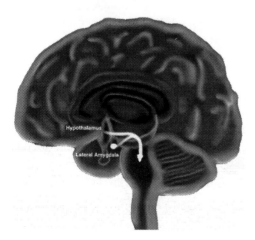

Figure 10.6 The "negative" motivational systems (Figures 10.6.7.8) are those that accompany the sense of frustration and involve the avoidance of certain disturbing stimuli.

This, he considered circumscribed and definite for every single object since it is connected to the infinite "open" network of imaginable objects through only the sense of hearing. The "sound image" (the word) of the object, acquired through the auditory system, of the corresponding thing (expressed by the mother's voice) is only subsequently connected to the motor image of the spoken word (the pronunciation or uttering of that word), and then to reading and writing it. For Freud, language acquisition follows the natural path of listening to the child's sounds pronounced (by the mother) that leads to naming a given object. Freud (1923) will say, returning to this theme long after his abandonment of neurology:

> The verbal residues essentially come from acoustic perceptions, so that in a certain way there is a specific sensory origin for the Preconscious system. For the moment their visual components can be neglected as secondary, generated as they are by the reading of the verbal representation; the same is true for the motor images of speech, which – except for the deaf and dumb – perform the function of auxiliary signs. *The word is essentially the mnestic residue of a word heard.*
>   (Freud, 1923, p. 20; emphasis added)

In the child, the first mnestic associations between the word heard and the spoken word are created, and through processes of consolidation and re-consolidation of memories, these traces become learned patterns (Alberini, 2005). From the illustration of the developmental steps, outlined very briefly here, of the first Freudian model of language acquisition, we can deduce that central to child development are the early relational processes between the child and the mother or caregiver. The child observes and perceives the maternal object in its components (visual, auditory, etc.), and at the moment of need *seeks* to repeat these experiences and recall from memory the experiences that have led to the need being satisfied (Sandler, et al., 1997). It has been stressed several times that the evolution of language represents a determining factor in the development of self-awareness, or consciousness of the Ego, that is, the ability to represent oneself in space and time and to build a conscious sense and narrative of one's personal history and finally of identity. According to Freud (1900), thanks to the acquisition of language, we become aware of our intrinsic mental activity, which is expressed in the form of words spoken internally (an internal dialogue).[6]

Freud (1891) therefore called *objects*, those representations of the *things* invested with affects. The representations of the objects, which present themselves as imagos (visual, auditory, etc.) that can be re-represented, according to Freud, at a higher level in secondary process thinking (*wort-vorstellung*). He believed that the value of words consisted in the fact that these, like all cognitive representations, derive from perception – in this case above all auditory – and have the property of making a certain "thing" conscious. Word representations also have the additional ability

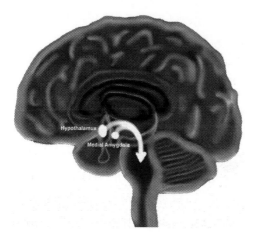

Figure 10.7 The ANGER system are the motivational systems of avoidance of stimuli felt as threatening for our affective homeostasis. Both see the amygdala as the coordination nucleus of these emotional excitations: the FEAR system in the lateral portion, while the ANGER system in the medial one of the amygdaloid nuclei.

to represent relationships between concrete objects of thought. The main value of words is to allow us to represent the relationships between things or to re-represent them in an abstract form and not (as Freud believed) to allow us to make conscious of the processes emerging from the repressed and the Id. This characteristic allows us to assume a separate observational vertex between things and the Self, hence, to think about things and to mentally manipulate them. Words allow us to carry out mental tasks, using our memories of past experiences and our thoughts, allows us to "travel" both in space and in time (recalling past experiences and projecting them into our future). Today we know that these memory residues make use of networks of semantic memories located in the cerebral cortex that are the result of childhood learning: they were fundamentally learned after birth both in terms of "things" (objects and their use in the world) and in terms of "word representations". Huth and colleagues (2012) have shown using functional magnetic resonance that this "cortical semantic space" actually exists: analogous to the schema proposed by Freud (1891), more than one hundred years ago, these semantic networks of representation of objects are distributed in "maps" that involve the whole cerebral cortex; this breakdown appears to be relatively homogeneous in the different subjects studied, an element that indicates to us that there is an inherited, genetic predisposition to the localization of these learned memories; furthermore, this distribution of the representations of objects significantly overlaps the cortical distribution of the meaning of words in both hemispheres brain (Huth et al., 2016; see Figure 10.7).

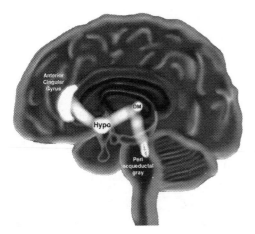

Figure 10.8 The **separation distress/sadness system** the bottleneck of this system is the anterior gyrus of the cingulate, but includes large subcortical regions, such as the hypothalamus (Hypo), the mid-dorsal nucleus of the thalamus (DM), and the periaqueductal gray. It is known that these sites are of great importance for the maintenance of a proximity or proximity relationship in the offspring of mammals.

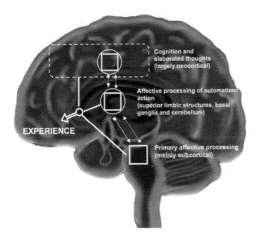

Figure 10. 9 The **"nested hierarchical model"** of learning processes according to Panksepp (1998) - The emotional and cognitive learning processes in development would derive from the resulting maturation of the primary, secondary and tertiary motivational processes, all nested into the other in hierarchical order. During the development of the child the primary processes "instruct" the higher-order learning centres (bottom-up control and modulation; arrows directed upward). Once consolidated, these higher-order learning modules regulate both primary emotional activity and secondary stereotyped reactions (top-down influences; arrows directed downward).

Words, therefore, play a decisive role within *reflexive consciousness* (also called secondary consciousness) in drawing the distinction between "me" and "not me," the differentiation between the Self and the other than Self. For the child, the acquisition of language represents an important developmental watershed that goes hand in hand with the establishment of body boundaries and the Ego. This abstract level of re-representation allows the subject of consciousness (the Self) to separate itself as an object from other objects (and therefore to imagine itself and to imagine plans of action congruent with its needs). Solms (2013), therefore, highlights three levels of the experience of Self:

a   The *affective level* corresponding to the affective primary conscious experience; it is the first phenomenal level of the Self as a subject, at the basis of the first-person perspective (e.g. the "me" that is frightened when threatened); this level in non-representational, it is a basic feeling of something.
b   The *perceptual level* of the Self, as one may regard oneself as a representation, as an object; it is the basis of the second-person perspective (that "me/you" I see when I look in the mirror);
c   The *abstract-symbolic* (or re-representational) *level* of the linguistic Self (the "me/ him/her" corresponding to my name) which acts as an object in relation to other objects and thereby contributes to the progressive building the third-person perspective of the world.

Damasio (1999) includes these higher cognitive aspects of consciousness in his definition of *extended or reflexive consciousness*. All these terms refer essentially to "consciousness of consciousness" (the capacity of being aware of one's own thoughts). The first level of the representation of the Self, as described earlier in the hydraulic analogy, constitutes "the ephemeral and fluid" activation of the affective consciousness, also referred to as the "liquid affective activation". The second level corresponds to the memories of things, objects, notions, concepts and events of the world. Finally, the third level is that of words and more abstract representations, stored in the matrices of cortical "mental solids" (Solms, 2013). These last two cortical levels become conscious only if "filled with the liquid flows" of primary subcortical affective consciousness. Therefore, the preschool child, who still lacks sufficient maturation of the orbito-frontal and pre-frontal cortex, possesses an unstable bond with reality testing, we could say that it confuses the internal reality with the external one, fantasies with perceptions. At first, due to the effects of the more ancient basal frontal structures, the child recognizes external objects, but they are still invested (*cathected*) in a narcissistic fashion, that is, they follow the laws of the pleasure principle and those of a desired internal reality: it is as if "the things of the world are part of us" and they have to behave "as if it they are us or as we wish," conforming to the magical thinking process of the child. As the somatosensory associative networks begin to develop, during learning, objects become integrated with their sensory components, based on contact with external reality, though they are still fragmented and confused with the initial "objects," narcissistically invested according to internal reality and fantasies. This ability to link concrete objects to experiences (which arrive from the senses directed towards external reality) and which creates the categories of "things" develops as a result of specialized and lateralized structures in the cerebral cortex. The areas involved are localized in the cortical convexity of the cerebral hemispheres, particularly the right side. Finally, cortical associative networks are formed that lead to the construction of symbolic objects (categories of "things") from concrete objects (a function in which the left parietal cortex may be particularly involved), and finally the association of the sound and motor images of words. These are the associative networks that are formed for the understanding of language (in Wernicke's area on the postero-superior temporal cortex) and for language production (in Broca's area of the operculum of the inferior frontal gyrus), both in the left cerebral hemisphere.

The importance of language for self-awareness has also been confirmed recently by neuroscientific studies. For example, Gerard Edelman (1992) argues that self-awareness, or higher-order consciousness, is related to the functioning of brain areas responsible for linguistic communication, such as Broca's, Wernicke's, and the supplementary motor areas. In particular, the flow of information from the frontal and prefrontal cortex, that reaches the neuronal centers of language, transforms our unconscious intentions into words that can be "heard internally" (thought) within the primary perceptual consciousness system. This system corresponds roughly to short-term (or working) memory. The ability of human beings to become aware of their thoughts and feelings and, especially, to transform concrete perceptions into abstract concepts, is strictly dependent on our language capacity. Language allows us to activate the perceptual trace not only of a particular object (for example the visual image of our father) but also of an entire class of objects (the audio-verbal traces of words that indicate categories such as "fathers" or "women" and so on). All these memory functions, so fundamental to a child's learning, are significant to the functions of the neocortex, where our knowledge of the world is based and which is also the result of our emotional experiences, the repetitions of perceptual experiences and our reflections upon them. Semantic memory is the network of associations and concepts that underlies our basic knowledge of the world: lexical meanings, categories, facts and statements, and so on (Schacter, 1996). This knowledge is stored as information expressed in "third person" form, as could be found in an encyclopedia. It includes pieces of objective information about the world and how it works. There is nothing "subjective" about semantic memory, in the sense that it is not represented as subjective experiences. Instead, it contains information that is typically shared within a society or cultural group. It often happens that we overlook the fact that we had to learn all these things and how to name them in early and later infancy.

Learning consolidation during the developmental age

The ultimate goal of learning processes is therefore to construct a predictive model that solves our problems in the external world once and for all and then to generate a matrix of memories that might ideally always work: to this end, the predictions are repeatedly confirmed by the feedback yielded by reality become increasingly automated (creating memories that become very similar to innate instincts). This memory consolidation, therefore, requires the gradual transfer of these processes from the cortical to the subcortical memory systems. These subcortical memory systems match the secondary motivational systems in the model developed by affective neuroscience (Panksepp and Solms, 2012). They are divided into two types. The first are learned processes, typical of "procedural" memories, and consist of non-representational associations. As such, they are not related to images or words; indeed, they are "non-declarative" memories, characterized by very slow learning through repeated series of experiences. They are, therefore "difficult to learn," but once learned also "hard to forget" and extremely rapid in their automated execution. These processes are typically involved in learning to read and write, for example. Secondly, there are the innate "affective" memory processes. Even the basic motivational processes highlighted by Panksepp can be modified by experience, but we should not forget that these structures are associated with immediate learning – learning that can be established based on a single exposure to stimuli and tending to become indelible. A child cannot learn twice from the experience of putting his fingers in an electric socket, and although nature has endowed him with an innate motivational system that signals pain, fear and unpleasant "surprise," it is unlikely that evolution could foresee this particular eventuality. This is the job of superimposed structures of secondary and tertiary learning systems that teach that this type of experience is harmful and therefore to be avoided. Once this type of experience has eventually been automated in the secondary processes (supported by structures associated mainly with the basal ganglia, cerebellum, and related circuits), these processes are not easily updated by the working memory (and thus the cognitive consciousness). They are efficient, inclined to be indelible, and "fast but dirty" (Ledoux, 1998). In other words, there is nearly no delay in their accomplishment (or deferral between stimulus and response); but at the same time they are not flexible, as they are not supported by "trial-and-error testing". They act like reflex arcs and are performed extremely quickly in an "all-or-nothing" (on/off) fashion, without any interpolation by thought processes. Although the primary organizing center of emotional responses resides in the deep subcortical areas of the core-Self (Figure 10.1), each emotional system possesses widespread connections with the higher limbic and cortical regions that constitute the most recently evolved portions of our brain. It is precisely these connections and branches that provide the degree of psycho-behavioral plasticity required for all kinds of emotional learning. That is, each emotional disposition is represented at different levels in the hierarchy of neuro-psychic architecture (Panksepp and Biven, 2012); and by overlapping and interacting with other emotions, these dispositions create more and more varied stratified and complex mental states and representations (such as the feelings of shame and guilt, dominance, humiliation, embarrassment and so on). While the deep subcortical areas of the core-Self are responsible for the most "unalloyed" expressions of affects and emotional responses, the maturation of the upper neocortical portions provides a greater degree of behavioral plasticity and more sophisticated learning. The association between affects, perception and motor skills becomes more and more complex during child development and is processed by areas that are more highly developed than the brain stem, bringing into play structures such as the thalamus, basal ganglia and mesial portions (along the brain's mid line) of the limbic system. The child then begins to associate emotional "value-signals" with successful approach and avoidance behaviors and thus begins to learn. What we mean by developmental "success" here is the memorization and consolidation of action of varying degrees of complexity that leads to the fulfillment of the needs identified by our "basic needs detectors"[7] – memorization that ultimately leads to the selective retention of the perceptual-motor memories of experiences that have proved effective in regulating our feelings of well-being and safety (Sandler, 1960).

Moving further up the scale of brain functions, we encounter even more highly evolved areas, such as the hippocampus and temporal areas connected to autobiographical knowledge (of the child's self in the space-time context of the world), which are functionally mature only after about the third year of life (Tulving, 2002). The adjacent ventro-medial portions of the orbito-frontal cortex, which link emotional experience to the specific representations of "things" in the world develop more fully in a bottom-up learning mode around the fourth/fifth year of life (Schore, 1996; Squire, et al., 1993). In this same period (i.e. at school-age), the cortical zones of language (Galaburda, 1982) and semantic memory (McKee and Squire, 1993) begin to function at a higher rate, while the prefrontal portions of the inhibitory control, planning and verification system, safeguarding our perceptions and behaviors, mature much more slowly (a maturation that comes to an end only at around the age of 25; Fuster, 1988).

Jaak Panksepp's neuroethological research indicates that the primary motor in the development of the higher cognitive functions is thus the subcortical emotional processes, which constitute a bridge between the body's homeostatic and visceral processes and the outside world. Basic emotions are the fundamental indicators that enable the person experiencing them to assign a corresponding signal-value (whether positive or negative) to the stimuli in the world and to his own behavior (Panksepp, 2008; Vandekerckhove, et al., 2014).

Most neuroscientific research on learning processes has used the behaviorist paradigms of classical conditioning (which essentially explores the perceptual side) and operational (mainly motor) conditioning. Regarding classical conditioning, we know that some temporal areas of the limbic system, such as the amygdala and hippocampus, play an essential role when stimuli or complex configurations of originally neutral stimuli acquire a new emotional value by virtue of their association with unconditional stimuli (Squire, et al., 1993). Most of the research in this regard has been done on fear conditioning, but the results of these studies can at least in part also apply to other emotional predispositions. In particular, the neurobiologist Josef LeDoux (1998, 2003), who has collaborated over a number of years with the Nobel Prize winner Eric Kandell, a neuroscientist but also an admirer of psychoanalysis, was able to demonstrate that when a neutral stimulus acquires the ability to trigger a fear reaction, by association with an electric shock, for example, the basolateral amygdala is activated and memory traces are formed inside it that connect the new stimulus to the emotional response.

The acquisition of these internalized action patterns, whether motor, mental, cognitive or affective, seems to depend on the correct functioning of the emotional seeking system with the meso-cortico-limbic dopaminergic circuit, which is one of its key components (Alcaro, et al., 2007; Haber, 2014). Indeed, the activation of this system in new or unfamiliar environmental conditions encourages the individual to explore the environment and act upon it in novel ways (Deyoung, 2013). When this exploratory activity produces a reward, the state of satisfaction perceived by the animal acts in such a way as to reinforce the memory traces of the events immediately preceding the reward, leading, after many repetitions, to the acquisition of a fixed procedure (Wise, 2004). As already mentioned, many of these skills are impressed so deeply during learning that they are not normally even considered to be aspects of memory: they are viewed as learned procedures, which behave as innate instincts that are reactivated and executed automatically at the appropriate moments. They depend on experiences that have been performed correctly and reinforced by numerous repetitions, which we might call practice. Constant repetition in the learning phase is particularly important in procedural memorization. Ideomotor skills, from walking to playing the piano, are (and must be) learned slowly and gradually at all levels. These skills (like riding a bicycle, for instance) are also extremely resistant to decay over time and require a degree of active inhibition to regulate and modulate adaptive behavior.

Of all the different types of procedural learning, those related to the dynamics of relationships and social communication are most directly involved in psychopathological phenomena and emotional disorders, influenced as they are by the dynamics of basic emotional systems. From this point of view, the large amount of data collected by Allan Schore (1994, 2003) shows the importance of cortico-limbic areas, in particular those located in the right brain hemisphere, in the processes of communication and emotional regulation between mother and child. These implicit early memories, encoded in the form of internal attachment operating systems, not only play an important role in modulating our emotional responses and our prelinguistic social communication patterns, but also constitute the unconscious memory base on which the Ego is structured in its relations with the outside world and therefore on which the whole scaffolding of our reflexive (self-conscious) personality rests (Beebe and Lechmann, 2002; Fonagy and Target, 1997, Stern, 2004).

The dynamic origin of DLD

The reconsolidation of the neural structures underlying the higher generative models of the cerebral cortex, therefore, requires the activation of the subcortical affective (conscious) arousal and only secondarily higher (conscious) cognition or "working memory" (which prompts conscious thinking). But, as mentioned above, there are limits to working memory (it has a variable capacity but tends to be restricted to 5–7 units of information; Engle, 2002) and therefore this accommodation of our predictive models generally encounters resistance (Solms, 2017): confirming one's beliefs requires less energy than changing them. Particularly during childhood, when the more sophisticated systems of emotional control are still undeveloped, this tiring work of dealing with intrapsychic conflicts and learning from reality (through the *perceptual inferences* used to update our adaptive procedures) is never fully accomplished in an effective and adaptive way and the internal adaptive solutions, which are generally very imprecise, generally prevail. In the early stages of the child's development, omnipotent thought processes of a narcissistic nature still predominate and this makes the child perceive and act in the world based on *active inferences*, that is, according to unconscious archaic methods: "I can't get to grips with any of this and it makes me suffer, but I can cope by either thinking it doesn't exist or that it has just gone away as if by magic".

Adaptive solutions of this type underlie the phenomenon of *repression* and all the primitive or secondary defenses deriving from it. As we saw in the previous section, we could say that all predictions made internally by the subject that are "legitimately" confirmed by reality (Solms, 2017) contribute to constructing the *cognitive unconscious* (that part of our consolidated unconscious cortical and subcortical functioning – that have been learned by taking into account predictive errors and subjected to the reality test and updated). The *repressed unconscious*, on the other hand, corresponds to the dynamic part of the mind that has been automated "illegitimately" (i.e. without taking into account reality tests and the predictive errors they entail, and resorting to premature or, to use child language, "magical" solutions; Solms, 2017). This part of the unconscious has been automated "illegitimately" because the child's immature Ego is overwhelmed by the demands of the Id (by its entropic engulfment), and cannot (by itself) find solutions that meet the criteria of reality testing: every psychosexual-stage conflict constitutes an example of an insoluble problem. The child is faced with a series of often irreconcilable emotional needs. Resistance to learning from experience (of which repression is the best known and most studied example) requires a premature withdrawal of cognitive consciousness in favor of premature automation of a "behavioral – procedural – algorithm," which is "premature" because it is consolidated without taking due account of and conforming to the reality principle. However, this premature automation solution triggers continuous attempts to confirm this "illegitimate" prediction in the face of an equal stream of predictive errors produced by external reality, with the associated release of free (affective) energy: the "return of the repressed" continues to activate affective subcortical centers and higher-order attentional and consciousness processes. Defenses are thus effective in by-passing cognitive consciousness but not affective consciousness: *this forms the foundations for developmental disorders and mental illness since every relational problem derives from a conflict meaningful to the child.*

The first possible outcome of this unsolvable contractual situation is that the child, for endogenous or environmental reasons, suffers from arrested development, and with his still immature resources he has no choice but to try to cut his losses stemming from these conflicts. The child thus finds himself grappling with his activated feelings, which signal the persistence of the problem of adapting to relational reality and remains psychically "blocked" by a problem that he cannot solve, thus wasting the precious but limited space of working memory and cognitive consciousness. This endless and repetitive cognitive loop gradually becomes a symptom, limiting the child's ability to use it effectively at school age to learn reading, writing and counting skills, for example. The child's learning experience is therefore very similar to his nutritional experience, where failure can again be seen as the consequence of "malnourishment," in which the child experiences feelings of resignation (of a depressive nature) generated by the loss of hope that his attempts to communicate will be understood (either by the adults around him or by himself). The child needs to attain inner safety, ability to handle feelings of separation, before acquiring the capacity to move freely in the more mature world of symbols and concepts (Sandler, 1960). These, for the child, represent the mental expression of a threatening sense of separateness, and thus of anxiety, which may unsettle his infantile predictive generative models and become too distressing (Miller, 2015).

The origins of the child's DLD, for the most varied reasons, would therefore lie in a maturation blockage (and a lack of due care and attention) from the early stages of narcissism to object relationship, where the pleasure principle and "magical thought" prevail. The child tends to draw upon "illegitimate" predictions to face reality, and if these solutions are automated and consolidated, they may lead to a persistence of different forms of infantile omnipotence (in line with the stance taken by psychoanalysis; see for example Bion, 1962). Alongside the many causes attributable to the outside world (as in trauma, bereavement, abuse or obvious neglect), the problem is also associated with two fundamental emotional factors endogenous to the child's relational development: the first (1) is the persistence of unstable nar-cissistic defenses that make the child fragile and beset by feelings of shame and inadequacy linked to the fantasy of being worthless (Miller, 2015); alter-natively, (2) the recurrence of even more archaic defensive solutions, linked to an unconscious fantasy of self-congratulatory omnipotence centered on the unconscious belief that he possesses magical knowledge, a kind of om-niscience. In short, the recurrent and dominant grandiose fantasy of the child with learning disabilities is often that of being a *misunderstood genius.*

Both of these relational situations are located on the spectrum of nar-cissistic wounds, in which the subjective experiences of the child can be placed on an "axis that oscillates from impotence to omnipotence". The child is subjected to a regime of an all-or-nothing type of response (feeling completely helpless, desperate or resigned, which leads the child to "give up" learning in the first place or, in the second, an equally maladjusted sit-uation where the child is secretly completely gratified, as well as convinced of being a sort of "magical scholar" and consequently that "there is no need to learn"). The problem, in the latter case, is that the child's failure to learn is revealed to the rest of the world, which of course does not understand the magical skills of the self-taught child. Naturally, there are indeed talented children who manage to learn by themselves, either because they have a special talent or thanks to greater than average cognitive components (in-telligence) or emotional tools (intuition). There is also another group of children who, precisely because they are sufficiently cognitively gifted, suc-ceed in learning but continue to feed their narcissistic fantasies and are emotionally immature. The problem with this group of children is that their narcissistic problem is overlooked by adults, precisely because they are good at school. These more intellectually gifted children, with apparently better school performance, are not immune from negative consequences in terms of emotional development: they also try to "get by in a bad situation" by tending to use omnipotent infantile thought, rendering their infantile fantasies automatic, even if they do not respect reality testing criteria. The problem here too is that the fantasized prediction (which is "illegitimate" according to the reality test) is treated in all respects "as if" it were real and effective and it, therefore, fails to activate consciousness. As a result, the child is resistant to updating (and reconsolidating) the generative model, holding fast to the blanket of self-satisfaction and pseudo-autonomy. These are the children who, for example in the latency stage, believe (and are so perceived by the family and the school) they have resolved their pre-genital conflict (so, for example, they might think they are self-taught geniuses, perhaps precisely on account of their cognitive learning success; Miller, 2015). These children then face emotional and relational problems, even serious ones, at a later age (one need only consider the frequent onset of psychosis in adolescence, for example), when reality inevitably returns to "knock on their emotional door," as affective arousal reemerges to con-stantly signal predictive errors.

Attention deficit hyperactivity disorder and the loss of meaning

Neuropsychology considers the superficial convexity of the frontal lobes of the neocortex to be the main site of the child's attentional capacities, abilities required for learning, such as concentration and the inhibition of impulsive activities (Fuster, 1988). According to cognitive scholars, the child learns to regulate his attention to focus on and absorb the proposed stimuli, to listen to lessons, to read and write and then later to take pleasure in studying, especially thanks to the maturation of these sophisticated and highly evolved portions of the cerebral cortex. This structure allows the child to develop extremely advanced abilities in order to be able to plan actions that we could ascribe to thinking ability, through inhibitory mechanisms that both boost the stimuli that come from the outside world and act as a "brake" on internal impulses. Such frontal skills include (a) imaginative abilities (the selection and organization of assimilated memories, as well as planning actions, which literally allows the child mentally to "travel" backwards to previous experiences but at the same time generating predictions about future opportunities), (b) reflective skills (developing an internal dialogue, asking questions and understanding how to get answers), (c) introspective skills (perceiving and understanding one's intentions and emotions) related to learning and (d) empathic skills (understanding the intrinsic meaning of what the teaching material intends to convey, appreciating others' intentions and motives). The integration of these skills allows the child to mature his predictive abilities and thus his decision-making and behavioral flexibility, thanks to the progressive use of a mode of thinking that is increasingly focused and tailored to the gratification of the learner's own needs according to the criteria gleaned from increasingly accurate reality testing.

Attention, understood as "attention directed at the outside world" (which is the source of all useful learning of "things" and "words"; Freud, 1891), is however intimately linked to conscious awareness. Only the activation effected by the subcortical motivational structures highlighted by Panksepp (1998) and thus the deep motivational systems can produce the level of attention (salience) necessary to start the processes of consolidation and reconsolidation of memories involved in learning. In particular, the complex molecular mechanisms that occur in the de-structuring of synaptic connections involved in learning new declarative knowledge (reconsolidation) require consciousness. Only in this way can the synapses (on which declarative memory updating relies) be "updated" and pass from the so-called "working memory" (whose more psychodynamic equivalent is cognitive consciousness) to long-term memory (with its declarative episodic and semantic components). This is the basis of organized learning and ultimately of the thinking skills required for the formal learning imparted to the child in his school career and is essential for the growth of social skills and awareness. Freud (1900) referred to consciousness as "a sensory organ for the perception of psychic qualities" and it is clear that today this only concerns *cognitive consciousness* (which we now regard as being associated with the cortical mechanisms of working memory). However, Solms' (2013) work has shown that cognitive consciousness is secondary to affective consciousness. The consciousness underlying attentional processes is primarily an excitatory affective function (arousal) and only secondarily a perceptive function. This means that the adaptive functioning of attention and concentration and the development of the activities that bring finalized actions to a successful conclusion during the child's development are based on the earliest ERTAS (*Extended Reticulo-Thalamic Activating System*); Watt, 1999). The primary processes supported by the seven basic motivational centers (with the SEEKING system playing the role of "manager" coordinating the other six emotional systems) are also essential for the attentional processes, for these emotional systems act as detectors, activators and coordinators of salience. A developmental alteration at any level of the hierarchical order of these affective-saliency-attentional systems has a sort of "domino effect" on all the most evolved memory regulation systems (the final generative models of cognitive predictions), especially in sites at the cortical level, predisposing the child to an attentional or a DLD disorder. In addition to governing the SEEKING system in attentional processes, what Panksepp (2007) has called the PLAY system appears to have another important role (see also Burgdorf and Panksepp, 2006). Panksepp's (2007) studies have pointed to a particular portion of the ERTAS, the *intralaminar nuclei of the thalamus* (see Figure 10.3), as a nodal crossroad of this system. The affective regulation provided by these PLAY structures enables the child to experience a sense of excitement and enthusiasm that acts as an impetus in the exploratory motor activities at the heart of the child's unregulated free PLAY. This recreational activity has an important role in development and is well known to constitute the evolutionary platform on which fantasies and thus play are expressed. In both animals and humans, the juvenile's PLAY system mimics in a safe and secure context the fundamental activities performed in adulthood (survival, self-maintenance and reproduction) in order achieve evolutionary success. The child's play activity therefore acts as a "mold" for the child to create the adaptive solutions and cognitive predictions most suited to his environment and development, through the representation of his fantasies compared with the real objects he plays with. The affective regulation carried out by the child's PLAY system also facilitates a more complete maturation of the frontal cortices (Panksepp, 2007). It is also known that specific drugs usually prescribed for attention deficit disorder act especially on the prefrontal cortex by pharmacologically compensating for the dysregulated action of lower (overactivated and disinhibited) regions on these cortical prefrontal systems. Amphetamine-like drugs, such as the much-discussed methylphenidate act upon the outward-directed attention component and inhibit the impulsiveness caused by the excess, inner-induced activation, in this way effectively counteracting the child's hyperactivity and concentration disorders. However, these favorable pharmacological outcomes do not come without a cost: it is well established that these drugs are also potent inhibitors of free play, and thus block an activity that ensures a more complete and physiological maturation of the prefrontal cortices (Vandekerckhove, Bulnes and Panksepp, 1997). These drugs are recognized in medical circles as being effective inhibitors of the child's sometimes disruptive agitation both at home in the family and at school. However, these drugs are not only effective because they increase hetero-direct attention and concentration, but also by inhibiting the child's impulsive outbursts within the dysregulated PLAY system. At the same time, according to some studies this drug-induced inhibition sets in motion a vicious circle, for it predisposes children subjected only to this type of "chemical treatment" to continue with the method as a way of avoiding conflicts. While on the one hand this reduces the externalizing symptoms of the child with ADHD, on the other there is evidence that prolonged administration of these excitatory drugs on the prefrontal cortex can make the child more likable to addiction later in life (this is especially true of those children who do not simultaneously receive psychological support that makes it possible for them to give meaning to their accentuated impulsiveness and hyperactivity; Nocjar, 1996; Robinson and Berridge, 1993).

Specificity of developmental learning disorders

The neurological standpoint has often clashed with psychoanalysis, frequently leading to sterile debates on the causes of DLD, with neuropsychologists regarding them as secondary deficits or alterations of higher cognitive functions supported by the cerebral cortex, while psychoanalysts (as for every psychological symptom) have always pointed to the relational component as triggering these interferences in learning from experience. How should we consider specific learning disorders if, as it is possible today, we want to combine a neurocognitivist perspective interested in relieving the child from his symptomatology with psychoanalytic methodology, which is intrinsically interested in understanding their inner meaning? We believe that affective neuroscience is providing the conceptual tools that will enable this goal to be reached. The construction of the child's internal reference schemes, the structuring of his perceptual skills, and integration with the real world, thus become increasingly intertwined as development procedes. This trend depends on the acquisition of predictive patterns of reality acquired by the child, who selects those that best suit what is required by his environment (for example, firstly by his care-givers and then by his educators). First of all, it must be said that we do not in fact possess the full scientific picture of how every child learns to read and write, since there is no single way to learn language. Learning a language, therefore the ability to read and write, derives from each child's ability to decode the "operating code" of a language, or how the child translates verbal messages, mainly and initially perceived through the auditory pathways (Miller, 2015).

The neuropsychology of reading disorders, in a nutshell and in line with the ideas of Freud's neuroscience period, tells us that language is organized in the brain according to multimodal somatosensory and proprioceptive-motor systems: all the main senses are included in linguistic coding and decoding neocortical areas. When the child learns to read, for example, he uses in particular the two ways available to the visual projection to decipher the meaning of things: in the early stages of reading, the first system to function is the dorsal occipito-parietal processing pathway – the "pathway of *where*-information" that informs us of the spatial configuration of the visual stimuli, matching the stimuli of the letters *seen* with phonemes (the written sign with verbal auditory representations) of the language *heard* (in the sense of memorized). This process therefore concerns the phonological decoding of the visual stimuli of a text. The ontogenesis of the ventral (parvocellular) visual pathway is more recent; it follows an inferior occipito-temporal path and is called the "*what*-information pathway," which enables allows an object to be identified through parallel matching between newly generated stimuli and previously stored information. This identification is then translated into a morpheme (the smallest unit of a word possessing meaning). The dorsal phonological decoding pathway then transforms the visual spatial representation into an auditory code (in the angular gyrus of both hemispheres) to convey this information to the Wernicke area (the well-known auditory language decoding area in the left cerebral hemisphere). This phonological decoding is then re-transmitted to Broca's language motor area for the production and vocal articulation of the word. Besides maturing later in development, the ventral pathway for word identification is also slower to mature and makes use of the dorsal pathway of spatial decoding in the subsequent stages of development between the first and third year of life before becoming completely operational. The late-developing ventral pathway then takes over.

In the case of reading, thanks to the late maturation of the ventral path (in its turn dependent on the first dorsal path functioning well), words begin to be recognized audio-visually: the written word starts to be read more accurately and more quickly, effective and automatic reading becomes possible (without the interpolation of conscience and attention). This maturation represents a good example of procedural learning (supported by affective regulation), as mentioned above. It must be added that in developmental dyslexia what appears to be the "cortical signature" of the disorder, appears fundamentally to be a deficit in audio-visual decoding (of the phonological pathway). This is accompanied by other peculiarities highlighted by functional magnetic resonance studies (fMRI; Joseph, Noble and Eden, 2001) of dyslexic children: in addition to the aforementioned hypoactivation of the posterior dorsal pathway, in particular in the left cerebral hemisphere, there is a hyperactivation of the anterior cortical zones of the left hemisphere and of the posterior zones of the right. These combined elements in the configuration of cortical activation seem to support the hypothesis that these distinctive signs accompanying dyslexic disorders in children are the expression "compensation" by means of neighboring functioning areas of the primary problem of dyslexia: the *phonological decoding deficit*. As is well known, the dyslexic child strives to pronounce the not fully recognized words that he reads and, however slowly or inaccurately he does so (hyperactivation of the left anterior areas of production and pronunciation of the word), he performs additional work in trying to recognize or decode the shape of the visual object represented by the written word (overactivation of the parietal areas of the right hemisphere). The fundamental deficit that "marks" developmental dyslexia in children therefore consists mainly of the maturative deficits of the phonological dorsal pathway (Demb, Poldrack and Gabrieli, 1999). What then ensures good functionality of this first cortical maturation consisting of the dorsal phonological pathway in the processing of reading-writing? To answer this question, we turned to the observations of Lovett and Barron (2008):

> The phonemes that make up a syllable are co-articulated with each other; the result is a largely overlapping representation between acoustic and articulatory aspects of the information relating to each phoneme. Phonemes are not physically distinct units from each other; they are nested in the syllables. Children [with defective phonological awareness] have *difficulty in using phonemes as separate mental objects*, objects that can then be associated with letters in the course of learning the correspondences between graphemes and phonemes.
>
> (Lovett and Barron, 2008, p. 802; emphasis added)

These authors refer here to the cortical and audio-visual decoding aspects of developmental dyslexia, but extending the above to the data emerging from recent research on the mechanisms of embodiment and onto how the child learns to differentiate between self and others (Fotopoulou and Tsakiris, 2017), we could hypothesize that behind the task of "using phonemes as separate objects" lie the fundamental processes of *separation between self and object* (of individuation and separation; Mahler, Pine and Bergman, 1978), a process closely linked to *mentalization* (Fonagy and Target, 1997). These processes require the assimilation of the primary processes of separation and identification occurring in body mentalization (embodied mentalization; Fotopoulou and Tsakiris, 2017). In order to separate objects and the symbols that represent them, things and words, the intrinsic processes of maturation need to have taken place at the emergence of the processes of separation of the Self (starting with the minimal Self), which is largely based on the first representations that the child has of his own body first, followed by his own mind, as distinct and separate from of other objects, whether they are animated (such as the mother) or inanimate (like the things or objects of his own "games," either mental – fantasies – or physical – in the external world). The direction of the acquisition of this important mentalizing skill – the ability to manipulate objects and words in one's imagination – must therefore be attributed to the development and progressive regulation of the primary attentional and motivational systems of the basic emotions described by Panksepp (1998). These systems, in particular the SEEKING and PLAY systems, are the primary structures in development and allow the maturation of the cortical structures at the origin of the child's ability to then "play," mentally manipulating words and things. The child's so-called DLD could therefore be traced back to a fundamental maturational deficit due to motivational dysregulation. Underlying these alterations, we can find dynamic mechanisms with an objective, attentional and relational foundation that have only secondary repercussions in the decoding, recognition and representation of particular procedural memories organizing cognitive processing in the cerebral cortex. If, on the other hand, the activations of the FEAR, RAGE or PANIC/SEPARATION DISTRESS systems prevail over the SEEKING system, then the so-called positive affects, the PLAY system or the CARE system, or the LUST system, that contribute to the formation of the Self, of separation between oneself and the other from oneself, can be interfered with or seriously compromised, leading the child to experience difficulties in mentalizing (in using his own thought, his own cognitive and reflexive consciousness later on), in decoding firstly the meaning of "objects" and of "words," then the intentions and motivation of significant others. This "primary confusion" (Weiss, 1960) can therefore continue to interfere with learning, where the well-known symptoms of dyslexia and dysgraphia may occur: the inversion of the form of the letters, the indistinctness of phonemes and graphemes and the failure to recognize morphemes (the first symbolic units with meaning) and all the symptoms typically present in the first phases of reading and writing, are all phenomena that can persist and consolidate as a specific learning disorder in the later stages of development.

Psychoanalytic therapy in learning and attention disorders

Attention deficit disorders (ADHD) and specific learning disorders (DLD) are included in the DSM-5 (American Psychiatric Association, 2013) among neurodevelopmental disorders. We have argued that they constitute a complex and heterogeneous problem of neuropsychodynamic origin, in which all the factors inherent in neurodevelopment should be considered, including especially psychic, emotional and relational development, as suggested by affective neuroscience, psychoanalysis and, in particular, neuropsychoanalytic studies. In fact, treatment for these disorders must eschew all preconceptions. This also does not exempt scholars and therapists who for example consider dyslexia to be caused exclusively by genetic factors (Hannula-Jouppi, et al., 2005) or by peripheral or central problems of vision (Galaburda, et al., 2006) from the need to constantly reappraise their theoretical models. There is a growing need for a more integrated therapeutic approach that takes into account how a child has developed and evaluates the specific disorder. Controlled relational experiences, whether deriving from experience of good maternal care or arise from psychotherapy, encourage the child to structure "internal organizers" (internal objects), which enable him to perceive and then comprehend aspects of the world that are cognitively and effectively endowed with meaning for the child. All being well (*rebus bene gestis*, if things are done well, as Freud used to say in Latin), the child is thus helped to give up the omnipotent and omniscient solutions typical of infantile narcissism, and these internal organizers, deriving from the relational experiences made by the child in his earliest childhood, enable the child, as if they were optical lenses, to obtain an increasingly shared and integrated picture of the outside world, even if this picture will never be immune to some distortion created by the child's inner world of fantasies and affects. As already mentioned, in psychoanalysis, we call these "lenses," *internalized object relations*, to be precise: "legitimately" automated "internal organizing" memories (that is, they help us achieve our evolutionary goals and our needs according to our needs and interests, but also in accordance with the reality principle). These organized internal referencing schemes (Sandler and Sandler, 1998) are essentially matrices of procedural memory, a "precipitate" of the multiple relationships engraved in the child's mind. These matrices allow the child progressively to acquire the ability to think according to the secondary process. The gradual integration of Ego functions and reality testing therefore consists in the growth of this verification and selection skill (implemented as we have seen, referring to perceptual and active inferences in illustrating the predictive coding model), and to choose among the most adaptive options offered by the environment.

The fundamental characteristic of cognitive functions (of the Ego) is well known to be the marked tendency to resolve these contradictions through conceptual synthesis and perceptual integration. The examination of reality and the examination of conceptual reality can therefore be regarded, at an increasingly complex level, as the legacy of this integration operation. These Ego processes can be considered primarily affective – generally when their operation leads the individual to predict and control what happens to him (inside and outside himself), with greater probability of success. It is in this sense that the individual's greater or lesser capacity for adaptation should be understood. The Sandlers (Sandler and Sandler, 1998) have however clearly stated that this adaptive organization is anything but linear and constant in each of us. Each adaptive reorganization is regularly confronted with the Ego's *natural resistance to change* (the updating of the generative models that structure our expectations, our beliefs and, ultimately, our view of the world). Each modification imposed upon the Self undermines the feelings of its narcissistic integrity (in the child as well as in the adult) and is therefore perceived as a threat, precisely because it needs revising – an effort that entails deconstructing and reconsolidating the very fabric of our Self: our views and memories. At these times "surprise" (internal entropy; Friston, 2010) increases and feelings of safety diminish. What is true for the child and his mental processes also applies to the development of scientific communities and therefore to scientific research itself. The scientist builds a theory or a model of the functioning of the external world by testing his hypotheses, then continuously modifies it on the basis of the verification of the observations he makes and his subsequent thought processes.

The research techniques adopted by the scientist are basically extensions – sometimes extremely sophisticated – of the sensory capacities underlying the examination of objective and conceptual reality (one need only consider the magnetic resonance that extends our vision to the inside the body). No branch of science is immune from perceptual distortions caused by unconscious affects and motivational pressures and from the use of defense mechanisms against an undesired reality. This is something researchers often forget. It is important for every scientist to be aware of the limits and potentials of the scientific method he/she adopts.

Psychoanalytic psychotherapy intends to favor emotional-relational development from another point of view, i.e. "by removing" SEEKING through continuous comparison between the current experience with the analyst (in the transference) and the feelings aroused by it, making the emotional-relational interferences that led to the formation of that symptom re-emerge, however specific it may appear (as happens in reading, writing and counting disorders). Setting aside sterile debates on the organic or environmental nature of its origins, any specific learning disorder, if viewed as a symptom of a (neuro-psycho-dynamic) conflict, can be dealt with exactly as it happens in the physiological development and normal psychological growth of the child in this double-folded perspective. In addition to stimuli and a context encouraging exposure to learning, the psychoanalytic approach also has much to offer: it brings relief to the child by making him face his fears, reducing their scale, and consequently dismantling his most strenuous defenses (automated predictions "illegitimately" and not in accordance with the reality principle). This occurs in a context of care provided by another human being, that is through a caregiver equipped with a properly regulated maternal (or psychotherapeutic) CARE system that helps the child tolerate psychological pain and frustration. In this way, even the dyslexic child can be helped to process what it is acting out in the *here-and-now* of the transference as a result of the procedural memories of repressed experience that can no longer be represented. In child psychotherapy, the child can be helped to re-problematize – or bring to his attention – the repetitive derivatives of repressed experience, which, in the transfer with the therapist, can now be re-lived in the current experience. This procedure, therefore, entails the reactivation (reconsolidation) of new cortical representations, which can then enter into the working-through made possible in the declarative memory domain (and reflexive tertiary processes of the prefrontal *cortices*), then becoming rethinkable. This process, in turn, allows these thoughts and fantasies to reconnect with the related effects in a tolerable way, (a) thanks to the fact that the child can now have a more neurobiologically mature brain than he had when these primitive "illegitimate" connections were established in early infancy, and (b) making use of the temporary help of another mind/brain (that of the analyst, for example, who acts as an auxiliary Ego) whose aim is to aid the child's development by revising his conflicts and the recurring feelings generated by them. The therapeutic process facilitates the generation of better (more adaptive) predictive models, with action plans more adherent to the child's current reality. All this takes time: after the symptom stops being repeated and the transference is interpreted (the process continues with the slow, tiring work of *working through*; see Freud, 1914), which leads to the creation of new procedural memories. The structuring of new connections, consolidating fresh generative models automatizing more realistic predictions, is a very slow process, as we have seen, both in infancy and increasingly so at later ages. As Mark Solms (2013) remarks:

> Those who propose faster treatments (or less frequent sessions) [in disorders consolidated in developmental age, do not know and] will therefore have to study better how [the psychodynamics and neurobiology of] learning really work.
>
> (Solms, 2017, p. 6; additions by the authors)

Psychoanalysis is both a therapeutic method and an example of ceaseless scientific research (Sandler, 1962). It constitutes a serious scientific attempt to understand our subjective life, that is, that unsharable part of our nature involving our subjective Self, which determines, with the choices and actions we perform, who we are. Just as the child makes a serious attempt to give gradually more plausible explanations concerning his internal and external reality, so motivated scientific scholars in the course of their research (and psychoanalysts, who are among them), also make equally serious attempts to reconstruct and understand this integration between inner and outer reality.

Notes

1 We owe to Valerie Sinason (1992) an interesting definition of "stupidity" in those suffering from deficits, disabilities or mental handicaps: the author traces the word "stupid" etymologically to the Latin *stupor*, a medical term that refers to the "lack of critical cognitive function combined with a level of consciousness in which the patient is almost incapable of responding to basic stimuli, such as pain". Similarly, a frustrating and painful intrapsychic relationship, if experienced as intolerable, can also elicit very specific disabling defenses, such as confusion regarding the letters, phonemes, and graphemes in numbers and words.

2 All seven primary emotional systems converge caudally (i.e., downwards on a horizontal plane in the brain) at two deep, subcortical points that are the Peri-Aqueductal Gray (or PAG) and the dorsal midbrain tegmentum. The PAG is an area of neurons located deep within the brain stem surrounding the cerebral aqueduct (hence the name), which consists of two sections: the ventral part generates extremely pleasant sensations, while the dorsal PAG gives rise to

intense psychic pain. The degree of pleasure and suffering determines the nature of the experience and account for the "basic meaning" of emotions. The second major body map is located very close to the first, in the dorsal tegmentum and in the roof of the mesencephalic brain stem. This region of the brain receives inputs from all the sensorimotor circuits and is therefore one of the "zones of convergence" between emotions and perceptual experience. These two areas of the midbrain together generate a rough representation of the whole person, the combination of two "virtual bodies": the internal visceral one (the periaqueductal gray) and the external somatosensory one (the dorsal tegmentum). Panksepp conceptually locates the core-self in this region of the brain, as it is here (superimposed like Russian dolls) that the basic self on which we build all the most complex representations of ourselves in relation to the world, is formed. The second reason why the short distance between these two body maps (visceral and somatosensory-musculoskeletal) is important is that it gives the area that generates emotions in the brain more direct access to the systems that perform actions. The *homunculus* in the dorsal tegmentum provides a combined sensorimotor map of the body, which generates our most primeval impulses to act (i.e., for instance, approach and avoidance behaviours, which are closely related to pleasure and sorrow, respectively). This calls to mind the highly significant fact that not only do we perceive the emotional experience, but we also express our emotions. Emotions are not just perceptual modalities directed inwards; they are also a form of visceral motor discharge.

3 Jaak Panksepp (1998) used capital letters to define his basic motivational systems to emphasize that these terms carry a far greater content than they have in everyday use on the grounds that they refer to distinct neuro-anatomical and functional systems, especially as regards the neuromediators that govern them.

4 Roughly speaking and with all due to the differences, Panksepp's description of affective primary processes may be conflated in Freudian models with the notion of *drive; and* the laws that govern drives and their fluctuations lead to the primary process mode of psychic functioning, which constitutes *primary process* in the psychoanalytic sense. As far as reality testing is concerned, according to the secondary process thinking as it is described in psychoanalysis, it loosely corresponds to what Panksepp describes as psychic functioning at the tertiary levels (see Figure 10.5). Panksepp's secondary (motor-affective procedural) learning corresponds approximately to the repetitive-compulsive workings of the unconscious.

5 Freud addressed these questions in a passage from 1915:

> Philosophers have stated that the intellectual enigma aroused in the primeval man by the image of death forced us to reflect and was the starting point of all subsequent speculation. It seems to me that in this the philosophers think too much ... like philosophers, and do not take sufficient account of the primary causation. I therefore believe I must limit and correct this statement: in front of the corpse of the killed enemy, the primeval man simply felt a sense of triumph and was not induced to worry about the mystery of life and death. Not an intellectual enigma, but *the emotional conflict in the face of the death of a loved one and yet also a stranger and hated person* has given way to human research. Psychology was born from this emotional conflict [of ambivalence]
>
> [Freud, 1915; emphasis added]

We see well expressed in Freud "the psychologist" the fundamental role of the primary effects: it seems that Freud is speaking to us, in outlining the bases of the psychology of the individual, of the primary motivational systems of ANGER, of maternal attachment (CARE system) and the primary infant attachment system (SEPARATION ANXIETY/SADNESS system).

6 According to Freud, before the acquisition of language we could only be aware of external perceptions, while the external mental activities remained excluded from consciousness.

7 These *basic needs detectors* are also integral part of the motivational systems and are mainly found in the hypothalamus, a structure that constantly monitors the delicate balance of our internal visceral body. Some hypothalamic regions act as "accelerators", others act as "brakes", increasing or decreasing the activity of the motivational systems. They make continuous "estimates" of the internal milieu in order to keep their homeostasis stable exactly as the thermostat of our heating does: in fact, one of these systems, for example, regulates our central body temperature. It ensures that our temperature remains in the correct range (a generally very narrow range). Similarly, there is a "detector" of thirst, one of hunger, of "sexual need" and in an increasingly complex way of "danger," of "proximity to the maternal object," and so on.

References

Alberini C.M. (2005), Mechanisms of memory stabilization: Are consolidation and reconsolidation similar or distinct processes?, *Trends in Neurosciences*, *28*(1), 51–56.

Alberini C.M. (2009), Transcription factors in long-term memory and synaptic plasticity, *Physiological Reviews*, *89*(1), 121–145.

Alcaro A., Huber R., Panksepp J. (2007), Behavioral functions of the mesolimbic dopaminergic system: An affective neuroethological perspective, *Brain Research Reviews*, *56*(2), 283–321.

Alcaro A., Panksepp J. (2011), The SEEKING mind: Primal neuro-affective substrates for appetitive incentive states and their pathological dynamics in addictions and depression, *Neuroscience & Biobehavioral Reviews*, *35*(9), 1805–1820.

Alcaro A., Panksepp J. (2014), Le radici affettive e immaginative del Sé. Un'indagine neuroetologica sulle origini della soggettività, [The affective and imaginative bases of the Self. A neuroethological study on subjectivity] In: Northoff G., Farinelli M., Chattat R., Baldoni F. (Eds.), *La plasticità del Sé. Una prospettiva neuropsicodinamica*, [*The plasticity of the Self. A neuropsychodynamic perspective*] (pp. 65–89). Bologna: Il Mulino.

American Psychiatric Association. (2013), *Diagnostic and statistical manual of mental disorders* (5th ed.). Arlington, VA: American Psychiatric Association.

Baddeley A.D., Hitch G. (1974), Working memory, *Psychology of Learning and Motivation*, *8*, 47–89.

Badgaiyan R.D., Sinha S., Sajjad M., Wack D.S., (2015), Attenuated tonic and enhanced phasic release of dopamine in attention deficit hyperactivity disorder, *PLoS One*, *10*(9), 1–14.

Beebe B., Lachmann F. (2002), Organizing principles of interaction from infant research and the lifespan prediction of attachment: Application to adult treatment, *Journal of Infant, Child, and Adolescent Psychotherapy*, *2*(4), 61–89.

Bion W.R. (1962), *Learning from Experience*. London: William Heinemann. [Reprinted London: Karnac Books].

Bion W.R. (1967), A theory of thinking. In: Bion W.R. (Ed.), *Second thoughts*. London: William Heinemann. [Reprinted London: Karnac Books, 1984].

Botvinick M., Cohen J. (1998), Rubber hand feels touch that eyes see. *Nature*, *391*(February), 756.

Bowlby J. (1988), *A secure base: Clinical applications of attachment theory* (Vol. 393). London: Taylor & Francis.

Burgdorf J., Panksepp J. (2006), The neurobiology of positive emotions, *Neuroscience & Biobehavioral Reviews*, *30*(2), 173–187.

Cai D.J. et al. (2009), REM, not incubation, improves creativity by priming associative networks, *Proceedings of the National Academy of Sciences (PNAS)*, *106*(25), 10130–10134.

Chomsky N. (1968), *Language and mind*. Cambridge: Cambridge University Press.

Chomsky N. (1988), *Language and problems of knowledge: The Managua lectures*. Cambridge: The MIT Press.

Clarici A. (2014), *Teoria e ricerca in psicoanalisi. [Theory and research in psychoanalysis]* EUT (Edizioni Università di Trieste), Trieste.

Craig A.D. (2009), How do you feel – now? The anterior insula and human awareness, *Nature Reviews Neuroscience*, *10*, 59–70.

Crystal J.D. (2012), Prospective cognition in rats, *Learning and motivation*, *43*(4), 181–191.

Dahan L, Astier B, Vautrelle N, Urbain N, Kocsis B, Chouvet G. (2007), Prominent burst firing of dopaminergic neurons in the ventral tegmental area during paradoxical sleep, *Neuropsychopharmacology*, *32*(6), 1232–1241.

Damasio A., Damasio H., Tranel D. (2012), Persistence of feeling and sentience after bilateral damage of the insula, *Cerebral Cortex*, *23*(4), 833–846.

Damasio A.R. (1999), *The feeling of what happens: Body and emotion in the making of consciousness*. Boston, MA: Houghton Mifflin Harcourt.

Demb J.B., Poldrack R.A., Gabrieli J.D.E (1999), Functional neuroimaging of word processing in normal and dyslexic readers. In: Klein R.M., McMullen P.M. (Eds.), *Converging method for understanding reading and dyslexia* (pp. 245–304). Cambridge: MIT Press.

Depue R.A., Collins P.F. (1999), Neurobiology of the structure of personality: Dopamine, facilitation of incentive motivation, and extraversion. *Behavioral and Brain Sciences*, *22*(3), 491–517; discussion 518–569.

Deyoung C.G. (2013), The neuromodulator of exploration: A unifying theory of the role of dopamine in personality, *Frontiers in Human Neuroscience*, *14*(7), 762.

Edelman G.M. (1992), *Bright air, brilliant fire: On the matter of the mind*. New York: Basic books.

Engle R.W. (2002), Working memory capacity as executive attention, *Currentdirections in Psychological Science*, *11*(1), 19–23.

Fonagy P., Target M. (1997), Attachment and reflective function: Their role in self-organization, *Development and Psychopathology*, *9*(4), 679–700.

Fotopoulou A., Tsakiris M. (2017), Mentalizing homeostasis: The social origins of interoceptive inference. *Neuropsychoanalysis*, *19*(1), 3–28.

Freud S. (1891), *On Aphasia*. New York: International Universities Press.

Freud S. (1900), The interpretation of dreams. *Standard Edition of the Complete Psychological Works of Sigmund Freud*, Volume IV and V. London: Hogarth.

Freud S. (1911), Formulations on the two principles of mental functioning. *The Standard Edition of the Complete Psychological Works of Sigmund Freud*, Volume XII. London: Hogarth, pp. 213–226.

Freud S. (1914), Remembering, repeating and working-through. *The Standard Edition of the Complete Psychological Works of Sigmund Freud*, Volume XII. London: Hogarth.

Freud S. (1920), Beyond the pleasure principle. *Standard Edition of the Complete Psychological Works of Sigmund Freud*, Volume 18. London: Hogarth, pp. 7–64.

Freud S. (1923), *The ego and the id. Standard Edition of the Complete Psychological Works of Sigmund Freud*, Volume 9. London: Hogarth, pp. 12–59.

Friston, K. (2005), A theory of cortical responses. *Philosophical transactions of the Royal Society B: Biological Sciences*, *360*(1456), 815–836.

Friston K. (2010), The free-energy principle: A unified brain theory?, *Nature Reviews Neuroscience*, *11*(2), 127–138.

Friston K. (2012), The history of the future of the Bayesian brain. *NeuroImage*, *62*(2), 1230–1233.

Fuster J.M. (1988), Prefrontal cortex. In: Irwin L.N., *Comparative neuroscience and neurobiology* (pp. 107–109). Boston: Birkhäuser.

Galaburda A.M. (1982), Histology, architectonics, and asymmetry of language areas, In: Arbib M. (Ed.) *Neural Models of Language Processes*, Cambridge, MA: Academic press, pp. 435–445.

Galaburda A.M., LoTurco J., Ramus F., Fitch R.H., Rosen G.D. (2006), From genes to behavior in developmental dyslexia, *Nature Neuroscience*, *9*(10), 1213–1217.

Haber SN. (2014), The place of dopamine in the Cortico-Basal ganglia circuit, *Neuroscience*, *282*, 248–257.

Hannula-Jouppi K., Kaminen-Ahola N., Taipale M., Eklund R., Nopola-Hemmi J., Kääriäinen H., Kere J. (2005), The axon guidance receptor gene ROBO1 is a candidate gene for developmental dyslexia, *PLoS Genetics*, *1*(4), e50.

Hartmann H., Rapaport D.T. (1958), *Ego psychology and the problem of adaptation.* Madison: International Universities Press.

Hobson J.A. (2009), REM sleep and dreaming: Towards a theory of protoconsciousness. *Nature Review in Neuroscience*, *10*(11), 803–813.

Huth A.G., de Heer W.A., Griffiths T.L., Theunissen F.E., Gallant J.L. (2016), Natural speech reveals the semantic maps that tile human cerebral cortex. *Nature*, *532*(7600), 453–458.

Huth A.G., Nishimoto S., Vu A.T., Gallant J.L. (2012), A continuous semantic space describes the representation of thousands of object and action categories across the human brain, *Neuron*, *76*(6), 1210–1224.

Janet P (1889), *L'automatismopsicologico.* Milano: Raffaello Cortina, 2013.

Joseph J., Noble K., Eden G. (2001), The neurobiological basis of reading. *Journal of Learning Disabilities*, *34*, 566–579.

Kandel E.R. (1999), Biology and the future of psychoanalysis: A new intellectual framework for psychiatry revisited. *American Journal of Psychiatry*, 156, 505–524.

Kaplan-Solms K., Solms M. (2002), *Clinical studies in neuro-psychoanalysis: Introduction to a depth neuropsychology.* New York: Other Press, LLC.

Kihlstrom J.K. (1987), The cognitive unconscious, *Science*, *237*, 1445.

Ikemoto S., Panksepp J. (1999), The role of nucleus accumbens dopamine in motivated behavior: A unifying interpretation with special reference to reward-seeking, *Brain Research Reviews*, *31*(1), 6–41.

Immordino-Yang M.H. (2015), *Emotions, learning, and the brain: Exploring the educational implications of affective neuroscience (the Norton series on the social neuroscience of education).* New York: W.W. Norton & Company.

Immordino-Yang M.H., Damasio A. (2007), We feel, therefore we learn: The relevance of affective and social neuroscience to education, *Mind, Brain, and Education*, *1*(1), 3–10.

LeDoux J. (1998), *The emotional brain: The mysterious underpinnings of emotional life*. New York: Simon and Schuster.

LeDoux J. (2003), *Synaptic self: How our brains become who we are*. New York: Penguin.

LeDoux J. (2015), *Anxious: The modern mind in the age of anxiety*. New York: Simon and Schuster.

Lovett M.W., Barron R.W. (2008), Developmental reading disorders. In: Feinberg T.E., Farah M.J. (Eds.), *Behavioral neurology and neuropsychology*. New York: McGraw-Hill, pp. 801–819.

Lu H., Zou Q., Gu H., Raichle M.E., Stein E.A., Yang Y. (2012), Rat brains also have a default mode network, *Proceedings of the National Academy of Sciences*, *109*(10), 3979–3984.

Luria A.R. (1976), *The working brain: An introduction to neuropsychology*. New York: Basic Books.

MacLean P.D. (1990), *The triune brain in evolution: Role in paleocerebral functions*. Berlin: Springer Science & Business Media.

Mahler M.S., Pine F., Bergman A. (1978), *The psychological birth of the human infant symbiosis and individuation*. New York: Basic Books.

Malcolm-Smith S., Koopowitz S., Pantelis E., Solms M. (2012), Approach/avoidance in dreams, *Consciousness and Cognition*, *21*(1), 408–412.

Mantini D., Gerits A., Nelissen K., Durand J.B., Joly O., Simone L., Sawamura H., Wardak C., Orban G.A., Buckner R.L., Vanduffel W. (2011), Default mode of brain function in monkeys, *Journal of Neuroscience*, *31*(36), 12954–12962.

McKee RD, Squire LR (1993), On the development of declarative memory, *Journal of Experimental Psychology: Learning, Memory, and Cognition*, *19*(2), 397.

Merker B. (2007), Consciousness without a cerebral cortex: A challenge for neuroscience and medicine, *Behavioral and Brain Sciences*, *30*, 63–134.

Miller JF (2015), *Do you read me?: Learning difficulties, dyslexia and the denial of meaning*. London: Karnac Books.

Nocjar C. (1996), Chronic amphetamine increases future reward seeking behavior of rats: Effect of SCH23390 or haloperidol co-treatment. *Unpublished Ph.D. Dissertation*, Bowling Green State University, Ohio: Bowling Green.

Panksepp J. (1998), *Affective neuroscience: The foundations of human and animal emotions*. Oxford: Oxford University Press.

Panksepp J. (2001), The long-term psychobiological consequences of infant emotions: Prescriptions for the twenty-first century, *Neuropsychoanalysis*, *3*(2), 149–178.

Panksepp J. (2007), Can PLAY diminish ADHD and facilitate the construction of the social brain?, *Journal of the Canadian Academy of Child and Adolescent Psychiatry*, *16*(2), 57.

Panksepp J. (2008), The power of the word may reside in the power of affect, *Integrative Psychological and Behavioral Science*, *42*(1), 47–55.

Panksepp J. (2011), Cross-species affective neuroscience decoding of the primal affective experiences of humans and related animals, *Public Library of Science (PLoS One)*, 6 (9), e21236-e21236.

Panksepp, J. (2014), The core emotional systems of the mammalian brain: The fundamental substrates of human emotions. In: Corrigal J. et al., (Eds.) *About a body: Working with the embodied mind in psychotherapy*. Hove: Routledge, pp. 14–32.

Panksepp J., Biven L. (2012), *The archaeology of mind: Neuroevolutionary origins of human emotions (Norton series on interpersonal neurobiology).* New York: W.W. Norton & Company.

Panksepp J., Solms M. (2012), What is neuropsychoanalysis? Clinically relevant studies of the minded brain, *Trends in Cognitive Sciences, 16*(1), 6–8.

Panksepp J, Watt D. (2011), Why does depression hurt? Ancestral primary-process separation-distress (PANIC/GRIEF) and diminished brain reward (SEEKING) processes in the genesis of depressive affect, *Psychiatry, 74*(1), 5–13.

Passamonti L., Terracciano A., Riccelli R., Donzuso G., Cerasa A., Vaccaro M., Novellino F., Fera F., Quattrone A. (2015), Increased functional connectivity within mesocortical networks in open people. *Neuroimage, 104*, 301–309.

Petkova A., Ehrsson H. (2008), If I were you: Perceptual illusion of body swapping. *PLOS ONE, 3*(12), e3832.

Roberts W.A. (2012), Future cognition in animals, *Learning and Motivation, 43*, 169–180.

Robinson T.E., Berridge K. (1993), The neural basis of drug craving: An incentive-sensitization theory of addiction, *Brain Research Reviews, 18*, 247–291.

Saling M., Solms M. (1986), On psychoanalysis and neuroscience: Freud's attitude to the localizationist tradition, *The International Journal of Psycho-Analysis, 67*, 397.

Sandler J. (1960), The background of safety, *The International Journal of Psycho-Analysis, 41*, 352–356.

Sandler J. (1962), Research in psycho-analysis—The Hampstead index as an instrument of psychoanalytic research, *The International Journal of Psycho-Analysis, 43*, 287–291.

Sandler J. (1976), Dreams, unconscious fantasies and identity of perception, *International Review of Psycho-Analysis, 3*, 33–42.

Sandler J., Dare C., Dreher A.U., Holder A. (1997), *Freud's models of the mind: An introduction* (No. 1). Sterling, VA: Stylus Publishing, LLC.

Sandler J, Joffe W.G. (1967), The tendency to persistence in psychological function and development, *Bulletin of the Menninger Clinic, 31*(5), 257.

Sandler A.M., Sandler J. (1998), *Internal objects revisited.* London: Routledge.

Schacter D.L. (1996), *Searching for memory: The brain, the mind, and the past.* New York: Basic Books.

Schacter D.L., Addis D.R., Hassabis D., Martin V.C., Spreng R.N., Szpunar K.K. (2012), The future of memory: Remembering, imagining, and the brain, *Neuron, 76*(4), 677–694.

Schore A.N. (1994), *Affect regulation and the origin of the self.* Hillsdale: Lawrence Erlbaum.

Schore A.N. (1996), The experience-dependent maturation of a regulatory system in the orbital prefrontal cortex and the origin of developmental psychopathology, *Development and Psychopathology, 8*(01), 59–87.

Schore A.N. (2003), *Affect dysregulation and disorders of the self (Norton Series on Interpersonal Neurobiology).* New York: W.W. Norton & Company.

Schore A.N. (2011), The right brain implicit self lies at the core of psychoanalysis, *Psychoanalytic Dialogues, 21*, 75–100.

Schwartenbeck P., Fitzgerald T., Dolan R.J., Friston K. (2013), Exploration, novelty, surprise, and free energy minimization, *Frontiers in Psychology, 4*, 710.

Seligman M.E. (2006), *Learned optimism: How to change your mind and your life.* New York: Vintage.

Sinason V. (1992), *Mental handicap and the human condition: New approaches from the Tavi- stock*. London: Free Association Books.

Solms M. (2000), Dreaming and REM sleep are controlled by different brain mechanisms, *Behavioral and Brain Sciences, 23*(6), 843–850; discussion 904–1121.

Solms M. (2013), The conscious Id. *Neuropsychoanalysis, 15*, 5–19.

Solms M. (2017), What is "the unconscious," and where is it located in the brain? A neuropsychoanalytic perspective, *Annals of the New York Academy of Sciences* (in press) 1–8.

Solms M. (2018), *The feeling brain: Selected papers on neuropsychoanalysis*. London: Routledge.

Solms M., Turnbull O. (2002), *The brain and the inner world: An introduction to the neuroscience of subjective experience*. London: Routledge.

Squire L.R., Knowlton B., Musen G. (1993), The structure and organization of memory, *Annual Review of Psychology, 44*(1), 453–495.

Stern D.N. (2004), *The present moment in psychotherapy and everyday life (Norton series on interpersonal neurobiology)*. New York: W.W. Norton & Company.

Tomasello M. (2003), *Constructing a language: A usage-based theory of language acquisition*. Boston, MA: Harvard University Press.

Tsakiris M. (2010), My body in the brain: A neurocognitive model of body-ownership, *Neuropsychologia, 48*, 703–712.

Tulving E (2002), Episodic memory: From mind to brain, *Annual Review of Psychology, 53*(1), 1–25.

Vandekerckhove M., Bulnes L.C., Panksepp J. (2014), The emergence of primary anoetic consciousness in episodic memory, *Frontiers in Behavioral Neuroscience, 7*, 210.

Vanderschuren L.J., Niesink R.J., Van Ree J.M. (1997), The neurobiology of social play behavior in rats, *Neuroscience & Biobehavioral Reviews, 21*, 309–326.

Watson J.B. (1930), *Behaviourism*. New York: Norton.

Watt D.F. (1999), At the intersection of emotion and consciousness: Affective neuroscience and extended reticular thalamic activating system (ERTAS). In: Watt D.F. (Ed.), *Theories of consciousness. Toward a science of consciousness III* (pp. 215–229). Cambridge: MIT Press.

Weiss E. (1960), *The structure and dynamics of the human mind*. Philadelphia, PA: Saunders.

Winnicott D.W. (1974), *The maturational processes and the facilitating environment: Studies in the theory of emotional development*. London: Routledge.

Wise R.A. (2004), Dopamine, learning and motivation, *Nature Reviews Neuroscience, 5*(6), 483–494.

11 The motivational trigger and the affective function in infantile dream

Claudio Colace

> *Now, if there is one thing you can be sure of, there is nothing more powerful than a child's desire... other than an Apache helicopter. An Apache helicopter is equipped with an automatic cannon and missiles. It is an incredibly extraordinary set of armaments. An absolute death machine. Be that as it may, John had chosen the perfect night to make a wish.*
>
> From the film TED (2012)

Introduction

Over the past 20 years, the research on dreams from an ontogenetic perspective has proved impressively useful for studying different aspects of the dreaming process. The research on young children's dreams has provided useful indications concerning, among other things, the role of wishes in dreams, the nature and development of "dream bizarreness" and other characteristics of dreaming.[1]

The first to realize that children's dreams can offer an extraordinary way to understand dreaming processes was Sigmund Freud, who studied the dreams of his children and grandchildren since he started developing his dream theory (Colace, 2010). Freud strongly maintained that explanations to several aspects of dreaming could be drawn from the study of infantile dreams (Freud, 1916–1917). Years later, the great usefulness of childhood dreams was also brought to light by Piaget (1962), who studied dreams in relation to the development of representative and symbolic activities in the child, and by Foulkes (1982, 1999) who carried out the first study on the REM dreams of children in a sleep laboratory, obtaining important indications on the process by which the child develops awareness and on those cognitive functions (visuospatial and symbolic skills) that are indispensable for accomplishing the dream experience.

The most recent studies are showing that children's dreams can represent a useful way for an in-depth study of the motivational determinants of dreaming and its possible function as *affective regulator* (Colace, 2010, 2013, 2017, 2021). Given their exceptional clarity of content and their direct connection with the dreamer's daytime experience, infantile dreams can also

DOI: 10.4324/9781003198741-13

provide clear feedback on the role of subjective motivational drives in triggering dreams, as *Affective Neuroscience* and *neuro-psychoanalytic studies* suggest.

After a brief introduction on Freud's observations about children's dreams (and their fortunes in empirical research), this chapter discusses the most prominent results of large-scale systematic research programs conducted on young children's dreams (Colace, 2006a, 2010, 2013). The chapter deals in particular with the role of wishes in triggering dreams and with the "affective re-establishment" (AR) function of dreams in children between 3 and 5 years of age. Finally, I will attempt to evaluate the extent to which the results of these studies converge with the results from *Affective Neuroscience* and *neuro-psychoanalytic research* on dreaming.

Infantile dreams: the Freudian lesson

The usefulness of studying children's dreams

In Freud's observations, the dreams of children up to five or a little more are often the clear and direct fulfilment of a (conscious) unfulfilled wish, coming from the child's real life, which has left behind a state of nostalgia, displeasure, regret or impatience. Freud suggests that dreams are instigated by a wish that finds hallucinatory fulfilment in the dream content. Wish is the motive force of dream. The peculiarity of infantile dreams is that wish-fulfilment is immediately evident (unlike in adult dreams) to the person who collects the dream report, with no need to interpret the dream content (Freud, 1916–1917). In other words, in order to understand the early dreams of children, there is no need to detect any latent content, since their meaning and function appear straightforwardly in their manifest content. It is however important, for a complete comprehension of dream meaning, to have information on the child's experiences in the previous day (Freud, 1916–1917, pp. 126–127). Theoretically, the most relevant aspect of Freud's observations is the proven effectiveness of infantile dreams in suggesting that at the basis of a dream there always seems to be a wish as the motive force that triggers it, and that the dream constitutes the attempt to fulfil such wish, albeit on a hallucinatory level.

From infantile dreams, Freud drew several deductions – many of which are general in scope – concerning crucial questions about dreams that have always been the subject of dream research and theory, such as the origin of dreams, the sense/senselessness of dreams, their validity or not as a psychic act, the general and individual meaning of dreams, as well as their function. In particular, from children's dreams we may observe that:

- Dreams are instigated by wishes
- The dream is a valid, meaningful and finalized psychic act

- Dreams are the hallucinatory fulfilment of a wish
- Not all dreams are instigated by repressed sexual desires
- The dream allows the continuation of sleep state
- Dream bizarreness is not an intrinsic feature of the dream process
- Not all dreams are bizarre
- All dreams are, in principle, interpretable.

Indeed, Freud regarded children's dreams as an extraordinary example and proof of his general theory of dream. Here is another strategic aspect of Freud's observations: the study of infantile dreams provides empirical support to his general dream theory through systematic "out-of-therapy" observations. On this point, Freud was very explicit in opening a path: children's dreams can be studied by psychologists who do not have a psychoanalytic training and, above all, they do not require the use of any interpretation technique in order to be understood (Freud, 1916–1917, pp. 126–127, 131).[2]

Fortunes of Freudian observations in the empirical research on children's dreams

Freud's observations on children's dreams call for two major considerations. In the first place, some systematic research on these dreams, conducted on large samples of children and dream reports, might represent an opportunity to assess the empirical consistency of the data on infantile dreams so widely used by Freud in the development of his general dream theory (Colace, 2010). Second, children's dreams (and here I also include the so-called infantile dreams of adults) are grounds where Freud's observations and hypotheses, including on dreaming in general, can be tested empirically by the same methods used in the classical ("academic") dream research (Colace, 2006b, 2009a, 2012; Colace & Boag, 2015a, 2015b). While young children's dreams do not need a psychotherapeutic setting nor an interpretation of their content in order to be understood, at the same time, they offer an opportunity to observe the motivational mechanisms of dream triggering and formation, here at "embryonic state", the same ones that exist, in more complex forms, also in adult dreams. Therefore, children's dreams provide an arena for comparing psychoanalytic assumptions with other theoretical models on dreaming, with the same methodologies of empirical research. By saying this, I do not mean that the use of the analytic setting as a tool for observation and clinical research does not equal in dignity the empirical-academic methodology. However, when Freud's theories on dreams are supported, even with the same experimental methods used in the classical research on dream/sleep, the latter can no longer accuse psychoanalysis, as it usually does, of not being scientifically grounded nor empirically testable (Hobson, 2013, 2015; Popper, 1959, 1963: on this topic see also: Colace, 2010; Colace & Boag, 2015a, 2015b).

Despite their importance, Freud's observations on infantile dreams were scarcely considered in the early empirical research on childhood dreams. For example, in the first research on children's REM dreams conducted at a sleep laboratory (Foulkes, 1982; Foulkes et al., 1967), despite the impressive number of variables into play, no detailed information on the children's experiences in the days preceding the dream was collected, which prevented Foulkes and his team from giving accurate results about the frequency of direct wish-fulfilment dreams, let alone about their nature.

The other few studies that followed on the dreams of young children failed to even mention Freud's works on childhood dreams and/or his observations on the wishful aspect of these dreams were not investigated at all (Hall & Domhoff, 1963; Domhoff, 1996; Resnick, Stickgold, Rittenhouse & Hobson, 1994).

The only exceptions showing some interest in Freud's observations come from authors who do not fall into the classical tradition of scientific research on sleep/dream and who however, through less systematic methodologies, arrive at substantially benevolent conclusions on the presence of clear wish-fulfilment dreams in young children (Coriat, 1916; Hill, 1926; Kimmins, 1920; Piaget, 1962).

Among them, Piaget's (1962) contribution appears relevant, being an author not psychoanalytically oriented. Piaget identified at least three types of childhood dreams that are in line with the Freudian thesis of direct wish-fulfilment dreams: a) dreams that fulfil wishes through the direct evocation of the desired result, b) dreams in which conscious symbols appear that represent things loved by the child, and c) dreams of painful events with a positive ending (for examples of these, see: Piaget, 1962, pp. 177–178) Other categories of dreams identified by Piaget are: dreams of punishment and self-punishment, complicated dreams (with secondary symbolism), and nightmares (Piaget, 1962, pp. 179–181).

In conclusion, the potential importance of Freud's observations on children's dreams continued to have little appeal for sleep and dream research until at least the early 1990s. Furthermore, up to that moment, no empirical research was conducted to verify the empirical validity of Freud's observations, and any judgment on them can be regarded as essentially biased (Colace, 2010).

Freud's observations and hypotheses about the dreams of young children have been analysed and described systematically and evaluated empirically in a series of studies since the early 1990s (Colace, 1997, 1998a, 1998b, 2006a; Colace & Tuci, 1996; Colace, Tuci & Ferendeles, 1997; Colace & Violani, 1993; Colace, Violani & Solano, 1993; for a summary, see: Colace, 2010), and thereafter in new research projects (Colace, 2013, 2017, in press; Colace et al., 2021; Mari, Beretta & Colace, 2018). The general purpose of those studies was to replicate Freud's observations on children's dreams and possibly broaden their empirical basis and the opportunities to make them more general and develop them further. Furthermore, those studies have proved to be a valuable research paradigm for the empirical testing of certain prominent assumptions of the Freudian dream model in general (Colace, 2006b, 2009a, 2010, 2012, 2013, 2021; Colace & Boag, 2015a, 2015b).

Systematic evaluation of the frequency of clear wish-fulfilment dreams in preschool children

The results of several systematic studies conducted on large samples of children and of dream reports, and of a recent longitudinal study on a single case, have given strong and consistent indications that dreams at preschool age (3–5 years) often present clear wish-fulfilment contents. The average percentage of this type of dreams, across the various studies, is 65% of all the dreams collected, greater when more information about the children's daytime are available (about 70%), and relatively lower where such information are less detailed (about 60%) (Colace, 2010, 2013, 2017, 2021).[3]

These dreams are clear and simple in their content and do not require interpretative and deductive readings to understand their meaning. They clearly show the representation, in a dream scenario, of the direct (non-symbolic) fulfilment of a (known) wish completely or partially unfulfilled, during the day. Through them, the dreamer experiences, albeit in a merely hallucinatory form, the real-time gratification of his/her wish (examples of these dreams are provided further on in the chapter).

The overwhelming presence of clear wish-fulfilment dreams in young children opens a possibility to engage in a direct study of the motivational determinants of the dream and to make hypotheses about their triggering mechanisms as well as their meaning and function, possibly stirring interest in the motivational aspects of dreaming, a long-neglected aspect of sleep and dream research.

Dream wishes and their fulfilment

The study of a large sample of clear wish-fulfilment dreams allowed us to gain insight into the nature and phenomenology of the wishes underlying children's dreams.

The wishes that are observed in children's dreams concern play/entertainment activities, the child's common imagery, including TV characters, cartoon and videogame heroes, social relationships with peers, activities with grandparents and parents, new and exciting experiences (e.g. first time on the snow, first time at the sea, a school trip, etc.) (Table 1).

Table 11.1 Real-life examples of wishes that appear in children's dreams

---

Oh, I wish I could play with my toy train!
Oh, I wish it were my birthday right away and I were receiving gifts!
Oh, I wish I could go underwater with the new mask!
Oh, I wish I could go camping at once at the mobile home!
Oh, I wish I were a dinosaur fighter!
Oh, I wish I were the hero of the video game!
Oh, I wish I could win the karate fight!
Oh, I wish I could have the scorpion miniature right away! (will be released only
  the following week)
Oh, I wish I could go to the amusement park (famous theme park)!
Oh, I wish it were already tomorrow, so I could see my favourite movie at school!
Oh, I wish I could play football again with mom and dad!
Oh, I wish I could play with my toy kitchen!
Oh, I wish I could celebrate my birthday party with my friends!
Oh, I wish I could see my friend healed!
Oh, I wish my grandfather could come home from hospital!
Oh, I wish I could talk to my brother! (recently lost)
Oh, I wish I could go to the pool again!
Oh, I wish I could see my dog again! (recently died)
Oh, I wish Mum could buy me the stickers!
Oh, I wish you could buy me the Bakugan (cartoon superheroes) and the track!
Oh, I wish I could play hide-and-seek again and chase each other at home with
  mom!
Oh, I wish I had Gameboy! (portable video game console)

The wishes that occur in the dreams are conscious (or preconscious) and were left completely or partially unfulfilled during the child's daytime experience. They are wishes that arose during the day and had a major emotional impact on the child. Of course, in many cases, these wishes are important and need to be fulfilled only from the perspective of a young child, who has less ability to desist from having a wish fulfilled and in whom the desired objects and situations are accompanied by intense and peculiar affective states. In other words, the strength of these wishes and the intensity of the affective states associated with them should be viewed in the context of the infantile psychic apparatus. A *specific strength of infantile wishes* that makes them capable of triggering dreams, even in the absence of an unconscious wish ally.

Sometimes, the dream expresses multiple motivational requests simultaneously. *Infantile dreams were observed that fulfil more wishes together*, and therefore appear *over-determined on a motivational level* (Colace, 2010, 2017, 2021). There is also the case of multiple dreams dealing with a single wish, i.e. *serial wish-fulfilment dreams*. Thus, a child's wish can appear in multiple dreams in the same night or in the same week. This is probably due to the strength of the wish in question and the associated affective state, that can occupy the life of the child for a certain period (even months) and appear in more than one dream (Colace, 2010, 2017, 2021).

Diurnal origin of children's dreams and their motivational and affective basis

||||As children's dreams allow us to observe directly the connections between the dream content and the diurnal experience of the dreamer, we may trace back the experiential (motivational and affective) and temporal conditions that prepare the dreams, and make hypotheses on what memory sources are involved in the construction of dreams, as well as on their triggering mechanisms and formation processes. It is therefore a matter of analysing the circumstances in which those wishes arise (and the associated affective states), which we assume to be at the origin of the dream.

Nature of the diurnal sources of dreams

The origin of wish-fulfilment dreams is invariably an emotionally important daytime experience. On the one hand, there is a strong wish, partially or completely unsatisfied, that triggers the dream and constitutes the motivational drive of its formation; on the other hand, this wish goes along with an intense affective state that has remained unprocessed, in a state of incomplete psychological resolution, and has therefore left untreated emotional portions (i.e., a certain arousal charge).[4] *Together, wish and affective state represent the motivational and affective basis of the dream, its conditions of existence.* The affective states observed have to do with a range of *displeasure/disappointment/regret/nostalgia* feelings due to the (partial or absolute) impossibility to achieve something desired, or of *surprise/excitement/happiness* feelings due to a pleasant, exciting and/or new experience (not achieved in full, or not as the child would have liked to). They may also be feelings of *impatience/excitement/urgency* for something that the child desires but that will only occur at a time that is regarded as too far a future in the child's mind (Colace, 2010, 2013, 2021).

Table 3 reports a few examples of a child's daytime experiences, the underlying wish and connected affective state, and the dreams that arose from them. Each of these diurnal experiences shows a logical and sensible connection with the content and meaning of the dream. The production and content of these dreams represent the result of a motivational and affective process that starts from a daytime situation with a strong motivational drive (represented by the wish), leads to an increase in the emotional load and finally, with the fulfilment enacted in the dream, ends in a situation of gratification of the wish and "settlement" of the original affective state occurred during the day. This concept will be resumed further on, in the part dedicated to the function of these dreams.

Table 11.2 The motivational and emotional basis of wish-fulfilment dreams

Daytime experience			Dream
Experience	Wish	Affective state	
A friend's party	To be at the party again	Sorrow	I dream of being at the party and drinking lemonade!
Conversation on an upcoming school trip	To go on a school trip	Excitement/ anticipation	I dream of being on a school trip
Repeated requests to have a sister	To have a little sister	Impatience	I dream that mom has a baby girl
Father's unexpected leaving the house	To see the father again	Frustration/ Sorrow	I dream that daddy comes back and hugs me
Lost kitten	To see the kitten again	Sorrow	I dream of playing with the kitten who has come home
Seeing snow for the first time	To be in the snow	Excitement/ Pleasure	I dream of making a snowman
Watching Hello Kitty cartoons on TV	To be with the cartoon character	Excitement/ Pleasure	I dream of being on Hello Kitty's hot air balloon
Viewing the places of the upcoming beach holiday	To go on holiday immediately	Excitement/ Impatience	I dream of being on holiday by the sea and by the pool

Temporal distance of the diurnal sources of dreams

A systematic analysis of the temporal distance of the diurnal sources of the dream suggests that its origin is often to be found in experiences had in the day preceding its occurrence (Colace, 2010, 2013, 2017, 2021; Mari, Beretta & Colace, 2018). Sometimes the diurnal sources can go back to a few days or a week earlier, more rarely they are events that occurred months earlier.

A more in-depth analysis shows that in some cases, even when the diurnal reference is something that happened (for the first time) a few days or even a week before, it lingers in the child's mind also in the following days, until the day before the dream where it is staged oneirically. It is therefore a diurnal residue relating to something that has persisted for a number of days with the child and that, at a given moment, finds its expression in the dream.

There are also cases of certain dreams that appear to have as diurnal source events or experiences dating back to three months earlier or even more, but that at a closer analysis showed those sources recalled, or update, somehow, precisely on the day before the dream (for example, by talking about what had happened months before, or by making experiences, on the day before the dream, that bring back the memory of what had happened previously (Colace, 2013, 2021).

These results are in line with Freud's observations that dreams appear to relate mostly to facts and experiences occurred on the day preceding them ("day residues") (Freud, 1900). Furthermore, what is observed in young children is similar to what is found in the dreams of adults that frequently relate to experiences from the day before the dream (i.e., day-residue effects) (Epstein, 1985; Nielsen et al., 2004; Nielsen & Powell, 1992).

In conclusion, the analysis shows that *the building elements for the formation of children's dreams relate to the memories of strong and recent emotional experiences, probably not sufficiently processed (or not psychologically coped with)*. The daytime experiences that the dream relates to are evoked again and then completed in a hallucinatory state, with a positive and satisfactory ending. Each night dream report appears to deal mainly with the most important experiences of the immediately preceding day. The same process is repeated every day/night. This concept will be resumed further on, in the part dedicated to dream function.

Modus operandi of wish-fulfilment dreams

The analysis of a large sample of simple wish-fulfilment dreams, and of the diurnal circumstances that determined them, clearly showed that not all wish-fulfilment dreams are of the same type. By analysing the relationship between the fulfilment of the wish in the dream and the daytime experience that the dream comes from, it was observed that *there are different forms of connection between dream and experience*. There can be a relationship of *inversion*, (the dream acting in lieu of the experience), *continuation* or *anticipation*. These three forms of relationship correspond to three modi operandi of the dream. Wish-fulfilment dreams can operate in order to *compensate, continue* (perpetuate, repeat), or *anticipate*. There are therefore three types of direct wish-fulfilment dreams, that I have called *compensation dreams, continuation dreams* and *anticipation dreams*.

In *compensation dreams,* we observe the fulfilment of a wish that derives from an objectively or subjectively negative daytime experience, for example, the loss of a loved one or a great sorrow for having lost the favourite toy. In the daytime experience, a given desire could not be fulfilled. In the case of the loss of a loved person, for example, it has become impossible to see him/her again. In these cases, the wish that is staged as fulfilled in the dream is the right opposite of what happened during the day. The relationship between dream and reality is a relationship of compensation, *consisting of an inversion* of real-life circumstances.

Q.II (14) -3 years, 9 months

A child whose father had died a few months before.

"I dreamed that I was with dad and mom and sister in the mountains, but then dad stayed up in the sky, but first he gave me a kiss and rubbed me with his beard".

Q.II (133) -3 years, 2 months

"I dreamed that I was playing with N. and A. (cousins)"

These are cousins who live abroad, with whom the child had been able to play during a previous holiday period in Italy, but as they had left this was no longer possible.

M.03. -4 years, and 7 months

The child dreams about going jumping, circumventing his parents' prohibition.

"I dreamed that I went to the jumping rides, you (dad) and mom told me not to go. But I went there, I jumped a lot, I went up in the air, up high in the air".

A few days before the dream, the boy had gone with his parents to a place with inflatable jumping rides. The parents, however, had forbidden him to jump because he should not sweat, since the week before he had had flu and cough, and this had happened also on the day before the dream. Even the day before the dream he had been at the playground but was not allowed to play with the bouncy castle, for the same reason.

Continuation dreams fulfil a wish that relates to pleasant diurnal circumstances (feelings of happiness, surprise, excitement) that were interrupted, or were too short compared to the child's expectations. These are experiences that do not last as long as desired. Therefore, in these dreams, (unlike in compensation and anticipation dreams), the wish re-enacted in the dream had been partially satisfied (although not enough) in the original diurnal experience. The relationship between dream and reality is a continuation of a pleasant diurnal experience, that may be resumed from the point where it was interrupted, or perpetuated or simply repeated. *In other words, these dreams bring an interrupted enjoyment to completion.*

Q.I (567) -4 years, 2 months

After visiting his grandparents' farm with its many animals, a child resumes the pleasant experience in the dream

"I dreamed the hens, rabbits and chicks moving all around me".

M.02.-4 years, 0 months.

"I dreamed about the new movie with the tow trucks [he is referring to the Cars movie, where there are tow trucks like the character of Tow Mater]. I was watching the movie".

The dream is about a DVD that the child had actually bought two days before and watched the evening before the dream. However, the DVD was only an episode taken from Cars, so it was much shorter than the original movie, which the child knows well. The child was probably startled, seeing that the movie didn't last long, he had expected it to last as long as the original Cars movie. When questioned, the boy said he was disappointed because the movie was so short, and added that it had been longer in the dream. The dream resumed, repeated and prolonged his pleasant daytime experience.

Q.II (28) -5 years, 6 months

"I dreamed that I was at school, I was at elementary school and they gave a sheet to me and my friend, a sheet we could draw on".

The child loves drawing and often asks for sheets of paper. Sometimes he secretly takes them from his father's desk, makes drawings on them and then gives them to his mother.

Anticipation dreams fulfil a wish that relates to a diurnal experience of wait/impatience for something pleasant that the child longs for but that will only occur in the future. The dream anticipates the event by enacting it immediately. Therefore, these dreams relate to something desired but totally unfulfilled. However, a form of imaginative prefiguration of wish fulfilment can also be fancied during waking state. The relationship between dream and reality is a relationship of anticipation. These dreams include those that may be called *dreams of impatience*, where the fulfilment of a wish that will be satisfied on the next day is enacted.

E. -4 years, 6 months

"I dreamed of grandfather's cows, one all black and one white and black. They were at grandfather's farm, but the farm was in a place I didn't know".

The child had not seen his grandfather for some time, and when he heard him on the phone he got the promise that he would see the cows on his next visit. His wish to spend some time with his grandfather and the animals was immediately fulfilled in the dream, anticipating the pleasant event that the child had had a glimpse of, but evidently deemed still too distant.

M.01. A 4-year-old boy dreams of being at his birthday party, scheduled to take place a few days later.

"I dreamed that we were at my party and my friends were there, we played soccer at the field and I kicked with my left foot".

M.05. A boy of 4 years and 8 months.

"I dreamed that the Befana brought me a Spiderman stocking, she left it on the sofa for me".

The child adds, "I can't wait for the Befana to come!" The evening before he had seen certain Befana stockings at the supermarket and he had liked the ones with Spiderman particularly. He had asked his parents to buy him one at once but his father, to his disappointment, had said, "Not now, M., you are going to get one from the Befana".[5]

It is noteworthy is that the dreams referred to herein as "compensation", "continuation" and "anticipation" dreams appear in the dream examples of several authors, who however do not make a clear distinction among them (Coriat, 1916; Freud, 1901; Hill, 1926; Kimmins, 1920). For example, a dream of continuation is that of Freud's daughter Sophie, of a "trip on the lake" that did not last long enough (Freud, 1901, pp. 20–21). Compensation dreams are also those described by Piaget: "At 5 years and 10 months (13), – she dreamt that her mother, who was ill, was better and admired one of her games" (Piaget, 1962, p. 178) or, again, "She dreamt she ate two eggs. At this time she was not allowed to have eggs, and was constantly asking for them" (Piaget, 1962, p. 178).

A more in-depth study of these different types of dreams will eventually provide useful indications about the different ways in which dreams can operate in relation to diurnal situations in order to "satisfy, resume and repair" unresolved experiences of unfulfilled wishes. On the other hand, the plurality of modi operandi of wish-fulfilment dreams, also confirmed by more recent studies (Colace, 2017, 2021; Mari, Beretta & Colace, 2018), is itself a tangible sign of the importance of wishes in triggering dreams.

Function of infantile dreams: the affective re-establishment hypothesis

The understandability of children's dreams, due to their clear content and direct connection with recent daytime experiences, made it possible to formulate a hypothesis on the possible function of these dreams.

As seen in the previous paragraphs, wishes that trigger dreams are clear and are accompanied by intense emotional states: imagine, for example, having to ask a child to give up on a much-desired toy, or on the strong desire to see his beloved grandfather, or even, to give up on seeing his first "fiancée". Take for example the case of a child who goes out to buy the Spongebob trolley he longs so much for (Spongebob being his favourite cartoon character) and then, to his enormous disappointment, he discovers that it is no longer in stock at the store that sells it.[6] His strong (unsatisfied) wish will be to buy the trolley for real, and the associated persistent affective state will be a feeling of disappointment/displeasure for not being able to buy it. It is plausible to assume that, at the time of going to sleep, the wish at unfulfilled state is such that it will continue to occupy the attention and interest of the child, pressing to be satisfied. The associated affective state (disappointment) will also remain persistent and perturbing (or exciting) because it was not processed ("settled" or "discharged" psychologically), and will probably dominate the emotional state of the child. *This binomial (unfulfilled wish/persistent affective state) is the basis of dream formation.* What the dream does is resume the wish and satisfy it in the form of lived experience (even if only at a hallucinatory level), which also allows the child to cope completely with the disturbing affective state (i.e., the unsettled portions of it).

All these dreams have the same triggering pattern and a certain final outcome or, so to speak, a certain achievement. Children's dreams *arise* because there is an unfulfilled wish that presses to be fulfilled, they *occur* because this will lead to the satisfaction of the wish and they *perform*, through the hallucinatory fulfilment of the wish, the function of discharging the disturbing affective state that the wish was originally accompanied by in the diurnal experience. Given these characteristics, we can infer that dreaming is a fully valid, meaningful and finalized psychic act, with a content that has a specific individual meaning and can by no means be considered, in its occurrence and in its contents, a random psychic event. The function of these dreams is therefore to allow the subject, through the fulfilment of his/her wish, to implement affective re-establishment through the decisive discharge of an intense and disturbing emotional state that originally arose with the wish (Colace, 2010, 2013, 2017, 2021; Mari, Beretta & Colace, 2018). The function of the dream is therefore to eliminate the stimulus that threatens the interruption of sleep (the wish), and settle the affective state allowing a complete psychological elaboration and resolution. I call this the *hypothesis of affective re-establishment (AR) function of dreams.*

Below are a few examples of how these dreams operate:

A little girl dreams of playing "fight" and "building a hut" with her father in her parents' bed, as she normally does every Sunday morning; however this has become impossible because her father has a broken leg.

Q-II (55) -5 years, 10 months
I dreamed that it was Sunday and daddy was at home and we played fight and building a hut on the big bed, but then I woke up and I remembered that daddy broke his leg and he can't play for now.

In this case, the daytime origin of the dream is represented by the (unfulfilled) "wish to play fight" and "building a hut" in the parents' bed with the father, and the emotional experience of displeasure/regret because this can no longer happen. The latter affective state remains unprocessed and perturbing. Now, what the dream does is "stage" a wish-fulfilment experience that allows the child to perform (even if only at hallucinatory level) that specific action (playing) that she cannot perform in the reality, and that implies the end, or so to speak the "settlement", of the unpleasant affective state. "Oh, how I'd like to play again!" becomes, in the dream, "I am actually playing", and this probably brings about the resolution of, or some relief from, the displeasure/regret associated with the wish.

In another example, a child dreams of happily going with his parents to a well-known marine theme park near Rome.

Q-II (29) -3 years, 7 months.

Mum, mum, I dreamed that you and I and daddy and my brothers went to Zoomarine, then there were the dolphins jumping, it was so much fun, then I dived into the dolphin tank and everyone laughed and I was so very, very happy

By the information obtained we learn that the boy had actually been at that park recently and was thrilled about it. The diurnal origin of this dream is this pleasant experience, associated to an affective state of excitement and happiness, not fully elaborated. The child resumes and repeats his experience in this *continuation dream*, staging it at a hallucinatory level (he goes again to the park), so as to relieve the state of (perturbing) excitement that is evidently still present.

A nice example of a dream with a clear affective recovery function was collected in a recent study (Mari, Beretta & Colace, 2018):

A 3-year-old child:

I dreamed N., she was with me on the lawn, she had come down from the sky because she died. She stayed with me a while, then she went away, she was gone.

From the information obtained we learn that N. is his grandmother's pet female dog. The child stays at his grandmother's place for most part of the day and the dog, that unfortunately had died some time before, used to be his playmate. In the dream, the fulfilment of the wish to see the pet again is enacted. Through the fulfilment of this wish, the dream allows the child to cope with the emotional state of displeasure and the emotional void caused by the loss of the pet. So the sorrow for the loss of the pet is likely to be relieved, implying affective reestablishment in the child.

This pattern is always repeated in the children's wish-fulfilment dreams.

The data show that the "disturbing" character of the affective state is not related to its degree of unpleasantness. Even states of excessive excitement, happiness and impatience can be "disturbing". It is probably the *intensity* of the affective state in itself that becomes "disturbing" from a given point on. Therefore, from a meta-psychological economic point of view, these dreams apparently discharge affective overloads, i.e., unprocessed portions of affective state that are disturbing in itself regardless of their nature (i.e., pleasant or unpleasant). *The "disturbing" character of the affective state lies therefore more in its quantity than in its quality.*

If the dream has the function of fulfilling a wish and coping with a disturbing affective state, then the emotions in the dream and upon awakening from it should tend to be positive and pleasant. A recent study has found that the predominant emotions in childhood dreams (self-assessed by the children themselves) are pleasant ones (being serene, calm, happy, or feeling good) and the general quality of the dream is assessed in most cases as "pleasant" (Sándor et al., 2015). Even in Foulkes' study (1982), where few oneiric emotions are reported, the most frequent type is "happiness". Honig and Nealis (2012) found that "joy" is the most frequent emotion in children's dreams; also, the emotional impact of dreams in the period of wake following the dream is classified as "positive" (41.8%) twice the number of times compared to "negative" (21.4%). Finally, compatible with the AR hypothesis, when young children report their dreams they often appear "serene" or "calm" rather than "upset" or in other emotional states (Colace, 2006a, 2013).

The AR hypothesis is consistent with Freud's statement that the dream is the fulfilment of a wish, and that the function of dreams, apart from safeguarding the sleep state, is to discharge unconscious drives (i.e., Robert-Freud's safety-valve hypothesis). While in adults what is coped with and settled is the load of unconscious drives, in children instead it is the problematic diurnal affective states that caused them a certain psychic imbalance. The stimulus (wishes vs. drives) and the affective states to be treated change; however, in both cases, the mechanism and intent of the dream is thought to be the same. When Freud says that the dream must have the function of settling a stimulus, he refers to the risk that the wish might interrupt the state of sleep. However, children's dreams show that what is treated through wish fulfilment is also the affective state associated with it, which ends up being relieved or dissipated.

Data on the temporal distance of the daytime sources of dreams can add further elements to the AR hypothesis (Colace, 2013, 2017, 2021). Children's dreams seem to act in order to cope with disturbing affective states that arose when the dreamer was awake, i.e. in the diurnal period that preceded the dream. Starting from this assumption, it may be plausibly assumed that nocturnal dreaming performs a task that affects *selectively* the disturbing affective load of the day just ended, and appears to have the function of resetting the functioning of the subject's psychological-emotional system, restoring its optimal conditions for the following day. Any repertoire of nocturnal dreams is therefore thought to have the function of coping with the daily affective load, a process that is presumably repeated every day. From this point of view, the AR hypothesis may also be called the *circadian* affective re-establishment hypothesis (Colace, 2017, 2021).[7] The AR function of infantile dreams, and the way AR is accomplished through the dreaming process (as a psychic act) also seems to be consistent with the so-called *hard* version of Freud's thesis of "dream as wish fulfilment": the dream, apart from representing the fulfilment of a wish, occurs *for the precise purpose of fulfilling a wish* (finalized and sensible psychic act) (Freud, 1900) (Figure 11.1).

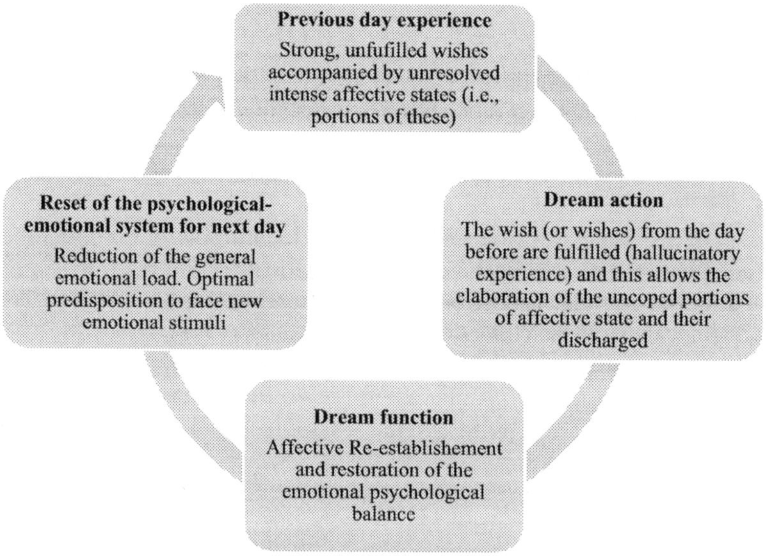

Figure 11.1 Circadian cycle of the Affective Re-establishment (AR) function of dreaming. A circular flow chart showing how dream dealt with unfulfilled wishes accompanied by unresolved intense affective states of the previous day. The wish (or wishes) is fulfilled (hallucinatory experience) and this allows the elaboration of the uncoped portions of affective state and their discharged. The dream allows an affective re-establishment and restoration of the emotional psychological balance. Now, the psychological-emotional system of child is reset and prepared for next day to face new emotional stimuli. The next day the process is repeated.

Comparison with theories on the adaptive/emotional function of dreaming

Several authors have formulated theories about dream functions, based on adult dreams had in particular life situations (e.g., a divorce), and/or based on particular categories of dreams, such as nightmares or recurring dreams, where dreams are thought to operate as adaptive emotion regulators (Breger, 1967; Cartwright, 2010; Fiss, 1980; Hartmann, 2011; Kramer, 2007). These theories have in common the general concept that dreams have the function of regulating variations in the intensity of emotions.

The AR hypothesis is in line with these theories, and suggests a certain continuity in the function of dream, from its early (infantile) forms (in children) to adult dreaming. It differs from them, however, in certain crucial aspects. In the first place, the AR hypothesis tries to explain specifically, for one dream of one individual, *how* affective re-establishment occurs and *what it consists of*; in other words, it tries to describe the modus operandi through which the dream acts in order to repair a perturbing diurnal emotional situation, defining which specific type of dream content performs this function (hallucinatory wish-fulfilment experience). Secondly, unlike the other theories, the AR hypothesis assumes that at the basis of dream triggering there is a specific (and identifiable) wish (i.e., the motive force and cause of dream) associated with a disturbing affective state, exactly the affective state that the dream tries to relieve by enabling its complete elaboration. Furthermore, emotional adaptive theories focus more on the way in which the dream is supposed to treat disturbing emotions, than on the possible role of motivations in triggering the dream, which for most of these theories is essentially activated by a cyclical, purely neurobiological trigger in the REM phase of sleep. Conversely, in the AR hypothesis, the function of the dream is linked to the causes that trigger it. The dream is thought to be activated by a motive force.

A general function of dream as an "emotional regulator" is apparently recognized by all authors, both in infantile and in adult dreams. In the dreams of children, however, the same inherent mechanisms of dream function occur in their most plain and elementary variants. From this point of view, *children's dreams are assumed to represent a simplified prototype, like a "small-scale" model, of adult dreams*, useful for a strategically advantageous research on the motivational and affective bases of dreams and of their possible function.

Comparison with recent theories on the emotional sleep/dream regulation function of dreaming

The AR hypothesis is in line with recent experimental data on the role of sleep/dream in the processing and discharging of the diurnal emotional load in order to restore the correct functioning of the individual's emotional system (for a review, refer: Deliens, Gilson & Peigneux, 2014; Tempesta, Socci, De Gennaro & Ferrata, 2018). It should be noted that many of these authors, although not psychoanalytically oriented, use such terms as *emotional load, discharge function* and *reset of the emotional system*, terms that are quite close to Freud's meta-psychological "economics" terminology, regarded by a majority as obsolete and valueless for research purposes (on this topic see: Colace, 2010; Colace & Boag, 2015a, 2015b; Hobson & McCarley, 1977; McCarley & Hobson, 1977; Michael, 2015; Solms, 2004, 2006).

For example, the AR circadian hypothesis is entirely in line with recent studies about the role of sleep/dream in the "dissipation" of the recent diurnal emotional load, thus enabling a reset of the brain's emotional reactivity system and reducing the threshold of subjective emotional reactivity on the next day (theory of emotional dissipation of dream/sleep (Van der Helm & Walker, 2009).

In line with this picture is also the Affective Network Dysfunction Model (AND) (Nielsen & Carr, 2017; Nielsen & Levin 2007) according to which dreams normally facilitate the regulation or "extinction" of negative emotions and emotional activation, while the jamming of this mechanism is evidenced by traumatic dreams. This latter type of dreams is said to be the result of an insufficient functioning of the connection between subcortical areas, the source of affective activation, and frontal areas, that should inhibit and moderate such activation during dreaming.

In their review of children's dreams, Sándor et al. (2014) recognize that Freud's hypothesis of the dream as a "safety-valve" is a "forerunner" of the AND model and conclude that the studies show that children's dreams have to do with their emotional issues. Furthermore, always according to these authors, the wish-fulfilment dreams reported may be interpreted as dreams that re-process the disturbing negative emotional stimuli and may therefore be regarded as in line with the assumption that dreams have the function of reducing the emotional load as pointed out by AR hypothesis.

Finally, the role of dreaming in the emotional regulation process was also suggested by Perogamvros and Schwartz (2012) in their Reward Activation Model. According to these authors, dreaming is the result of the amplification and activation of the mesocortic/mesolimbic dopaminergic system caused by a selective reactivation (during sleep) of memories that have high emotional and motivational value for the dreamer.

The AR hypothesis on the function of dream combines the notion of dream as the fulfilment of a wish (*what the dream does*) with that of "affective discharge" of and/or coping with disturbing emotions (*what is the dream for*), and considers the latter as one of the functions of dream, in the attempt to reconcile Freudian psychoanalytic concepts with the new theories on the function of sleep/dream as a re-arranger and dissipator of emotional experiences, and with data from modern affective neuroscience.

In conclusion, the results of the studies on children's dreams (Colace, 2010, 2013, 2017, 2021; Mari, Beretta & Colace, 2018) show that the observations of Freud and other seldom mentioned authors who conducted clinical and quantitative studies on young children's dreams (Coriat, 1916, Hill, 1926; Hug-Hellmuth, 1919; Kimmins, 1920; Banchieri, 1912: De Sanctis, 1899; Doglia & Banchieri, 1910–1911) receive substantial empirical support and consistent development, in particular concerning the motivational activation of dreams (the role of wish as motive force of dream) and the role of the day residues as the memory sources which dreams originate from, as well as the affective regulatory functions of these dreams (Despert, 1949; Grotjahn 1938).

Infantile dreams, affective neuroscience and neuro-psychoanalysis

The data on the frequency of clear wish-fulfilment dreams, the clear presence of a variety of wishes underlying them, the phenomena of motivational over-determination of dreams, serial wish-fulfilment dreams, the evidence of different modi operandi of wish-fulfilment dreams, as well as the affective function of dreams, suggest that the motivational factor is strongly involved in the triggering of infantile dreams.

Ultimately, children's dreams tell us clearly that *the matter dreams are made of is motivational and affective*. These dreams are extraordinarily effective in showing that the triggering and production of dreams is to be found in the motivations of the individual dreamer. Any model on dreaming, psychoanalytically oriented or not, should consider these results, which are in favour of a general reconsideration of the role of motivational factors in triggering the dream. On the one hand, at the empirical level, these studies on children's dreams are completely consistent and convergent with the knowledge base of psychoanalysis and, on the other hand, from a methodological standpoint, the results of these studies imply an objective legitimization of "psychoanalytic setting" as a valid context and instrument for observation and research.

Moreover, as Freud found, the infantile way of dreaming is not exclusive to young children. Infantile dream in adults are activated by the presence of a very strong wish or need, that, although not the expression of a strong unconscious request, possesses an extraordinary force that triggers a dream. A similar force is inherent to normal wish/needs that have become abnormal following severe deprivations, such as during food/water deprivation, in a laboratory setting or in natural circumstances (Colace, 2009b). Furthermore, such a force capable of triggering infantile dreams may also be inherent in a pathological wish such as in the case of *drug craving* in drug-addicted patients. I have described *drug dreams*, or dreams about drug use, in drug-addicted patients as an expression of the strong craving for drugs, that have precisely infantile characteristics, i.e. brevity, formal plainness and direct presence of the wish to use drugs (Colace, 2004, 2014; see also Colace, 2020).

It is worth pointing out that even in the presence of a pathological wish, such as drug craving in an addict patient, the pathological wish itself acts as a stimulus capable of triggering a dream (drug dream), especially in conditions of deprivation from the drug of abuse, so powerful that the wish, already strong per se, becomes even more impetuous (Colace, 2014). There are, therefore, different categories of so-called *infantile dreams of adults,* showing characteristics very similar to those of young children, that are equally valuable for a systematic study of the role of motivations in the dream process (Colace, 2009b, 2014, 2020).

The lack of interest in the motivational aspects of dreaming, especially in pure neurobiological models such as those of Hobson (Hobson, 1988; Hobson & Friston, 2012), cognitive models (Antrobus, 1978; Foulkes, 1978) and neurocognitive models (Crick & Mitchison, 1983; Seligman & Yellen, 1987) has reversed its trend following the development of research areas that have highlighted the importance of emotions and motivations in the dream process, although starting from different perspectives. For example, the use of brain visualization techniques in dream research (PET or Positron Emission Tomography, fRMI or Functional Magnetic Resonance) proved, during REM dream activity, the activation of brain areas that are part of the limbic system (mesocortic/mesolimbic dopaminergic system) (Braun et al., 1997; Maquet et al., 1996; Nofzinger et al., 1997) involved in basic emotions and motivations (Panksepp, 1998; Panksepp & Biven, 2012). Moreover, the recent neuropsychological approach to dreaming (Solms, 1997, 2000; Solms & Turnbull, 2002) showed, through the use of the clinical/anatomical method (research on the dreaming of patients with various brain pathologies and/ or deficits) that the essential neuroanatomical structures involved in the primary generation of dreams (damage to these areas produces a total cessation of dreaming) are the parieto-temporo-occipital junction and the limbic white matter of the ventromesial quadrant of the frontal lobes that accommodates the mesocortic/mesolimbic dopaminergic pathway, the most important portion of the so-called SEEKING system (Pankseep, 1998) that, when activated, triggers motivated behaviours, curiosity, interest, "appetitive" states such as hunger, thirst, craving for drugs and that, according to some authors, (Solms & Turnbull, 2002; Yu, 2001) closely recalls the Freudian concept of "libido" (Johnson & Mosri, 2016). Solms, therefore, affirmed that these results are in line with what was hypothesized in the Freudian dream theory as a peremptory expression of a wish (Solms, 2000; Turnbull & Solms, 2007).

Furthermore, the recent developments of affective neurosciences, that made it possible to obtain clearer evidence of the neurobiological and neuroanatomical substrate whose activation seems to be the counterpart the motivational trigger of dreaming, might raise further interest in the motivational aspects of dreaming. In fact, *Affective Neurosciences* (LeDoux, 1994; Panksepp, 1998; Panksepp & Biven, 2012; Plaff, 1999) brought a definition and description, apart from the SEEKING system, also of the other so-called basic emotional systems (e.g., CARE, PLAY, PANIC, RAGE, FEAR and LUST) (Panksepp, 1998; Panksepp, Clarici, Vandekerckhove & Yovell, 2019) (on this topic see other authors' contributions in this volume).

Children's dreams provide direct access to the subjective experience of dreaming and can represent a way to find convergent phenomenological feedback (wish at the base of dreams, ways of fulfilment, etc.) for the evidence coming from the aforementioned studies on the SEEKING system and its role in triggering dreams found in clinical neuropsychological studies.

The SEEKING system activity is well suited to represent the neuroanatomical and neurobiological counterpart of the young child's typical behaviours of curiosity, appetite and wish towards the outside world and of his direct and irrepressible way of living wishes in his waking experience as much as in his dream experience. These are wishes that have remained unfulfilled and that press for their satisfaction, and in respect of which the SEEKING system provides the necessary energy to activate what can satisfy them. On the other hand, the wishes of young children and the *way* they wish (with force, thrill and excitement) seem to be precisely the expression of a condition of pleasure connected to euphoric excitement that leads to the activation, intended as "expectation of satisfaction", of the SEEKING system.

In this perspective, the triggering of dream in young children caused by wishes lived strongly and intensely may be seen as an example of subjective, idiographic confirmation of the neurobiological activity of the SEEKING system and of its role in triggering dreams.

Such convergence of data coming from different areas of study is in line with the Freudian model of dream, which assumes that the dream originates from a wish, that is its motive force, and that the dream is a finalized and significant psychic act of the individual.

The research on children's dreams that show the motivational trigger of the dream and its role in easing the disturbing affective load suggest, consistently with the neuro-psychoanalytic research and the study on the motivational systems of affective neuroscience, that a motivational approach to dreaming is valuable and needed, recovering certain key concepts of the Freudian model, which, as the evidence shows, has some empirical utility and heuristic vitality in the explanation of the dream process.

Ultimately, what the research on children's dreams suggests is the validity of and the need for a motivational approach to dreaming, a perspective that has already been legitimated at neuroanatomical level by affective neurosciences and by the clinical neuropsychology of the dream.

Conclusions

The further development of studies on children's dreams promises to give indisputable contribution – as to the phenomenology of the wishes that underlie dreaming – about how these trigger dreams and about the functions of the latter for the destiny of the wish and of the affective state associated with it, as well as the effects of dreams on the emotional system after awakening. These studies will allow researchers to investigate, in parallel with affective neurosciences and neuropsychology of dreaming, the motivational and affective bases of dreams.

Notes

1 On dream bizarreness see: (Colace, 2010; Colace & Violani, 1993; Colace, Violani & Solano, 1993; Colace, Doricchi, Di Loreto & Violani, 1993; Colace & Tuci, 1996; Foulkes, 1982; 1999; Resnick, Stickgold, Rittenhouse & Hobson, 1994; Sándor, Szakadát,Bódizs, 2016); role of wishes in triggering dreams and research on the diurnal sources of dreams (Colace, 2010; 2013, 2017, in press; Liberty, 2017); self-representation in the dream (Baudet, 1990; Colace, Violani & Tuci, 1995; Colace, 2006; Colace, Demurtas, Testa, Angiletti, unpublished raw data; Colace, Tuci & Ferendeles, 2000; Foulkes, 1999; Honig & Neals,2012; Kráčmarová & Plháková, 2012; Resnick, Stickgold, Rittenhouse & Hobson, 1994; Sándor, Szakadát, Kertész, & Bódizs, 2015); the effects of neurocognitive, cognitive and personality development on the form and content of the dream (Colace, 2009a, 2010, 2021; Colace & Violani, 1993; Colace, Violani & Solano, 1993; Foulkes, 1982, 1999; Gartner, 2014; Honig & Nealis, 2011; Maggiolini, Di Lorenzo, Falotico, Gargioni & Morelli, 2020; Sándor, Szakadát, Bódizs 2016; Sándor, Szakadát, Kertész & Bódizs, 2015); function of the dream (Colace, 2010, 2013, 2017, 2021; Mari, Beretta & Colace, 2018) For a review of the studies on the dreams of young children see: (Ablon & Mack, 1980; Catalano, 1990; Colace, 2010, in press; DeMartino 1953; Despert, 1949; Sándor, Szakadát & Bódizs 2014); For a general introduction on the usefulness of studies on dreams in childhood, see Colace (2010; 2013b).
2 Freud was the first to anticipate an ontogenetic approach to the study of the dream process. This approach is currently widespread in psychology where the so-called evolutionary trajectories of psychic processes and/or functions are studied (Natale, 2015).
3 The quantity and quality of the information about the child's diurnal experience were found to be fundamental for identifying the wish underlying the dream and for a full understanding the dream. Improvements to the method of collecting such information (e.g., interviewing the parents immediately after the child reported his/her dream and asking to be as exhaustive as possible in telling the diurnal experiences that were apparently the background of the dream, might lead to find a further increase in the frequency of wish-fulfilment dreams.
4 On this aspect, Freud suggested that children's dreams are a reaction, in sleep, to a daytime experience that has aroused and left in the child an affective state as regret, nostagia, disappointment, sorrow for denied enjoyment, or for a unresolved wish or a state of impatience (Freud, 1900, pp. 128–130, 1901, p. 644, 1916–1917, p.128).
5 The "Befana" is a good old witch who flies on a broomstick and brings gifts to children in the night before the Epiphany (January 6), just like Santa does in the night before Christmas. Peculiar to Italy, the Befana tradition has now spread across the country but was originally restricted to the Rome area. The Befana typically brings stockings full of sweet snacks, chocolates and candy, which in the days preceding the Epiphany are usually sold ready-made at cafes and grocery stores.
6 This is a simplification. The boy had went out to buy a Spongebob sticker that he intended to place on a trolley (since the original Spongebob trolley was impossible to find); unfortunately, he was unable to obtain both the sticker and the trolley on which to apply the sticker.
7 On the possible circadian influences on dream formation, see, Nielsen (2011).

References

Ablon, S. L., & Mack J. E. (1980). Children's dreams reconsidered. *Psychoanalytic Study of Child, 35*, 170–217.

Antrobus, J. S. (1978). Dreaming for cognition. In A. M. Arkin, J. Antrobus, & S. J. Ellman (Eds.), *The Mind in Sleep: psychology and psychophysiology* (pp. 569–581). Hillsdale: Erlabaum.

Banchieri, F. (1912). I sogni dei bambini di 5 anni. *Rivista di Psicologia, VIII* (4), 1–8.

Baudet, D. (1990). *Encountering the Monster: pathways in children's dreams*. New York: Continuum.

Braun, A. R., Balkin, T. J., Wesenten, N. J., Carson, R. E., Varga, M., Baldwin, P., Selbie, S., Belennky, G., & Herscovitch, P. (1997). Regional cerebral blood flow throughout the sleep–wake cycle—an (H2O)-O-15-PET study. *Brain, 120*, 1173–1197.

Breger, L. (1967). Function of dreams. *Journal of Abnormal Psychology Monograph, 72*(5), 1–28.

Cartwright, R. (2010). *The Twenty-four Hour Mind: the role of sleep and dreaming in our emotional lives*. New York: Oxford University Press.

Catalano, S. (1990). *Children's Dreams in Clinical Practice*. US: Springer.

Colace, C. (1997). I sogni dei bambini nella teoria psicodinamica: un contributo teorico e sperimentale. [*Children's Dreams in Psychodimamic Theory: a teorical and experimental contribution*]. Unpublished Ph.D. Dissertation. Depertment of Psychology. University of Bologna, Italy.

Colace, C. (1998a). Sulla valutazione della credibilità dei sogni raccontati dai bambini: uno studio preliminare. *Psichiatria dell'infanzia e dell'adolescenza, 65* (1), 5–18.

Colace, C. (1998b). Wish-fulfillment in dream reports of young children. *Sleep, 21* (3 suppl.), 286.

Colace, C. (2004). Dreaming in addiction. A study on the motivational bases of dreaming processes. *Neuro-psychoanalysis, 6* (2), 167–181.

Colace, C. (2006a). Children's dreaming: A study based on questionnaire completed by parents. *Sleep and Hypnosis, 8* (1), 19–32.

Colace, C. (2006b). Commentary on "Freudian Dream Theory, Dream Bizarreness, and the Disguise-Censor Controversy (S. Boag)". *Neuro-Psychoanalysis, 8* (1), 24–27.

Colace, C. (2009a). *The Study of Bizarreness in Young Children's Dreams: a way to test the disguise-censorship model*. Poster presented at X International Congress of Neuropsychoanalysis, Parigi, France, 26–29, giugno 2009.

Colace, C. (2009b). Gli studi sull'effetto della frustrazione dei bisogni primari sul sognare e la recente ricerca e teoria sui processi onirici. *Psycofenia, XII* (20), 49–72.

Colace, C. (2010). *Children's Dreams: from Freud's observations to modern dream research*. New York: Routledge.

Colace, C. (2012). Dream bizarreness and the controversy between the neurobiological approach and the disguise censorship model: The contribution of children's dreams. *Neuropsychoanalysis, 14* (2), 165–174.

Colace, C. (2013). Are wish-fulfilment dreams of children the royal road for looking a the functions of dreams? *Neuropsychoanalysis, 15* (2), 161–175.

Colace, C. (2014). *Drug Dreams. Clinical and Research Implications of Dreams about Drugs in Drug-addicted Patients*. New York: Routledge.

Colace, C. (2017). *The Early Forms of Dreaming: a longitudinal single-case study on the dream reports of a child from the age of 4 to the age of 7.* Poster presented at The 18th Annual Congress of the International Neuropsychoanalysis Society, London, England July 13, 2017–July 15, 2017.

Colace, C. (2020). Gambling dreams in pathological gambler outpatients: A pilot study, August 2020. *Addicta The Turkish Journal on Addictions, 7* (3), 174–179. DOI: 10.5152/ADDICTA.2020.20053.

Colace, C. (2021). *The Dreams of a Child. A Case Study in Early Forms of Dreaming.* In press, Routledge.

Colace, C., & Boag, S. (2015a). Persisting Miths surronding Sigmund Freud's dream theory: A reply to Hobson's critique to scientific status of pychoanalysis. *Contemporary Psychoanalysis, 51* (1), 107–125.

Colace, C., & Boag, S. (2015b). The empirical study of infantile wish-fulfillment dreams. A reply to response of Allan J. Hobson. *Contemporary Psychoanalysis, 51* (1), 132–134.

Colace, C., Ceccarelli, V., Demurtas, G., Testa, A., & Angiletti, M. (2021). Nuove osservazioni sui sogni dei bambini piccoli. *Unpublished Manuscript.*

Colace, C., Doricchi, F., Di Loreto E., & Violani, C. (1993). Developmental qualitative and quantitative aspects of bizareness in dream reports of children. *Sleep Research, 22,* 57.

Colace, C., & Tuci, B. (1996). Early children's dreams are not bizarre. *Sleep Research, 25,* 147. University of California, Los Angeles, 1996.

Colace, C., Tuci, B., & Ferendeles, R. (1997). Bizarreness in early children's dreams collected in the home setting: Preliminary data. *Sleep Research, 26,* 241. University of California, Los Angeles, 1997.

Colace, C., Tuci, B., & Ferendeles, R. (2000). Self-representation in young children's dream reports. *Sleep (Abstract supplement 2), 23,* A176–A177, 1198.D.

Colace, C., & Violani, C. (1993). La bizzarria del sogno infantile come correlato della capacità di provare sensi di colpa. *Psichiatria dell'infanzia e dell'adolescenza, 60* (4–5), 367–376.

Colace, C., Violani, C., & Solano, L. (1993). La deformazione-bizzarria onirica nella teoria freudiana del sogno: indicazioni teoriche e verifica di due ipotesi di ricerca in un campione di 50 sogni di bambini. *Archivio di Psicologia, Neurologia e Psichiatria, 54* (3), 380–401.

Colace, C., Violani, C., & Tuci, B. (1995). Self – Representation in dreams reported from young children at school. *Sleep Research, 24,* 69.

Coriat, I. H. (1916). *The Meaning of Dreams.* Boston: Dodo Press.

Crick, F., & Mitchison, G. (1983). The function of REM sleep. *Nature, 304,* 111–114.

Deliens, G., Gilson, M., & Peigneux, P. (2014). Sleep and the processing of emotions. *Experimental Brain Research, 232* (5), 1403–1414.

De Martino, F. (1955). A review of literature on children's dreams. *Psychiatric Quarterly, 1* (suppl.), 1–12.

De Sanctis, S. (1899). *I sogni. Studi clinici e psicologici di un alienista.* Torino: Bocca.

Despert, J. L. (1949). Dreams in children of preschool age. *The Psychoanlaitic Study of Child, 3–4,* 141–180.

Doglia, S., & Bianchieri F. (1910–1911). I sogni dei bambini di tre anni, L'inizio dell' attivita onirica. *Contributi psicol, I,* 1–9.

Domhoff, G. W. (1996). *Emotions, Personality, and Psychotherapy. Finding Meaning in Dreams: a quantitative approach.* New York and London: Plenum Press.

Epstein, A. W. (1985). The waking event-dream interval. *American Journal of Psychiatry, 142,* 123–124.

Fiss, H. (1980). Dream content and response to withdrawal from alcohol. *Sleep Research, 9,* 152.

Foulkes, D. (1978). *A Grammar of Dreams.* New York: Basic Books.

Foulkes, D. (1982). *Children's Dreams, Longitudinal Studies.* New York: Wiley-Interscience Publication.

Foulkes, D. (1999). *Children's Dreaming and the Development of Consciousness.* Cambridge and London: Harvard University Press.

Foulkes, D., Pivik, T., Steadman, H. S., Spear, P. S., & Symonds, J. D. (1967). Dreams of the male child: An EEG study. *Journal of Abnormal Psychology, 72,* 457–467.

Freud, S. (1900). *The Interpretation of Dreams.* S.E., 4–5. London: Hogarth Press.

Freud, S. (1901). *On Dreams.* S.E., 5. London and New York: Norton & Company, Inc.

Freud, S. (1916–1917). *Introductory Lectures on Psycho-Analysis.* S.E., 15/16. London: Hogarth Press.

Gartner, Y. (2014). *Immature Recall Ability in Dream Reporting with Children Aged 3–5.* Faculty of Humanities, University of Cape Town. Unpublished Master Dissertation.

Grotjahn, M. (1938). Dreams observation in Two-Year, four-mouths-old Ba-by. *The Psychoanalytic Quarterly, 7,* 507–513.

Hall, C. S., & Domhoff, B. (1963). Aggression in dreams. *International Journal of Social Psychiatry, 9,* 259–267.

Hartmann, E. (2011). *The Nature and the Functions of Dreaming.* New York: Oxford University Press.

Hill, J. C. (1926). *Dreams and Education.* London: Methuen & Co.

Hobson, J. A. (1988). *The Dreaming Brain* (p. 319). New York: Basic Books.

Hobson, J. A. (2013). Ego ergo sum: Toward a psychodynamic neurology. *Contemporary Psychoanalysis, 49* (2), 142–164.

Hobson, J. A. (2015). Dreams and consciousness: Response to Colace and Boag. *Contemporary Psychoanalysis, 51* (1), 126–131.

Hobson, J. A., & Friston, K. J. (2012). Waking and dreaming consciousness: Neurobiological and functional consideration. *Progress in Neurobiology, 98* (1), 82–98.

Hobson, J. A., & McCarley, R. W. (1977). The brain as a dream-state generator: Activation-synthesis hypothesis of dream process. *American Journal of Psychiatry, 134,* 1335–1348.

Honig, A. S., & Nealis, A. L. (2012). What do young children dream about? *Early Child Development and Care, 182* (6), 771–795.

Hug-Hellmuth, H. (1919). *A Study of the Mental Life of the Child.* Washington: Nervous and Mental Diseases Publishing.

Johnson, B., & Mosri, F. D. (2016). The neuropsychoanalytic approach: Using neuroscience as the basic science of psychoanalysis. *Frontiers in Psychology 7,* 1459, DOI: 10.3389/fpsyg.2016.01459.

Kimmins, C. W. (1920). *Children's Dreams, an Unexplored Land.* New York: Longmans, Green and Co.

Kráčmarová, L., & Plháková, A. (2012). Obsahová analýza dětských snů. *E-psychologie* [online], *6* (4), 1–13 [cit. vložit datum citování]. Dostupný z www: http://e-psycholog.eu/pdf/kracmarovaplhakova.pdf. ISSN 1802-8853.

Kramer, M. (2007). *The Dream Experience: a systematic exploration.* London: Brunner-Routledge.

LeDoux, J. E. (1994). Emotion, memory and the brain. *Scientific American, 270* (6), 50–57.

Maggiolini, A., Di Lorenzo, M., Falotico, E. Gargioni, D., & Morelli, M. (2020). Typical dreams across the life cycle. *International Journal of Dream Research, 13* (1), 17–28.

Maquet, P., Peters, J. M., Aerts, J., Delfiore, G., Degueldre, C., Luxen, A., & Franck, G. (1996). Functional neuroanatomy of human rapid-eye movement sleep and dreaming. *Nature, 386* (6596), 163–166.

Mari, E., Beretta, M., & Colace, C. (2018). L'appagamento di desiderio e il ristabilimento affettivo nel sogno infantile: nuove osservazioni. *Psychofenia, XXI* (37–38), 17–28.

McCarley, R. W., & Hobson, J. A. (1977). The neurobiological origins of psychoanalytic dream theory. *American Journal of Psychiatry, 134,* 1211–1221.

Michael, T. M. (2015). *Freud's Theory of Dreams: a philosophico-scientific perspective.* Lanham, MD: Rowman & Littlefield.

Natale, V. (2015). Prefazione. In C. Colace (Ed.), *Iniziazione ai sogni dei bambini. Introduzione allo studio scientifico dei bambini* (pp. 11–13). Roma: Edizioni Mediterranee.

Nielsen, T., Kuiken, D., Alain, G., Stenstrom, P., & Powell, R. A. (2004). Immediate and delayed incorporations of events into dreams: Further replication and implications for dream function. *Journal of Sleep Research, 13,* 327–336.

Nielsen, T. A. (2011). Ultradian, circadian, and sleep-dependent features of dreaming. In T. Nielsen, M. Kryger, T. Roth, & W. C. Dement (Eds.), *Principles and Practice of Sleep Medicine* (pp. 576–584). New York: Elsevier.

Nielsen, T. A., & Carr, M. (2017). Nightmares and nightmare function. In M. H. Kryger, T. Roth, & W. C. Dement (Eds.), *Principles and Practice of Sleep Medicine* (6th ed., pp. 546–554). Philadelphia: Elsevier.

Nielsen, T. A., & Levin, R. (2007). Nightmares: A new neurocognitive model. *Sleep Medicine Reviews, 11,* 295–310.

Nielsen, T. A., & Powell, R. A. (1992). The day-residue and dream-lag effects: A literature review and limited replication of two temporal effects in dream formation. *Dreaming, 2,* 67–77.

Nofzinger, E., Mintun, M., Wiseman, M., Kupfer, D., & Moore, R. (1997). Forebrain activation in REM sleep: An FDG PET study. *Brain Research, 770,* 192–201.

Panksepp, J. (1998). *Affective Neuroscience: the foundations of human and animal emotions.* Oxford: Oxford University Press.

Panksepp, J., & Biven, L. (2012). *The Archaeology of Mind: neuroevolutionary origins of human emotion.* New York: W. W. Norton & Company.

Panksepp, J., Clarici, A., Vandekerckhove, M., & Yovell, Y. (2019). Neuro-evolutionary foundations of infant minds: From psychoanalytic visions of how primal emotions guide constructions of human minds toward affective neuroscientific understanding of emotions and their disorders. *Psychoanalytic Inquiry, 39* (1), 36–51. DOI: 10.1080/07351690.2019.1549910.

Perogamvros, L., & Schwartz, S. (2012). The roles of the reward system in sleep and dreaming. *Neuroscience and Biobehavioral Reviews, 36,* 1934–1951.

Plaff, D. W (1999). *Drive: Neurobiological and Molecular Mechanism of Sexual Motivation*. Cambridge: MIT Press.

Piaget, J. (1962). *Play, Dreams and Imitation in Childood*. New York and London: W.W. Norton & Company.

Popper, K. (1959). *The Logic of Scientific Discovery*. London: Hutchinson.

Popper, K. (1963). *Conjectures and Refutations. The Growth of Scientific Knowledge*. London: Routledge.

Resnick, J., Stickgold, R., Rittenhouse, C., & Hobson, J. A. (1994). Self-representation and bizarreness in children's dream reports collected in the home setting. *Consciousness and Cognition, 3*, 30–45.

Sándor, P., Szakadát, S., & Bódizs, R. (2014). Ontogeny of dreaming: A review of empirical studies. *Sleep Medicine Reviews, 18*(5), 435–449.

Sándor, P., Szakadát, S., & Bódizs, R. (2016). The development of cognitive and emotional processing As Reflected in children's dreams: Active self in an eventful dream signals better neuropsychological skills. *Dreaming, 26* (1), 58–78.

Sándor, P., Szakadát, S., Kertész, K. & Bódizs, R. (2015). Content analysis of 4 to 8 year-old children's dream reports. *Frontiers in Psychology, 6*, 534. DOI: 10.3389/fpsyg.2015.00534.

Seligman, M., & Yellen, A. (1987). What is a dreaming? *Behavior Research Therapy, 25* (1), 1–24.

Solms, M. (1997). *The neuropsychology of dreams: a clinico-anatomical study*. Mahwah: Lawrence Erlbaum Associates Publishers.

Solms, M. (2000). Dreaming and REM sleep are controlled by different brain mechanisms. *Behavioral Brain Science, 23* (6), 843–850.

Solms, M. (2004). Freud returns. *Scientific American, 290*, 83–88.

Solms, M. (2006). Dream debate. Should Freud's dream theory be abandoned? Hobson (yes) vs Solms (no). Presented to the Conference "Toward a Science of Consciousness", held in April at Tucson, Arizona.

Solms, M., & Turnbull, O. (2002). *The Brain and the Inner World: an introduction to the neuroscience of subjective experience*. New York: Other Press.

Tempesta, D., Socci, V., De Gennaro, L., & Ferrara, M. (2018). Sleep and emotional processing. *Sleep Medicine Reviews, 40*, 183–195. DOI: 10.1016/j.smrv.2017.12.005.

Turnbull, O., & Solms, M. (2007). Big issues, little issues... and non-issues. *Cortex, 43* (8), 1116–1121.

Van der Helm, E., & Walker, M. P. (2009). Overnight therapy? The role of sleep in emotional brain processing. *Psychology Bulletin, 135* (5), 731–748.

Yu, C. K. (2001). Neuroanatomical correlates of dreaming. II: The ventromesial frontal region controversy (dream instigation). *Neuropsychoanalysis, 3*, 193–202.

Index

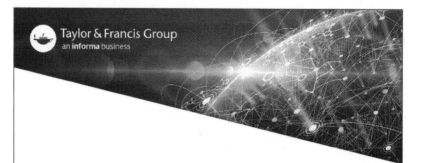